Making Modern Spain

Campos Ibéricos:
Bucknell Studies in Iberian Literatures and Cultures

Series editors:
Isabel Cuñado, Bucknell University
Jason McCloskey, Bucknell University

Campos Ibéricos is a series of monographs and edited volumes that focuses on the literary and cultural traditions of Spain in all of its rich historical, social, and linguistic diversity. The series provides a space for interdisciplinary and theoretical scholarship exploring the intersections of literature, culture, the arts, and media from medieval to contemporary Iberia. Studies on all authors, texts, and cultural phenomena are welcome and works on understudied writers and genres are specially sought.

Recent titles in the series:

Making Modern Spain: Religion, Secularization, and Cultural Production
Azariah Alfante

Space, Drama, and Empire: Mapping the Past in Lope de Vega's Comedia
Javier Lorenzo

Dystopias of Infamy: Insult and Collective Identity in Early Modern Spain
Javier Irigoyen-García

Founders of the Future: The Science and Industry of Spanish Modernization
Óscar Iván Useche

Shipwreck in the Early Modern Hispanic World
Carrie L. Ruiz and Elena Rodríguez-Guridi, eds.

Calila: The Later Novels of Carmen Martín Gaite
Joan L. Brown

Indiscreet Fantasies: Iberian Queer Cinema
Andrés Lema-Hincapié and Conxita Domènech, eds.

Between Market and Myth: The Spanish Artist Novel in the Post-Transition, 1992–2014
Katie J. Vater

For more information about the series, please visit bucknelluniversitypress.org.

Making Modern Spain

Religion, Secularization, and Cultural Production

AZARIAH ALFANTE

LEWISBURG, PENNSYLVANIA

Library of Congress Cataloging-in-Publication Data

Names: Alfante, Azariah, author.

Title: Making modern Spain : religion, secularization, and cultural production / Azariah Alfante.

Description: Lewisburg, Pennsylvania : Bucknell University Press, 2023. | Series: Campos ibéricos: Bucknell studies in Iberian literatures and cultures | Includes bibliographical references and index.

Identifiers: LCCN 2023011505 | ISBN 9781684484959 (paperback ; alk. paper) | ISBN 9781684484966 (hardback ; alk. paper) | ISBN 9781684484973 (epub) | ISBN 9781684484980 (pdf)

Subjects: LCSH: Caballero, Fernán, 1796–1877—Criticism and interpretation. | Bécquer, Gustavo Adolfo, 1836–1870—Criticism and interpretation. | Pérez Galdós, Benito, 1843–1920—Criticism and interpretation. | Pereda, José María de, 1833–1906—Criticism and interpretation. | Christianity in literature. | Christianity and literature—Spain. | Literature and society—Spain—History—19th century. | Secularization—Spain—History—19th century. | Spain—Intellectual life—19th century. | LCGFT: Literary criticism.

Classification: LCC PQ6509.Z5 A68 2023 | DDC 860.9/005—dc23/eng/20230727

LC record available at https://lccn.loc.gov/2023011505

A British Cataloging-in-Publication record for this book is available from the British Library.

Copyright © 2024 by Azariah Alfante

All rights reserved

No part of this book may be reproduced or utilized in any form or by any means, electronic or mechanical, or by any information storage and retrieval system, without written permission from the publisher. Please contact Bucknell University Press, Hildreth-Mirza Hall, Bucknell University, Lewisburg, PA 17837-2005. The only exception to this prohibition is "fair use" as defined by U.S. copyright law.

All photos by the author unless otherwise indicated.

All Scripture quotations are from the Douay-Rheims Bible.

References to internet websites (URLs) were accurate at the time of writing. Neither the author nor Bucknell University Press is responsible for URLs that may have expired or changed since the manuscript was prepared.

♾ The paper used in this publication meets the requirements of the American National Standard for Information Sciences—Permanence of Paper for Printed Library Materials, ANSI Z39.48-1992.

bucknelluniversitypress.org

Distributed worldwide by Rutgers University Press

For my beloved grandmother, Marina Fajardo Quintana

What are the roots that clutch, what branches grow
Out of this stony rubbish? Son of man,
You cannot say, or guess, for you know only
A heap of broken images, where the sun beats,
And the dead tree gives no shelter

—T. S. Eliot, "The Burial of the Dead"

Contents

List of Illustrations   XI
Note on Orthography and Translations   XIII

Introduction   1

1   Modern Matter: Disentailment and the Religious
    Question   13

2   At the Heart of the Nation: Domestic Well-Being and
    Spiritual Patrimony in Cecilia Böhl de Faber's *La gaviota*
    (1849), *La familia de Alvareda* (1856), *Callar en vida y
    perdonar en muerte* (1856), and *Lágrimas* (1862)   38

3   The Hallowed, the Haunting: Remembering and Restoring
    the Sacred Precinct in Gustavo Adolfo Bécquer's *Historia de
    los templos de España* (1857), *Cartas desde mi celda* (1864),
    and *Leyendas* (1858–1864)   66

4   A New Vital Force: Reconstructing Spain's Spiritual Body in
    Benito Pérez Galdós's *Doña Perfecta* (1876), *Gloria* (1877),
    Mendizábal (1898), and *Montes de Oca* (1900)   97

5   The Abyss and the Mount: Questions of Faith, Family,
    and Tradition in José María de Pereda's *El Tío Cayetano*
    (1858–1859 and 1868–1869), *Blasones y talegas* (1869), *De tal
    palo, tal astilla* (1880), and *Sotileza* (1885)   129

Final Reflections   161

Acknowledgments   169
Notes   171
Bibliography   199
Index   215

Illustrations

1. Portico, Campo de San Francisco, Oviedo   2
2. Monasterio de Piedra, Saragossa   14
3. Monasterio de San Jerónimo de Buenavista, Seville   49
4. Cloister, Monasterio de San Juan de los Reyes, Toledo   71
5. Portico, Museo de Bellas Artes, Seville   162

Note on Orthography and Translations

All nineteenth-century text citations have been standardized in accordance with modern Castilian. Thus, *v* replaces *b* (*socabar* becomes *socavar*), *j* replaces *g* (*enagenación* becomes *enajenación*), and *x* replaces *s* (*esclaustración* becomes *exclaustración*). I have added punctuation marks and accents where missing in the original.

Unless otherwise noted, all translations are my own.

Making Modern Spain

Introduction

An archway stands in the middle of the Campo de San Francisco in Oviedo, Spain. Moss and fine roots envelop its crumbled stone. Within a busy park, it looks out of place, with no sign around it to inform those passing by of its origin and former function. This otherworldly structure, once a convent portico, recalls French historian Pierre Nora's remark: "We speak so much of memory because there is so little of it left." According to Nora, nowadays we speak only of *lieux de mémoire*, or "sites of memory," because *milieux de mémoire*, or "real environments of memory," no longer exist.[1] The site of memory, much like this ruined portico, figures as a fragment. It was once part of a whole, and that whole was once part of a milieu. I consider this threshold a prompt, an aperture into a discussion of memory, culture, and history.

Monuments and historical edifices, extant or ruined, speak much about the past. Yet, often overlooked, they have ceased to occupy a place in the collective consciousness. As the Austrian writer Robert Musil once remarked, "Monuments possess all sorts of qualities. The most important is somewhat contradictory: what strikes one most about monuments is that one doesn't notice them. There is nothing in the world as invisible as monuments."[2] It is a lack of knowledge, an unawareness of historical context, that distinguishes the site from its environment of memory. For Nora, *lieux de mémoire* are essentially remains, products of the "deritualization of our world"; that is, the obsession of society with its own transformation and renewal and its privileging of the new over the old, the future over the past.[3] Lewis Mumford avows that monuments, despite their superficial veneer of fixity, are "hollow echoes of an expiring breath" in that they no longer represent the impulses of modern civilization. As Mumford puts it, "If it is a monument it is not modern, and if it is modern, it cannot be a monument."[4] From Musil's and Mumford's perspectives, the monument either stays invisible

1

Figure 1. Portico, Campo de San Francisco, Oviedo.

or stands out of place. But its hiddenness or incongruent appearance can only be perceived through a lack of familiarity, remembrance, and information. Hence, Nora suggests that *lieux de mémoire*, due to their lack of real referents—or rather, their self-referentiality—play a double role: while they are closed in upon themselves, they are also permanently open to a wide range of possible significations.[5]

This wealth of possibility that Nora perceives in the monument has the potential to pique one's interest, leading one down the path of research, reflection, and

INTRODUCTION

discussion. Ruminating on the ruined portico, I consider that it symbolizes a rupture between its edificial past and present condition. The park once belonged to the thirteenth-century convent of San Francisco, and the portico itself was part of the conventual church of San Isidoro.[6] The ecclesiastical expropriation laws under Juan Álvarez Mendizábal in 1836 led to the convent's secularization, transforming it into the first general hospital of Asturias.[7] Such legislation was symptomatic of the liberal attempt to modernize the Spanish nation politically, economically, and culturally. Hence, the convent's fate was decided by a series of events, circumstances, and ideas arising from the religious question in nineteenth-century Spain.

This study concerns cultural responses to the so-called religious question in nineteenth-century Spanish writing. Through analyzing a selection of novels, plays, essays, prose texts, and letters, I will illuminate aspects of the morphing and conflicted relationship between Catholicism and various constituents of the Spanish nation regarding the place of religion and its external elements: the ecclesial buildings, places, persons, and goods that comprise the Church's tangible and visible apparatus.[8] I argue that the liberal attempt to modernize the nation through disentailment—the forced confiscation of assets—constituted an economic mechanism with profound sociocultural implications that particularly pertained to class mobility, the exclaustration and destitution of Spanish religious communities, and the loss of faith among the Spanish population. I will examine these issues more closely in chapter 1.

This work integrates literary analyses and discussions of historical events and contexts with a theoretical framework encompassing culture, religion, and memory. I will explore how the religious question arose out of the tensions between a politically and economically fractured Spain in need of modern reforms and a staunch traditionalist resistance. Substantiating my analyses of parliamentary, journalistic, and clerical discourses, I will examine selected works by four Spanish writers: Cecilia Böhl de Faber (who wrote under the pseudonym of Fernán Caballero, 1796–1877), Gustavo Adolfo Bécquer (1836–1870), Benito Pérez Galdós (1843–1920), and José María de Pereda (1833–1906). As part of the intellectual and artistic production that assisted in facilitating the consolidation and institutionalization of Spain's national culture, literature was an indispensable manner of understanding "the national spirit" and the sociopolitical implications of its destiny, the so-called "problema de España"[9] [problem of Spain]. Regarding their works, I propose to foreground the conflict between organized religion and secularization by examining their representations of collective, individual, external, and internal expressions of spirituality manifest in the sociopolitical events of nineteenth-century Spain and the cultural reactions to these realities.

A key recurrent theme throughout my study is disjuncture. This notion of disjoining represents the liberal attempt to challenge religious and social traditions through modern reforms and to "dismantle" religious buildings and communities through disentailment. The image of the ruin in the works of Böhl, Bécquer, and Pereda embodies this idea of rupture, which aptly describes the literal and symbolic break between modernity and tradition, the inward and the outward, especially in terms of Spain's religious and social fabric. The ecclesial building therefore is a motif of Spain's Catholic history and identity.

This study aims to contribute to debates on the intersections between culture, politics, and religion in nineteenth-century Spain. I propose to illuminate particularly the understudied cultural ramifications of ecclesiastical expropriation, the social implications of exclaustration (the suppression and expulsion of Catholic religious communities), and the issues surrounding the shifting valorization and signification of religious beliefs, edifices, and properties. I therefore take a different approach to other studies on disentailment and the religious question, which focus solely on the legal, political, and artistic aspects of these phenomena, although I am also indebted to such scholarship.

Overview of Nineteenth-Century Spain

Before embarking on studies related to the religious question, I will outline the chronology of salient historical landmarks of nineteenth-century Spain, which I divide into three sections for the purposes of this study: 1800–1830, 1830–1860, and 1860–1900. Critical stages in these periods include the declaration of new constitutions, the Carlist Wars, disentailment laws, and major shifts in the political arena regarding monarchy and republicanism. I expand on these issues in chapter 1.

The Napoleonic occupation of Spain began with the French invasion in 1808, during which José I (Joseph Bonaparte) reigned after Fernando VI's brief period of rule in 1808. In 1812, the first liberal Constitution of Cádiz was promulgated, only to be abrogated by Fernando VII upon returning to the throne in 1814.

The Liberal Triennium (1820–1823) took place after the revolt of lieutenant colonel Rafael del Riego to reestablish the Constitution of Cádiz. Although the Liberal Triennium saw Ferdinand VII giving way to constitutionalism, this would end after the French invasion in 1823, which restored him to absolutist power. The so-called Ominous Decade ensued until Fernando VII's death in 1833. By then, Spain's colonial losses in the Americas had triggered a web of economic, political, dynastic, and social crises that relegated the former imperial power to a "second-rate" nation in Europe.[10]

Fernando VII's daughter, Isabel II, ascended the throne in 1833; acting as regents were her mother, María Cristina, until 1840 and General Baldomero Espartero (1793–1879) until 1843. Isabel II's reign saw the rise of the Liberal Revolution, particularly through the promulgation of the Constitution of 1837 and the ascendance of the prime minister Mendizábal, whose disentailment laws were enacted in 1836.

INTRODUCTION   5

The Revolutionary Sexenium (1868–1874) commenced with the 1868 Revolution, known as La Gloriosa, and Isabel's deposition and exile to France. General Francisco Serrano headed the provisional government in 1869. After the brief rule of Amadeo I in 1871–1873, the short-lived First Spanish Republic was proclaimed (1873–1874). The Bourbon monarchy was restored under Alfonso XII from 1874 to 1885 and his son Alfonso XIII from 1886 to 1931, with his mother, the queen consort María Cristina, acting as regent from 1885 to 1902.

STUDIES ON THE RELIGIOUS QUESTION AND DISENTAILMENT

Most studies on the religious question in nineteenth-century Spain have centered on historical research, as evident in the works of Raymond Carr, José Álvarez Junco, Francisco Tomás y Valiente, and Adrian Shubert. Regarding disentailment, Francisco Simón Segura asserts that this religious, social, and economic phenomenon still requires more scholarly attention.[11] Francisco Tomás y Valiente states that laws of disentailment started under Carlos IV and Prime Minister Manuel Godoy in the late 1700s.[12] Such liberalizing economic measures were mirrored previously during the reign of the preceding monarch, Carlos III, in the proposals of politicians like Pedro Rodríguez de Campomanes, whose project to stem the growth of ecclesiastical mortmains was condemned by the Church. Throughout the nineteenth century, the main pieces of legislation concerning ecclesiastical expropriation were Mendizábal's decrees in 1836 and 1837, Espartero's law in 1841, and Madoz's law in 1855.[13] A primary concern raised at the Cortes of Cádiz was the national debt, which totaled 7,000 million reales in 1808 due to the war effort and increased to more than 19 billion in 1827.[14] Tomás y Valiente concludes that later in the century, disentailment was essential for facilitating the shift from the ancien régime to a capitalist, bourgeois revolution.[15]

Little addressed to date, however, are literary responses to disentailment's confiscatory policies and their concomitant ethical and sociocultural impacts. Francisco Javier Ramón Solans signals that the experience and perspectives of the clergy regarding political, social, economic, and cultural changes remain to be explored.[16] While almost all studies on disentailment mention the expulsion and transferal of not only priests but also friars and nuns, how these religious orders experienced exclaustration individually and collectively continues to be an arguably neglected aspect. To date, the social experience of exclaustration can be gleaned from recent research as well as from a few extant primary sources penned in nineteenth-century and early twentieth-century Spain.

These sources include an anonymous poem and two biographies, which provide glimpses into the virtually silent "afterlives" of exclaustrated nuns and clergy. The poem, titled "Representación que a la reina de las virtudes la Caridad dirige un quilibet exclaustrado, con solo el objeto de hallar el socorro y alivio de ella," was published in Madrid in 1838.[17] An exclaustrated friar's plea for aid, the text details his poverty and solitude. Eustasio Esteban's 1919 biography, *El siervo de Dios Fr. Diego José de Rejas: Religioso agustino exclaustrado de la provincia de Andalucía; Posiciones y artículos para la causa de su beatificación* [The servant of God Fr. Diego José de Rejas: Exclaustrated Augustinian religious of the province of Andalusia; Opinions and articles for the cause of his beatification], gives an overview of the life of exclaustrated Augustinian friar Diego José de Rejas (1807–1867). He taught Latin and humanities until the suppression of his monastery, after which he moved into a house with other excloistered friars, to return later to his family in Huelma, Jaén. He lived a life of destitution given that, being only twenty-eight years old, he did not qualify for the pension, which was only assigned to ordained priests above the age of forty, according to the 1837 law of suppression.[18] Another exclaustrated friar was the Dominican Claudio Sancho de Contreras (1811–1886). During the Napoleonic occupation and then under the 1836 disentailment laws, his community was forced to abandon the convent of Santa Cruz in Segovia. From this religious house, established in 1218, Sancho de Contreras was credited with safeguarding a chalice that had been a gift from the Catholic Monarchs to the Dominicans of Segovia. Although they no longer lived together, the excloistered Dominicans continued to uphold their vocations, meeting for religious ceremonies and administering spiritual and material aid to one another.[19]

Intrigued by the disregard for the human factor of exclaustration in scholarly debates, Antonio Iturbe Saíz questions the fate of the 32,000 friars and 15,000 nuns who were expelled from their communal abodes and religious ways of life:

> Se vieron de la noche a la mañana en la calle, con un sueldo miserable, cuando lo cobraron, con sus ideales de vida destrozados, con sus compañeros dispersos. Claro que no todos fueron fieles a sus ideales religiosos y que muchos se metieron en política o lucharon a favor de los carlistas. Pero de ahí a concluir que había que exterminar a esta clase social como apestados, hay una diferencia.[20]
>
> [They suddenly found themselves out on the street from one day to the next, with a meager salary, when they received it, with their life's dreams destroyed, with their companions scattered. Certainly, not all were faithful to their religious ideals, and many were involved in politics or fought for the Carlists. But between this situation and the conclusion that one had to exterminate this social class as pariahs, there is a difference.]

Iturbe Saíz's consideration of the religious orders as a social class sheds light on the changing understanding of the role of nuns and clergy in Spain. It is worth noting that in nineteenth-century Spain, the religious orders did not make up a large percentage of the population. José María Antequera wrote that Spain had 2,051 male religious houses, 1,075 female religious houses, and 92,927 cloistered

INTRODUCTION

individuals at the start of the century. Religious orders at that time thus comprised less than 1 percent of a nationwide population of 10,164,096.[21] According to José Manuel Cuenca, by 1826, the number of religious orders decreased to 37,363 regular clergy and 23,552 nuns.[22] The exclaustration of these individuals would not have meant as much to the rest of the Spanish populace as it would have to the nuns and monks themselves, whose expulsion signified an irreversible change in their spiritual lives and the religious focus of their identities to which they had been "called."[23] The impact of disentailment and exclaustration on clergy is implicit in Bécquer's texts and mentioned specifically in the works of Böhl, Galdós, and Pereda.

Much of the scholarship on disentailment has been largely quantitative, focusing primarily on political, legal, and economic analyses. In his study on disentailment, Germán Rueda comments that the first monographs on Mendizábal's and Espartero's disentailment legislation dealt solely with the financial aspects of auctioned goods.[24] Of greater interest to architects, art historians, and professionals of the heritage sector in recent times have been case studies throughout Spain that illuminate aspects of Spain's artistic patrimony, much of which has changed over the years. One prime example of the quantitative and artistic approach to disentailment in recent bibliography is Francisco Martí Gilabert's *La desamortización española* [The Spanish disentailment, 2003], which outlines the political, economic, social, and cultural effects of ecclesiastical confiscation. This study delineates the historical background of disentailment: the politics of Godoy, confiscatory measures, and the Spanish Church's financial resources.[25] It examines Mendizábal's laws of disentailment, the auction system, the abolition of the *diezmo* [tithing system], the sale of properties belonging to the secular clergy (clerics not associated with a religious order), and the consolidation of ecclesiastical confiscation.

Changes were taking place throughout the West in the nineteenth century, with new ideas developing about religion and its place in modern society. The tenets of the Enlightenment that infused the intellectual trends of Krausism, positivism, and rationalism pointed toward a "natural" religion of humanity. This brand of interior and rational spirituality would differ from the "theatrical," dogmatic, and heavily corporeal aspects of Catholicism, a religion of "real presence."[26] Spanish Catholicism, as Mary Vincent remarks, has had a history of both public presence and personal belief.[27]

EXCARNATION AND SECULARIZATION

Essential to my study is Charles Taylor's notion of excarnation, which he defines as a form of secularization that strips away embodied, "enfleshed" forms of religious life in favor of a perceived internal, private, and unseen spiritual core.[28] The idea of excarnation therefore indicates the removal of a substance or something that fills a void. I suggest that Taylor's thesis is useful for approaching the rationale behind disentailment, which, by seeking to modernize and economically bolster the Spanish nation, also shaped approaches to religion. The latter would prove problematic, given that the Catholic faith melds both the corporeal and the spiritual in its theological and liturgical aspects, as is expressed primarily through the dogma of the hypostatic union: Christ's twofold natures of divinity and humanity.[29] Crucial therefore to the Catholic sensibility is its visual culture.[30] What Álvarez Junco underlines as the visible, external, and public nature of Spanish Catholicism—its Baroque, counterreformist character—would be challenged by Enlightened, internalized versions of faith.[31]

The impact of disentailment on Spain's sociocultural fabric forms part of the nation's cultural memory.[32] Often overlooked are the collective experiences of the affected monastic and conventual communities, the Spanish Catholic population, and Spanish society as a whole. The first sector mentioned would have disagreed with disentailment more than other religious, social, and political groups in Spain. Böhl, Bécquer, and Pereda address the social ramifications of disentailment and exclaustration in their literary texts through somber themes such as loss and oblivion.

My study focuses on literature because of its capacity to provide, as Astrid Erll and Ann Rigney remark, a "mimesis of memory" in that it renders observable the process of memory.[33] This observation is valuable in understanding perceptions and recollections of expropriated and abandoned ecclesial sites and their former religious communities. In his interpretation of the relationship between religion and cultural memory, Jan Assmann argues that religion seeks to "maintain the world" through ritual coherence; that is, the rendering sacred of visible media such as symbols, edifices, sites, and images.[34] Catholicism involves a particularly transformed cultural memory in which the scriptures and the priesthood are witnesses to the sacred, to be passed down as canonical institutions throughout the generations.[35] Drawing on Assmann's remark that "all culture is a struggle with oblivion," I consider that religion and literature are concerned with memorialization. Writing, a system of notation, connotes the passing down of "markers" of memory to curtail the influences of forgetfulness, change, and disintegration.[36] The very act of recording through writing, Assmann argues, renders it an innate cultural medium of retrospection.[37]

Today the polyvalent term *culture* refers to the arts, refinement, and manifestations of human intellect and taste as well as the distinct amalgam of ideas, customs, and a way of life that characterizes a certain group, people, society, nation, or time. The myriad definitions of *culture*, Michael Thompson, Richard Ellis, and Aaron Wildavsky note, are constant matters of debate. On the one hand, culture may comprise a series of "mental products" such as values, beliefs, symbols, and ideologies; on the other hand, it may refer to the lifestyle, relations, and attitudes of a certain people.[38]

INTRODUCTION

E. Inman Fox argues that culture is the interpretation of ways of thinking, feeling, and believing. Hence, culture is, overall, the search for meaning.[39] Moreover, the *Oxford English Dictionary* acknowledges the multiple origins of *culture* in French and Latin. In medieval times, the French term referred to cultivation and husbandry, while later it meant the development of language, literature, and education. The French *culture* was derived from the classical Latin etymons *cultūra* [to cultivate] and *cultus* [worship, veneration]. Set in primarily agricultural areas, Pereda's novels demonstrate the similarities between cultivation and religion, which recall the scriptural call for the development and nourishment of faith, particularly in the parable of the sower. Cultivation, which includes tilling the land and growing plants, suggests an organic process of progress and development. Furthermore, the religious meaning of culture (*cultus*) is manifest in the institutionalized spirituality of nineteenth-century Spain and is particularly apparent in the works of Bécquer, Böhl, and Pereda.

As mentioned above, I will interweave my textual analyses with a discussion of theories pertaining to cultural memory, collective memory, and heritage. Cultural memory has burgeoned in the area of cultural studies, as Mieke Bal observes.[40] The performativity of cultural remembrance lends itself to nostalgia, which, if critically tempered and historically informed, can be both productive and uplifting, given that nostalgia is a structure of relating to the past.[41] Regarding collective memory, I draw on Maurice Halbwachs's seminal work *On Collective Memory*, which highlights the relevance of the visible and corporeal in cultural recollection. As he puts it, "There is hence no memory without perception."[42] The act of remembrance can never be purely interior and individual, since any collective memory draws on the ideas of others and external factors such as individuals and objects.[43] Signposting collective memories, according to Halbwachs, are established landmarks and concrete images, which sustain our ideas.[44] This observation is similar to Nora's notion that one must have the will to remember *lieux de mémoire*.[45] Such an attachment of responsibility to the act of remembrance is striking. As Nora remarks, "Memory attaches itself to sites, whereas history attaches itself to events."[46] It is the interplay of memory and history that creates these *lieux de mémoire*.

My study on religious memory, a conjunction of cultural and collective memories, leads to a consideration of heritage studies. Nora's "duty" of remembrance and Halbwachs's notion of collective religious memory demonstrate that material spaces generate meaning. This idea contends Laurajane Smith's statement that all heritage is intangible.[47] For Smith, it is "meaning-making" that creates the heritage site.[48] Yet the religious site assumes another dimension because it is rendered sacred through consecration, which is the ritualized conferral of sacred value.[49] This process is important to consider, as it illuminates the value of a spiritual edifice.

Remembering these disentailed and confiscated buildings and their anterior purposes, I will also stress in my analysis a sociology of ruins. Crucial to my understanding of ruins and their role in the selected writings of Böhl and Bécquer is Kieran Flanagan's assertion that ruins disturb.[50] Hence, they are not only sites of a bygone era but places that can still hold sway in the public consciousness. A significant layer of symbolism envelops ecclesiastical ruins, given their spiritual purpose. In Anne Janowitz's study of ruins as topoi in English Romantic poetry, ruins are depicted not only as evidence of "ineluctable genesis and decay" but also as challenges to the structure of the present by conjuring an unforeseeable repetition of the past. Janowitz claims that longing supersedes memory.[51] Nostalgia, therefore, unites the icon of the ruin with memory studies.

Chapter 1 concerns the ways in which various constituents of the Spanish nation perceived the religious question in terms of Catholic belief and practice. I will lead into a definition of the religious question and examine the hotly contested notion of the Two Spains. This concept is debated due to varying political cultures within Spanish liberalism, which included moderates, progressives, democrats, federalists, republicans, federal republicans, radical republicans, and reformist republicans.[52] Referring to the differing visions regarding Spain's future, this concept denotes the political, intellectual, and spiritual clashes between tradition and modernity. Subsequently, I will focus on ecclesiastical disentailment and its contemporary historiography. I will first outline legislation and events pertaining to ecclesiastical confiscation and exclaustration before analyzing a selection of parliamentary speeches, periodical essays, and clerical responses that focus on these realities. Such literary reactions to disentailment will serve to highlight the conflicting views that radical liberals and conservatives had of the Spanish Church and its apparatus: its property, the secular clergy, and the religious orders (monks, friars, and nuns).

Chapter 2 focuses on four novels by Cecilia Böhl de Faber (Fernán Caballero): *La gaviota* [The seagull, 1849], *La familia de Alvareda* [The Alvareda family, 1856], *Callar en vida y perdonar en muerte* [Silence in life and forgiveness in death, 1856], and *Lágrimas* [Tears, 1862].[53] Böhl's depictions of Spanish village life and customs have seen her categorized as a figure of the literary movement known as *costumbrismo*, which features popular verse, dictums, and songs to communicate social attitudes and norms.[54] In my examination of Böhl's novels, I will foreground her nostalgia for Spain's religious heritage, to which she ascribes qualities of piety and glory. Of paramount importance to the maintenance of Spanish patrimony is the family unit, which Böhl depicts as ideally safeguarding religious and moral values and norms. Thus, her traditionalist writings exalt Spain's purportedly devout past by portraying modern liberal ideas as foreign and harmful. Juxtaposing the Andalusian village with a Madrid seen as progressive and individualistic, Böhl accentuates the boundary between traditional life and modern pursuits. As I later point out, this dichotomous representation of the *pueblo* [people] and the capital is also manifest in the works of Bécquer, Galdós, and Pereda.

INTRODUCTION   11

Chapter 3 centers on Bécquer's writings: *Historia de los templos de España* [History of the temples of Spain, 1857], *Cartas desde mi celda* [Letters from my cell, 1864], and *Leyendas* [Legends, 1858–1864]. While architectural and monumental ekphrasis was a contemporary literary trend, Bécquer's highly personal and poetic reflections in *Historia* render vital the ecclesial building's role in Spain's national identity and heritage. In his study of Toledo's ancient churches, synagogues, and mosques, Bécquer highlights the town's historically religious landscape and depicts its monastic and ecclesial buildings as landmarks of Spain's monarchical and chivalric history. Like Böhl, Bécquer laments the inability to return to this idealized past.

Bécquer expresses the same nostalgic sentiment in *Cartas*, written during his convalescence from tuberculosis in Saragossa's Monasterio de Veruela. In these letters, he portrays religious faith and Spain's artistic past as the cornerstones of its national heritage. Such reflections are amplified in his *Leyendas*, where Bécquer elevates the presence of the divine and the supernatural by utilizing Gothic and Romantic elements. In the tales "La ajorca de oro" [The golden bracelet, 1861], "El miserere" [The Miserere, 1862], and "El beso" [The kiss, 1863], Bécquer deploys medieval, monastic, and otherworldly settings to embody the spiritual realm. I argue that these fantastical stories, which channel the sentiments of his *Historia* and *Cartas*, constitute a defense of the unseen and the sacred in what Bécquer believed was an increasingly rationalistic and materialistic society.

Chapter 4 examines, in the works of Benito Pérez Galdós, the rationalist goal to reconcile faith and modern pursuits through a new brand of spirituality. Galdós's *novelas de historia* [historical novels] and *novelas de tesis* [thesis novels] reveal the contested conceptions that traditionalist, moderate, and progressive sectors of Spanish society had of Spain's national future. Most significantly, I will argue that Galdós articulates the need for a vital force, which comprises an inward spirituality as opposed to the incarnational and dogmatic nature of Catholicism, to invite the realignment of national priorities and mindsets in accordance with progressive ideology.

Galdós pursues this notion of vital force in four novels: *Doña Perfecta* (1876), *Gloria* (1877), *Mendizábal* (1898), and *Montes de Oca* (1900). *Doña Perfecta* and *Gloria* are ideological novels that deal with religious intransigence and the perceived conflict between orthodoxy and progress. Galdós's historical novels, *Mendizábal* and *Montes de Oca*, are based on their respective eponymous figures: Juan Álvarez Mendizábal (1790–1853), Spain's main proponent of extreme disentailment legislation, and Manuel Montes de Oca (1803–1841), a statesman who supported the regency of Isabel II's mother, María Cristina de Borbón-Dos Sicilias. Having written these two novels after the restoration of the Bourbon monarchy in 1875, Galdós employs fictitious characters to discuss key sociopolitical issues surrounding religion and society in nineteenth-century Spain. Finally, this chapter will focus on Galdós's play *Electra* (1901), which draws on the marital symbolism prevalent in *Doña Perfecta* and *Gloria* to portray the clash between orthodoxy and rationalism.

Chapter 5 analyzes José María de Pereda's novels *Blasones y talegas* [Blazons and sacks, 1869], *De tal palo, tal astilla* [Like father, like son, 1880], and *Sotileza* (1885) together with several of his essays in the weekly periodical *El Tío Cayetano* [Uncle Cayetano, 1858–1859 and 1868–1869], which he co-founded. Pereda's works elucidate the status of religious belief and practice in Spain and the implications of social reforms for traditional ways of life. His essays in *El Tío Cayetano* denounce ecclesiastical disentailment, while his novels articulate the fundamental ties between belief and belonging. In *Blasones y talegas*, Pereda criticizes the restructuring of social hierarchies, rendering such transformations as symptomatic of modernity, which he regards as impious, heretical, and invasive in Spanish society. A response to Spain's sociopolitical situation, as Raquel Gutiérrez Sebastián notes, *Blasones y talegas* was written after the 1868 Revolution.[55]

It was in response to Galdós's representation of religious intransigence in *Gloria* that Pereda published *De tal palo, tal astilla*, in which familial relationships are portrayed as laying the foundations for the cultivation of religious beliefs and traditions. As in the works of Böhl and Galdós, the family unit in Pereda's novels acts as a microcosm of the Spanish nation, as does the village community, which he depicts as a bucolic refuge from the entanglements of modern infrastructure and commercial enterprise. Pereda's idealization of the village community is heightened in his eponymous novel *Sotileza*, which concerns the inhabitants of a small town in Santander, northern Spain. In all three novels, Pereda forges a connection between faith and family.

In my final reflections, I offer my insights on principal themes in my chosen texts to illuminate understudied facets of the tensions between religion and the modern nation. I will also highlight my study's relevance to the contested place of religion and ecclesiastical edifices in Spain today, touching on recent events pertaining to the observance and visibility of Catholicism. I hope that this study will serve as an interdisciplinary platform of inquiry into the significance of sacred buildings nowadays and as a springboard for future discussions on cultural and religious heritage.

CHAPTER 1

Modern Matter

DISENTAILMENT AND THE RELIGIOUS QUESTION

Figure 2, a photograph taken at the Monasterio de Piedra [Monastery of Stone] in Saragossa, shows a plaque that recalls Mendizábal's disentailment law and testifies to the monastery's resultant damage and loss. The memento's language is emotionally charged. The phrases "templo destruido" [destroyed temple] and "imágenes mutiladas" [mutilated images] depict the monastery's confiscation as a tortuous experience before it passed into private ownership. Ecclesiastical edifices such as this monastery are still extant nowadays, either in various states of ruin or transformed into new edifices. Other church buildings were said to be "desaparecidos" [disappeared], according to the gallery labels at the Museum of Salamanca, built in 1835 to house artwork taken from Salamanca's decommissioned religious buildings.

The abovementioned adjectives, which refer to destruction, mutilation, and disappearance, not only personify the ecclesiastical edifices they describe. They also connote the social experiences of trauma arising from their secularization. Cathy Caruth writes that *trauma* was originally the Greek word for "wound," an injury inflicted on a body. The notion that trauma was an injury to the psyche was a Freudian innovation.[1] Freud likened melancholia to "an open wound."[2] I posit that the corporeal metaphor of the "damaged" religious building in the monastery's plaque corresponds with that of the Church, defined as the mystical body of Christ.[3] The intertwining of the spiritual body and the building expresses itself fully in the monastic and conventual community. Members of the clergy and religious orders, expelled by laws of suppression, were forced to find anew their places in a world that they had renounced on entering religious life. The respective suppression and secularization of religious communities and buildings, therefore, were perceived as traumatic experiences.

A pattern of disjuncture interlaces the historical events of expropriation and exclaustration. The physical dismantling of the religious edifice and the

13

Figure 2. Monasterio de Piedra, Saragossa.

communal separation from the monastery resulted from the seismic social tensions between liberal and traditionalist sectors in nineteenth-century Spain around the so-called religious question: the sum of ideological, material, and spiritual ruptures between the old order and the new. The breaking away from the old Spain to construct the new nation entailed a process of fragmentation, an aspect to which I will return in chapter 2 on Bécquer. The fragmenting of the

MODERN MATTER

old "matter" of religion, as depicted in figure 2, encapsulates the process of excarnation, the stripping away of the visible and material substance of religion.

Combining its aforesaid religious and material connotations, the edifice features throughout this study as a motif that illustrates the construction of Spain's intertwined national and spiritual identity. This initial chapter will examine in detail the building blocks that comprised the religious question. I will first outline the economic and political contexts of nineteenth-century Spain. Focusing on a selection of discourses from political, journalistic, and clerical spheres, I will then delineate the legislative and historiographical backgrounds behind ecclesiastical confiscation and exclaustration, which represented the tensions between liberal and traditionalist sectors in the Spanish nation. The liberals comprised the *moderados* [moderates] and *progresistas* [progressives]. Fox asserts that the more conservative moderates sought a limited bourgeois revolution in the interests of an elite, and the more forward-thinking progressives stressed the secularization of society and the advancement of industry and commerce for the good of the proletariat.[4]

ECONOMIC STABILITY IN NINETEENTH-CENTURY SPAIN

Nineteenth-century Spain experienced immense political upheaval and socioeconomic crises. As Jaime Vicens Vives states categorically, this century was characterized by a "spirit of reform."[5] The War of Independence against France (1808–1814) produced devastating results for Spain, exacerbated by not only its colonial losses but also the confluence of foreign plunder, agricultural failures, and widespread famine.[6] In 1808 and 1809, José I decreed the suppression of religious orders and the expropriation and reconversion of their properties into national assets, primarily to pay for the French military occupation of Spain. Previously, Carlos IV had implemented disentailment measures in 1795 but had made an agreement with Pius VII beforehand.[7] Governments under Fernando VII and Isabel II addressed Spain's national debt through the expropriation and selling of religious and civil buildings, labeled *manos muertas* [mortmains] due to their perceived inability to garner national revenue.[8]

At the start of the nineteenth century, a small middle class was already emerging alongside a liberal Spanish intelligentsia with shared political and economic interests, chief among them being the construction of Spain's national identity and sovereignty in response to the vacuum of power in the later years of the French invasion. The Cortes of Cádiz, convoked in 1810 as the national assembly during the Napoleonic occupation of Spain, proposed a series of reforms to solve the nation's financial problems. These modifications imitated the bourgeois ideal, aiming to eliminate legal feudalism in rural areas and contribute to an economic expansion by confiscating ecclesiastical property and suppressing guilds.[9] The Cortes's decree on June 17, 1812, echoed those of José I's foreign government in that assets of ecclesiastical communities were seized again.

Stanley G. Payne holds that the liberal Constitution of 1812 was the most reasonable bridging attempt between the old order and the modern in its goal to secure economic, political, and national stability.[10] It aimed to incorporate the liberal principles of the Enlightenment throughout Western Europe while taking care not to disparage elements of religious and cultural tradition.[11] Proponents of the Enlightenment had criticized the *manos muertas*, considering them hindrances to progress.[12] The Constitution of 1812 signaled the start of a lengthy and rocky road toward the progress envisioned by the liberals of the Cortes and the radical liberals or *exaltados* [extremists] of the 1820–1823 Liberal Triennium.[13] Liberals were thus divided: the moderates supported a revision of the constitution to involve monarchical involvement with the government; the radical liberals decried further limitations in defense of the integrity of the constitution.[14]

Accompanying the political and economic reforms necessary for the construction of Spain's sovereign nationhood was the religious question. In five of Spain's constitutions in the nineteenth century, Catholicism featured as the religion of the State and the Spanish people. Article 12 of the Constitution of 1812 proclaimed that Catholicism was the "perpetual" religion of Spain, while article 10 of the Constitution of 1837 and article 11 of the Constitution of 1845 stipulated the Spanish nation's obligation to maintain the observance of Catholic worship and ministry. Although the Constitutions of 1869 and 1876 repeated the statements of the former, they also promoted tolerance for the private practice of other faiths, which indicated a growing awareness of the changing spiritual fabric of the Spanish nation.

At the start of the nineteenth century, the Church in Spain had participated in the collective resistance against the invading French army and France's perceived heterodoxy. As I will point out later, Böhl, Bécquer, and Pereda illuminate the impact of this foreignness on Spain's interlaced cultural and religious identity. During the French invasion, members of the Spanish clergy mobilized the so-called *pueblo* [Spanish people] against the foreign troops. In Andalusia, the Capuchin friar Rafael de Vélez witnessed public calls for the defense of the faith and the monarchy, evident in slogans such as "¡Viva María Santísima, viva Jesucristo, viva su fe, su religión, viva Fernando VII, mueran los franceses!" [Long live Holy Mary, long live Jesus Christ, long live his faith, his religion, long live Fernando VII, death to the French!]. In reaffirming its support for the Spanish monarchy and Catholic faith, the Church disparaged Napoleon and the anticlerical and radical ideas of the French Revolution.[15]

While the Church emphasized the conservation of Spain's religious past and identity, perceived to be under assault from the influx of foreign forces and ideas, Spanish liberals sought to respond to the fractured advent of modernity. Fernando VII's oscillation between absolutism and constitutionalism revealed the nation's tug-of-war between tradition and modernity, although the energy, support, and success of opponents of absolutism were more important in these

MODERN MATTER

political swings. While his return symbolized Spanish independence, the triumph of the monarchy, and a national victory, his reinstatement of the Spanish Inquisition largely disappointed the liberals who had helped him regain the throne.[16] Liberal exiles returning to their homeland after the death of Fernando VII brought with them political and economic ideas, nationalistic goals, Romantic visions, and the cultural mythologies of France and England.[17] Equipped with new philosophies and ideas, Spanish liberals were determined to reshape Spain's identity to pave the way for its future.

LIBERALISM AND THE SPANISH NATION

The liberal construction of the modern nation, as Fox maintains, involves the combination of the veridical with the mythical.[18] The nation, operating at the service of nationalism, is characterized by a remembered common past, cultural and linguistic ties, and an alleged equality between members. This rhetoric of sameness and sharedness demonstrates therefore that the nation is essentially an artifact composed of popular convictions, loyalties, and solidarities.[19] From the perspective of liberalism, Fox states that the people of a nation are an active political subject.[20] The civil order, justice system, and economic structure provided by a liberal government demand the solidarity of its citizens, who therefore experience a sentiment of belonging to the nation.[21] This sense of belonging, however, would become problematized in the sociopolitical context.

Spanish liberalism was beset by crises in political, social, and spiritual spheres. Such predicaments were evident in the divisions between Spain's past and present and between the Spanish people and their religious identity. In an essay published in *El Pensamiento de la Nación* on June 4, 1845, the Spanish philosopher and political theorist Jaime Balmes wrote that the rise of liberalism was responsible for what he perceived as Spain's identity crisis. Spain in the mid-nineteenth century hardly resembled France and England, whose politics the nation had supposedly adopted, yet it was nothing like the old Baroque Spain of Felipe II either.[22] Writing from a conservative and Catholic perspective, Balmes proceeded to challenge what he considered was the liberal dismissal of Catholicism, reaffirming that religion was at the core of Spain's legal and cultural identity:

> ¿No se descubre aquí la España antigua con sus sentimientos monárquicos y religiosos, luchando contra los que intentan transformarla a viva fuerza? De todo esto prescindieron los liberales; no se tomaron la pena de atender a lo que existía, antes de ensayar la realización de lo que a ellos les halagaba. Comenzaron por zaherir a la religión, cuando la religión era lo más popular que había en España; comenzaron por atacar a las clases privilegiadas, y muy particularmente al clero, cuando el clero se formaba del mismo pueblo, cuando los conventos eran un asilo para muchos hijos del pueblo . . . cuando el pueblo estaba

en incesante contacto, en íntima relación con la Iglesia, no solo en lo tocante a lo religioso, lo que se enlaza con la vida entera, sino también en lo concerniente a educación, instrucción y hasta medios de subsistencia.[23]

[Is not the old Spain, with its monarchical and religious sentiments, fighting against those who attempt to transform it forcefully to be found here? The liberals dispensed with all this. They did not endeavor to care for what had previously existed before attempting to execute what gratified them; they began by mocking religion when religion was what enjoyed the most favor among the Spanish people; they began by attacking the privileged classes, and particularly the clergy, when the clergy were part of the same people, when convents were a sanctuary for many children of the people . . . when the people were in ceaseless contact, intimately connected to the Church, not only in a religious sense, which links to life in its entirety, but also in matters concerning education, instruction, and even their livelihoods.]

The distinction that Balmes makes between the Two Spains reflects not only the division between the clergy and the government but also that between the Church and the liberal intelligentsia.[24] While the new Spain of the liberals was nascent, Balmes recognized its growing strength: "Es su parte más inquieta, que más se agita, que más suena en todos los negocios públicos"[25] [It is what is most restless, most unsettled, and makes the most noise in public affairs].

For the traditionalist Balmes, the liberals aimed to transform the meaning of religion. While many liberals and progressives believed in the social functions of religion, what nature this role would take was a question that was, for the most part, unresolved. As Balmes saw it, comprising "the new Spain" were two supposedly anarchical factions united in their pursuit of individualism and rationalism and distinct only in their approach to the past:

La España nueva se encamina a sustituir la incredulidad a la fe, el goce a la moral, la teoría a la tradición, el interés privado a los antiguos vínculos sociales . . . se divide en dos fracciones; unos quieren anarquía en las ideas y anarquía en los hechos; otros anarquía en las ideas, de[s]potismo legal sobre los hechos. . . . Ambas fracciones empero convienen en quitar toda influencia a la España antigua, solo que la una la quiere tomar a su servicio, la otra la quiere oprimir sin rodeos. Pero ya sea con unos, ya sea con otros, es evidente para todo hombre observador que se tiende a tra[n]sformar enteramente la España [antigua].[26]

[The new Spain is heading toward replacing faith with disbelief, morality with pleasure, tradition with theory, ancient social bonds with private interests . . . it is divided into two factions; some want anarchy in ideas and deeds; others want anarchy in ideas and legal tyranny over events. . . . Both factions, nevertheless, agree to completely disempower the old Spain, with the sole difference being that one faction desires to have it in its service; the other, to oppress it without further ado. Irrespectively, however, it is evident to all observers that there is a tendency to transform old Spain entirely.]

Balmes's reference to "the old Spain" evokes the interconnection between the Catholic religion and tradition. Representing contesting national mythologies, for Santos Juliá, the Two Spains denoted a deeply national and constitutional battle between the young and old, the living and the official.[27] Álvarez Junco similarly juxtaposes these two mythologies of Spain: the liberal-progressive quest for liberty and democracy and the national-Catholic emphasis on unity and monarchical authority.[28] Conversely, William J. Callahan considers that the metaphor of the Two Spains is inadequate because the conceptualizations of the Spanish nation and its Church were numerous and multifaceted, which testifies to the political (and, I add, religious) fragmentation that accompanied and characterized the century.[29] For his part, Xavier Andreu Miralles considers the "Two Spains" a problematic interpretation because it overlooks the ambivalence and complexity with which Spanish authors approached Europe and modernity. He identifies, instead, a wide gamut of gray areas in which Spanish authors did not deny the advances of European nations like France and England; however, few were inclined to accept that principal features of the Spanish nation had to be sacrificed for the sake of progress.[30]

Spain was not an isolated instance in its yearning for self-determination and freedom from the old order, given that neighboring Western European nations were also undergoing societal and religious reforms and sharing in the widespread antagonism toward the anciens régimes.[31] Since these revolutions took place in historically Catholic societies, the papacy was involved in the turmoil. On September 15, 1864, the Italian king Victor Emmanuel II and Napoleon III signed the September Convention, which stipulated that the Italian government had to respect papal territory.[32] In that same year, Pius IX published the encyclical *Quanta Cura*, which was accompanied by the *Syllabus of Errors* (1864), a document demonstrative of the Church's intransigence, which outlined eighty ideological and theological divergences from the Catholic religion manifest in the rise of modern liberalism.[33]

The proliferation of theories and concepts from the French Revolution and the Enlightenment had fermented in Europe to such an extent that by the nineteenth century, a good number of Spanish politicians and intellectuals were espousing liberal ideas. The neo-Catholic party emerged in the mid-1850s, promoting the restoration of Spanish religious unity.[34] Politicians and theorists such as Juan Donoso Cortés, the Marquis of Valdegamas, reflected much of the Spanish, neo-Catholic, integrist stance against liberalism, as in texts like his *Ensayo sobre el catolicismo, el liberalismo y el socialismo considerados en sus principios fundamentales* [Essay on Catholicism, liberalism, and socialism considered in their fundamental principles, 1851], which criticized the novel trends of liberalism and socialism. As Begoña Urigüen states, Donoso's correspondence with the papal hierarchy contributed to the elaboration of the *Syllabus*, to which the neo-Catholics looked in their determination to keep pure and untainted "la Iglesia verdadera frente a las protestas de confesionalidad de los católicos contemporizadores con las 'luces del siglo'"[35] [the true Church against all protests of Catholics, who opposed the confessional Church and embraced "Enlightenment principles"]. Pope Pius IX was commended by the neo-Catholics for his integrist outlook, which paralleled Donoso's traditionalist principles: apocalyptic catastrophism, antimodernism, and the dichotomy between God and society, religion and politics, the Church and civilization.[36]

The traditionalist Catholic view of Spain as the champion of orthodoxy is mirrored in the words of the conservative historian Marcelino Menéndez y Pelayo in his *Historia de los heterodoxos españoles* [History of Spanish heterodoxies, 1880–1882]: "España, evangelizadora de la mitad del orbe, España, martillo de herejes, luz de Trento, espada de Roma, cuna de San Ignacio"[37] [Spain, evangelizer of half of the world; Spain, the hammer of heretics, light of Trent, sword of Rome, cradle of Saint Ignatius]. For Menéndez y Pelayo, dogmatic uniformity was synonymous with the nation's religious unity. These principles would later buttress national Catholicism in twentieth-century Francoist Spain, which was premised upon a Catholic national identity, shared interests between the Church and the State, and providentialism (the belief that all events on earth are controlled by God).[38]

Historiography of Disentailment

In my introduction, I declared that historiography on disentailment has mostly been quantitative. Vicens Vives recommended a systematic study driven by a "scientific attitude" as opposed to sentimentalist polemics to answer the "delicate question" of the true impact of disentailment on Spanish society.[39] Yet, as Rocío Román Collado explains, disentailment was not only an economic venture but also a sociocultural undertaking.[40] For Vicens Vives, scholarly responses to ecclesiastical and civil (secular property) disentailments from the 1800s to the 1950s were mainly adverse. Catholic historians and politicians generally considered ecclesiastical confiscation a grave act of pillage, indicative of irreligion and injustice, while collectivist and socialist-leaning intellectuals regarded civil disentailment in the same way, viewing the destitution of peasants as directly resulting from the manipulation of individualist theories of property.[41] These purportedly polemical writings provide glimpses into the understudied perceptions of a complex issue that transcended economics and interlaced spiritual and social fallouts.

Various political and ideological conflicts contributed to disentailment. Mendizábal's anticlericalism culminated in the imposition of severe disentailment laws, especially as a result of the Spanish clergy's alignment with the Carlist cause.[42] What therefore exacerbated the nation's divisions were the three Carlist Wars (1833–1840, 1846–1849, 1872–1876), in which the Carlists supported the claim of Fernando VII's brother, Carlos María Isidro de Borbón (1788–1855), to the Spanish throne instead of Fernando's daughter, Isabel II. The Carlists' observance of the Salic law, which excluded females from royal succession, indicated their advocacy for a return to the ancien régime.[43] Resisting these traditionalist principles, the liberal bourgeois revolution imposed ecclesiastical disentailment as a politico-economic measure, causing a strain in relations between the Church and the State and between the State and the Vatican.[44]

Under successive governments' disentailment laws, the Church lost its power not only to acquire new goods but also to possess and maintain ownership over its buildings due to their transformation into national goods.[45] The government's confiscatory measures placed Spain at odds with the pope, given its defiance of established Church doctrine.[46] Two royal decrees enforced the confiscation of ecclesiastical goods to ease the debt caused by the Peninsular War. A decree under José I on August 18, 1809, suppressed religious orders and took over their properties during the war. The Cortes of Cádiz, by a decree on September 13, 1813, declared buildings formerly belonging to the Jesuits and other suppressed convents and monasteries to be national goods, only to have some of these goods restored to convents with the return of Fernando VII. The Liberal Triennium, however, saw the reestablishment of the disentailment laws of 1813, which suppressed all convents with fewer than twelve resident members and prohibited the Church's acquisition of new property. The decree of October 1, 1820, also reduced the number of any religious orders that were not already suppressed.

After Fernando VII's death, of the anticlerical laws under Mendizábal, three prominent ones stood out. The decree of February 19, 1836, put up for sale the properties of suppressed religious communities; the decree of March 8, 1836, called for the suppression of all convents; and two royal decrees on July 29, 1837, nationalized the secular clergy's properties and claimed that assets pertaining to suppressed monasteries, convents, congregations, and religious houses and colleges would be sold to pay off the national debt. Under Espartero, the law of September 2, 1841, put up for sale all the properties of the secular clergy, leading to the expropriation of 62 percent of the clergy's assets.[47] Espartero had become prominent due to his defeat of the Carlists in Aragón and Catalonia in 1840 and took over the regency of Spain after the exile of María Cristina de Borbón-Dos Sicilias until his overthrow in 1843.[48] According to Shubert, Espartero's regency aimed to establish a streamlined Church subservient to the State that entailed expropriation, exclaustration, and the reorganization of parishes and dioceses and limited contact between the Spanish Church and Rome.[49]

The suppression and expulsion of religious orders and clergy from their residences demonstrate Mendizábal's government's emphasis on economic utility. In an 1812 decree from the Cortes of Cádiz, monastic orders with fewer than twenty-four members were appended to the list of the nation's profitable assets. Three of the Cortes's more radical measures saw ecclesiastical communities prohibited from acquiring any revenue-producing property and obliged such orders to sell part of their lands, while *diezmos* [ecclesiastical tithes] were also seized, even though these had already been reduced by 50 percent.[50] The economic consequences of disentailment resulted in destitution for some religious communities. For many nuns, there was a constant delay in pensions, as evident in the session of July 4, 1840, in the Congress of Deputies, when the situation of the convent of Santa Cruz in Santander was brought up.[51] There the nuns, "tal vez ... las monjas más miserables y desgraciadas de la Península" [perhaps ... the most miserable and unfortunate nuns of the Peninsula], had no provisions.[52] The impact of expropriation and exclaustration elicited criticism from the public toward the government. In September 1840, a communiqué from the Junta Provisional de Gobierno spoke of plans to direct some funds to wartime widows and nuns, while the periodical *El Corresponsal* called for the establishment of an association to collect donations for exclaustrated nuns. Martí Gilabert also notes that from Seville came the plea for "pan para las monjas"[53] [bread for the nuns].

Two agreements between Rome and Spain attempted to soften the disentailment laws: the 1845 Agreement, which stipulated the Spanish government's restitution of confiscated ecclesial properties and the Holy See's acknowledgment of the private buyers' proprietorship over acquired goods, and the 1851 Concordat between the Holy See and the Spanish government, which called for the Church's rights and patrimony to be respected.[54] As Carolyn P. Boyd maintains, the Spanish moderates and conservatives largely accepted the Catholic equation of national identity with religious unity as part of their agreement with the Church from the 1850s onward.[55] The concordat was canceled, however, by Madoz's 1855 disentailment law, which resumed the sale of ecclesiastical properties. Following the 1868 Revolution, disentailment laws that same year again suppressed the Jesuit order and other religious communities and secularized and nationalized all convents founded since 1837.[56]

THE SPANISH CHURCH'S PERSPECTIVE ON DISENTAILMENT

That ecclesiastical confiscation was mostly a battle of principles rather than mere economics was the stance taken up by the nineteenth-century moderate jurist and politician Santiago Tejada y Santamaría, who saw confiscation as an issue not only of accounting but also of religious and moral import.[57] The Church's perception of disentailment as sacrilege testifies to the sacredness of its properties, designated for worship and charitable activities. The politician and lawyer Juan

MODERN MATTER

Martín Carramolino wrote in *La Iglesia de España económicamente considerada* [The Spanish Church economically considered, 1850] that expropriation damaged the Church's ancient patrimony.[58] His treatise on the Church's economic independence drew on the traditional, orthodox conception of the Church's pastoral mission, which would require earthly resources for its fulfillment:

> Siendo la Iglesia, como queda ya sentado, una sociedad perfecta e independiente de toda otra autoridad temporal, debe contener dentro de sí misma todos los medios necesarios para conseguir su fin, que es la bienaventuranza de sus hijos en la vida eterna y como para obtenerla no hay otro camino que la profesión de la fe de Jesucristo, cuya religión exige indispensablemente un culto externo, requiere templos, altares y ornamentos; necesita de ministros exclusivamente dedicados a enseñar, corregir y consolar al hombre, acompañándole sin cesar y en todos los pasos y situaciones de la vida, desde la cuna hasta el sepulcro como debe socorrer por obligación divina a los pobres, que es la pensión irredimible con que le gravó Jesús al fundarla: y en fin como es una entidad política, una persona moral, un cuerpo social con necesidades físicas y materiales para su conservación.[59]

> [Since the Church, already established, is a perfect society independent of all other temporal authorities, it must contain within itself all necessary means to achieve its goal, which is the happiness of its children in eternal life, and because to achieve it there is no other way but to profess the faith of Jesus Christ, whose religion essentially demands a display of worship. It requires temples, altars, and ornaments; it needs ministers exclusively dedicated to teaching, instructing, and consoling humankind, accompanying them continuously without end and in all stages and situations in life, from the cradle to the grave just as it must help the poor by divine obligation, which is the irreversible duty with which Jesus charged the Church upon founding it, and finally, because it is a political entity, a moral person, a social body with physical and material needs for its conservation.]

Martín Carramolino's understanding of the Church as a political, moral, and social body reveals the intricate connections between religion and the Spanish nation.[60] His reference to the Church's obligation toward the poor criticizes the lack of opportunities for charity work resulting from expropriation and the exclaustration of priests and nuns. This dearth also reflected a public distrust, as Yongjiao Yang, Iain Brennan, and Mick Wilkinson suggest that charities rely on such for their existence and social legitimization. Religious charities were deemed to benefit only believers rather than the broader society.[61]

The disunity evident in the clerical hierarchy's conflicting perspectives on disentailment is yet another instance of the lengthy debates on directives for the Church. Conservative clerics committed to upholding the Church's proprietorship of its buildings and goods were considered by their liberal counterparts to be privileging papal and ecclesial authority. Hence, more than a theological and liturgical reform, the confiscation of Church goods was regarded as a deeply political measure on various levels.

Clerics both reformist and reactionary took to the press to voice their concerns. Several letters were responses from clergymen such as Hermano Bartolo, who replied to a pamphlet written by another cleric, who wrote under the pseudonym "El Solitario" [The Solitary One]. In El Solitario's 1813 work, titled *Juicio histórico-canónico-político de la autoridad de las naciones en los bienes eclesiásticos* [Historical-canonical-political judgment of the authority of nations over ecclesiastical goods], the forward-thinking author supported the abolition of ecclesiastical bodies, the reduction of clergy numbers, and the view that the Catholic Church was overly pious. Like the liberal members of parliament, El Solitario approved of the State's ownership of all the nation's goods, especially the Church's property:

> El legítimo dominio de los bienes eclesiásticos reside en el Soberano, quiere decir: en la universalidad de los individuos que componen una Nación a quien está radicalmente anexa la Soberanía, y que en fuerza de autoridad legislativa que le compete, permite a la Iglesia poseer bienes temporales.[62]

> [The legitimate dominion over ecclesiastical assets resides with the sovereign; that is, with the universality of individuals who comprise a nation to whom the sovereign is fundamentally attached, and who, by the power of the legislative authority that he holds, permits the Church to possess temporal goods.]

In contrast, for the more conservative Hermano Bartolo, the Church's authority was evident in scripture, church councils, and patristic writings. In his rebuttal to El Solitario, Hermano Bartolo deploys discourses like those of the Church in order to validate that institution's ownership of its goods. More significantly, he addresses the Spanish people, reminding them of their spiritual and filial obligation to the Church's main authority, the Holy Father:

> ¡Pobre Solitario! Llegará un día en que caiga la venda fatal de tus ojos, y veas el abismo que has abierto con la fuerza de tus monstruosas opiniones. . . . Oye y oigan los españoles todos. Tu escrito es un libelo contra los Papas, contra la curia y corte Romana, contra el clero, y contra los derechos de la Iglesia ¿Qué te propones probar? ¿La autoridad de las naciones en los bienes eclesiásticos?[63]

> [Poor Solitary One! The day will arrive when the fatal blindfold falls from your eyes and you see the abyss that you have opened with the power of your monstrous opinions. . . . Listen, and let all Spaniards listen. Your writing is a libel against the popes, against the Roman curia and court, against the clergy, and against the rights of the Church. What do you propose to prove? The authority of nations over ecclesiastical goods?]

MODERN MATTER

Subsequently, Hermano Bartolo utilizes the motif of the edifice to demonstrate the Church's historical authority:

> El edificio de la Iglesia es incontrastable según la palabra de eterna verdad, y no está sujeto a vacilaciones ni vaivenes. ¿Y por qué? Porque también lo es la piedra o el cimiento sobre que se levanta; siendo punto incontrovertible que no puede ser firme el edificio si no lo es el cimiento sobre el cual se apoya.[64]

> [The Church's edifice is unyielding, according to eternal truth, and it is not subject to hesitations or fluctuations. Why? Because the stone or foundations on which it rests share these properties; it is indisputable that the building cannot be strong if the foundations that support it are also not strong.]

Hermano Bartolo deploys the metaphor of the edifice to evoke not only the image of the confiscated ecclesial building but also the Church's spiritual foundations and its doctrinal emphasis on eternity. The gradual disassembly of this edifice, Hermano Bartolo warns, will eventually lead to the erasure of public expressions of faith:

> Forzosamente amanecerá el día en que veamos abolido todo el culto de Dios: porque no teniendo los ministros con que subsistir han de abandonar el altar, el púlpito, el confesionario y el respeto de sagrados ministerios para entregarse á otros destinos que los provean de alimento y vestido, y socorran las demás necesidades de la vida.[65]

> [Inevitably, the day will come when we will see all worship of God abolished, because without ministers to ensure their survival, the altar, pulpit, and confessional will be abandoned, together with the respect for sacred offices, and its ministers will embrace other jobs that provide them with food, clothing, and life's daily necessities.]

This admonition reflects the traditionalists' concern for the future of Catholicism, given that the clergy formed an essential part of Catholic identity.

Indicative of the divisions between the Catholic clergy were their differing viewpoints on disentailment. In 1875, the journalist and writer Gabino Tejado, in a sardonic critique of liberal Catholicism, divided the Spanish clergy into "los *prudentes* y los *exagerados*" [the *prudent* and the *fanatics*][66]; that is, the liberals who supported expropriation and the clergy who did not:

> Condénese desde el púlpito la culpable codicia que del ayuda de cámara de nuestro *prudente* hace un ladronzuelo doméstico: ¿qué cosa más puesta en razón? Pero ¡pobre predicador si [se] le ocurre llamar robo sacrílego a la desamortización de bienes de la Iglesia, decretada sin consentimiento de ella por un Parlamento demagógico—¡Qué *Exageración*! ¡Eso es usurpar las

atribuciones de la potestad civil; eso es perturbar el Estado; ¡eso es comprometer a la Religión, mezclándola con la política![67]

[Condemn from the pulpit the blameworthy greed that turns our *prudent one's* manservant into a domestic thief: Could anything be more reasonable? But woe betide the preacher should he happen to call the disentailment of ecclesiastical goods a sacrilegious robbery, decreed without the Church's consent by a demagogical parliament—what an *exaggeration*! This is to usurp the powers of civil authority. This is to perturb the State. This is to compromise religion, mixing it with politics.]

Such members of the clergy who supported Rome were labeled neo-Catholic, absolutist, and ultramontane.[68] These ideological divisions between the Catholic clergy, Tejado argues, are generated by the commingling of religion and politics. This criticism demonstrates the many-sided, problematic nature of the religious question.

The Spanish Parliament's Perspective on Disentailment

The role of the clergy was a principal topic of debate in parliament, which indicates the impact of religion on Spain's sociopolitical configuration. Joaquín Casalduero states, therefore, that what characterizes the modern age "no es la multiplicidad de sentimientos y de ideas sino la necesidad de transformar la sociedad . . . dando lugar a una nueva Institución—el Parlamento—que reúne a los que gobiernan y la oposición"[69] [is not the multiplicity of feelings and ideas but the need to transform society . . . giving rise to a new institution—the parliament—that brings together those who govern and the opposition]. A key topic in a session of the Congress of Deputies on June 15, 1840, was liturgical and clerical resources. Article 11 in the 1837 Constitution stipulated that the State would maintain these.[70] First raised on June 5, 1840, this matter was debated in subsequent sessions, which shed light on the economic and cultural significance of issues relating to the maintenance of worship and the clergy. In that first session on June 5, 1840, Vicente Sancho criticized the excess of the clergy while announcing the nation's obligation to support its upkeep, albeit with a greater frugality in its expenses:

¿Cuánto hemos de dar, pues, para mantener el culto y clero? La contestación en términos generales es fácil de dar: todo lo que se necesite, nada más que lo que se necesite. Todo lo que se necesite, señores, porque los gastos a que se han de aplicar los fondos que vamos a votar son gastos de tal naturaleza que no pueden sufrir escasez sin que se cause escándalo en los españoles que son católicos; pero no se debe dar más que lo que necesite.[71]

[How much should we give, then, to maintain worship and the clergy? The answer in general is easy: everything that is necessary; nothing more than what

MODERN MATTER 27

is necessary. Everything that is necessary, gentlemen, because the expenses that these funds will pay and on which we will vote are expenses of such kind that they cannot be wanting without proving scandalous for Spaniards who are Catholics. But one must not give more than what is necessary.]

This call for wise spending mirrors the government's emphasis on utility for the good of the nation's economy. Yet the high costs inherent in Catholic worship problematized this pursuit of thriftiness, as Sancho remarked: "Nosotros queremos que el culto que se ejerza en España [concuerde] con la pompa y dignidad que requiere la índole de nuestra religión" [We want the way in which Spaniards worship to dovetail with the pomp and dignity befitting our religion]. To demonstrate the excess in clergy, Sancho compared statistics from France with those from Spain: "¿En Francia para 32 millones de católicos bastan 123 millones, y en España para 12 han de ser precisos 212? ¿Nosotros hemos de dar para el gasto espiritual 17 reales 22 mrs. por persona al año, y a los franceses les basta con 3 rs. y 28 mrs.?"[72] [In France, for 32 million Catholics, 123 million is enough. And in Spain, is 212 necessary for 12? Must we spend 17 reales and 22 maravedis annually on spiritual expenses per person, while the French get by on 3 reales and 28 maravedis?]. By stating that France kept to a strict budget for public worship, he pointed out that the same was possible for Spain. The reduction of excessive clergy was therefore perceived as imperative for the State's economic health.

The difficulty in defining the real benefits and uses of Catholicism was to be expected in a nation in pursuit of progress. The Church's role and nature in society grew increasingly harder to define, and the advent of modernization and urbanization challenged its sphere of influence.[73] A fundamental facet of the modern Spanish nation was the provision of adequate instruments for its survival.[74] The government's focus on what it considered to be practical and beneficial would soon extend to the ecclesial sphere, where the usefulness of fundamental elements of the Church—its liturgy and hierarchical authority—were questioned. Raymond Carr notes that during the nineteenth century, the Spanish Church was flawed in its distribution of ecclesial resources among its ministers. While parish priests took on many pastoral duties, they were seriously undereducated and underfunded.[75] According to Callahan, the ecclesiastical commission formed by the Cortes in August 1820 sought to change this calamitous situation, providing parish priests with decent salaries by reducing the high salaries of cathedral deans. However, the commission considered the regular clergy (friars or clerics who belonged to religious orders) to be too numerous and useless. This perception of the religious orders led to the resuppression of the Jesuit order and the closure of 801 convents and monasteries in less than two years.[76]

From another angle, the moderate politician and dramatist Francisco Martínez de la Rosa defended the clergy's right to its property.[77] According to Richard

Stites, the moderates defended private property, centralization, and order.[78] In a session on June 15, 1840, Martínez de la Rosa remarked,

> No puedo, sin embargo, dejar de hacer una reflexión, que me parece de suma gravedad, y es que todos los que han hablado han reconocido que el derecho del clero a sus fincas, a los predios rústicos y urbanos que posee es una *propiedad* en todo el rigor de la palabra. Se ha dudado si merece ese título . . . pero respecto de los predios rústicos y urbanos, de las fincas que ha adquirido el clero con títulos los más legítimos, por los medios reconocidos por las leyes, por los Códigos, por la voluntad de los Monarcas, por la a[c]quiescencia de los pueblos, por todos cuantos medios hay para asentar la propiedad, esta cuestión se puede decir que está decidida ya.[79]

> [I cannot, however, not observe, because it seems to me of the utmost gravity, that all those who have spoken have recognized that the clergy's right to their buildings, to the rustic and urban properties that they possess, constitutes property in every sense of the word. It has been doubted that it warrants this title . . . but regarding the rustic and urban properties, the buildings that the clergy has acquired for the most legitimate reasons, by means recognized by laws and codes, the will of the monarchy, and with the approval of the people, by all available means of securing property, one may say this matter has already been settled.]

Although Martínez de la Rosa supported the clergy, emphasizing their right to proprietorship, he still concurred with the government's suppression of religious orders such as the Jesuits. Thus, like other liberals, he perceived little utility in the religious orders.

Martínez de la Rosa's discourse adhered to the emphasis on worship and clergy in the Constitutions of 1812 and 1837, in which there was no mention of the religious orders. He urged members of parliament to reflect further on the potential impact that the reduction of the clergy's properties would have on the character of Spanish society:

> ¿Es por ventura el clero una corporación que puede desparecer, que puede extinguirse por el voto de los legisladores? . . . No; y esta circunstancia es particular, única tal vez. La existencia del clero no está a nuestra merced . . . la ley fundamental establece el principio de la necesidad de mantener el culto y clero; en el mero hecho de que justísimamente ha asentado la religión como la piedra angular del edificio social; en el mero hecho de que la Constitución ha consagrado el principio de la religión católica, la Nación española no puede quedar sin culto y sin ministros del santuario.[80]

> [Is the clergy perchance a corporation that can disappear, that can be eliminated by the legislators' vote? . . . No, and this circumstance is particular,

MODERN MATTER

perhaps unique. The existence of the clergy is subject to our whims . . . the fundamental law establishes the principle of the need to maintain worship and clergy; in the mere fact that this law has most justly established religion as the cornerstone of the social edifice, in the mere fact that the constitution has consecrated the principle of the Catholic religion, the Spanish nation cannot be without worship and ministers of its shrines.]

On describing religion metaphorically as the "social edifice's cornerstone," Martínez de la Rosa articulated the clergy's utility as the foundation of Spain's spiritual architecture. While understanding the need for the Spanish nation to solve its economic problems, he held that the clergy was fundamental to the national purpose, given that "la religión necesita culto y el culto ministros; sin eso no hay religión ni nada. Sin indemnización previa, no se puede privar al clero de sus propiedades, no; sin indemnización es un despojo"[81] [religion needs worship and worship needs ministers; without this, there is no religion or anything. Without prior compensation, one cannot deprive the clergy of their properties, no; without compensation, it is plunder]. The singular emphasis on religious ministers, evident in the Constitutions of 1812 and 1837 and in Martínez de la Rosa's remarks, indicates the liberals' distinct conceptualization of the Spanish Church. Martínez de la Rosa's elision of the religious orders reveals their downplayed role in Spanish religion and society. These religious communities thus became legally disjoined from the ecclesial body.

The question of clerical proprietorship arose again in a session on July 20, 1841, with the politician Joaquín Francisco Pacheco outlining the differing attitudes toward ecclesiastical goods. While sectors of the government maintained that the Church's property belonged to the State, Pacheco vehemently declared that the Church was a legal entity. As he saw it, the disentailment laws on clerical property suggested an undermining of the clergy's authority:

La cuestión primera, señores, es si tenemos derecho para despojar al clero, para arrancarle, como se ha dicho aquí, los bienes que poseía. . . . Son bienes nacionales, se ha dicho por la comisión . . . son bienes que administraba el clero, pero que pertenecían al Estado. . . . Yo digo, por el contrario, que el clero poseía los bienes con intención de dominio, que el clero tenía en estos bienes toda la propiedad que una corporación de su clase, sancionada por las leyes. . . . Pues qué, ¿puede ser propietaria una compañía de seguros, y el clero de la Iglesia española no podía serlo?[82]

[The first question, gentlemen, is if we have the right to deprive the clergy, to strip them, as it has been said here, of the goods they possess. . . . According to the commission, they are national goods . . . they are goods that the clergy administrates but that belong to the State. . . . I say, on the contrary, that the clergy possessed such goods with the intention of administering them, that the clergy has in these goods all the property typical of a corporation of their kind, sanctioned by the laws. . . . Well then, if an insurance company can own goods, cannot the clergy of the Spanish Church do the same?]

Pacheco would ultimately state, as seen below, that expropriation was a form of persecution. Such a condemnation of State law illustrates the divisiveness brought about by the laws that called for the reduction of the clergy's property. Pacheco signals that this financial imposition does not contribute to the Spanish nation's progress:

> Este gobierno, que persigue, que trata tan mal al clero católico de España, repito, no traerá con semejante conducta ningún bien a la Nación. . . . Ellos dicen: nosotros queremos dotar al clero, no queremos que perezca; pero no queremos tampoco que tenga bienes porque abusa de ellos en mal de la causa pública. Véase aquí cómo el pensamiento de la ley es una idea no económica sino más bien de persecución.[83]

> [This government, which persecutes and maltreats Spain's Catholic clergy, I repeat, will not bring in the same way any good to the nation with such behavior. . . . They say: we wish to endow the clergy, we do not want them to die; however, we also do not want them to possess goods because they abuse them to the detriment of the public cause. Observe here how the principle of the law is not an economic idea but rather one of persecution.]

Most significantly, he concludes that the laws regarding the clergy's ownership of property reflected a religious and social issue rather than an economic one. It is evident therefore that politicians such as Pacheco took to heart the impact of legislation on the clergy.

Disparaging the legislation of Mendizábal, whom he portrays as "tan empeñado en la venta de los bienes del clero, que parece su única idea, su solo objeto, que parece que ve en esto la salvación y bienaventuranza del país" [so determined to sell the clergy's goods that it seems to be his only idea, his sole objective, that it seems he considers in it the salvation and happiness of the country],[84] Pacheco discloses his concern for the fate of the clergy and their properties. He repeatedly poses the rhetorical question of the legislation's supposed convenience:

> Es conveniente, se dice, la enajenación; ¿pero a quién es a quién conviene? Yo bien sé que es conveniente a alguien, puesto que se pretende con tal empeño: ¿más es conveniente, repito, para la Nación? Yo bien sé que es conveniente para los que especulan con los fondos públicos; yo bien sé que es conveniente para los poseedores de ciertos capitales más o menos cuantiosos, que tratan de adquirirse grandes utilidades con ellos: esto está fuera de toda duda. ¿Pero es conveniente, vuelvo a preguntar, a la Nación? Tal es la pregunta que sus Representantes, que sus Diputados se deben hacer.[85]

MODERN MATTER 31

[It is said that expropriation is appropriate, but for whom? I know that it is
advantageous to someone, given that it is sought with such determination. But
I repeat, Is it more beneficial to the nation? I know that it is advantageous to
those who speculate with public funds; I know that it is advantageous to those
who possess a certain capital, more or less substantial, and who try to acquire
significant personal benefit. This is beyond any doubt. But I ask again: Is it
advantageous to the nation? This is the question that its representatives, its
members of parliament, must ask.]

Pacheco urges his fellow politicians to ruminate on the idea of disentailment
and its real beneficiaries, declaring that the enterprise would cause the nation
"grave perjuicio"[86] [serious damage]. He implies, therefore, that the Spanish
nation would be disunited, since only a few of its members would benefit from
ecclesiastical confiscation at the expense of members of the Spanish Church. This
anticipated repercussion contested incipiently the idea of the "national good,"
which held different meanings for opposing sides of the debate.

Regarding Pacheco's speech as "incendiary," the politician Agustín Argüelles
conversely justifies disentailment by referring to the Spanish nation's economic
problems and the clergy's role in the Carlist Wars.[87] He states, "Persecución del
clero. . . . Tengo poco que añadir a lo dicho; la persecución no es al clero; el clero
nos ha perseguido a nosotros, y nosotros le hemos retribuido con toda genero-
sidad, no hemos tomado jamás medidas de excepción contra él"[88] [Persecution
of the clergy. . . . I have little to add to what has been said. The persecution is not
directed at the clergy; it is clergy who have persecuted us, and we have repaid
them with generosity. We have not taken any exceptional measures against them].
Pointing to the country's debt, Argüelles regards ecclesiastical assets as national
goods subject to the market: "Si obligada la Nación a proceder a la venta de los
bienes eclesiásticos como un medio subsidiario para salir de los apuros del día,
se han de poner en venta de esta o de la otra manera"[89] [If the nation is obliged to
proceed to the sale of ecclesiastical goods as an additional means to resolve the
current predicaments, they must be put up for sale one way or another].

In response to Pacheco's recognition of the authority of Rome on ecclesiastical matters, Argüelles expresses his conceptualization of the Catholic religion
as a more internal and personal experience and not as an institution. This attitude, which I develop in greater detail in my fourth chapter on Galdós, characterized the progressive liberals' perception of religion. It is evident, then, that
Spain's traditional spiritual architecture was being exposed to ideological and
material transformations:

¿Y qué derechos tiene la corte de Roma en España? ¡La religión! La religión,
señores, reside en la conciencia, y nada tiene que ver con las canonjías,
ni con las prebendas eclesiásticas reservadas, ni con recomendar a tal o tal

Prelado para que tenga un beneficio, ni con vender por dinero indulgencias ni perdones. Esa no es la religión que yo profeso, yo soy tan católico como el Sr. Pacheco, aunque no soy romano en ese sentido; profeso la religión de Jesucristo como él la ha enseñado, y soy miembro de la Iglesia católica, que no es otra cosa que la reunión de los fieles, en cuyo número me cuento.[90]

[And what rights does the court of Rome hold in Spain? Religion! Religion, gentlemen, resides in one's conscience, and it has nothing to do with canonry, or with privileged ecclesiastical perks, or with recommending such and such a prelate for a benefit, or with selling indulgences and pardons. This is not the religion that I profess. I am just as Catholic as Mr. Pacheco, although not Roman in that sense. I profess the religion of Jesus Christ as he has taught it, and I am a member of the Catholic Church, which is nothing but a gathering of the faithful among whose number I count myself.]

It is evident that Argüelles's speech reveals his rejection of the material or incarnational matter of religious doctrine as well as his negation of papal authority in national affairs. Pacheco's response to Argüelles underlines their opposing perspectives on religion, which continued to be a subject of intense debate: "Ha hablado el Sr. Argüelles de su religión; y sobre este punto yo dejo al Congreso y a la Nación que lo juzguen"[91] [Mr. Argüelles has spoken of his religion, and on this point, I defer to the congress and the nation to judge him].

Due to the Church's loss of the protective political ambience afforded by the absolute monarchy and its apparent inability to respond adequately to the social ramifications of industrialization and modernization, religion could no longer be valued as a common heritage by the Spanish populace. Instead, it became a serious point of conflict.[92] Fueling the bitter debate between the traditionalists and liberals within the Church was the introduction of a "new theology" and "natural religion" at the turn of the nineteenth century. These two key factors of an increasingly liberalizing Christianity had formed the subject of the Italian ex-Jesuit Bonola's 1789 anti-reform work *The League of Modern Theology with Modern Philosophy*, the Spanish translation of which was published in 1798. It circulated among traditionalists, who sought to maintain past institutions and privileges and eradicate internal and external heterodoxies.[93]

THE SPANISH INQUISITION

Another major change that took place in the early nineteenth century in Spain concerned the Inquisition, abolished and reinstated on several occasions. The Spanish Tribunal of the Holy Office of the Inquisition, the principal judicial institution focused on extirpating heresy (teachings not in conformity with Catholic dogma), was a point of conflict for the Spanish nation and its political and

MODERN MATTER

religious identity until its abolition in 1834 under Isabel II. Its existence, stemming from the Catholic Monarchs in 1478, was primarily a matter of religious and political authority. In 1808, Bonaparte had suppressed the Inquisition, considering it an encroachment on the monarchy. Likewise, the Spanish assembly at Cádiz abolished it in 1813, declaring it incompatible with the nation's liberal constitution and restoring jurisdictions to bishops and secular judges.[94] This proposed elimination triggered lengthy debates that took into consideration the liberty of the press, which would challenge the Inquisition's authority on doctrinal matters. On July 21, 1814, following the restoration of the Spanish monarchy when the Peninsular War ended, Fernando VII reestablished the Inquisition, declaring that the safeguarding of religious orthodoxy was crucial to the preservation of the kingdom's stability.

The Inquisition was therefore regarded by conservative Catholics as an important political and religious court for preventing the fermenting of the errors introduced by Napoleon's foreign, non-Catholic troops. Unsurprising, therefore, was the narrative that Julián Juderías termed *La leyenda negra* [The Black Legend], which attacked the social and political customs and life of the "inquisitorial" Spanish people.[95] The idea of a fanatical Spanish people first circulated in the mid-sixteenth century during Spain's religious wars in France and the Low Countries.[96] Daniel Muñoz Sempere adds that several Spanish authors' works, such as Francisco Cabello y Mesa's 1811 drama *La Inquisición* [The Inquisition], reiterated the same images of the Inquisition, which demonstrated its centrality to Spanish liberal ideology.[97]

The inquisitor general from 1814 to 1818, Francisco Javier Mier y Campillo, denounced the novel doctrines that had "infected" Spain during the French occupation.[98] A similarly vehement attitude was taken up by Jerónimo Castillón y Salas, bishop of Tarazona from 1815 to 1835 and inquisitor general from 1818 to 1820, who wrote a letter of exposition in June 1823 to Pope Pius VII about the role of the Inquisition in preserving Spain's religious unity. The bishop stressed that its reestablishment was vital due to the "errores revolucionarios" [revolutionary errors] of the Freemasons ("aquella secta" [that sect]), which he regarded as damaging to religious and monarchical stability across Europe.[99]

SPANISH RELIGIOUS UNITY

Central to the religious question was the debate on the nature and type of the State's official Church and religion.[100] The 1812 Constitution generated discord between reactionaries and reformers to the detriment of the country's religious unity, a historical cornerstone of the Spanish Church. The religious question would remain as such throughout the century, mirroring the reactive construction of the nation's identity, which Álvarez Junco regards as defensive and hardly proactive.[101] Spain's religious identity was undergoing a process of intense change and reform, which encompassed spheres that ranged from the secularization of the Church's properties to the devotional life of religious adherents. Callahan points out that a combination of social and cultural factors, particularly anticlericalism and evolving (and devolving) patterns of religious belief and practice, led to the friction between Church and State, as I have signaled above.

Moreover, landless laborers in the south, radical movements of industrial workers in the major cities, and the educational inadequacy and elitism of the clergy inspired a "mass dechristianization."[102] According to Shubert, the nineteenth-century Church in Spain was smaller and poorer; rural clergy received little, although much-needed, intellectual and catechetical formation; and vocations dwindled.[103] Callahan adds that aspects of folk piety (popularized religious beliefs and customs) misinterpreted Church doctrines.[104] The most violent expressions of anticlerical discontent included the massacre of friars in Madrid on July 17, 1834, and, decades later, the Tragic Week of 1909.[105] While Callahan argues that pious practices such as the growing veneration of the Sacred Heart of Jesus and the rosary diverted the populace from the gospel and Catholic Mass, I argue that these devotions served to bolster the people's open attachment to their religious faith. Devotionalism was prevalent in the nineteenth century, ranging from individual practices to public ceremonies and associations.[106] These public and visible practices stem from the incarnational nature of Catholicism, which was manifest in its visual culture, a significant facet of this religion. Ángel Luis López Villaverde and Julio de la Cueva Merino state that in the latter part of the nineteenth century, during the papal office of Leo XIII, Catholic organizations such as pious associations, labor unions, pilgrimages, and the religious press proliferated to confront modern liberal society and its secularizing processes.[107] Cueva Merino argues that, recognizing its potential, the Church drew on an "arsenal" of public manifestations of faith in the fight against secularization. Yet this mobilization was not limited to Spain, given that, as Cueva Merino points out, the Marian devotions of the nineteenth century arose from apparitions in Paris, Lourdes, and La Salette.[108]

Transnational pilgrimages facilitated these public religious displays, starting with France during the 1870s, when Catholic monarchists responded to the sociopolitical turmoil arising from the Franco-Prussian War, the Paris Commune, and the proclamation of the Third French Republic with reparational pilgrimages.[109] During the Revolutionary Sexenium (1868–1874), the period following the overthrow of the Bourbon monarchy in Spain, the Spanish congress proposed new legislation on secularization: the suppression of Jesuit and religious orders founded after 1837, restrictions on religious orders, and the approval of civil marriage.[110] Hence, following the model of French Catholic mobilization, the Carlists pioneered a pilgrimage of legitimist Catholics to Lourdes in 1869 as a public counterrevolutionary act of atonement.[111]

Symptomatic of the friction between the clergy and the government was the attitude toward the 1812 Constitution, which signaled the potential of the State

MODERN MATTER

to influence clerical authority, given the constitution's requirement of utmost loyalty. For clerical officials of monarchist loyalties, this devotion to constitutionalism undermined monarchical authority. At the beginning of the Liberal Triennium in 1820, many clergymen refused to swear loyalty to or speak of the constitution during Mass, in defiance of the government's order. The bishop of Orihuela, Simón López, appealed to the Spanish government, stating that he could not comply with its mandates, since doing so would contribute to the confusion between divine and secular matters. Along with other clerics, he was exiled.[112] Nevertheless, David Martínez Vilches argues that liberal clergy defended the constitution in their sermons, which demonstrated the imbrication of politics and theology. Vicente Almiñana y Portes of Alicante delivered a religiopolitical allocution in 1820 to his fellow citizens on the sacredness of the constitution, stressing its enshrining of the faith as the state religion. Similarly, Antonio Romero of Cádiz delivered a sermon on how the 1812 Constitution provided spiritual direction and encouraged good citizenhood.[113]

Also at stake were the boundaries between ecclesiastical and civil authorities regarding the Church's liturgical life. The bishop of Ceuta and Capuchin friar Rafael de Vélez opposed the 1812 Constitution because he disagreed with the ecclesiastical commission's dictating of what was considered necessary for worship and the general vulnerability of the Church to the government's orders. This commission, formed on April 11, 1811, proposed the return of precious objects to the treasury, claiming that the use of silver and gold was unnecessary for worship.[114] Vélez denounced the government's appropriation of ecclesiastical goods, drawing on the scriptural juxtaposition of the secular (Caesar) and the divine (God):

Demos a Dios lo que es suyo y al César lo que le pertenece. La Iglesia tiene sus propiedades, el estado las suyas: la seguridad recíproca del imperio y del sacerdocio exigen que cada uno se contenga en la posesión de sus bienes y de sus derechos respectivos. El estado ha subvenido en todo tiempo con larga mano a las necesidades de la Iglesia y de sus ministros: la Iglesia ha cumplido con el deber de acudir al estado, vendiendo hasta los vasos sagrados destinados al culto. En el primer caso los príncipes, los pueblos, los fieles cumplen con una de sus primeras obligaciones, respecto de Dios, de su religión y de sus ministros; y en el segundo, estos ministros llenan el primer deber que les imponen la sociedad, el estado, la religión, el evangelio mismo.[115]

[Let's give to God what is his and to Caesar what belongs to him. The Church has its properties; the State its own. The reciprocal security of the empire and the priesthood demands that each act with restraint regarding assets and its respective rights. The State has generously met the needs of the Church and its ministers. The Church has fulfilled its duty of turning to the State, selling even its sacred vessels destined for worship. In the first case, princes, peoples, and the faithful fulfill one of their primary obligations: respect God, his religion, and his ministers. In the second case, ministers carry out the first duty that society, the State, religion, and the very gospel impose on them.]

The liberal government's emphasis on usefulness dictated its administration of social and material resources. This emphasis on utility and activity was symptomatic of the construction of nationhood, which Anthony D. Smith regards as a modern innovation. The utilization of resources for the purposes of production distinguishes the modern nation from its perennialist counterpart, the latter resting on an ancestrally based culture composed of allegedly inherent and immemorial qualities.[116] The Western paradigm of the modern nation stresses the political nature of the nation, constructing a framework of functions administered between leaders and citizens.[117]

This emphasis on usefulness partially formed the rationale behind ecclesiastical expropriation and the suppression of religious orders. A rising and "useful" bourgeoisie was pitted against the nobility and the Church, both considered to pertain to the so-called unproductive classes that owned two-thirds of Spain's land.[118] Maryellen Bieder states that ecclesiastical fallow lands were appropriated for husbandry, thus freeing up land for individual development from which the bourgeois entrepreneurs and more affluent classes were able to profit.[119] The Vatican and the State agreed in the 1851 Concordat that in return for the Vatican's recognition of the sale of appropriated ecclesiastical property, the Spanish Church would retain its authority over the nation's education system, imposing its doctrinal orthodoxy and subsidizing clergy.[120] However, as María G. Moreno Antón points out, the 1855 disentailment laws under Madoz failed to honor such arrangements.[121]

According to Simón Segura, Mendizábal's progressive laws of disentailment were generally regarded as extreme: "Hay casi unanimidad en considerar que la desamortización de Mendizábal se realizó con falta de moderación y de forma atropellada"[122] [It is almost unanimously agreed that disentailment under Mendizábal was carried out hurriedly and without moderation]. Tomás y Valiente states that Mendizábal's intertwining of confiscation, ecclesiastical reform, the national amortization of debt, and his defense of Isabel II rendered him the archetype of liberal and anticlerical politics.[123] The moderate and progressive liberals were mostly antagonistic toward the clerics, especially at the start of the Carlist Wars. Throughout history, the Church generally objected to disentailment, with exceptions such as the agreement between Pius VII and Carlos VI, as mentioned in my introduction. Marcelino Menéndez y Pelayo noted that church councils such as those of Constantinople (381), Toledo (400–702), and Basel (1431–1449), together with the first Council of the Lateran (1123), condemned the practice of disentailment as "sacrilege."[124] Menéndez y Pelayo himself denounced Mendizábal's disentailment policies, labeling them a "despojo del patrimonio de San Pedro"[125] [looting of Saint Peter's patrimony].

To conclude, the religious question and the so-called Two Spains depicted the underlying tensions that emerged with the burgeoning conflict between a traditional and a modern world. The national debt, Fernando VII's alternation between absolutist rule and forced adherence to liberal constitutionalism, the Carlist Wars, and the disentailment laws of progressive governments were all political circumstances that shaped reforms and witnessed challenges to the Church's hierarchical leadership and religious influence. The ideas of social utility and activity dictated the State's plans for the economic, political, and religious future of Spain. The parliamentary speeches of such figures as Martínez de la Rosa, Pacheco, and Argüelles elucidate the government's divided views on the role of the clergy and religious properties. Within the Church itself, a "civil war" was being waged between traditionalists and liberal clergy, who sought reforms to adjust to what they deemed were the inevitable demands of a modern era. From the perspective of reactionary members of the Church hierarchy and laity, the economic and political changes brought about by secularization policies were antithetical to the Church's evangelical mission. This traditionalist approach to the Church's function in Spanish society is marked in the literary works of Cecilia Böhl de Faber, to which I turn in the following chapter. In her novels, she upholds an idealized image of a traditional, religious Spain to promote its conservation and denounces individualist ambition, which she depicts as a symptom of the progressive, revolutionary ideology that imperils national stability.

CHAPTER 2

At the Heart of the Nation

DOMESTIC WELL-BEING AND SPIRITUAL PATRIMONY IN CECILIA BÖHL DE FABER'S *LA GAVIOTA* (1849), *LA FAMILIA DE ALVAREDA* (1856), *CALLAR EN VIDA Y PERDONAR EN MUERTE* (1856), AND *LÁGRIMAS* (1862)

In Cecilia Böhl de Faber's novels, certain religious and cultural values and institutions are at stake. She depicts the traditional institutions of marriage and family as hallmarks of stable future generations. As we will see in *Lágrimas*, religion and family are threatened by the burgeoning positivism espoused by the emerging middle class.[1] Romantic and familial unions appear to have more to do with the future than the past, given their concern for the passing down of traditions. Böhl, however, ties the past to the future through the very bonds of body and blood that underpin the Church's sacramental rituals of the Eucharist and matrimony. Religious and social laws, customs, and traditions purport to keep these bonds intact in order to guarantee the stability of the Spanish nation. Throughout her writings, Böhl depicts the concrete and symbolic aspects of marriage and family, associated with the domestic sphere, and the Catholic faith as elements of the national patrimony.[2]

As a writer with antiliberal leanings, Böhl was particularly engaged in the political and ideological battles of the day.[3] Marieta Cantos Casenave maintains that her works echo Catholic concerns about Spain's budding laicism.[4] Her novels reacted against prevailing liberal ideologies that produced social, political, and economic changes in a slowly modernizing Spain. Böhl draws on historical settings and events in Spain, specifically those relating to civil wars and disentailment, and her narrative voice discusses the general ideological and socioeconomic phenomena that contributed to the causes, courses, and consequences of civil conflict and ecclesiastical confiscation. As Carmen Bravo-Villasante maintains, Böhl's writings were marked by an "elogio de virtudes cristianas y el anatema contra la desamortización"[5] [praise for Christian virtues and anathema against disentailment]. Likewise, Böhl scholars such as Derek Flitter, Susan Kirkpatrick, and Javier Herrero consider her Catholic traditionalism to be the

AT THE HEART OF THE NATION

main characteristic of her writing. I will contribute to the scholarship on Böhl by examining the parallels between the (de)sacralization of family and marriage in Böhl's novels and the privatization of religious establishments. Central to these associations is the notion of foreignness, which Böhl develops through characterization and didactic style. Extraneous persons, ideas, and interests appear to threaten the core of families and marriage, which function as both basic components and icons of the Spanish nation.

In this chapter, I will analyze four of Böhl's novels that delve into aspects of Spanish national identity and spiritual patrimony: *La gaviota* (1849), *La familia de Alvareda* (1856), *Callar en vida y perdonar en muerte* (1856), and *Lágrimas* (1862). I will first examine Böhl's life and literary, political, and intellectual influences and then explore how her conservative ideas responded to movements such as the Enlightenment, Romanticism, and costumbrism as well as atheist and anarchist challenges. Of paramount importance in my discussion is the Romantic theme of transgression, which Böhl criticizes heavily in her characterization and portrayals of marriage, family, and parenthood. Transgression signals an active movement, a breaking of barriers set by religious doctrines and cultural norms. Böhl's characters, as I will argue, enact these transgressions as they move within and outside of their places of residence. The provincial space—their hometowns—foregrounds the interplay between center and periphery, the secular and the religious, and public and private. In the context of excarnation, the rupture between these realms echoes the separation between the body and the soul. The break between the sacred and the secular in matters of family and tradition, Böhl articulates, carries significant implications for the nation's spiritual heritage.

Finally, I will investigate the symbolic and material connections between these philosophical, social, and familial issues with regard to the Church in Spain. Böhl depicts the Church as the nation's spiritual reservoir and identity marker. Families and matrimonial unions, she elaborates, depend heavily on religious belief. Böhl therefore draws a parallel between the secularization of religious establishments and the apparent degradation of sacralized marital and familial unions. Such a consideration of nineteenth-century Spain's social relations is crucial to a wider understanding of ecclesiastical confiscation as a generator of profound sociocultural and class tensions. It is through this lens that Böhl centers on peasants and the religious orders. According to Gabriel Tortella, these were the main communities who bore the brunt of ecclesiastical disentailment, while its beneficiaries were the affluent classes and aristocracy.[6] Böhl highlights this multifaceted reality in her characterization and attention to historical and ecclesiological detail.

Although Flitter mentions in passing Böhl's critical stance against disentailment, manifest in three of her novels—*La gaviota*, *Callar en vida y perdonar en muerte*, and *Lágrimas*[7]—I consider that *La familia de Alvareda* also deals with the same topic.[8] In their Andalusian towns, the families in these novels are affected by, or are involved with, the closing or trespassing of religious establishments. In *La gaviota*, the monastery at Villamar is closed; in *Lágrimas*, the convent is sold; and in *La familia de Alvareda*, the church in Alcalá Guadaíra is raided. Similarly, in her short novel *Callar en vida y perdonar en muerte*, Böhl sharply censures the systematic ruin of religious dwellings to laud the inhabitants of Val de Paz who reject the "luces" [enlightened ideas] of the age and choose to live traditionally.[9]

Böhl's Catholic beliefs explain her investment in, and concern for, the spiritual and material aspects of the Church. Íñigo Sánchez Llama notes that Böhl received support from the institutional neo-Catholics, especially the lawyer, politician, and journalist Cándido Nocedal (1821–1885), whose prestige in the cultural sphere enabled him to address the topic of Catholic unity in the 1854 Congress of Deputies.[10] In 1856, Nocedal assisted in devising the Ley de Imprenta [Print Law], which aimed to bring about a re-Catholicization of Spanish society through moralizing literature. The neo-Catholics believed that the aristocratic values and religious devotions contained in such literature would foster national cohesion.[11] Nocedal praised Böhl's novels in particular as displays of aesthetic beauty and patriotism because they perceivably rendered a great service to the nation:

> Fernán Caballero es [un] vivo ejemplo de que son verdaderas aquellas palabras suyas . . . en medio del torpe materialismo que va invadiendo los espíritus, cual las crecientes olas de un diluvio universal, en que perecerán nuestras inteligencias, hay seres cuyas almas arden como divinas almas en las iglesias.[12]

> [Fernán Caballero is a living example of the truth of her words . . . amid the crass materialism that invades our spirits, like the rising tide of a universal deluge in which our intelligence will perish, there are beings whose souls burn like divine souls in the churches.]

Two Romanticisms

Like Bécquer, Böhl also drew on traditionalist Romanticism and was especially influenced by contemporary German critics. Family and faith played a prominent role in this interest. As a devout Catholic convert, her German father, a Hamburg native and Andalusian-based merchant, Johann Nikolaus Böhl de Faber (1770–1836), defended the conservative version of German Romanticism that stressed aesthetic and moral value in anything reflecting the organic and traditional *Volksgeist*—popular beliefs, ideas, and sentiments—of Catholic Spain.[13] He followed the ideas of the German scholar and poet August Wilhelm Schlegel (1767–1845), who, in his 1809 Vienna lectures, regarded Spain's Golden Age as the representation of the Romantic soul of the Spanish nation unscathed by Enlightenment doctrine and French influence.[14] From the end of the Liberal Triennium, two schools of Romanticism developed: a more traditional one in Spain and another, more liberal current formed by Spanish exiles in England and France.[15] Romanticism consoled both liberal exiles and supporters of the restoration of the Spanish monarchy after the War of Independence because it premised the hope of a Spanish national future.[16]

In the nineteenth century, Spain was divided by multifaceted political stances and tensions, which were exacerbated by domestic military conflicts and increasing secularization. In *Ruin and Restitution*, Philip W. Silver describes the notion of the Two Spains as powerful conservative forces obstructing liberal advances.[17] Between 1834 and 1844, Romanticism was immersed in bourgeois efforts to establish political and ideological hegemony. Yet contrary to the accepted belief in an alleged "liberal romanticism," Silver argues that Romanticism in Spain was predominantly conservative due to the pact between an "anaemic bourgeoisie" and a powerful nobility.[18] Although agriculture led the economy in the nineteenth century, agricultural technology had not yet advanced due to the delayed industrialization of other economic sectors. Consequently, Spanish traditionalism prevailed over genuine liberalism and a liberal Romanticism that would have helped instill bourgeois values of nationalism, freedom, and individual subjectivity.[19]

In contrast with this traditionalist depiction of Romanticism, Jo Labanyi asserts that many scholars have regarded Romanticism as the literary manifestation of liberalism in Spain and other countries.[20] Flitter, who defines Spanish Romanticism as mostly traditionalist, concedes that the 1830s and 1840s saw a greater, albeit brief, radical leaning in Romantic writings, as exemplified in the literary works of José de Espronceda, Mariano José de Larra, Ángel de Saavedra (Duque de Rivas), and Antonio Alcalá Galiano.[21] Hence, as Herrero and Flitter suggest, Spanish Romanticism had two different faces, which to a certain extent opposed each other. Labanyi notes that the French strand of Romanticism, influenced by the anticlericalism and militant secularism of the French Revolution, was more individualistic than its Protestant English counterpart, which took individualism for granted.[22] As Kirkpatrick suggests in her analysis of Ángel de Saavedra's 1835 Romantic play *Don Álvaro, o la fuerza del sino* [Don Álvaro, or the force of fate], the instability of the individual subject indicates Spain's lack of a Protestant tradition.[23] For Labanyi, Spanish Romanticism in general would dramatize the person's conflictive relation to the family unit, which restricts the development of autonomous selfhood.[24] Böhl thus premises her critique of Romantic individualism upon what she perceives as threats to marriage and the family.

The individual's impact on familial stability denotes the collective obligation to protect and foster a kind of national selfhood. This collective identity in Romanticism stems from the thought of Johann Gottfried Herder (1744–1803), who believed in the importance of safeguarding genuine, autochthonous, national traditions in culture and literature. According to Herder, an indomitable awareness of identity was indispensable for the nation to preserve itself: "Get to know yourself, for others know you and abuse you. Seize yourself so that you may not be seized by others."[25] Due to the modern state's bureaucracy and rigid stratification, which inhibited individualism and nonconformity, Herder was critical of its "machine." Instrumental in restoring what he perceived to be the stifled, original voice or expression of a putative national essence of the *Volk* [people] was a recovery of its literary past.[26]

In the quest to revive the past, Herder therefore urged Romantic writers to forgo foreign—mainly French—influences and focus instead on the Middle Ages and the sixteenth century. Flitter states that this cultural efflorescence of medieval Spain and the Spanish Golden Age was particularly endorsed by the German poets and literary critics August Schlegel and his brother, Friedrich.[27] Böhl too supported this traditionalist branch of Romanticism, which disparaged the cultural and ideological "specter of social disintegration" and thus challenged its liberal counterpart.[28]

BÖHL'S TRADITIONALISM AND *COSTUMBRISMO*

Böhl's traditionalist novels pertain to the literary movement of *costumbrismo*, popular in Spain from the late eighteenth century to the mid-nineteenth century.[29] Seeking a national "essence" that would represent all regions, it defied the individualism promoted in liberal Romanticism as well as the universalist, cosmopolitan tendencies of the Enlightenment.[30] A salient feature is its creation of colorful comedic sketches that portray the manners and customs of a particular age and region, using characters who appear as representative types.[31] Paradoxically, this particular conceptualization of an "authentic" Spanish culture associated with peasants contrasts with Böhl's own foreign, upper-class roots.[32] Like her German father, Böhl found inspiration in the so-called *Volksgeist* of Spain and thus sought to portray its national "essence" through the examination of "lo popular" [the popular], an interest that differed from her father's concentration on Spanish medieval literature.[33] Böhl was also inspired by her Spanish mother, Frasquita Larrea (1775–1838), who was a less-known yet important figure of the European Romantic literary movement. Teresa González Pérez states that Larrea witnessed the French occupation of her hometown in Cádiz, Chiclana de la Frontera, between 1806 and 1810. Consequently, she upheld "la trilogía Dios, Patria, Rey" [the God, country, king trilogy] in her traditionalist writings and helped establish the Sociedad Patriótica de Damas [Ladies' Patriotic Society] in 1811 to support the Spanish war effort.[34]

Drawing on her parents' traditionalism and cultural interests, Böhl articulates in her novels the moral need to preserve "enduring examples of Spanishness" for future generations. Such an agenda, Alison Sinclair asserts, was

AT THE HEART OF THE NATION

common for many regional writers. Yet this pursuit of cultural preservation also led to idealization.[35] Idealized images of the Spanish nation were an element of *costumbrismo*, which, according to Joaquín Álvarez Barrientos, rested on the traditional concept of imitation, which requires the reproduction of an observed reality of distinct types of people and situations. Given that *costumbrismo* tended to emphasize imitation and the acknowledgment of differences, as a cultural movement it clearly displayed political and ideological undercurrents that worked to fashion nationalism. As Álvarez Barrientos explains, "La costumbrista es una literatura renovadora, según las tendencias europeas del momento, pero de ideología nacionalista frente al liberalismo que parece querer disolver el espíritu nacional sobre el que sustentan los valores que se creen auténticamente españoles y cuya defensa van a asumir el arte y la literatura costumbristas"[36] [Costumbrism is a renovating literature, according to the contemporary European tendencies, but of a nationalist ideology against a liberalism that seems to want to dissolve the national spirit that sustains values believed to be authentically Spanish and whose defense would be taken up by costumbrist art and literature]. As a traditionalist form of literature, *costumbrismo* sought to challenge what it regarded as the liberal dismantling of the national spirit.

In its aim to conjure an allegedly authentic representation of Spanish identity, *costumbrismo* assumed a dual approach: to combat numerous external influences (especially French) and to challenge their negative images of Spain.[37] Spain's Black Legend and alleged backwardness and disorder were exaggerated in the French press.[38] Such foreign portrayals had begun in the late eighteenth century through the rapid and unchecked proliferation of French periodicals and pamphlets and worsened during the War of Independence in the early nineteenth century.[39]

Among the foci of *costumbrismo* was the representation of proximities in time and space; that is, whatever seemed to be close and recent, whether urban, rural, or provincial.[40] Böhl, however, does not conflate the urban, rural, and provincial in her stories but foregrounds the peasant inhabitants of rural Andalusia to evoke a traditional feudal society. Rural areas, located away from what is central, metropolitan, and a potential crucible for working-class upheavals, are the spaces privileged in Böhl's writings as conducive to the conservation of a particularly traditional Spanish heritage.[41]

The significance of family and province as metaphors for and markers of unity and patrimony within the context of nationalism is crucial for my analysis of *La gaviota*. As I will discuss, Böhl pursues the ramifications of breaking these traditional, unified social structures and spaces through what the narrator perceives to be foreign influences. The principal impediments to the former's cohesion are adultery and avarice. Adultery disturbs the familial stability afforded by marriage, while avarice destroys the physical and spiritual home of the religious edifice.

LA GAVIOTA, THE PROVINCE, AND NATIONAL IDENTITY

La gaviota concerns the young German surgeon Fritz Stein, who, after offering his services in the civil war between Carlists and Isabelline troops, receives the help of Tía María, her family, and the exclaustrated Fray Gabriel in the village of Villamar in Cádiz. Stein marries the young Marisalada (nicknamed "La gaviota"), the daughter of a local fisherman, Pedro Santaló. Encouraged by the Duke of Almansa, Marisalada, an accomplished singer, travels to pursue fame and wealth in Seville and Madrid. In Madrid, however, she embarks on an adulterous affair with the bullfighter Pepe Vera, causing the brokenhearted Stein to move to Cuba, where eventually he perishes from yellow fever. When Pepe Vera dies accidentally in the bullring, Marisalada returns to the province of Villamar.[42] Having lost her singing voice, she ends up living with a barber, Ramón Pérez, who squanders her money.

In Böhl's novels, the province is a microcosm—as well as synecdochically a part— of the Spanish nation. The narrator of *La gaviota*, speaking in first-person plural, represents the collective voice of "nuestra Patria" and establishes in the prologue the novel's aim of conjuring an intimate nationalistic image of the Spanish people and their language, beliefs, lore, and traditions.[43] It is in the rural communities of the Andalusian region that Böhl explores the concatenations of ideas of national patrimony, community, and religious and social norms to dispel stereotypes of Spain in European Romanticism.[44] Andalusian archetypes, including bandits, gypsies, and bullfighters, were depicted in both European and Spanish Romantic narratives, rendering Spain "medio oriental, a la vez sensual, temible y risueña"[45] [almost oriental, sensual, terrifying, and promising]. Scholars have observed that throughout the 1840s, many Spanish authors accepted the fundamental elements enshrined in their national mythology, thus casting doubt on Spain's capacity to join the modern world.[46]

Andreu Miralles argues that Böhl ultimately subverts characters with such traits by denying their stereotypical representation in her work.[47] As I point out later in this chapter, these characters depict values in relation to the worlds in which they are anchored: the present or the past. At the beginning of *La gaviota*, the narrator divides the Spanish people into categories in accordance with their devotion to their homeland. The classification of these groups, who are unified by ethnicity yet divided in their attitudes toward national culture and history, problematizes the notion of a single cohesive Spanish people. Böhl centers on Villamar to reveal the extent to which the liberal revolution had impacted the lives of its ordinary inhabitants, criticizing it and illuminating, in turn, a traditional and devout exemplar for the Spanish nation.

The region and the province, Ian Duncan argues, are territories that depict a "concentrated version" of what Benedict Anderson has termed the "imagined community."[48] In deploying an idyllic rural south that contrasts with modernized

AT THE HEART OF THE NATION

45

and industrialized cities, Böhl foregrounds religious communities, peasants, and agricultural laborers. As Tortella notes, most of these groups were victims of disentailment and subsequently demonstrated their unrest through uprisings.[49] Böhl's representation of these groups in her writings illuminates what she considers to be important to Spain. As a traditionalist, she underscores Catholicism's role in quotidian life.

In a letter to her friend, the Spanish dramatist Juan Eugenio Hartzenbusch (1806–1880), Böhl justified her interest in articulating religious matters in her novels, explaining that they should not be relegated to the private sphere:

> Los señores quieren relegar (¡y gracias!) las cosas y palabras de Dios a los sermones, que no oyen, y a las Iglesias donde no entran. Pero, ¿dónde más estética, más poesía, más drama, más saber, más pureza, más enseñanza que en los asuntos religiosos?—¿Cuáles, por Dios, nos atañen de más cerca, hablan más al alma y al corazón? Y no quiero a la Religión atrincherada en una fortaleza, la quiero como el pueblo Español, en todo.[50]

> [Gentlemen wish to relegate (and be grateful!) God's matters and words to sermons, which they do not hear, and to the churches, where they do not enter. But where else can you find more aesthetic, more poetry, more knowledge, more purity, more teaching if not in religious matters? What, for goodness' sake, concerns us more, speaks more to the soul and the heart? I do not want religion barricaded in a fortress; I want it like the Spanish people—in everything.]

As a fierce critic of ecclesiastical confiscation, Böhl recognized the role of the novel in demonstrating the aesthetic, dramatic, and dogmatic appeal of the Catholic religion. Hence, *La gaviota* was essentially propagandistic, and the costumbrist genre would prove fertile ground for her social commentaries.[51] By foregrounding sentiment and religion, Böhl conveys her literary objective to provide a spiritual perspective on faith and tradition through the more intimate domains of family and home in the Spanish province.

The province in Böhl's fiction plays a crucial role in the nation's spiritual and moral character because the observance of age-old cultural and religious customs is more visible there. This perceptible spiritual life, represented as beneficial to the provincial community, contrasts with the rationalist, utilitarian depiction of *manos muertas*, civil and ecclesiastical properties considered impractical in the liberals' pursuit of Spain's progress. According to Duncan, the representation of the province or region in Victorian literature has three possible functions: "[It] may represent an authentic site or source of national identity—a distillation of the nation; or it may take the place of a larger national identity that has failed; or it may register a wholesale disintegration of the categories of home: origin, community, belonging."[52] Consequently, the province has the potential to represent, replace, or reflect the presence, disruption, or absence of national identity. I posit that these three interpretations of the roles of provinces and regions apply to *La gaviota*, where Marisalada's physical movements from rural to urban (Villamar to Seville and Madrid) and then from urban back to rural demonstrate the complex relations between the center and the periphery, the sum and its parts, and represent the political and cultural movements that are associated with modernity but also provoked the displacement of many. The provincial village is socioeconomically inferior to the urban center—the purported site of modernity—and progress, wealth, and fame. Nonetheless, Böhl ultimately privileges Villamar, a refuge from modernity and a minute constituent of the Spanish nation, over the more advanced metropolitan centers of Seville and Madrid, in line with her traditionalist views.

Ferran Archilés observes that nineteenth-century novels served to locate and situate the nation, allowing it to (re)create its own space according to that of its regions: "La construcción simbólica de la nación se hizo en paralelo a la construcción de la región, también en España"[53] [The symbolic construction of the nation was undertaken in parallel to the construction of the region, also in Spain]. As stated, Böhl's narratives take place in the southern Spanish region of Andalusia—specifically, in the imaginary village of Villamar. Despite its fictionalization, Villamar mimics ordinary rural life, ordered by social customs and Catholic beliefs, and the events that occur there mirror the extent to which civil and ecclesiastical disentailment affected Spanish society.

In her preface to *La gaviota*, Böhl reveals the novel's objective: to provide a genuine portrait of Spanish society to challenge the prevailing assumptions of foreigners. "Quisiéramos que renaciese el espíritu nacional" [We want the national spirit revived], she declares, vehemently supporting the notion of Spain's "resurrection."[54] To what extent, then, do Böhl's writings respond to external perceptions of Spanish society? Were her works more reactive to these foreign views, or did they equally extend to a criticism of those Spanish people who somehow contribute to these perspectives? What versions, and visions, of Spaniards were at stake? Böhl declares that she writes about Spain's people so that others may better appreciate the meaning of their Spanish nationality:

> Ahora bien, para lograr este fin, es preciso, ante todo, mirar bajo su verdadero punto de vista, apreciar, amar y dar a conocer nuestra nacionalidad. Entonces, sacada del olvido y del desdén en que yace sumida, podrá ser estudiada, entrar, digámoslo así, en circulación, y como la sangre, pasará de vaso en vaso a las venas, y de las venas al corazón.[55]

> [Now then, to achieve this end, it is necessary, above all, to examine our nationality from its true perspective and to appreciate, love, and promote it. Only then, rescued from the oblivion and disdain in which it lies immersed,

AT THE HEART OF THE NATION

can it be studied—to enter, let us say, into circulation and, like blood, to pass from vessel to vessel to the veins and from the veins to the heart.]

Blood, circulation, and the heart connote the nation as an organic body that depends on sustenance for its survival. This organic metaphor also anticipates the figure of the German surgeon, Fritz Stein, who enters Spain to offer his services during the war.

Although Stein is a foreign individual, he is of value to the Spanish people. Portrayed positively as a surgeon, he "cures" the nation during its civil wars. He has no difficulty entering into the families of Tía María and Marisalada, making his home in Villamar, and substituting his German name with the Spanish "Federico." Hence, Fritz, a foreigner, loses his foreignness when he joins the families of Villamar. Conversely, when Marisalada leaves her hometown for the cities, she becomes a "stranger" to her own family and Villamar's inhabitants.

The Value(s) of Faith in *La gaviota*

The hallmarks of home—in Duncan's words, "origin, community, belonging"[56]— are foregrounded in the narrative when Stein meets Tía María's family and the evicted Fray Gabriel, who all inhabit a damaged and confiscated convent in Villamar. The convent originally belonged to Fray Gabriel's community of friars, who are now displaced. The religious origins and purposes of this home in Villamar no longer correspond with the present reality. What Böhl identifies as truly alien to the Spanish people—represented by the rural microcosm of Villamar's inhabitants—are nontraditional ideas and government mandates. In the nationwide confiscation of religious dwellings, Böhl identifies positivism, materialism, and irreligion as the main ideological culprits, which she characterizes as un-Spanish.

Consequently, Böhl's immediate emphasis on the protection of patrimony in her novels privileges the religious edifice, especially convents and churches. A prominent theme in her works is the desacralization of sacred institutions through their purchase, sale, and transformation into secular places.[57] Such elements are highlighted in episodes that describe Stein's perambulations through Seville. After watching a bullfight in Seville with Marisalada, Stein takes a walk alone around the city, passing by several sites that disentailment has transformed. He sees the convent of the Pópulo, now a prison. He comes across the convent of San Laureano, where Fernando Colón, "hijo del inmortal Cristóbal"[58] [son of the immortal Christopher], founded a school and established its observatory. Not too far from this site, on the riverbank, stands the monastery of San Jerónimo, whose statue, *San Jerónimo penitente* [Saint Jerome Penitent] by Pietro Torrigiano, is now installed in a museum: the Museo de Bellas Artes in Seville, a former convent. Sighting these places prompts Stein to reflect on their present value:

48   MAKING MODERN SPAIN

¿Habrían hecho los antiguos artistas tantas obras maestras, si en lugar de consagrarlas a la veneración de las almas piadosas, a recibir su culto y sus oraciones, hubieran sabido que su paradero había de ser un museo donde estarían expuestas al frío análisis de los amigos del arte y de los admiradores de la forma?[59]

[Would the artists of old have created such masterpieces if, instead of consecrating them for veneration by pious souls to receive their worship and prayers, they had known that their location would be a museum where they would be exposed to the cold analysis of friends of art and admirers of form?]

The "cold analysis" of religious works denotes the modern rationality and lack of religious sentimentality that characterizes the museum space. Böhl's narrative voice considers that the scrutinizing of cultural artifacts and objects of monetary and artistic value undermines the primarily religious purposes of these masterpieces. The shift in their target group, from religious believers to aesthetes, reflects the secular transformation of the religious abode into a building for public service and interest. This change in valorization constitutes a characteristic of modernity.

Similar thoughts run through Stein's mind as he views the Capuchin friars' monastery, constructed on the site of the alleged first church built in Spain by the apostle Saint James, as well as the convent of La Trinidad, also abandoned in 1835 due to disentailment. He praises the convent of Los Remedios and the people who amassed funds to construct the temple. Stein holds this attitude in high regard, considering it a "magnífico ejemplo de abnegación, de entusiasmo religioso y de inteligencia artística"[60] [magnificent example of self-sacrifice, of religious enthusiasm, and of artistic intelligence], to finally remark, "¡Dios mío!, ¡es posible—se decía aludiendo a la guerra—que a aquello lo llamen gloria y a esto—aludiendo a los toros—lo llamen placer!"[61] ["Goodness gracious! Can it be possible," he said, alluding to war, "that they call this glory, and"—alluding to the bulls—"that they call this pleasure!"]. True glory and pleasure, to Stein's way of thinking, stem from the establishment and appreciation of edifying historical sites. He thus serves to articulate Böhl's standpoint that the very people who now utilize religious buildings and articles are diminishing the latter's original, higher purpose.

Soon after he is taken in, Stein spends more time with Fray Gabriel, surveying the damage inflicted by negligence on a nearby church. He expresses profound melancholy on seeing the abandoned religious site. The macabre undertones of the language in the following passage suggest a state of mourning for the loss of the holy edifice:

¡Dios mío! . . . ¡Qué espectáculo tan triste y espantoso! ¡A la tristeza que produce todo lo que deja de existir se une aquí el horror que inspira todo lo que

Figure 3. Monasterio de San Jerónimo de Buenavista, Seville. Courtesy of Sevilla&Me.

merece de muerte violenta a manos del hombre! ¡Este edificio, alzado en honor de Dios por hombres piadosos, condenado a la nada por sus descendientes!

[My God! . . . What a sad and atrocious scene! United with the sorrow that arises from everything that ceases to exist is the horror inspired by everything that deserves to die a violent death at the hands of man. This building, which devout men erected in God's honor, now condemned to oblivion by their descendants!][62]

Acknowledging the significance of this church as a site and symbol of a bygone intensity of faith, Stein's haunting references to homicide and condemnation cast the State, the property sellers and buyers, and those who have trespassed sacred spaces and communities through the acts of expropriation and exclaustration as accomplices in these grave crimes against holy bodies.

Fray Gabriel does not cease to observe the rules of his religious vocation. When Manuel urges him to eat, since "ya no hay conventos, reglas ni ayunos" [there are no longer any convents, rules, or fasts], Fray Gabriel maintains the practice of fasting in penance: "Usted me ha de perdonar . . . pero yo no dejo de ayunar como antes, mientras no me lo dispense el padre prior"[63] [You must excuse me . . . but as did before, I'll continue to fast until the prior exempts me from it]. The monastic vow of obedience still stands for Fray Gabriel, despite the absence of his prior, his religious superior. In contrast, before Stein and Marisalada leave Villamar, the Duke of Almansa presents gifts to the members of Tía María's family except to "el pobre" [the poor] Fray Gabriel. To the duke, the quiet friar is effectively invisible, and like his exclaustrated contemporaries, "se quedó sin nada"[64] [he ended up with nothing]. Fray Gabriel continues to voice his desire to restore his monastery, and in a conversation with the war veteran Don Modesto, he prioritizes faith, symbolized in the monastery, over Don Modesto's castle: "Muy cierto . . . que la tía María tiene que pedir al santo cosas de más entidad que reedificar las paredes del Castillo. Mejor sería pedirle que rehabilitase el convento"[65] [Quite right . . . Aunt Maria must ask the saint for things of greater consequence than rebuilding the walls of the castle. It would be better to ask the saint to restore the convent]. At the end of the novel, Don Modesto mourns the death of Fray Gabriel, who never lived to see his monastery restored to its original state.

Disentailment, from Böhl's point of view, concerns all Spaniards, whose forebears built the nation's religious buildings, and its heritage, for future generations. Continuing their legacy is seen as an act of respect and a prime social and spiritual responsibility. The narrative voice didactically ascribes an idealized universality and perenniality to the role of religion in culture:

> Conservad, españoles, y respetad los débiles vestigios que quedan de cosas tan santas como inestimables: ¡No imitéis al mar Muerto, que mata con sus exhalaciones los pájaros que vuelan sobre sus olas, ni, como él, sequéis las raíces de los árboles, a cuya sombra han vivido felices muchos países y tantas generaciones![66]

> [Conserve, Spaniards, and respect the fragile vestiges that remain of things as holy as they are inestimable: do not imitate the Dead Sea, which kills with its exhalations the birds that fly over its waves or, like the Dead Sea, wither the roots of the trees, in whose shade many countries and generations have lived happily!]

These natural images of birds and trees stress the life and rootedness that the sacred affords, while the melding of the spiritual and physical represents the holistic importance of religion to the Spanish people. Indeed, the tree connotes life and its continuation, both spiritual (the biblical tree of life) and physical (a provider of oxygen). The narrator urges the Spanish people to focus on not only the earthly world but also eternal life, their spiritual destiny. The Dead Sea, which kills seagulls and trees, alludes to Marisalada ("the salted sea") and the "outside world" that destroys her, causing her to abandon her family and their beliefs. The death of the tree—a familial icon prominent in Böhl's writings—illustrates the end of a genealogy.

I posit that an analogy of the rupture between society and the Church can be seen in the separation that arises between Marisalada and her father. Marisalada's nickname—"La gaviota"—not only describes her carefree personality but also depicts her as a bird accustomed to frequent flights over the sea, a portrayal that signifies a lack of interest in the figurative nests of home and family. When she

AT THE HEART OF THE NATION

travels with the duke to metropolitan Seville, she leaves behind her impoverished father, Pedro Santaló. The onomastic significance of Pedro Santaló is telling, as he takes his name from Saint Peter, the first pope and Holy Father. It is unsurprising that Pedro is a fisherman just as Peter was, evoking also the title given by Christ to Peter and his brother Andrew as "fishers of men."[67] Marisalada's flight from her home thus denotes, on a symbolic level, the flight of certain sectors of the Spanish people from the Catholic Church toward materialism. She thus becomes a "foreigner" to Villamar. In convincing Marisalada and Stein to leave with him, the duke asks them, "¿Podéis decidiros a quedaros para siempre apegada a vuestra roca, como esas ruinas?"[68] [Can you decide to stay forever attached to your rock, like these ruins?]. This "rock" not only describes a seagull's rocky dwelling but also recalls Peter's name, Cephas, meaning the "rock" on which Christ founded the Church.

With regard to the Church, another avian symbol—birds in a nest—illustrates the situation of religious communities forced out of their homes through exclaustration. When Stein brings up the popular belief that Spain has too many convents, Tía María becomes suspicious of him and, on an acerbically sarcastic note, derides the State's perceived plan to erase the presence of religion from the public sphere through disentailment: "Destruyamos el nido, para que no vuelvan los pájaros"[69] [Let us destroy the nest so that the birds do not return]. This nest alludes to the home of the evicted religious individuals whom Fray Gabriel represents.

LA FAMILIA DE ALVAREDA AND RELIGIOUS SYMBOLISM

Expropriation, an act that trespasses the sacred precinct of the religious establishment, is essentially an act of transgression. This Romantic manifestation of individualist defiance is prominent in Böhl's novels, whose characters endanger the health of their marital, familial, and communal relationships by disobeying established authority and crossing boundaries. In *La familia de Alvareda*, to which I now turn, Perico Alvareda marries Rita against his mother's wishes. Rita, however, is secretly in love with Ventura, to whom Perico's sister Elvira is engaged. Furious, Perico murders Ventura, flees the village of Dos Hermanas in the province of Seville, and joins a group of bandits led by Diego, with whom he accidentally kills the son of a countess, his family's benefactor. In their attempt to raid the church of Alcalá de Guadaíra with the help of a gypsy woman, they are caught. Consequently, the authorities in Seville execute Perico and the bandits.

Given the importance of the gypsy and bandit in Andalusian cultural traditions, these archetypes feature prominently in Böhl's costumbrist discourse.[70] The portrayal of banditry, as Ben Dodds asserts, reflected the general lack of consensus on the legitimacy of authority in nineteenth- and twentieth-century Spain.[71] The figures of the bandit and gypsy mirror a position outside the laws that govern Spanish society. As for the gypsy woman, she is a symbol of Andalusia, an exotic locale that contrasted with the allegedly civilized worlds of modern European cities.[72] These portrayals of social alienation, another Romantic trope, follow the Rousseauian model of individualism.[73] Böhl's characterization aligns with a more conservative Romanticism in that she depicts the individualist Perico as a transgressor rather than as the hero in liberal terms. Through this pitting of self against society and the use of Andalusian stereotypes, Böhl accentuates Perico's double alienation: as a bandit alienated from not only civil society but also his group of outlaws for opposing sacrilege. Guilty of killing Ventura and the countess's son, Perico hesitates to commit the sacrilege of trespassing and robbing a church, an act evocative of ecclesiastical expropriation. In vain, Perico, along with other men, begs Diego not to enter the church. Diego, however, is indifferent to the fact that entering and looting a church is a form of desecration:

> —¡El atentado en la casa de Dios! Dijo el primero.
> —¡Despojar un sagrario! añadió otro.
> Ea, callarse, gritó Diego: ¿a qué viene ya eso? A lo hecho pecho. Andemos.[74]

> ["Attacking the house of God!" said the first.
> "Pillaging a sanctuary!" added another.
> "Come on, be quiet," shouted Diego. "What are you on about? What's done is done. Let's go."]

Böhl's text portrays the church of Alcalá de Guadaíra as "altamente sublime" [profoundly sublime], a place of great heights and depths with its "inmensas y aterradoras" [immense and terrifying] naves, "gigantes de piedra" [stone giants], and high fillets.[75] The darkness adds a haunting dynamic to this silent space. In describing the church, the narrator centers on the main altar as the symbol of the three theological virtues in Catholicism—faith, hope, and charity:

> El altar mayor, aún perfumado de incienso de las flores de la mañana, y cuyas vislumbres chispean en las tinieblas; el altar, universal centro de la Fe, trono de la Caridad, refugio de la Esperanza, esplendor pródigo de dulcísimos consuelos, amparo del desvalido, atrae los ojos, los pasos, los corazones![76]

> [The high altar, still perfumed with incense from the morning's flowers, and whose gleam sparkles in the darkness. That altar—universal center of the faith, throne of charity, refuge of hope, prodigious splendor of the sweetest consolations, refuge of the helpless—appeals to the eyes, footsteps, hearts!]

The following image of the tabernacle's solitary flame evokes the isolation of religious belief: "Ante el tabernáculo arde la lámpara, solitaria, guardiana del sagrario, sin más objeto que alumbrar, porque la luz es el conocimiento de Dios"[77] [Before the tabernacle burns the lamp—alone, guardian of the sanctuary, with no purpose but to light, because light is the knowledge of God]. In the secularizing

AT THE HEART OF THE NATION

era, this imagery is apt. Yet despite the lamp's nebulousness, it remains eternal: "Lámpara santa y misteriosa, suave y constante holocausto, llama permanente, como la eterna misericordia, que arde como el amor, silenciosa como el respeto, alegre y tranquila como la esperanza"[78] [Holy and mysterious lamp, a gentle and constant sacrifice, a permanent flame, like eternal mercy, that burns like love, silent as respect, as cheerful and calm as hope]. The specks of light, in their fragmented state, indicate a quiet, constant activity as they seemingly animate the frames of the altar space: "Los destellos y reflejos de esta luz recortan y abrillantan algunos puntos salientes de los follajes y molduras del dorado retablo, dándoles la apariencia fantástica de ojos que velan en religioso insomnio"[79] [The glimmer and reflections from this light break up and enhance the protrusions of the foliage and frames of the golden reredos, giving them the fantastic appearance of eyes that keep watch in holy sleeplessness].

Using the Romantic interplay of shadow and light, Böhl juxtaposes the dark, transgressive nature of the novel's bandits and gypsy with the light of earnest religiosity, of knowing and fearing God. The complete silence and stillness of the scene are amplified here to increase the gravity of its imminent disturbance. The macabre and the supernatural combine, plunging the religious site into a state between the earthly reality of death and the otherworldly uncertainty of dreams, given that the space and quiet, in the face of a looming interruption, "forman como una suspensión de la vida, que no es la muerte, que no es el sueño; pero que tiene de aquélla la solemnidad, de éste la dulzura"[80] [seemingly suspend life, which is neither death nor a dream, yet has the former's solemnity and the latter's sweetness].

Family Dynamics and National Order
in *La familia de Alvareda*

The profanation of the sacred depicted in *La familia de Alvareda* is a symptom of the parallel systematic breakdown of its families and traditional order, as in the other novels studied in this chapter. The story presents the experiences of the Alvareda family, headed by pious and moralistic parents, Ana and Juan Alvareda. Before his death, Juan counsels Perico:

> A tu cargo quedan tu madre y hermana; vela sobre la una y guíala; déjate guiar por la otra. Siempre viví en el santo amor de Dios, y pensé en la muerte; así la veo llegar sin espanto y sin sorpresa. Acuérdate de mi muerte para no temerla; todos los Alvaredas han sido hombres de bien; en tus venas corre la misma sangre española, y en tu corazón viven los mismos principios católicos que los hicieron tales. Sé cual ellos, y vivirás dichoso y morirás tranquilo.[81]

> [Your mother and sister remain under your charge. Watch over one and guide her; let yourself be guided by the other. I have always lived in God's holy love

and thought about death; in this way, I can see it arrive without terror or surprise. Remember my death so as not to fear it. All Alvaredas have been men of goodwill. In your veins runs the same Spanish blood and in your heart live the same Catholic principles that made them such. Be like them, and you will live happily and die peacefully.]

His last words constitute a passing down of the Alvareda family's identity, formed by a marriage between race, or "sangre española" [Spanish blood], and religion. The symbol that represents the Alvareda family is the orange tree, described at the beginning of the text as "ese gran señor, ese hijo predilecto del suelo de Andalucía, al que se le hace la vida tan dulce y tan larga"[82] [this great lord, this predilect son from the soil of Andalusia, to which he makes life so sweet and long]. A source of food, medicine, and delight, the tree is a family heirloom. According to Javier Herrero, the family's house and tree form an enclave that conveys a mythic, paradisiac quality.[83] The orange tree and its surroundings contribute to the stability and continuity of the Alvareda family's way of life. Such stable and permanent locales and their natural landmarks, Timothy W. Luke notes, serve to contain or project traditional practices.[84] As the family's inheritance, the orange tree serves as a reminder of the generations who have gone before, coalescing them into an idealized image of a perennial family unit: "Cuando el cura, hermano de su mujer, le embromaba y daba calma sobre la antigüedad y no interrumpida filiación de su linaje, [Juan] respondía sin alterarse y sin que vacilase su convicción ni un instante, que todos los linajes del mundo eran antiguos"[85] [When the priest, his wife's brother, teased him and made light of antiquity and uninterrupted ancestry of his lineage, Juan responded without getting upset or wavering in his convictions even for a moment, because all lineages in the world were ancient]. Yet the enormous orange tree, as the deceased Juan Alvareda liked to boast, was planted during the expulsion of the Moors by one Alvareda, a soldier in the employ of the saint and king Fernando.[86] This idea of spiritual superiority is manifest also in the writings of Bécquer and Galdós, although with differing implications.

With her husband's death, Ana now heads the family. Raised by her priest brother, she is portrayed as devout, stern, dignified, and virtuous. Ana's name recalls the mother of Mary and the grandmother of Christ—Santa Ana—who is also the patroness of Dos Hermanas.[87] Observable in Ana's maternal character is her moral rigidity, conveyed through her costumbrist use of proverbs and pious sayings. Such oral traditions point to the regional transmission of cultural patrimony, given that the *refrán* [proverb], as Antonio Gómez Yebra remarks, was the "fruto de la sabiduría de un pueblo"[88] [fruit of the wisdom of the people]. This legacy of wisdom indicates a heightened moralism that melds social and religious norms and enshrines them as traditions. In this

AT THE HEART OF THE NATION   55

way, the oral transmitter and receiver connect with their past, respecting an
obedience considered indispensable to authorities and their teachings.

When, despite Ana's disapproval, Perico insists on marrying Rita, his
mother warns him, "La que es mala hija es mala casada"[89] [A bad daughter
is a bad spouse]. Portrayed as "vana, ligera, cristiana fría e hija ingrata"[90] [a
vain, flighty, cold Christian and ungrateful daughter], Rita lacks the qualities
necessary for the continuation and preservation of the Alvareda family. In fact,
her unappealing traits, it is intimated, would only destroy it. If Perico marries Rita, Ana warns him, it will be too late to turn back. Notwithstanding his
mother's admonition, Perico, like Marisalada in *La gaviota*, follows his own
desires. It is this criticism of the liberal Romantic exaltation of unrestrained
passion that informs much of Böhl's work.[91] As I mentioned earlier, Böhl renders Perico's excessive individualism antiheroic and dangerous to both himself
and his immediate family.

Once wedded to Perico, Rita figures as the agent of the Alvareda family's collapse. Described as an unkind, mischievous daughter-in-law, she openly displays
her dislike of Ana. While her two children are running around the stable, Rita
sings as she does the laundry. While singing is a national custom and tradition, it
is especially significant in Andalusia, where, as the narrator states, "cada cual tiene
en su memoria tal archivo de coplas y tan variadas en sus conceptos, que sería
difícil se diese una cosa que se quisiese expresar y no se hallase en una copla el
modo de hacerlo"[92] [each person has in their memory an archive of sayings that are
so varied in terms of ideas that it would be difficult to say something one wanted
to express without finding in a refrain a way of doing so]. Referring to the biblical figures, Adam and Eve, Rita utilizes this practice to mock her mother-in-law:

Quien tuviera la dicha
De Adán y Eva,
Que jamás conocieron
Suegro ni suegra.[93]

[Whoever might experience the happiness
Of Adam and Eve,
Who knew neither
Father nor mother-in-law.]

Clearly not considering herself part of the Alvareda family, Rita derides Ana and
Elvira in a pert yet imprecatory song:

De suegras y cuñadas
Va un carro lleno:
¡Qué lindo cargamento
Para el infierno![94]

[Bearing mothers-in-law and sisters-in-law
There goes a full cart:
What a lovely load
Headed for hell!]

Here, Rita's contemptuous words, which make light of harrowing matters like hell, unsurprisingly evince her oxymoronic character as a "cristiana fría"[95] [cold Christian]. Blending dark humor and damnation in "una hermosa voz, bien modulada y clara"[96] [a beautiful voice, well modulated and clear], which recalls that of *La gaviota*'s Marisalada, Rita embodies indulgence and profanity in open defiance of Ana's religious devotion, moral principles, and maternal authority.

Ventura too shares in Rita's self-indulgent personality, choosing to go against his mother's wishes by pursuing the married Rita because, as he declares, the best fruit for him is "la prohibida"[97] [the forbidden one]. Just as Rita mentions in her song the biblical "first parents," Adam and Eve, Ventura's scriptural reference to forbidden fruit also evokes these figures, whose disobedience in the pursuit of individual desire led to humanity's fall. In drawing irreverently on the defiance of Adam and Eve, Rita and Ventura extol the perversion of the sacred. Expressing a kind of radical Romantic exile in their departure from familial and marital ties, which Böhl censures, Rita and Ventura reject religious teaching, familial obligation, and social norms. The breaking of their covenant with God signifies their flouting of authority, both divine and earthly, and, ultimately, their estrangement from God. Hence, their symbolic departure echoes that of the double exile of Adam and Eve from the paradise of the Garden of Eden and the eternal paradise of heaven, which constituted the punishment for their transgressions.

The interrupted wedding of Ventura and Elvira in the first part of the novel portends their marital instability. In turn, this instability is symbolic of a wider disruption at the national level in the French invasion of Andalusia in 1810, which saw Dos Hermanas and Seville surrender to José I's forces and suffer the effects of disentailment imposed by the French monarch.[98] By incorporating this historical event into the narrative, Böhl underlines the national instability that a hostile foreign invasion brings. Likewise, the matrimonial unions that Perico and his sister Elvira had each hoped for, along with the intactness of the Alvareda family, are intruded on by extramarital affairs. The results are disastrous to the individuals and the social unit to which they ideally belong. Böhl's costumbrist emphasis on ordinary life and traditionalist discourses against unchecked progressivism are embodied in the happenings in *La gaviota*'s Villamar and *La familia de Alvareda*'s Dos Hermanas, whose cultural edifices are besieged. Both texts present the family as built on the sacramental institution of marriage, cast as the nucleus of society and the cornerstone of the nation.

AT THE HEART OF THE NATION

57

On all levels of the text, Böhl censures what she perceives to be an irreligious, secularist ethos. The narrative voice makes this criticism explicit in the following passage, which describes events after Ventura's death:

> Tocó entonces la campana el toque de la agonía. Toque solemne, toque lúgubre, voz de la iglesia que avisa al hombre que uno de sus hermanos lucha entre angustias, fatigas y congojas, y va a comparecer ante el tremendo tribunal. Grave saeta con la que la iglesia dice a la multitud que bulle encenagada en intereses frívolos que tiene por importantes, en pasiones pasajeras que sueña eternas: "Paraos un momento por respeto a la muerte, por consideración a vuestro semejante que va a desaparecer de la tierra, como desapareceréis vos mañana."[99]

> [The bell then tolled the chime for the dying. A solemn toll, a mournful ring, the voice of the church that warns men that one of their brothers is struggling against anguish, fatigue, and distress and will appear before the awe-inspiring tribunal. A grave sacred song with which the church speaks to the multitude that swarms depravedly in frivolous interests that it deems important, in fleeting passions that it dreams of as eternal: "Stop for a moment to respect death, out of consideration of your brother who is about to disappear from the earth, just like you will vanish tomorrow."]

The *saeta*, a heartfelt dirge pertaining to the flamenco tradition with Jewish and Arabic roots and sung especially during Holy Week in Andalusia, mourns the death of Christ as well as the members of his Church. In Böhl's text, the church bells and *saeta* together serve as a memento mori, stressing fraternal unity due to the brevity of life. This textual call to prayer and the remembrance of death then turns to a criticism of the Enlightenment, which championed scientific rationalism to curtail the influence of the Church. Here Böhl's narrator holds that the response to the inevitability of death is to be found in religion, not in Enlightenment philosophies: "Pero esa voz que hablaba de muerte, esa voz que decía: *¡rogad y acordaos!* era intempestiva en el siglo de las luces. ¡La ilustración acordarse de la muerte! ¡Eso queda bueno para los cartujos! Y la ilustración mandó callar a la iglesia, porque su voz le importunaba"[100] [But that voice that spoke of death, that voice that said "Pray and remember!" was inopportune in the age of the Enlightenment. The Enlightenment remembering death! This was only good for the Carthusians! And the Enlightenment ordered the Church to be silent because its voice irked it].

Death, which marks the fragmentation of the physical as well as familial body, reinforces the significance of marital and familial unions. Böhl's novels insist that the family, in accordance with Teresa Brennan and Carole Pateman's thesis, is traditionally a model and symbol for authority relationships throughout society in that it bases itself on a need for intactness for the good of itself and its members.[101] Even *La gaviota*'s Fritz Stein, the lone military surgeon, integrates himself into the homes and families of Tía María and Marisalada. In contrast, in *La familia de Alvareda*, Rita and Ventura's affair, which causes Perico to kill the latter, ruptures the family. To follow personal ambitions that do not correspond with the family's creeds and expectations, as in the cases of Marisalada and Rita, only leads to the family member's downfall and the family's disgrace.

Callar en vida y perdonar en muerte: Positivist Materialism Under Attack

Whereas in *La gaviota*, Böhl criticizes what she perceives to be avarice in the buying, selling, and demolition of religious dwellings, in *Callar en vida y perdonar en muerte*, a short murder mystery, Böhl condemns the influences of the positivist age on the character of Don Andrés while exalting the steadfast Christian ways of Rosalía and her mother, Mariana. The novel tells the story of a house where an old woman, Doña Mariana, was the innocent victim of a murder. Doña Mariana's daughter, Rosalía; her son-in-law, Don Andrés Peñalta; and her grandchildren abandon their shared house and move to a distant province as a result. Years later, Rosalía discovers that the murderer was actually her husband, Don Andrés. A former captain, the self-serving Don Andrés dedicates himself to several successful businesses, one of them being the demolition of convents to sell their materials at a low price.

The village where Mariana and Rosalía live, Val de Paz, is, as its name denotes, a harmonious place due to its religious traits and, it is intimated, remains untainted by the "siglo de las luces" [Enlightenment]: "En este pueblo español, rancio, cristiano, viejo, tan alegre y pacíficamente alumbrado por las luces de sus altares y por las del sol, no habían penetrado las del siglo"[102] [In this Spanish town—time-honored, Christian, old, so happy and peacefully lit by the light of its altars and the sun—the lights of the century had not penetrated]. At the center of the idyllic village is an intact church that has not been profaned. This situation is disrupted by the arrival of Captain Don Andrés and his "horde" of soldiers, an animalistic group whose militants are a major threat. Böhl's sardonic description of Don Andrés reflects her rejection of modernity and condemnation of his lucrative business of purchasing and selling convent materials:

> En una palabra, llegó a ser una *notabilidad* y el tipo del ciudadano moderno, esto es, gran expendedor de frases retumbantes salpicadas de términos heterogéneos, celoso apóstol de la moralidad, ferviente pregonador de la filantropía, arrogante antagonista de supersticiones, entre las que contaba la observancia del domingo y días festivos; preste de la diosa *Razón*, arcipreste de *San Positivo*, gran maestre prosopopeya, profesor en las modernas *nobles artes* del menosprecio y del desdén, hábil arquitecto de su propio pedestal.[103]

AT THE HEART OF THE NATION 59

[In a word, he had become a *notable person* and the epitome of a modern citizen—that is, a great purveyor of bombastic phrases interspersed with heterogenous terms, a zealous apostle of morality, a fervent proclaimer of philanthropy, an arrogant enemy of superstition, among which he counted the observance of Sundays and feast days; a priest of the goddess *Reason*, an archpriest of *Saint Positive*, a great master of pomposity, a professor in the *noble arts* of contempt and disdain, a skilled architect of his own pedestal.]

Böhl's sarcastic juxtaposition of phrases denoting traditional religious worship— "domingo" [Sunday], "días festivos" [feast days], "arcipreste" [archpriest], "apóstol" [apostle]—with others reflective of modern rationalism and positivism criticizes people like Don Andrés, who deify their desires and themselves. The title of "arquitecto de su propio pedestal" [architect of his own pedestal], which conveys his hubristic self-regard, is antithetical to the religious people who humbly constructed the convents and monasteries to honor God. In this perverted kind of litany, Böhl establishes that the devastation of ecclesiastical buildings is not so much an act of destruction as a flagrant substitution.

Throughout her novels, Böhl vehemently criticizes the Enlightenment, the legacy of which she perceives as a threat to spiritual concerns in an increasingly materialist modernity. Consequently, the main aim of Böhl's *Lágrimas* is to educate the entire Spanish people about the detrimental mindset of positivism. As its narrator admonishes its readers,

> ¿No se sabe allá el moderno significado de esta palabra, lector? Pues te la diré. Esta denominación es un cinismo que indigna . . . es la bandera que enarbola descaradamente lo material sobre lo espiritual . . . es en fin, la quijada de burro con la que el siglo XIX cae sobre los restos de las cosas y sentimientos grandes y elevados de los tiempos de fe, de entusiasmo y de caballerismo.[104]

> [Is not the modern meaning of this word known there, reader? Well, I will tell you. This denomination is a cynicism that outrages . . . it is the flag that brazenly hoists the material over the spiritual . . . it is, in short, the scourge that falls on the remains of great and lofty things and feelings in times of faith, enthusiasm, and chivalry.]

Böhl's reference to the flag suggests the burgeoning nationalist tendencies of the century. The bicolor red-yellow flag (*Rojigualda*), a major yet often disputed symbol in Spain's nationalist imagery, was first adopted by the Spanish Navy in 1785, and its prominence spread during the nineteenth century.[105] Böhl alludes to this nationalist symbol in her critique of what she perceives as the Spanish State's embracing of positivism, which she regards as a factor in the downfall of Spain's reputation as a Catholic country. Inspired by the Enlightenment, the positivist, as Böhl's narrator pronounces, "no quiere existencias modestas y tranquilas: esto es contra la dignidad de las luces y el *decorum* de la ilustración"[106] [does not want modest and peaceful existences: this runs counter to the Enlightenment's dignity and *decorum*]. Contrasting sharply with these "hombres superiores"[107] [superior men] are the lowly and uneducated, whom the narrative voice regards as truly the happiest due to their lack of earthly ambitions and preoccupations:

> Hay seres eminentemente felices y envidiablemente dichosos. Son estos los que con una excelente salud, una situación mediana, en la que nada ahorran, pero en la que tienen su pan asegurado, alejando así esperanzas doradas y temores negros, en un círculo limitado de objetos y de ideas, sin conocer un libro ni de vista, sino el catecismo, tienen la existencia exterior arreglada como un reloj, y la interior tranquila como una balsa de aceite.[108]

> [There are eminently happy and enviably joyful beings. These are those who, with excellent health and average circumstances, in which they do not save anything but in which they have enough to eat, removed from golden hopes and dark fears, in a limited circle of objects and ideas, without any knowledge of books other than the catechism, have a material life that runs like clockwork and a soul of absolute peace.]

Böhl's emphasis on simplicity and truth privileges the peasantry, whom Böhl and her father perceived as the source of pure, genuine Spanish traditions.[109] This bucolic image of simplicity and piety conflicts with Romantic individualist exaltations of passion and desire. Böhl's criticism of self-gratification stems from her insistence that it destroys the family unit first and subsequently the nation.

The repercussions of unrestrained ambition on familial unity are prominent in Böhl's *Lágrimas*. The novel opens with the death of the wife of the merchant Don Roque la Piedra during a stormy voyage from Havana to Cádiz. Before her death, the woman begs Don Roque, a gambler and troublemaker, to take care of their daughter, Lágrimas, and to treat her better than he did his spouse. Due to Lágrimas's weak constitution and asthma, Don Roque decides to remain in Cádiz and send Lágrimas to Seville. There she lives with other girls under the care of nuns at a convent. In the end, Lágrimas, bewailing her father's practice of buying, dismantling, and converting religious houses, perishes from tuberculosis.

At the beginning of the novel, Lágrimas's mother laments leaving her native Cuba to join her husband on his business trip to Spain. This episode demonstrates the tension between the mother's sentimental, rooted nostalgia and the father's dogged expediency. The mother's description of an exhausted, fallen, and ruined Europe alludes to that continent's perceived spiritual fatigue due to its industrial advancement:

> ¡A Dios, pues, para siempre, mi suave país, verde y rico como la esperanza! Te dejo por la exhausta y caduca Europa, caída en infancia, cubierta de ruinas y

AT THE HEART OF THE NATION   61

llena de recuerdos, que son las ruinas del corazón. ¡A Dios mis árboles altos
y frondosos, que no taló aun la mano de los hombres! ¡A Dios mis puros ríos,
cuyos cristales no enturbian ni esclavizan aun las construcciones de la invadi-
ente industria! ¡A Dios mis espesos manglos [*sic*], que crecéis fuertes y serenos
en la amargura de las aguas del mar![110]

[Farewell, then, forever, my sweet country, green and rich like hope! I leave you
for an exhausted and dying Europe, fallen in infancy, covered in ruins and full
of memories, which are the ruins of the heart. Farewell, my tall and leafy trees,
which the hand of man has not yet felled. Farewell, my pure rivers, whose crys-
talline waters have still not yet been spoiled or enslaved by the constructions
of an invading industry! Farewell, my dense mangroves that grow strong and
serene in the bitterness of the ocean's waters!]

The Americas and Europe, the New World and the Old, form a binary: the Americas are cast as lush and teeming with life, while Europe is dying. The images of
pure rivers, trees, and mangroves deeply rooted in the sea suggest a perenni-
ally paradisiac landscape, similar to the Alvareda family's orange tree enclosure,
untainted by the machines of modernity. After her farewell, evocative of a sol-
emn requiem, the devout mother perishes.[111] Like Ana in *La familia de Alvareda*
and Tía María in *La gaviota*, she represents the repository of a living tradition
that cannot thrive or survive in the modern environment. Crossing the ocean
between the Old World and the New does not prove to be a viable transition, thus
designating the apparent impossibility of bridging (past) tradition and (present)
modernity.

Don Roque's plan to close and sell convents constitutes the secularization of
the sacred in viewing these as practical investments, which the narrative voice
censures in the following description of him and his associates: "Sentados sobre
la suntuosa gradería del altar mayor, discutían sobre el modo de degradar más
pronto esa portentosa obra de la piedad de los antepasados, y arrancarle lo solo
que le quedaba: la austera majestad de la soledad, la profunda melancolía del
abandono"[112] [Seated on the sumptuous steps of the main altar, they discussed
how to degrade in the quickest possible way that magnificent work of piety built
by their ancestors and how to tear away the only thing that remained: the aus-
tere majesty of solitude, the profound melancholy of abandonment]. While the
verbs *degradar* [degrade] and *arrancarle* [uproot] connote a violent uprooting,
equally significant is the fact that these men discuss the building's fate on the
altar steps—the passage toward the highest and most important site in a church.
As the narrator laments, "¡Oh Dios mío! . . . Si hay quien nos pueda culpar, por
levantar nuestra débil voz gritando tus propias palabras: *dad a Dios lo que es
de Dios, y al César lo que es del César*"[113] [Oh, my God! . . . If someone could blame
us for lifting up our weak voices and shouting your words: *give to God what is*

God's and to Caesar what is Caesar's]. The pronoun *nos* [us] and possessive adjective *nuestra* [our] connote an imagined spiritual community or nation under threat, while the scriptural reference to God and Caesar, also evident in the clerical defense of ecclesiastical buildings that I outlined in chapter 1, denounces the secular appropriation of religious sites.

The narrative voice therefore condemns those involved in purchasing and dismantling holy edifices:

> ¿Qué derecho tenéis a destruir lo que otros labraron? ¿Creéis poder, como Dios a las olas del mar, decir a los sentimientos de los fervientes, hasta aquí llegaréis? Si la generación presente condena en sus obras a la generación que labró, día llegará en que la generación venidera condene con harta más razón sobre ruinas, a la generación que destruyó.[114]

> [What right do you have to destroy what others have cultivated? Do you believe you can, like God to the waves, tell the sentiments of the fervent, "This is as far as you go"? If the present generation condemns in its works the generation that constructed all this, the day will come when the future generation will condemn with greater reason, over the ruins, the generation that destroyed it all.]

Here the narrator emphasizes the inextricable bond between the church building and what it represents and the preceding generations who worked on building it. The architectural connotations of building and labor demonstrate that the task of the present generation is to conserve the work of the past for those to come.[115]

Building up the nation's spiritual patrimony rests on valuing appropriately the religious edifice. With the secularization of such buildings, there is no place for the sacred, as is evident in the men's disregard for the church's holy images: "Pasaron delante de la capilla del Señor del Socorro y delante del cementerio, y ni la imagen de Dios ni la de la muerte, distrajeron un momento la atención de estos hombres de su negocio. . . . Eran hombres *positivos*"[116] [They passed in front of the chapel of the Lord of Succor and in front of the cemetery, and not even the image of God or that of death distracted for one moment these men from their business. . . . They were *positive* men]. The narrator concludes that these men, focusing entirely on their business, are oblivious to religion. Böhl's critique of positivism is thus premised upon her perception of its spiritual implications. The businessmen's incessant search for material gain renders them blind to the existence of the sacred.

What might be the future of the church, or "santo palacio,"[117] is a question taken up by the characters of Don Modesto and Rosita, who also appear in *La gaviota*. When Don Modesto informs Rosita that it will become a factory, she replies, "¡Jesús me valga! . . . ¡Una fábrica del templo del Señor!"[118] [May Christ save me! A factory of the temple of the Lord!]. Likewise, in her last letter to her friend in Seville, Reina, Lágrimas denounces her father's plan to purchase a convent for its assets:

AT THE HEART OF THE NATION

Te he dicho que este pueblo es bonito sin tener pretensiones de serlo; es un grupo de casas bajas rodeadas a la iglesia que descuella grave, y parece con su paz y su silencio un rebaño de fieles arrodillados alrededor de una cruz. Cerca hay un soberbio convento que ha comprado mi Padre. ¿No te suena extraño al oído eso de *comprar un convento* como una vara de paño? No he querido ir a verlo porque me daría mucha tristeza entrar en él.[119]

[I have told you that this town is pretty without being pretentious; it is a group of low houses surrounding the church that stands out solemnly, which seems in its peace and silence like a congregation of faithful kneeling around a cross. Nearby, there is a proud convent that my father has purchased. Does it not sound strange to you, this *purchasing of a convent* like a yard of fabric? I have not wanted to go and see it because it would make me sad to enter it.]

The nostalgic tones of Lágrimas's letter criticize the conversion of sacred spaces to public properties through government decrees. In the following passage, Lágrimas's sentimental recollection works to reconstruct the lost wholeness of the demolished sanctuary:

¡Silencio hosco en las bóvedas en que sonaban himnos y preces al Señor! ¡Qué dolor ver el tabernáculo en donde se entronó la Majestad, llenando de respeto, de amor y de consuelo los corazones, vacío y frío, esparcir desconsuelo y asombro! Prefiero ir al convento de Santa Ana; allí los cantos de las monjas, las flores, el incienso, las luces, los rezos de los fieles, todo consuela al corazón y redobla nuestro fervor, como en coro y acompañada se levanta la voz más firme y confiada.[120]

[What a gloomy silence in the vaults in which hymns and supplications resound to the Lord! What sadness seeing the tabernacle where His Majesty, filling hearts with respect, love, and consolation, is now empty and cold, sowing grief and horror! I prefer to go to the convent of Saint Anne; there the nuns' singing, the flowers, the incense, the lights, the prayers of the faithful—everything there consoles the heart and increases our fervor, just as in chorus and, accompanied, lifts up the most resolute and trusting voices.]

Pondering the ruins, devoid of sound and content, Lágrimas rues the deformation of these divine sites into lesser, secular chattels. Böhl's depictions of these ecclesiastical ruins exemplify Flitter's description of Mendizábal's disentailment program as a "destructive legacy."[121] By contrasting the strands of irreligion and materialism in her society with the perceived spiritual vigor of past ages, Böhl exposes that destruction as not only a physical appropriation and ruin of religious edifices but also a spiritual calamity. Since religious buildings figure as visible monuments of the Church's apparatus and Spain's historical landscape, they form part of its spiritual legacy. Thus, as I have stated earlier, Böhl maintains that profanation is not so much the elimination of the sacred as its replacement and perversion. This transformation, from her point of view, threatens the spiritual patrimony built by the Spanish Church and its affiliates, an important heritage intended for continuity.

For its role in the confiscation of the Church's buildings, Böhl therefore casts the government as a formidable adversary, underlining its capability to impose extreme disentailment legislation. In *Lágrimas*, Böhl satirizes the historical figure of the politician Pascual Madoz, whose disentailment laws took place in 1855, through the speech defects of the Galician Tiburcio: "No *esh eshtraño*, no *shepais* donde eshtá shituado un pueblo tan deschconocido que lo ha omitido en su diccionario, el sheñor Madozzz"[122] [It is not strange. You do not know where such an unknown town is situated because Mr. Madoz has omitted it from his dictionary]. In having this fictionalized Madoz render invisible the little town of Villamar, Böhl illustrates the vulnerability of the forgotten provinces at the hands of the federal government. Although the Andalusian-raised Lágrimas does not know where Villamar is located, the allusion to Madoz ironically shows that for the Spanish government, Villamar is in plain sight and cannot escape its laws.

CONCLUSION

Böhl's four novels, *La gaviota*, *La familia de Alvareda*, *Callar en vida y perdonar en muerte*, and *Lágrimas*, uphold traditions by denouncing spiritual and material profanation in the forms of desecration and despoil. In *La familia de Alvareda*, the foreign invasion of the Spanish nation parallels the overthrow of religious buildings and monastic communities through disentailment legislation in *La gaviota*. In both novels, infidelity overwhelms the joint matrimonial body. This pattern of besiegement assumes a different role in *Callar en vida y perdonar en muerte* and *Lágrimas*, where the demolition of convents endangers domestic relationships. In both these novels, female religious faith, originating primarily from maternal figures, is both challenged and tested. Thus, Böhl's novels condemn the defiance of the sacred, which leads to the negative transformation of sacred sites and the ruin of the traditional institutions of marriage and family.

Rearranging Flitter's formulation of "destructive legacy," I consider that in Böhl's texts, this legacy of destruction originates from a destruction of legacy. Böhl's conceptualization of ruined heritage applies not only to the material demolition of sacred spaces but also to the breakdown of traditionally sacred institutions due to unrestrained individual desire and ambition. For Böhl, the replacement of religious buildings with secular utilities for national economic advancement constitutes an irreparable damage to a spiritual heritage, while the rejection of marital fidelity demonstrates the undermining of religious teachings and the breakdown of the family.

AT THE HEART OF THE NATION

The motif of the family in Böhl's novels operates on two levels: it is the fundamental unit of society and a microcosm of the nation. Excessive individualism debilitates the microcosmic family unit, which is itself at the mercy of a modernizing society that claims to prioritize the nation. I have posited that Böhl foregrounds the collapse of intimate marital and familial unions to reveal the social, cultural, and spiritual consequences for the national body. Her concern for the nation's religious patrimony thus arises from her traditionalist perspective, in which matrimony, the family, and religious observance are sacralized and intertwined due to their crucial role in the spiritual and sociocultural formation of future generations. Drawing on elements of Catholic dogma, conservative Romanticism, and *costumbrismo* in the forms of dictums, scriptural references, songs, and traditions, Böhl allows her characters not only to transmit received wisdom but also to defy it, albeit to their detriment.

As Böhl's novels have demonstrated, the authoritative religious and cultural apparatus of the traditionalist Catholic province struggles to resist the modern ideas and values that beleaguer it. In my following chapter, I will turn to the works of Bécquer. Both conservative Catholic writers, Böhl and Bécquer convey differing strands of nostalgia for certain aspects of Spain's spiritual past. While Böhl seeks to restore elements of Spanish religious devotion, Bécquer reflects on the function of the sacred in Spain's morphing social and cultural landscape.

CHAPTER 3

The Hallowed, the Haunting

REMEMBERING AND RESTORING THE SACRED
PRECINCT IN GUSTAVO ADOLFO BÉCQUER'S *HISTORIA
DE LOS TEMPLOS DE ESPAÑA* (1857), *CARTAS DESDE
MI CELDA* (1864), AND *LEYENDAS* (1858–1864)

Remembrance is fundamentally a form of narration. As the French psychologist and philosopher Pierre Janet once remarked, "Memory is an action: essentially, it is the action of telling a story."[1] While Böhl commemorated Spain's religious and regional traditions by drawing on the thought of Schlegel and Herder in her costumbrist writings, Gustavo Adolfo Bécquer was inspired by the conservative French Romantic writer François-Auguste-René Chateaubriand (1768–1848), who defended Catholicism and commemorated France's sacred sites and monuments in his opus *The Genius of Christianity* (1802), written while in exile in England during the French Revolution.[2] Like Chateaubriand, Bécquer expressed his concerns regarding the political, spiritual, and cultural state of Spain through the lens of artistic traditionalism.[3] Bécquer's nostalgia for a bygone, sacred world drew from Chateaubriand and the Romantic writer Walter Scott, who approached ruins with a deeply spiritual imagination.[4]

The term *nostalgia*, derived from the Greek *nostos* [to return home] and *algia* [painful feeling], was first coined by Johannes Hofer in a 1688 Swiss medical thesis. Utilizing displaced soldiers as an example, Hofer defined *heimweh*, the soldiers' languishing for home, as a medical condition or disease.[5] Thus, nostalgia was originally understood as pain. Barbara Cassin goes on to affirm that nostalgia is the "pain of return," which is twofold in that the individual suffers while far away from home and must endure this suffering in order to return home.[6] For his part, Flanagan asserts that "the plight of disconnection between place and 'elsewhere' often finds expression in properties of exile and nostalgia."[7] Svetlana Boym asserts that nostalgia, in relation to the past and one's home or community, tends to be expressed in two ways: reflective nostalgia, which focuses on rebuilding and filling the gaps in memory (*nostos*), and restorative nostalgia, which emphasizes loss and longing (*algia*). Reflective nostalgia centers

THE HALLOWED, THE HAUNTING   67

on "human finitude" and the irrevocable nature of the past.[8] I posit that Bécquer is reflectively fixated on ruined edifices, focusing on the experience of individual and cultural remembrance.

I argue that Bécquer draws from both reflective and restorative nostalgia because he simultaneously ponders the very finitude and disintegration of a sacred home in a reflective nostalgia and exhibits restorative nostalgia in an artistic, symbolic sense pertinent to cultural memory. Bécquer's nostalgia stems from a search for connections between religious belief—a characteristic of Spain's social and cultural past, which provided Bécquer with literary inspiration—and the landscape of modernity.

As I will develop throughout this chapter, Bécquer's works examine the religious question through his artistic engagements with sacred architecture, his constant and wistful remembrance of Spain's religious history, and his use of the fantastic and the sublime to elucidate the sacred. In particular, as indicated in my introduction, I probe Bécquer's conceptualizations of the sacred space in three of his works: *Historia de los templos de España* (1857), *Cartas desde mi celda* (1864), and *Leyendas* (1858–1864). The first two parts are thematically connected because they analyze *Historia* and *Cartas*, two texts centered on Bécquer's observation of convents, monasteries, and churches.[9] The first section on *Historia* deals primarily with metaphor and religious symbolism in relation to Toledo's Monasterio de San Juan de los Reyes. I focus specifically on San Juan de los Reyes because of its spiritual and historic significance to Toledo. Deploying the corporeal metaphor of the Church, Bécquer personifies the damages and negligence inflicted on Catholic religious buildings and communities, as seen in Toledo. Furthermore, Bécquer's reflections on these ruins reveal their role as a "prism of the past," as Flanagan puts it. The ruin, Flanagan states, acts as a medium that clarifies and distorts history. Hence, the ruin becomes a space for the viewer's subjectivity, "a shifting spectacle" dependent on the viewer's expectations. At the mercy of the ruin's openness to interpretation is the knowledge of its true origin, which is often incompletely told.[10]

In my analysis of his *Cartas*, I discuss how Bécquer pays homage to mysticism, which defies temporal restrictions of time through its emphasis on eternity. Here I base my discussion of mysticism on Michel de Certeau's theories. Alluding to the Spanish mystics, who lived within their cloistered communities and traveled to found monasteries and convents, Bécquer commemorates Spain's less conventional religious heritage. His reflections on historical monastic sites are pertinent to this act of remembrance, given that many clergy and nuns were exclaustrated due to the laws of disentailment and the suppression of convents and monasteries. By physically producing, and literarily situating, his writings within the precincts of churches and the dwellings of religious communities, Bécquer calls attention to the wavering flame of memory, symptomatic of the fallout from political decisions in Spain, to which he personally alludes in his *Cartas*.

Yet, although Bécquer ponders the very finitude of home, he also exhibits restorative nostalgia in an artistic, symbolic sense pertinent to cultural memory. Rubén Benítez argues that in his *Historia*, Bécquer undertakes an artistic reconstruction of sacred monuments, privileging beliefs, ideas, and sentiments over historical documents.[11] Bécquer conveys, therefore, a spiritual homesickness in his *Historia*. He reiterates the sentiment of yearning in *Cartas*, an epistolary work wherein he foregrounds the historical events and spiritual attitudes that contributed to this inability to return to the physical home of the abbey and the spiritual home of the ruined or neglected church. The inhabitants of confiscated monasteries and convents—members of religious communities—could not go back to their residences. Moreover, lay religious believers, like Bécquer, were deprived of the sacred ambience of conventual spaces, which had now become lodging for travelers as opposed to the places of worship that they once were.

Bécquer describes the modern world as a place of unoriginality and unending materialist desire due to rapid industrialization. Tom Lewis situates Bécquer's response to the emergence of Spanish modernity as "one of the first textualizations of powerfully felt emotions in the context of new social experiences."[12] The growing, bustling city with its novelties was one of the environments that Bécquer's writings aimed to question and transcend. In comparison, Sarah Sierra considers that Bécquer himself was a moderate, appreciating the benefits of modernization while remaining loyal to Spain's religious and cultural heritage like most liberals.[13]

Finally, Bécquer's focus on the historical and spiritual appeal of the sacred buildings peaks dramatically in his *Leyendas*. Here I discuss Bécquer's use of Gothic terror and the Romantic sublime, concepts that highlight sound, silence, and privation. Although Bécquer is not, strictly speaking, a Romantic writer, he inherits and draws on the legacy of the Romantic movement. Antonio Risco's readings of the *Leyendas*, alongside Tzvetan Todorov's analysis of fantastical literature, form part of my framework for understanding the workings of horror in Bécquer's tales.

Romanticism and National History

Silver asserts that Bécquer's work was characterized by a late conservative, Catholic, medievalizing Romanticism.[14] His texts convey, this critic declares, the idea that "the past is unrecoverable, and yet its interpretation remains a matter of spiritual life and death."[15] Religious and spiritual matters are intertwined in Bécquer's writings, as he identifies the religious edifice as a tangible and visible expression of the supernatural realm. Although he was as fervent a Catholic as Böhl and a more sophisticated moralist, Silver maintains that Bécquer articulated through various genres what was arguably the dilemma of the century: the pressing demands of modernization, which, in turn, were imperiling Spanish

THE HALLOWED, THE HAUNTING

religious and cultural institutions and traditions. Imitating Chateaubriand's contemplation of religious architecture, Bécquer addresses the relationship between the divine and the created worlds through a reflection based on piety, not melancholy.[16] Drawing on Silver's argument, I posit that Bécquer's conveying of religious nostalgia is an act of sacralization, whereby he melds the artistic and cultural meanings of religious sanctuaries by "conjuring" a bridge between their past and present states. While Benítez declares that "el observador no ejerce una actividad libre"[17] [the observer does not perform a free activity], I maintain that Bécquer goes beyond the role of a mere spectator in his *Historia* and *Cartas* to assume that of a creator, closely examining and interpreting the inner lives of the temples of Toledo and the Monasterio de Veruela.

NATIONAL MONUMENTS IN *HISTORIA DE LOS TEMPLOS DE ESPAÑA*

During Spain's nineteenth century, the significance of buildings for the nation's history was paramount. Confirming this importance was, for instance, Patricio de la Escosura's *España artística y monumental: Vistas y descripción de los sitios y monumentos más notables de España* [Artistic and monumental Spain: Views and description of Spain's most famous sites and monuments, 1842], which provided illustrations and accounts of religious and civil sites and monuments throughout Spain, such as the sepulchres of the Castilian noble Álvaro de Luna, the Cathedral of Zamora, the monastery of Santa María de las Huelgas in Burgos, the former synagogue Santa María la Blanca in Toledo, and the Cathedral of Toledo. Escosura lauds Toledo in particular as a place built by the religious piety of Spain's ancestors.[18]

In 1857, a twenty-one-year-old Bécquer published his ambitious *Historia de los templos de España*, dedicated to Isabel II and other State and Church officials. This unfinished work indicates his strong religious convictions and mystic nature as well as his personal interests and determination as a young writer.[19] It is important to note that Bécquer opened his *Historia* with Toledo, beginning with a description of and reflection on San Juan de los Reyes. I argue that Bécquer does not seek to conceal his sentimental and personal conceptualization of the religious buildings in *Historia*. Rather, he presents a highly subjective and imaginative poetic response, assuming the roles of the solitary thinker, the studious artist, and the creative poet.[20] Bécquer's artistic skills, evident in his apprenticeship as a painter, helped form the foundation of a sensitive and observant poet. Thus, imitating a pictorial artist, Bécquer describes sacred buildings in great detail, guided by his Catholic beliefs.[21]

Indeed, I posit that Bécquer's literary "dismantling" of the sacred site into its concrete, aesthetic, historical, and religious facets doubly evokes the actions of breaking and salvaging, which can be seen as mirroring his unresolved state of trauma. Through the eyes of a thinker, artist, and poet, Bécquer endeavors to present himself as a witness to the silent, disembodied ruins of an increasingly secularizing Spain. Apart from San Juan de los Reyes, *Historia* also features the synagogues of Nuestra Señora del Tránsito and Santa María la Blanca, the old mosque of Cristo de la Luz, and a wide range of then existing Catholic churches, convents, monasteries, beguinages (houses for lay religious women), chapels, sanctuaries, and religious communities.

Going beyond giving an account of each building's background and architectonic features—elements principal, if not primary, to any historico-architectural text—Bécquer represents them as essential components of Spain's variegated spiritual histories. From the beginning, he discloses the thoughts and sentiments that underpin the entire work in question: "La tradición religiosa es el eje de diamante sobre el que gira nuestro pasado"[22] [Religious tradition is the diamond axis on which our past rotates]. I consider that Bécquer's subjective responses to the fates of historic religious buildings demonstrate his concern for the sacred precinct, a space associated with the redemptive properties of a religious faith under threat. From a time of perceived excessive secularization and political upheavals, Bécquer's text looks back to a past when faith constituted the source of social unity rather than disunity and of communion, not disharmony. For Rubio Jiménez, Bécquer's *Historia* represents a literary attempt to rescue a sacralized world from destruction and oblivion.[23]

The Catholic Monarchs proclaimed their descent from the Visigoth monarchy, which saw that Toledo was its ancient political and spiritual center. It was at the Third Council of Toledo that the Visigoth king Reccared renounced Arianism and converted to Catholicism. Since then, Peter Linehan states, "Spain's spiritual awakening has been, and continues to be, dated to the metaphorical act of national baptism which III Toledo is held to have represented."[24] Consequently, to commemorate their victory at the Battle of Toro in 1476, which consolidated the union of the two most important kingdoms in the Peninsula, Castilla and Aragón, the Catholic Monarchs founded San Juan de los Reyes, a temple intended as the founders' mausoleum.[25] The establishment of the monastery, dedicated to Saint John the apostle, began in the fifteenth century under the monarchs' direction.[26] The inscription of the lower cloister of San Juan de los Reyes describes the monastery as an icon of unification and orthodoxy:

> Este monasterio fue edificado por mandato de los católicos y muy excelentes reyes D. Fernando y Doña Isabel . . . a honra y gloria del rey del cielo, y de su gloriosa madre y de los bienaventurados San Juan Evangelista y del Sacratísimo San Francisco, sus devotos intercesores; y dentro de la edificación de esta casa ganaron el reino de Granada y destruyeron la herejía.[27]

> [This monastery was built by order of the very excellent Catholic Monarchs Don Ferdinand and Doña Isabella to honor and glorify the king of heaven and

Figure 4. Cloister, Monasterio de San Juan de los Reyes, Toledo.

his glorious mother and the blessed ones, Saint John the Baptist and the most holy Saint Francis, their devout intercessors. And in building this house, they won the kingdom of Granada and destroyed heresy.]

Associated with its founding monarchs, the monastery embodied political and spiritual imperialism, which concentrated on uniting its kingdoms, reforming clergy and nuns, and evangelizing in overseas colonies. The monarchs' decision to establish the monastery as a mausoleum would change in 1504, when Isabel and Fernando chose the royal chapel of Granada as their place of interment to memorialize their victory over Islam, their defense of the Catholic religion, and the union of Spain's principal kingdoms.[28]

During the War of Independence, Toledo was an important strategic location for French troops due to its proximity to the capital. To prepare for their arrival in April 1808 under General Dupont, the town's citizens were ordered to prepare lodgings, and the town decided that convents would be adequate places. Hence, the religious were shifted to other convents. The authorities of San Juan de los Reyes implemented measures regarding the closure of the convent chapel and the retrieval of its books and possessions in case of plunder.[29]

Bécquer depicts San Juan de los Reyes—a concrete symbol of Spanish Catholicism and monarchical power—as a core facet of Spain's national history and identity. This monastery is, therefore, not only an artistic monument but also a symbol of Spain's dual role as mystic and *conquistador* [conqueror]. This union of what Nora terms *lieux de mémoire* with Spanish national history illustrates the extent to which history guides cultural memory.[30] It must be remembered that the 1812 Constitution wedded Spanish nationality to the Catholic religion.

For the French, Nora writes, the first annals of power in France consisted of the royal chapel, the Fleury Abbey, and Saint Benoît sur Loire, with Saint-Denis as a necropolis of the kings and Reims as the city of the royal anointing.[31] Similarly, Bécquer writes about the history of Spain first, considering San Juan de los Reyes a key monument in Spain's political history. He poignantly emphasizes the holiness of the monastery, lamenting the reality of its obscurity. It is on this notion of the deliberate, politically motivated forgetting of the sacredness of religious space that Bécquer seems so fixated.

According to Pedro Navascués Palacio, Bécquer was the first to call attention to San Juan de los Reyes, thus preventing its total oblivion.[32] In fact, Navascués Palacio posits, Bécquer's Romantic prose influenced the decision to create the Comisión de Monumentos [Commission for Monuments], even if it took until 1881 for the architect and sculptor Arturo Mélida to restore the building's "lost dignity."[33] The monastery building had suffered damages from French troops and later lost its inhabitants, members of the Franciscan order, through the 1835 exclaustration act.[34]

Bécquer describes the building as worthy of intellectual, artistic, and poetic attention despite its former devastation, demonstrating that literary and visual art can fill the chasm created by loss and damage. He apostrophizes the precincts as well as the sacred figures to whom these buildings have been specifically dedicated, beckoning them to acknowledge his presence: "Silenciosas ruinas de un prodigio del arte, restos imponentes de una generación olvidada, sombríos muros del Santuario del Señor, heme aquí entre vosotros"[35] [Silent ruins of an artistic wonder, extraordinary remains of a forgotten generation, somber walls of the sanctuary of the Lord, here am I among you]. Invoking a supernatural power, Bécquer confers upon himself the authority and responsibility of speaking for these voiceless elements from the past. *Heme aquí* educes the reply of Moses to the Lord God in the book of Exodus 3:4: "Here I am," Moses says, acknowledging and responding to the presence of the divine. Assuming the prophetic persona of Moses, Bécquer authorizes himself to carry out and receive the commands of the past and to re-create its images through the fragments that inspire his poetic imagination and voice. He decries the forgetting of these hollowed and hallowed spaces, given their high cultural significance, which he explicitly describes with the words *prodigio* [wonder] and *imponentes* [extraordinary]. With this poetic invocation, he aestheticizes the ruin and foreshadows the fantastical events that take place in the holy settings of *Leyendas*.

Moreover, Bécquer addresses these buildings in the present tense as if he were directly speaking to the dead. It could only mean that for him, the dead have not disappeared entirely. Such a stilling of time conveys an attempt to preserve an

THE HALLOWED, THE HAUNTING

essential reality. The Catholic sacralization of the dead premises the hope of their resurrection. In light of this theological concept, Bécquer emphasizes in *Historia* the poet's ability to retrieve what seemingly belongs to a bygone era: "El poeta, a cuya invocación poderosa, como al acento de un conjuro mágico, palpita en sus olvidadas tumbas el polvo de cien generaciones; cuya imaginación ardiente reconstruye sobre un roto sillar un edificio, y sobre el edificio, con sus creencias y sus costumbres, una edad remota"[36] [The poet, at whose powerful invocation, like the sound of a magic spell, beats in their forgotten tombs the dust of a hundred generations pulsates in forgotten tombs; whose burning imagination reconstructs from a broken stone slab a building, and on the building, with its beliefs and customs, a distant age]. Literature takes on the act of renewal, but for both writer and reader, the act of renewal is also a duty. The written word tasks the reader with conjuring images mentally in the absence of intact visual realities, thus restoring them through the imagination.

Bécquer lends a poetic sensibility to the image of the sold, ruined abbey, which appears as a decrepit object but remains replete with artistic, historical, and religious significance. His speaking to the monastic complex as if it were a human person can be analyzed on three levels of signification: the cruciform church as a sign of Christ's body, the sacred building as a house for the living, and the church as a resting place for the dead and sanctified. On the symbolic potential of the body, Mary Douglas has remarked, "The body is a model which can stand for any bounded system. Its boundaries can represent any boundaries which are threatened or precarious."[37] In his description of San Juan de los Reyes, Bécquer utilizes anatomical terms, describing its body and the nerves of its vault.[38]

This apt organic metaphor of the body in relation to San Juan de los Reyes acknowledges the amalgam of earthly and celestial bodies in the church space. Relics of martyrs are placed in the altar stone, situated in the sanctuary that is the head of the church. In the chapels between the aisles and the nave, the body of the church, are shrines to the saints and sepulchres. The church, by virtue of its primarily cultic function, separates itself from the secular world. Duncan G. Stroik points out that the church's role is twofold: it is a *domus Dei* [house of God] and a *domus ecclesiae* [house of the people of God].[39] Drawing on Stroik, I consider that the same can be said of the abbey of San Juan de los Reyes, which has its own church and is also a home for people who dedicate themselves to religion. The liturgical locus and the religious house are, therefore, sanctuaries. Both consecrated sites give each other meaning.

In *Historia*, Bécquer regards the temple of San Juan de los Reyes as the manifestation of religious tradition, the study of which will help synthesize the "eje de diamante" [diamond axis], the invincible foundation and core of a shared past.[40] He acknowledges the myriad individuals who created the monastic complex, from the builders who constructed it, to the artists who decorated it, to the archivists who stored history and knowledge in it:

74   MAKING MODERN SPAIN

Por último, cuando nos hayan revelado sus secretos las artes, cuando desci-
fremos el Apocalipsis de granito que escribió el sacerdote en el santuario y
aparezcan a nuestros ojos esas generaciones gigantes que duermen bajo
las losas de sus sepulcros, arrojaremos sobre el confuso caos de tan diferentes
ideas un rayo de la fe que creara, y este será el *fiat lux* que disipará las sombras
de ese pasado desconocido.[41]

[Finally, when the arts have revealed to us their secrets, when we decipher the
apocalypse of granite that the priest wrote in the sanctuary, and when those
colossal generations that sleep beneath the gravestones of their tombs appear
before our eyes, we will cast over the confusing chaos of such different ideas
a ray of faith that creates, and this will be the "let there be light" moment that
dissipates the shadows of that unknown past.]

By referring to *fiat lux* [let there be light], Bécquer alludes to the creation story
in the book of Genesis. Taking on a quasi-divine role as literary creator, he
aligns himself with the monastery's builders: "El convento de San Juan de los
Reyes, en sus distintas cualidades de página histórica, de edificio monumental y de fuente de la poesía, goza el triple privilegio de hablar a la inteligencia
que razona, al arte que estudia, al espíritu que crea"[42] [The convent of Saint
John of the Kings, in its distinct qualities as historical narrative, monumental building, and source of poetry, enjoys the threefold privilege of speaking
to the intelligence that reasons, the art that studies, the spirit that creates].
He also subsequently refers to the Tower of Babel, the biblical tower that God
destroyed to punish its builders for their hubris. This scriptural reference may
be interpreted as alluding to the Spanish nation in political and spiritual turmoil. Bécquer cautions against human ambitions, juxtaposing the collective
giant of religious beliefs with the small, rickety Babel of secularization: "Acaso
cuando, ya reunidos sus fragmentos, pongamos en pie el coloso de las creencias, sus gigantes proporciones humillen y confundan la raquítica Babel de la
impiedad"[43] [Perhaps when, once its fragments are reunited, we raise up the
titan of belief, its colossal proportions will humiliate and confound the emaciated Babel of impiety].

For Bécquer, these fragments belong to the unifying structure of religious
belief. The recovering and reuniting of these fragments is an act of remembrance.
Apropos of narrative memory and the remaking of individual and collective
selves, Susan Brison asks, "How does one remake a self from the scattered shards
of disrupted memory?"[44] According to her, the performative role of speech is
indispensable for recovering from trauma because "saying something about a
traumatic memory does *something* to it."[45] The trauma survivor, Brison continues, experiences a "figurative dismemberment," which involves the shattering of
assumptions; the severing of the temporalities of past, present, and future; and a

THE HALLOWED, THE HAUNTING

disruption of memory.[46] It follows, then, that to construct a narrative is to gather up these shards in an attempt to reconstruct the damaged self.[47]

Recalling Brison's likening of shattered memory to shards, the fragments that Bécquer envisages assembling designate the physical and spiritual brokenness of the confiscated building that his commemorative writing will restore:

> Los años de la devastación, al pasar sobre sus muros, le han grabado el sello de ruina y de grandeza que lo caracteriza, y la hiedra que se mece colgada de los parduscos y fuertes machones de su ábside; los carcomidos y tradicionales hierros que, a manera de festón arquitectónico, rodean sus robustos pilares; los calados doseletes que arrojan una sombra misteriosa sobre la frente de sus rotos y mudos heraldos de granito; la majestad y la esbeltez de la espaciosa y única nave de su iglesia.[48]

> [The years of devastation, on passing over its walls, have engraved on it the seal of ruin and grandeur that characterizes it and the ivy that sways, clinging to the strong brownish buttresses of the apse. The decayed traditional wrought ironwork, like an architectural decoration, surrounds its robust pillars; the soaked canopies that cast a mysterious shadow on the foreheads of its broken and mute heralds of granite; the majesty and slender lines of the spacious and unique nave of the church.]

The idealized, robust pillars that hold the sacred building together have not prevented the formation of broken, mute heralds of granite. The silencing of these shattered angelic messengers suggests that the convent's foundations and the spiritual ideals that it represents have been shaken. Nevertheless, the verb *grabar* [to engrave], alluding to inscription, depicts the ruin as a palimpsest. Such a description portrays the ruin as a site worthy of reflection, which appeals to the Romantic sensibility.

Following Bécquer's detailed description of the convent's architectural and semantic (de)composition, he concludes with a personal ode to the building and its history, which might be read as a headstone epitaph: "El alto silencio del abandono vive ahora en vuestros muros, entre cuyos sillares crece la hiedra que da sombra al nido de la golondrina, hecho de leves plumas sobre el dosel de las estatuas"[49] [The resounding silence of abandonment now lives within your walls, while between slabs of stone grows ivy that gives shade to the swallow's nest, made of light feathers over the canopy of the statues]. Furthermore, Bécquer laments that the holy space has now faded into oblivion and obscurity. Faith and religious devotion buttressed the monastery's ability to stand strong for many centuries. With the dawn of the modern age, however, the monastery and the religion that it symbolizes must compete with the liberal pillars of industry and commerce. As Bécquer continues, the invasive forces of war ("legiones extranjeras" [foreign legions]; "corceles" [steeds]) and avarice, which are theoretically contrary to the premises of religion, debilitate the monastery's structure on a physical level and eclipse its presence in the public sphere. Thus, Bécquer's religious beliefs and nationalist sentiment result in his threefold opposition to foreign intervention, anti-Catholic sentiment, and modern liberalism:

> Envueltos en el olvido y la oscuridad, pasáis luego a través de una y otra generación hasta que las legiones extranjeras profanan vuestros umbrales. Bajo las santificadas bóvedas que sólo habían recibido la nube del incienso o las preces de los religiosos, retumban el sonoro golpear del ferrado casco de los corceles, el ronco son de los atambores y el metálico choque de las armas. Temblando los ecos, repiten los libres cantares de los campamentos y el nocturno grito de alarma de los vigías.[50]

> [Enveloped in oblivion and obscurity, you then pass from one generation to the next until the foreign legions profane your doorsteps. Under the holy vaults that had only received clouds of incense or the prayers of the religious resound the loud beating of the ironclad hooves of the steeds, the raucous sound of drums, and the metallic clash of weapons. The reverberations of echoes repeat the free chants of the encampments and the sentries' nocturnal cry of alarm.]

Bécquer then invokes the mute, dormant statues around him: "¡Mudas estatuas que me rodeáis! ¡Guerreros que dormís inmóviles en vuestros nichos de piedra! Vosotros debisteis de temblar de indignación aquel día y llevar vuestras heladas manos a las espadas de granito que penden aún en vuestros cinturones"[51] [Voiceless statues that surround me! Warriors who sleep motionless in your stone niches! You must have trembled with indignation that day and lifted your frozen hands to the swords of granite that still sway at your waists]. By personifying the inanimate statues of the church of San Juan de los Reyes, Bécquer points to the desecration ("las carcajadas, los juramentos, las blasfemias" [the guffaws, the profanities, the blasphemies]) of avaricious individuals, those who "siguen el oro"[52] [pursue gold]. I touch again on this literary technique below in *Leyendas*, where the personification of sculptures also serves to signal and reinforce the supernatural milieu of the church. There Bécquer emphasizes that avarice is blasphemous and thus antithetical to a temple's function.

Bécquer's commanding, incensed tone transforms his reflection into an elegy, which, according to David Kennedy, "presents everything as lost and gone, or absent and future."[53] Nineteenth-century Romantic elegy, Kennedy notes, involves outbursts of anger as well as repeated phrases.[54] As Bécquer takes on the role of an elegiac poet, he mourns the building and its present condition. In combining the building's history with a poetic lament for its dilapidated state, he expresses a desire for the restitution of the religious faith that San Juan de los Reyes denotes. This longing for an idealized, stabilizing faith continues in several of his *Cartas*, to which I now turn.

THE HALLOWED, THE HAUNTING

77

CARTAS DESDE MI CELDA: BÉCQUER'S DEBT TO MYSTICISM

Between 1863 and 1864, Bécquer and his brother, Valeriano, an artist like their painter father, José Domínguez Bécquer, stayed in the Monasterio de Veruela, founded by the Cistercian order and nestled among the fields and mountains of Moncayo in Saragossa.[55] As Bécquer recovered from tuberculosis, he wrote his epistolary work, *Cartas desde mi celda*, and sketched while Valeriano produced *Espedición [sic] de Veruela* [Trip from Veruela], an album of drawings and paintings of their daily lives and surroundings.[56] Up to forty of their drawings, which formed most of their artistic output during their stay, were of the Monasterio de Veruela. I hold that throughout their artistic journeys there, both revealed their anxiety about the effects of progress on tradition, of which the sacred, haunting space of the monastery was emblematic.[57]

It is relevant that Bécquer wrote *Cartas*, published in the periodical *El Contemporáneo* [The Contemporary] in 1864, in the actual monastery of Veruela. A prince of Aragón, Don Pedro Atarés, founded the famous monastery after witnessing the apparition of the Virgin of Veruela, who allegedly rescued him in a storm. Jesús Rubio Jiménez states that this monastery was abandoned thrice: in 1808 during the Napoleonic invasion, in 1820 by the Cortes's abolition of monastic orders, and in 1836–1837 through Mendizábal's disentailment laws. Ever since the first period of pillaging and abandonment, the monastery buildings gradually deteriorated, and their possessions were dispersed or destroyed. In 1844, the *Boletín de la Provincia de Zaragoza* [Bulletin of the Province of Saragossa] advertised the monastery's auction, and the entire monastery was put up for sale.[58]

Surrounded by high mountains, Veruela was a site par excellence for prophetic reference. Marlon B. Ross declares that to speak from the mountain is the ultimate experience of the sublime, where the individual tests the power and limits of self, stresses the solitude of self-questing, and pits the self against nature's power. Biblically, prophets communicated with God on these high places. It was on Mount Horeb that God commanded Moses to lead his people to safety and then offer a sacrifice on the same mountain (Exodus 3:12), and it was on Mount Sinai that Moses received the Decalogue from God (Exodus 20). Most significantly, in his Sermon on the Mount, Jesus reinforced moral teachings from the Beatitudes to respect what was sacred. In Ross's words, "It is from mountains that prophets proclaim their truths; for the poet-prophet the mountain symbolizes the necessary solitude of the leaders of men and the necessary stance of truth— its transcendence, its elusiveness, and its immense might."[59]

Although the monastery was destroyed during the French occupation of Toledo, Bécquer states in his description of Veruela's monastery that it remains, for the most part, intact: "El monasterio se conserva en buen estado y es objeto de continuas visitas de artistas, anticuarios y extranjeros, que van allí a admirar la severidad y sencillez grandiosa de este asilo, consagrado, en tiempos más piadosos, a la contemplación divina"[60] [The monastery is kept in good condition, and it is the object of continual visits from artists, antique dealers, and foreigners, who go there to admire the architectural austerity and grand simplicity of this sanctuary, consecrated, in more pious times, to the contemplation of the divine]. However, Bécquer points out that the edifice's primary purpose as a monastic abode has been replaced by tourism activities, thus signaling its break from a worshipful, divine past. Throughout *Cartas*, Bécquer conveys his sentiment of yearning on relating his daily experiences and thoughts in the first person and turns such musings into a patriotic reminiscence of "*nuestra* vieja España"[61] [our old Spain]. As Smith categorically states, memory is bound to a place, particularly a homeland.[62] This idea of binding suggests defiance toward an unstable, changing modern world, driven by utility, activity, and mobility.[63] Bécquer's reference to "our old Spain" privileges ideals of permanence and antiquity, a trend common in Romanticism. The deeply melancholic undertones of his second, fourth, and tenth letters in particular, on which my analysis focuses, are suffused with religious nostalgia and yearning for the medieval past, perceived as more enduring.

In his second letter, Bécquer describes the monastery's surroundings as an ambience conducive to a mystical experience, a "flight" from the world. Hearing its various bells brings relief, alleviating his anxieties about the contemporary political climate and national concerns. From the problematic public arena, Bécquer retreats to the interior realm of his soul:

> La campana del monasterio, la única que ha quedado colgada en su ruinosa torre bizantina, comienza a tocar la oración, y una cerca, y otra lejos, estas con una vibración metálica y aguda, aquellas con un tañido sordo y triste, les responden las otras campanas de los lugares del Somontano. . . .
>
> Ya todo pasó. Madrid, la política, las luchas ardientes, las miserias humanas, las pasiones, las contrariedades, los deseos; todo se ha ahogado en aquella música divina. Mi alma está ya tan serena como el agua inmóvil y profunda.[64]

> [The monastery bell, the only one that remains hanging in its ruined Byzantine tower, begins to ring for prayer, and from near and far—the latter, with a metallic and sharp vibration; the former, those with a muffled, sad peal—the bells from other the places throughout Somontano respond. . . .
>
> Everything has now passed. Madrid, politics, fiery struggles, human miseries, passions, enmities, desires—everything has been drowned out by that divine music. My soul is already as serene as the water, motionless and deep.]

Bécquer's attention to the bells and their impact on the auditory environment evokes the medieval custom of ringing church bells to summon the monastic community and laity to prayer in late classical antiquity. Early Christians could only worship privately until the fourth century with the Edict of Milan, after

THE HALLOWED, THE HAUNTING

which bells appeared in Western Europe as a common feature in liturgy and daily life. While Saint Pachomius's Egyptian rule made use of trumpets for calling members to prayer, Saint Benedict's rule in Italy employed the *signum*, the medieval word for "bell."[65] Bells eventually began to measure secular life, signaling commercial dealings and working hours in medieval Europe.[66]

The historic and monastic origins that these sounds evoke effectively conjure an image of an enduring religious past. Furthermore, the aural network that the simultaneous chimes form across the area signals a closing of distance, bringing together communities to answer the harmonious call of religion. I suggest that Bécquer's *Cartas* urge a retreat to the observance of faith. It may seem that this work signifies a personal spiritual experience of the individualist Romantic type, which navigates from the external trappings of religion and dogma. Yet it is crucial to point out that Bécquer upholds the icons of organized religion in his response to the bells and the "santuario del Señor" [the sanctuary of the Lord]. This milieu contributes to a spiritual recall that beckons a union with the past. The internal aspects of the Catholic religion, which Bécquer's passage above presents in theological terms, such as *alma* [soul], *divina* [divine], and *oración* [prayer], contrast starkly with the external panorama of political conflict. As I have signaled before, Catholicism was recognized constitutionally as the official religion of Spain, part of the national "body," yet exclaustration and expropriation threatened religious orders and Church assets. Prompted by the bells, the secular world ceases to perturb Bécquer. The phrase "todo se ha ahogado" [everything has been drowned out] effectively illustrates the way in which the divine overrides all earthly affairs, secondary to matters of the soul.

Bécquer's above-cited recourse to the symbol of deep, still waters is of mythical and spiritual significance. As Mircea Eliade notes, Asiatic and Oceanian mythologies recognized water's power to give life and death.[67] Christianity conferred new religious values on this archetypal image, which recalls not only Noah and the deluge that cleansed the world but also the baptism of Christ in the River Jordan and his institution of baptism as a sacrament.[68] Hence, the purifying nature of water is highlighted in its ability to "wash away sins."[69] According to the patristic writings of the early Christian Church, water bore a soteriological value and not just a cosmological one, bringing forth life in its natural and supernatural sense. Water as a natural, life-giving, and life-preserving element is a signifier of salvation. Eliade asserts that water is "*fons et origo*, the reservoir of all the potentialities of existence; they *precede* every form and *sustain* every creation."[70] Given that the theological foundation of all creation is God, Bécquer's symbol of profound waters signals God's fluid presence from time immemorial.

In *Bécquer tradicionalista* [Traditionalist Bécquer], Benítez asserts that Bécquer was associated with the moderates, an appraisal also shared by Sierra.[71] Yet

Benítez also points out certain contradictions in Bécquer's political and cultural mindset; while he was concerned about social injustice and disparities and believed in the goal of modern progress, he was equally vehement on the matter of tradition and religion.[72] It is thus probable that during the restoration of moderate rule in 1856, Bécquer's political mindset altered in that he began to favor the notion of a society originating from "la idea religiosa" [the religious idea] and supported the view that the monarchy was an expression of religious unity.[73] From 1860 onward, Benítez argues, Bécquer was a neo-Catholic in his criticism of extreme liberalism, which he saw as disregarding traditional values and the Catholic religion that had inspired important monuments in Spain's history.[74] In his second letter, Bécquer's criticism of Madrid as a hub of unchecked human ambition now reflects his artistic traditionalism that, as Benítez notes, took on political overtones to oppose the "piqueta demoledora del progreso"[75] [destructive pickax of progress].

In his *Cartas*, Bécquer declares that the miseries brought about by the tensions between Church and State and society's loss of social interest in Catholicism signal a break with the nation's past. In his fourth letter, he depicts the tensions between modernity, with its emphasis on the future, and the past, with its national traditions:

> Yo tengo fe en el porvenir. . . . No obstante, sea cuestión de poesía, sea que es inherente a la naturaleza frágil del hombre simpatizar con lo que perece y volver los ojos con cierta triste complacencia hasta lo que ya no existe, ello es que en el fondo de mi alma consagro, como una especie de culto, una veneración profunda por todo lo que pertenece al pasado, y las poéticas tradiciones, las derruidas fortalezas, los antiguos usos de nuestra vieja España, tienen para mí todo ese indefinible encanto.[76]

> [I have faith in the future. . . . Nevertheless, be it a matter of poetry or be it inherent in man's fragile nature to sympathize with all that perishes and turn his eyes with a certain sad complacence toward what no longer exists, the fact is, in the depths of my soul, I consecrate, like a kind of worship, a profound veneration for everything that belongs to the past. And poetic traditions, ruined fortresses, old uses of our old Spain have, for me, all that undefinable enchantment.]

That Bécquer confirms his faith in the future reveals that he is not pessimistic toward it. According to Joe Bailey, pessimism finds expression in avoiding the future, "using the past as a tool."[77] Instead, Bécquer's attitude toward Spain's religious and cultural history is accompanied by an attempt to harmonize tradition with the demands of modern life. Bécquer's commemoration of the past was, for him, a moral obligation, and establishing a compromise between past and future was better than blindly accepting excessive innovation.[78] This ascription of

THE HALLOWED, THE HAUNTING

responsibility to remembrance echoes Nora's notion that one must have the will to remember sites of memory.[79]

In the above passage, Bécquer also expresses a profound sense of grief at the ruin of churches, which are both sanctuaries and strongholds of religion. He regards the destruction of these holy places as an act of barbarism that demolished a people's past and annihilated wonder. Bécquer compares the convenience of technological innovations and the advancement of communications with the cost of losing the nation's past identity, beliefs, and way of life: "A medida que vuela por los hilos telegráficos, que el ferrocarril se extiende, la industria se acrecienta y el espíritu cosmopolita de la civilización invade nuestro país, van desapareciendo de él sus rasgos característicos, sus costumbres inmemoriales"[80] [While all flies through telegraphic wires, the railroad expands, industry grows, and the cosmopolitan spirit of civilization invades our country, its characteristic features and immemorial customs are slowly disappearing from it]. In referring to "nuestra vieja España" [our old Spain], Bécquer brings up the importance of traditions for future generations: "¡Quién sabe si nuestros hijos a su vez nos envidiarán a nosotros, doliéndose de nuestra ignorancia o nuestra culpable apatía para transmitirles siquiera un trasunto de lo que fue un tiempo su patria!"[81] [Who knows if our progeny in turn will envy us, hurt at our ignorance or our blameworthy apathy in transmitting to them at least an impression of what was, for a time, their homeland!].

As does Böhl, Bécquer describes the modern world as a place of unoriginality and unending desire, representing the processes of industrialization through phrases such as "caminos trillados" [worn-out paths] and "ansia de las innovaciones" [thirst for innovation].[82] Bécquer's yearning for monastic solitude and simple living recalls Fray Luis de León's sixteenth-century poem "Vida retirada" [A secluded life], the opening lines of which privilege the tranquility of living away from the world: "¡Qué descansada vida / la del que huye del mundanal ruido[!]"[83] [Such a tranquil life it is / that he who flees from worldly noise leads!]. Fray Luis de León was an important figure of the Spanish poetic tradition for moderate Spanish Romantics. Bécquer himself looked to the Golden Age poets Fray Luis de León, Garcilaso de la Vega, and San Juan de la Cruz for their emphasis on the interior life.[84]

What has impeded the expression and pursuit of all things spiritual, Bécquer asserts, is ignorance, vandalism, and envy in times of war:

> Al contemplar los destrozos causados por la ignorancia, el vandalismo o la envidia durante nuestras últimas guerras; al ver todo lo que en objetos dignos de estimación, en costumbres peculiares y primitivos recuerdos de otras épocas se ha extraviado y puesto en desuso de sesenta años a esta parte; lo que las exigencias de la nueva manera de ser social trastornan y desencajan; lo que las necesidades y las aspiraciones crecientes desechan u olvidan, un sentimiento de profundo dolor se apodera de mi alma.[85]

[On contemplating the destruction caused by ignorance, vandalism, or envy during our latest wars, on seeing all that, in objects worthy of esteem, in particular customs and primeval memories of other ages, has been lost and abandoned for the last sixty years—what the demands of the new ways of society disrupt and displace, what the growing necessities and aspirations discard or forget—a feeling of deep sadness overwhelms my soul.]

The nation's heritage, with its cultural customs, memories, and monuments, is subject to oblivion. Economic and political agendas have led individuals to overlook the distinct and sacred role of churches and abbeys, which results in their damage and neglect.[86] Such destruction provokes, as Bécquer's text affirms, a sense of deep pain, a wound to the soul on personal and collective levels.

Bécquer therefore criticizes a society based on appearances at the expense of religious belief, depicting this modernized Spain as a materialistic body that has disposed of its religious self, its soul. The disorder and disruption of the past that have resulted from Spain's modernizing transformation, Bécquer's text suggests, destabilize its present and future, which liberals premised on stability and order.[87]

Bécquer's reference to his own soul in his fourth letter ("un sentimiento de profundo dolor se apodera de mi alma" [a feeling of deep sadness overwhelms my soul]) recalls mystical writing and especially the verse of San Juan de la Cruz, Carmelite friar and noted figure of the Counter-Reformation. San Juan de la Cruz's poem "Llama de amor viva" [Living flame of love] expresses the intimate communication between the soul and God. The first stanza describes the soul's bond with God as a "llama de amor viva" [living flame of love] and develops imagery of life, light, and heat to oppose the loss represented by motifs of death, darkness, and cold:

¡Oh llama de amor viva
que tiernamente hieres
de mi alma en el más profundo centro!,
pues ya no eres esquiva,
acaba ya, si quieres;
rompe la tela de este dulce encuentro.[88]

[Oh living flame of love
that tenderly injures
my soul in its deepest center!
Because you are no longer aloof,
finish now, if you wish;
tear the veil of this sweet encounter.]

In his "Cántico espiritual" [Spiritual canticle], San Juan de la Cruz depicts the anguish of the soul, depicted as a yearning bride, for God, the biblical heavenly bridegroom:

THE HALLOWED, THE HAUNTING

ESPOSA

¿Adónde te escondiste,
Amado, y me dejaste con gemido?
Como el ciervo huiste,
habiéndome herido;
salí tras ti clamando, y eras ido.[89]

[BRIDE

Where did you hide yourself?
Beloved, and left me to wail?
You fled like the deer,
having injured me;
I went after you, crying out, and you were gone.]

Michel de Certeau discerns the dialogic discourse in this mutual search: "*I* and *thou*: two terms whose difference, regained and maintained, will be lost in the relation that posits them."[90] The *I*, de Certeau states, is both figurative and a figure, a symbolic representation.[91] The fusion that the soul and God seek, and the language used to define their relationship, annuls the heterology between them. Symbolic of the soul's anguish and indicative of its impatient longing to be united with God is its injury, indicated in "habiéndome herido" [having injured me]. The soul's fervent longing is amplified in its search for the hidden "ciervo" [deer], which is representative of God.

Mysticism, as de Certeau categorically states, is the anti-Babel in that mystics seek a common language after language has been shattered.[92] This common medium of expression is necessary for dialogue, which, as de Certeau defines it, is between God and the soul. In contrast with the chaotic event of the fall of the Tower of Babel, which, as Bécquer noted in his *Historia*, was a botched attempt to reach the heavens, mysticism starts at a lower height. The search for God in the heavens is one of spiritual longing and love, not ambition.

There exists a relationship between mysticism and ruins in that the latter are often the milieu of the former. Due to the religious and socioeconomic struggles brought about by wars and the Reformation, Christians in the sixteenth and seventeenth centuries witnessed the humiliation of the Christian tradition and the disintegration of a "sacred world." Therefore, ruins—symbols and products of destruction and decay—permeated the writings of mystics. Set against these ruins was God, who remained free from "the erosion of time." Unlike his signs on earth, God was permanent and immovable. Thus ruins and pain are interpolated into the mystical vision. Their connotations of loss (ruins) and trauma (wound) ultimately depict a void. It is this chasm that the mystic and believer must traverse. In de Certeau's words, the faithful "were leading lives of exile, hounded from their land by the defilements of history."[93] Mystical language represents the

84 MAKING MODERN SPAIN

collective experiences of this abandonment of home and the inauguration of wandering.

The message that Bécquer puts forward in his *Cartas* is that the realm of spiritual faith—visibly defined by the abbey—is in danger of oblivion. Yet he warns the liberal Spaniards who aim to construct their own progressive world that their vision of a unified, advanced, national future has been destabilized. What has caused this structural debilitation is the State's uprooting of the religious foundations of Spain's national history. This act of appropriation creates further confusion, as religious sites have become objects on which values antithetical to their original spiritual design have been imposed.

The tenth and final letter, not published in *El Contemporáneo* like the previous nine, presents a general recollection of Bécquer's time in Veruela, which he describes as a place built by a now waning faith. Here he criticizes the Spanish government's excessive focus on the economy to the detriment of the nation's spiritual health, which he regards as crucial for a changing world and for the premises of national identity enshrined in the Constitutions of 1812, 1837, 1845, and later, 1869. Summing up the final image of the holy ruins of Veruela, Bécquer stresses that the buildings constitute a metaphor of absence in that they are speechless due to the trauma that they have suffered and are in a state of solitariness because they have been directly abused, ignored, and forgotten. Bécquer describes the faith that constructed this divine complex, a faith that has petered out like a dying flame, he fears, because of the century's positivism and excessive focus on the economy:

> Todo es silencio, soledad y olvido en estas veneradas ruinas. La fe que, como llama viva, levantó esta oración de piedra, hoy, poco a poco, se extingue y apaga en los pechos. Este siglo positivista y burgués solo rinde culto al dios Dinero, y es su romanza preferida el sonido del oro acuñado.[94]

> [All is silence, solitude, and oblivion in these venerated ruins. The faith that, like a living flame, erected this prayer of stone, today, little by little, is becoming extinguished in all hearts. This positivist and bourgeois century only renders worship to the god Money, and its preferred ballad is the sound of minted gold.]

By reiterating the images of light and heat encapsulated in the "llama viva" [living flame] of divine faith, Bécquer reveals the gravity of the gradual extinction of religious beliefs.

The State's seizure and economic "revaluing" of ecclesiastical buildings contribute to this slow death. The task of remembering the faith becomes more difficult. Thus, Bécquer envisages the abbey as a space of "olvidadas tumbas" [forgotten tombs], indicative of "una edad remota" [a distant age].[95] Now that the religious inhabitants of the monastery of Veruela have gone, both they and their former

THE HALLOWED, THE HAUNTING

home are not what they were. The image of the tombs represents both their religious selves and their sacred place. For Jane Donohoe, the erecting of memorials is "our responsibility to the dead."[96] If the dead have ceased to be their human selves by virtue of their departure from their place, what do the living owe them? I interpret Bécquer's memorialization of the confiscated and damaged religious buildings as an act that counters the positivism that has supplanted the Catholic faith of old. For Auguste Comte, the founder of positivism, theological and mythological religion proved incompatible with the positivist spirit, which privileged modern industry and science to challenge superstition, fear, and blind obedience.[97]

Lamenting a faith that grows cold in the hearts of his fellow Spaniards, Bécquer's allusions to the work of San Juan de la Cruz are fitting. The Carmelite friar sought to reform his monastic community by calling for, like Bécquer, a rekindling of faith within. In his *Cartas*, Bécquer represents the Monasterio de Veruela as a locus that is conducive to a mystical union between the soul and God. The neglect and ruin of such an edifice, Bécquer asserts, would eliminate this possibility of spiritual unification between earthly subjects and the divine, which he sees as a necessary cornerstone for political and national unity.

Sacred Horror and the Supernatural in Bécquer's *Leyendas*

In stark contrast to the century's rationalist and positivist ideals that seek to "illuminate" the world, fear and darkness dominate the otherworlds of Bécquer's *Leyendas*. In these tales, Bécquer conveys the emotion of fear and the image of darkness as aesthetic facets and as indicative of a poetic sensibility. His imagined scenarios constitute what Marlon B. Ross calls "the attempt to stabilize the world." Such a process of stabilization seeks to uncover the "total vision" of the world that the individual self tends to limit; the anxiety of the poet can only be countered, therefore, by "going out of self" and entering the sublime "outer expanse."[98] This vast new world of possibilities is Bécquer's medium, one in which religious faith and positivism conflict. Continuing the stringent criticism of positivism depicted in his *Cartas*, Bécquer's *Leyendas* foreground the grave consequences of the privation, abuse, and desertion of religious spaces. His imagined castigations of death and madness on his stories' perpetrators can be interpreted as symptomatic of an attempt to restore order.

Bécquer's *Leyendas* has been the subject of several studies, most of which stress his imaginative application of aspects of Romanticism, the Gothic, and the sublime. Fernando Darío González Grueso states that while Bécquer valued the fruits of scientific advancement in the age of modernity, he maintained that science could never truly explain the origins of morality and civilization.[99] Necessary for the earthly preservation of divine law are sacred boundaries. I consider that Bécquer's *Leyendas*, set in Catholic sites, address the consequences of their transgression.

In my reading of three *Leyendas*, "La ajorca de oro," "El miserere," and "El beso," I will first analyze the depiction of the church and the abbey's physical status. I will then examine how these texts develop aspects of the sublime and horror, concepts important to Gothic and Romantic literature. In incorporating the theme of the sublime, Bécquer aims to foreground the supernatural identity of the religious spaces that are profaned.

The principal settings for "El miserere" and "El beso" are ruined churches or cathedrals. Through these damaged religious edifices, Bécquer sets the scene for his didactic tales. On the literary and sociological function of ruins, Flanagan remarks, "By their nature, ruins disturb. They stand as witnesses to the genius of man to construct and also to destruct."[100] Like those in *Historia* and *Cartas*, the ruins in Bécquer's tales serve as not only aesthetic backdrops but also telling reminders of their historical significance. By accentuating their ruined state through traits of Gothic and Romantic literature, Bécquer compels the reader to ponder the causes of their damage and decay. Flanagan observes that guilt and melancholy in Gothic literature often emerge as common reactions to what is lost, fractured, and left behind in a ruined condition.[101] As for Romanticism, it sought to resurrect a supernatural world that the modern empiricist and rationalist ideologies "discounted so capriciously."[102] These otherworlds feature as superior and invincible realms in Bécquer's stories.

In his *Leyendas*, Bécquer describes the religious spaces as they would have appeared in the mid-nineteenth century. Given that Spain was officially a Catholic country, religious sites, doctrines, and rituals would have been familiar to ordinary Spaniards. Nevertheless, in Bécquer's seemingly familiar sanctuaries, the most frightening things occur. Such occurrences, ostensibly impossible in real life, do not perplex the typical Catholic, for whom supernatural realms affix to the earthly world. Bécquer's use of folklore also points to popular superstitions, which were commonly believed by the majority in the centuries leading up to the Enlightenment.[103] More specifically, the Protestant polemic against Catholicism heightened during the Reformation, defining the Catholic customs and rituals of consecration—the rendering sacred of matter such as water, salt, and oil for sacramental purposes—as "unscriptural, superfluous, or erroneous."[104] This ritualistic conferral of sacredness on objects buttresses Bécquer's contemporary critique of personal gain at the Church's expense.

Bécquer's "La ajorca" elucidates the materialist ambitions underlying disentailment in its critique of greed, depicted in Pedro Alfonso de Orellana's attempt to steal a golden bracelet. The archbishop of Toledo had donated it to the Virgen del Sagrario in the Cathedral of Toledo, an act implying consecration through its association with the Virgin Mary.[105] The objective of Pedro's sacrilege is to gain the affection of the capricious and extravagant María Antúnez, who covets the bracelet. Pedro is therefore torn between his loyalties to the two Marys. Much of his fear derives from his recognition of the Virgen del Sagrario as Toledo's

THE HALLOWED, THE HAUNTING 87

patroness and thus a venerated figure of authority for him and his people. One night when Pedro enters the cathedral, he finds himself surrounded by hordes of statues who confront him with pupilless eyes, causing him to faint with fright. The next morning, Pedro is found at the foot of the altar holding the bracelet and boisterously acknowledging the Virgin Mary as its rightful owner instead of María Antúnez.

Set in a ruined monastery, "El miserere" also lambasts covetousness. It tells the story of a traveling musician, who, through the Cistercian monks of the Fitero abbey, learns of the famous old monastery, whose religious inhabitants were murdered by a jealous nobleman's son. Out of envy for these monks, who were the recipients of the nobleman's inheritance, the son and his fellow bandits damaged the monastery and left no one alive. These acts of pillage and murder took place on the night of Holy Thursday. According to local folklore, every Holy Thursday since then, the monks' ghosts have congregated in the monastery's ruins to sing the miserere, a penitentiary Latin hymn: "Miserere mei, Deus" [Have mercy on me, oh God].

The third tale, "El beso," focuses on the transgression of sacred boundaries. During the Napoleonic occupation, a French captain and his troops move into a ruined church in Toledo. By again situating his story in Toledo, historically the spiritual and political center of old Spain, Bécquer accentuates the dangers of foreign invaders, whose trespassing in the abandoned church denotes an attack on Spain's religious and national safety and honor and traditional Spanish values. One night, the young captain tells his companions that every night during their stay in the cathedral, he would hallucinate and see a statue of a lady, Doña Elvira de Castañeda, kneeling before the sepulchre of her husband, an old warrior. The next night, the captain shows the statue of the lady to his companions and, in a drunken stupor, advances toward the woman, who starts to appear like a real human. Before the captain can kiss her, however, the statue of the warrior suddenly strikes him with his stone gauntlet.

The transformation of statues recalls both European folklore and Spanish literary tradition.[106] The statue of the commander, Don Gonzalo de Ulloa, animates in Tirso de Molina's 1616 play *El Burlador de Sevilla* [The libertine of Seville] and José Zorrilla's 1844 play *Don Juan Tenorio*. According to James Mandrell, the statue of Ulloa acts as an agent of God's will.[107] Similarly, the statue in Bécquer's "El beso" performs a castigatory role in striking the crude captain. This final scene is also a show of masculine prowess and national dominance, in which the Spanish warrior-statue defeats the foreign captain.

The particularity of Bécquer's religious tales lies in the frequent encounter between the supernatural and the natural, the divine and the earthly. His religious horror stories establish a dialectic between modern disbelief and ancient belief. Antonio Risco holds that fantasy constitutes an attraction toward what is unknown.[108] Bécquer's *Leyendas*, in their exploration of themes of belief, doubt, reality, and the supernatural, compel one to rethink the nature of reality, its limits and its irruptive possibilities. The present-day reader might, along with Risco, assume that Bécquer's characters in his *Leyendas* conjure the outlandish episodes in their own minds due to their superstition. In his discussion of "La ajorca," Risco suggests that Pedro's nightmarish scene can be interpreted as a projection of mental images.[109] After all, Pedro Alfonso de Orellana is described as a superstitious and valiant young man.

Furthermore, it is important to note that Bécquer's stories from his *Leyendas* are also nocturnal episodes, with the churches' exteriors just as dark as their interiors. Imagery of darkness and lightness features largely in these three legends to express uncertainty, terror, and mystery, in line with Romantic tropes. In his 1757 essay *A Philosophical Enquiry into the Sublime and Beautiful*, Edmund Burke observed that obscurity was necessary to produce terror and hence awe in art. "When we know the full extent of any danger," Burke explained, "when we accustom our eyes to it, a great deal of the apprehension vanishes."[110] The absence of light occludes the sense of vision to create an atmosphere of mystery that suspends rational judgment: "It is our ignorance of things that causes all our admiration, and chiefly excites our passions. Knowledge and acquaintance make the most striking causes affect but little. . . . The ideas of eternity, and infinity, are among the most affecting we have, and yet perhaps there is nothing of which we really understand so little, as of infinity and eternity."[111] Such incomprehensible notions of eternity and infinity are particularly expressed in religious belief.

In his discussion of Burke's philosophical argument on aesthetics, Thomas Weiskel asserts that the idea of the sublime, associated with the vague or obscure, arose as a philosophical reaction to the impact of the Enlightenment in the eighteenth century. The sublime, Weiskel signals, accentuates individuals' epistemic limits, compelling them to feel lost in the surrounding vastness and inviting them to consider what is solely comprehensible through faith. For Burke, obscurity exercised a greater affective appeal than clarity.[112] The emotional experience of the sublime was an opportunity to embrace other dimensions of the human psyche and spirit. Bécquer's works, centered on the serious matter of religious belief, corroborate Weiskel's notion of the sublime as something not easily discernible for the individual.

In "La ajorca," Bécquer portrays the church and monastery as sublime, grand, and mysterious sites. Before Pedro steals the golden bracelet from the Virgen del Sagrario, the Cathedral of Toledo is described as a forest.[113] This sublime image of a natural space serves to accentuate the insignificance of the narrator and reader, inspiring reverential awe: "¡La catedral de Toledo! Figuraos un bosque de gigantescas palmeras de granito que al entrelazar sus ramas forman una bóveda colosal y magnífica, bajo la que se guarece y vive, con la vida que le ha prestado el genio, toda una creación de seres imaginarios y reales"[114] [The Cathedral of Toledo! Imagine a forest of gigantic granite palm trees that, interlacing

THE HALLOWED, THE HAUNTING

their branches, form a colossal and magnificent vault under which one takes refuge and experiences, with the life granted by the genius, an entire creation of imaginary and real beings]. The contrast between the images of inanimate stone and living forest denotes the dual nature of the cathedral, a symbol of timelessness and transcendence through the ages and an oasis of spiritual growth. The Cathedral of Toledo, like every Catholic worship site during the disentailments, is under threat of oblivion.

Bécquer sums up this gradual loss in an analogy that contrasts light with shadow: "Las moribundas lámparas . . . brillaban en el fondo de las naves como estrellas perdidas entre las sombras"[115] [The moribund lamps . . . shone at the end of the naves like stars lost among the shadows]. Developing the interplay of light and shade, Bécquer describes the clash between darkness and light as a "lucha" [battle] in which darkness appears to dominate. These images of light and dark lend themselves as interchangeable metaphors for contemporary ideological conflicts featuring the light of divine faith versus an ostensibly progressive but inherently backward materialism: "Figuraos un caos incomprensible de sombra y luz, en donde se mezclan y confunden con las tinieblas de las naves los rayos de colores de las ojivas, donde lucha y se pierde con la oscuridad del santuario el fulgor de las lámparas"[116] [Imagine an incomprehensible chaos of shadow and light in which the colored shafts of light from the ogives mingle and merge with the shadows of the naves, where the glow of lamps struggles and becomes lost in the darkness of the sanctuary].

Such a struggle between the forces of light and darkness also features in "El beso," where the deserted monastery is lit by "la escasa claridad de una linterna [que] luchaba trabajosamente con las oscuras y espesísimas sombras"[117] [the dim light of a lantern that battled with difficulty against the dark, dense shadows]. The ruined Toledo church in "El beso" is damaged, its doors broken down for firewood. The church resembles a graveyard in which ghostlike statues and total silence predominate. Starting with the words "Según hemos dicho" [As we have said], Bécquer establishes the narrator as a witness who gives testimony to a trauma. The traumatic event to which the narrator alludes is the Napoleonic occupation, the effects of which are visible in the broken "body" of the dismantled church:

> La iglesia estaba completamente desmantelada: en el altar mayor pendían aún de las altas cornisas los rotos jirones del velo con que lo habían cubierto los religiosos al abandonar aquel recinto . . . en el pavimento, destrozado en varios puntos, distinguíanse aún anchas losas sepulcrales llenas de timbres, escudos y larga inscripciones góticas, y allá a lo lejos, en el fondo de las silenciosas capillas y a lo largo del crucero, se destacaban confusamente entre la oscuridad, semejantes a blancos e inmóviles fantasmas, las estatuas de piedra que, unas tendidas, otras de hinojos sobre el mármol de sus tumbas, parecían ser los únicos habitantes del ruinoso edificio.[118]

90   MAKING MODERN SPAIN

[The church was completely dismantled: in the main altar, there still hung from the high cornices the ripped shreds of the veil with which the religious had covered it upon abandoning that place; . . . on the ground, destroyed in various places, wide sepulchral slabs could still be distinguished, with countless crests, shields, and large Gothic inscriptions; and there in the distance, at the end of the silent chapels and along the transept, there stood out confusingly in the darkness, similar to white, motionless ghosts, stone statues that—some prone, others kneeling on the marble of their tombs—seemed to be the only inhabitants of the dilapidated edifice.]

In the following passage from "La ajorca," Bécquer employs the image of stone in a way that recalls Böhl's depiction of Pedro Santaló from *La gaviota* by referring to the stone of "nuestra religión" [our religion]—that is, the rock of Saint Peter, to whom Christ entrusted his Church. The image evokes "nuestros mayores" [our elders], from Christ's disciples to the ancestors of Spanish Catholics, who passed down the faith to future generations:

Figuraos un mundo de piedra, inmenso como el espíritu de nuestra religión, sombrío como sus tradiciones, enigmático como sus parábolas, y todavía no tendréis una idea remota de ese eterno monumento del entusiasmo y la fe de nuestros mayores, sobre el que los siglos han derramado a porfía el tesoro de sus creencias, de su inspiración y de sus artes. En su seno viven el silencio, la majestad, la poesía del misticismo y un santo horror que defiende sus umbrales contra los pensamientos mundanos y las mezquinas pasiones de la tierra.[119]

[Imagine a world of stone—immense like the spirit of our religion, somber like our traditions, mysterious like its parables—and you still will not have the remotest idea of that eternal monument of the enthusiasm and faith of our elders, upon which the centuries doggedly showered the treasure of their beliefs, their inspiration, and their arts. In its bosom live silence, majesty, the poetry of mysticism, and a sacred horror that defends its doors from worldly thoughts and the earth's petty, miserable passions.]

Bécquer's narrator describes the cathedral as a spiritual treasure and a place of majesty, perhaps indirectly alluding to the divine kingship of Christ and the queenship of the Virgin Mary. Again, he associates the metaphor of poetry with the interior mystical experience.

I argue that the most significant aspect of these legends is the "santo horror" [sacred horror] to which Bécquer alludes in the above passage. This terror acts as an overwhelming supernatural force that conflicts with humankind's earthly interests and ambitions. That this horror takes place in the cathedral, the principal church of a diocese, is a hierarchical symbol of the Church's divinity, to which

THE HALLOWED, THE HAUNTING

Bécquer ascribes an unmatched significance. This privileging of religious faith over the secular world in a vertical hierarchical structure also features prominently in Pereda's works, which form the subject of my fifth and final chapter.

From adoring the magnificence that the Cathedral of Toledo exudes, Bécquer proceeds to compare its present state to its historical role as a place devoted entirely to Catholicism's rich liturgical traditions. The following aesthetic references to the biblical symbols of monarchy and dignity, such as gold, precious stones, fine cloth, and tapestries, serve to elevate the cathedral's function, melding the holy sanctuary with the palace of Christ, the King of kings:

> Pero si grande, si imponente se presenta la catedral a nuestros ojos a cualquiera hora que se penetra en su recinto misterioso y sagrado, nunca produce una impresión tan profunda como en los días en que despliega todas las galas de su pompa religiosa, en que sus tabernáculos se cubren de oro y pedrería; sus gradas, de alfombras, y sus pilares, de tapices.[120]

> [But if the cathedral presents itself grandly and impressively to our eyes whenever we enter its mysterious and sacred precinct, it never causes as marked an impression as on those days when it displays all the finery of its religious pomp, when its tabernacles are covered with gold and gemstones, its steps with carpets, and its pillars with tapestries.]

Bécquer then underscores the vibrancy of the cathedral's emphasis on the sacraments, conjuring an ethereal atmosphere perceptible through the senses of sight, hearing, and smell. This overly multisensorial aspect of the Catholic religion is due to its aestheticization, a legacy of the Baroque Counter-Reformation in Spain. The bright light of silver lamps, the floating cloud of incense, and the haunting flurry of choral voices, organ music, and bells serve to illustrate the ambience of what the narrative voice perceives as a properly used holy space:

> Entonces, cuando arden despidiendo un torrente de luz sus mil lámparas de plata; cuando flota en el aire una nube de incienso, y las voces del coro y la armonía de los órganos y las campanas de la torre estremecen el edificio desde sus cimientos más profundos hasta las más altas agujas que lo coronan, entonces es cuando se comprende, al sentirla, la tremenda majestad de Dios, que vive en él, y lo anima con su soplo, y lo llena con el reflejo de su omnipotencia.[121]

> [Then, when its thousand silver lamps burn, emitting a torrent of light, when a cloud of incense floats in the air and the voices of the choir, the harmonious tones of the organs, and the tower bells cause the edifice to tremble from its deepest foundations to the tallest spires that crown it, that is when one can understand, upon feeling it, the tremendous majesty of God, who lives in it, and animates it with his breath, and fills it with the reflection of his omnipotence.]

Underpinning Bécquer's description of the cathedral is God's living majesty, which connotes resurrection, revivification, and reanimation. The "soplo" [breath] that gives life to the edifice will demonstrate its restorative power in the story's climax.

Pedro's theft constitutes an appropriation of items reserved for cultic functions. Sacred images, or any ornament or object used in worship, Flanagan asserts, require an authority to constitute them, which explains the significance of dedicatory rituals. These rituals, which confer meaning on the sacred image, establishing its purposes and recognizing and validating its boundaries, are all the more necessary when images are decontextualized temporally or intentionally. The modern plunder of religious objects excised them from their holy milieux in acts of transgression that would go unacknowledged in a society indifferent to such thefts.[122] Thus, Pedro's removal of the bracelet from the Virgen del Sagrario can be read as a metaphor for expropriation in general.

Pedro's theft—an avaricious and sacrilegious deed in the cathedral—receives a supernatural penalty. Upon entering the cathedral, he is overcome by fear, which causes him to pause in his steps from time to time. Such hesitation, Todorov maintains, characterizes the fantastic, which thrives on the emotion of uncertainty.[123] Pedro's uneasiness in advancing toward the altar—what Todorov calls a wavering between total faith and total incredulity[124]—suggests that Pedro has entered a strange world that blurs the real and the imagined:

> La catedral estaba sola, completamente sola y sumergida en un silencio profundo. No obstante, de cuando en cuando se percibían como unos rumores confusos: chasquidos de madera tal vez, o murmullos del viento, o, ¿quién sabe?, acaso ilusión de la fantasía, que oye y ve y palpa en su exaltación lo que no existe; pero la verdad era que ya cerca, ya lejos, ora a sus espaldas, ora a su lado mismo, sonaban como sollozos que se comprimen, como roce de telas que se arrastran, como rumor de pasos que van y vienen sin cesar.[125]

> [The cathedral was empty, completely empty, and submerged in a deep silence. Nevertheless, from time to time, one could sense some confusing murmurs: cracking of wood, perhaps, or whispers of the wind, or who knows what? Perhaps a fantastical illusion that hears and sees and beats in its exaltation what does not exist. But the truth was that now nearby, now far off, now behind him, now beside him, they sounded like suffocated sobs, like the caress of fabrics that dragged along the floor, like a murmur of footsteps that incessantly come and go.]

After taking the golden bracelet, Pedro opens his eyes and cries out when he beholds the cathedral filled with statues. Here Bécquer presents a paradox: these supposedly inanimate objects are now living, staring at Pedro with pupilless eyes and wearing long invisible robes. The cathedral transforms into a site where the impossible becomes possible and where the supernatural supersedes the natural:

THE HALLOWED, THE HAUNTING   93

La catedral estaba llena de estatuas, estatuas que, vestidas con luengos y no vistos ropajes, habían descendido de sus huecos y ocupaban todo el ámbito de la iglesia y lo miraban con sus ojos sin pupila.

Santos, monjes, ángeles, demonios, guerreros, damas, pajes, cenobitas y villanos se rodeaban y confundían en las naves y en el altar . . . mientras que, arrastrándose por las losas, trepando por los machones, acurrucados en los doseles, suspendidos en las bóvedas, pululaba, como los gusanos de un inmenso cadáver, todo un mundo de reptiles y alimañas de granito, quiméricos, deformes, horrorosos.[126]

[The cathedral was full of statues, statues that, dressed in lengthy and invisible robes, had descended from their niches to occupy the whole of the church and were watching him with pupilless eyes.

Saints, monks, angels, demons, warriors, ladies, pages, cenobites, and villains thronged and mingled in the naves and at the altar . . . while, crawling over the stones, climbing over the buttresses, curled up on the dossals, suspended from the vaults, they swarmed, like worms on a massive corpse, an entire world of granite reptiles and vermin, chimerical, deformed, horrifying.]

The Romantic is a signifier, Philip Shaw declares, for that which goes beyond reason.[127] The shocking scene is unbearable to watch and hard to comprehend and ends with Pedro fainting on the ground: "Ya no pudo resistir más. Las sienes le latieron con una violencia espantosa; una nube de sangre oscureció sus pupilas; arrojó un segundo grito, un grito desgarrador y sobrehumano, y cayó desvanecido sobre el ara"[128] [He could not resist any longer. His temples beat with a terrifying force; a cloud of blood darkened his pupils, he let out a second scream—a heartrending, supernatural scream—and fell unconscious on the altar]. Juxtaposed with the previous silent ambience of the cathedral is Pedro's supernatural scream: an irruption of fear in a sacred place rendered incomprehensible to humans. Similarly, in "El beso," before the French captain collapses at the foot of the sepulchre, his scream, "un grito de horror en el templo"[129] [a scream of horror in the temple], contrasts with his peers' previous laughter. Yet again, the musician in "El miserere" lets out "un grito horroroso"[130] [a terrifying scream] on fainting. These screams herald the consequences of trespassing the boundaries between the holy and the profane.

Given that in these instances, broken silence signals a supernatural presence, "El miserere" distinctly portrays the presence of the monks' souls by way of liturgical music, chants, bells, and a church organ. The musician hears the mysterious sound of unseen bells on the night that he visits the abandoned monastery:

Transcurrió tiempo y tiempo, y nada se percibió: aquellos mil confusos rumores seguían sonando y combinándose de mil maneras distintas, pero siempre los mismos.

"¡Si me habrá engañado!," pensó el músico; pero en aquel instante se oyó un ruido nuevo, un ruido inexplicable en aquel lugar, como el que produce un reloj algunos segundos antes de sonar la hora: ruidos de ruedas que giran, de cuerdas que se dilatan, de maquinaria que se agita sordamente y se dispone a usar de su misteriosa vitalidad mecánica, y sonó una campanada ..., dos ..., tres ..., hasta once.

En el derruido templo no había campana, ni reloj, ni torre ya siquiera.[131]

[Time passed by, and nothing could be seen. Those thousands of confusing murmurs continued to sound, and in a thousand different ways, but always the same sounds.

"I must have been deceived!" thought the musician. But at that moment, a new noise was heard, an unexplainable sound in that place, like the one produced from a clock a few seconds before striking the hour: sounds of wheels turning, ropes expanding, machinery vaguely stirring and preparing to utilize its mysterious mechanical vitality. And a chime sounded ... two ... three ... to eleven.

The ruined temple had no bell, no clock, not even a tower.]

The musician then sees the monks, whose corpses have come to life. Dressed in their habits, they move toward the miraculously reconstructed monastery to chant the miserere. For the curious musician, the whole scene is a phantasmagoria of horror: "Todo pareció animarse, pero con ese movimiento galvánico que imprime a la muerte contracciones que parodian la vida, movimiento instantáneo, más horrible aún que la inercia del cadáver que agita con su desconocida fuerza"[132] [Everything seemed to become animated, but with that electrifying movement that lends death contractions that parody life—an instantaneous movement more horrible still than the inertia of the corpse that moves with an unusual strength]. As Terry Castle notes, phantasmagorical spectacle has displayed its symbolic potential ever since its origin during the Enlightenment.[133] Its chief characteristics were unfamiliar and claustrophobic surroundings, Gothic strangeness and terror, a "rapid phantom-train of images," and the spectator's resultant disorientation and powerlessness. This sensational quality, Castle underlines, is manifest in nineteenth-century Romantic writings.[134]

I argue that Bécquer's portrayal in "El miserere" of monks coming to life is also a literary act of remembering the clergy and religious whose spiritual lives came to an end because of their exclaustration. Bécquer's tale invites readers to equate the monks' deaths with the expulsion of the religious in real life. Bécquer's "El beso" also recalls these figures, just as his *Historia* remembers the ancestors and builders of ancient, confiscated convents, monasteries, and churches. This act of recollection connects the dead with the living, those who can still remember and write about these figures of religion. As Shoshana Felman puts it, "Life for

THE HALLOWED, THE HAUNTING   95

the dead resides in a remembrance (by the living) of their story; justice for the
dead resides in a remembrance (by the living) of the injustice and the outrage
done to them. History is thus, above and beyond official narratives, a haunting
claim the dead have on the living, whose responsibility it is not only to remember but to protect the dead from being *misappropriated*."[135] Like Donohoe, Felman asserts the importance of commemorating the dead and ensuring that their
memory is not abused. The connection between trauma and the dead is one of
silent remembrance. Since the dead can no longer verbalize for themselves, it
can be agreed that "the relation between history and trauma is speechless."[136]
The traumatized, who constitute the subjects of history, are deprived of the
means to communicate their victimization.[137] In the case of ecclesiastical confiscation, the afterlives of exclaustrated priests, monks, and nuns remain, for the
most part, silent and unknown. The monks of the deserted Toledo monastery in
"El beso" have long gone. Their consecrated lives, just like their abodes, seem to
have disappeared.

Bécquer's narrated legends, with their use of otherworldly imagery, prof-
fer a warning. Ossified memory leads to the profanation of the religious space,
which then causes petrification and madness. Actions of stumbling and collapse
occur in all three legends. This downward movement connotes the biblical fall
from grace, the fall of humankind in the Garden of Eden, and the collapse of
established meaning. It is the act of falling that emphasizes the traumatic state in
which the trespassing characters find themselves. Citing Sigmund Freud, Caruth
remarks that trauma is the consequence of a fall or accident (*Unfall*): "Between
Unfall, the accident, and the 'striking' of the insight, its *auffallen*, is the force of
a fall, a falling that is transmitted precisely in the unconscious act of leaving."[138]
In "La ajorca," Pedro faints on the altar, overwhelmed by the swirling panoply
of reanimated statues. The musician in "El miserere" collapses onto the earth
and hears nothing more. With blood streaming from his eyes, mouth, and nose,
the captain in "El beso" falls at the feet of the sepulchre, only to be killed by the
statue of the warrior with one strike of his stone gauntlet. Witnesses to these falls
are not only the protagonists but also other characters in the selected tales. The
churchgoers who find the insane Pedro lying before the altar, the monks who
discover the dead musician in "El miserere," and the French soldiers who witness the strange death of their captain in "El beso" therefore function as internal
"readers" of these admonitory phenomena.

CONCLUSION

I have proposed that Bécquer's works convey an active religious nostalgia. Using
Boym's and Flanagan's respective theories on nostalgia and ruins, I have indicated the significance of Bécquer's artistic restoration. I have examined Bécquer's
conceptualizations of the ecclesiastical space in three of his works, which are set

in or depict religious sites and monuments. In *Historia*, I analyzed the image of the body in describing the church and abbey as well as Bécquer's role as poet and elegist to demonstrate his artistic involvement with the inner lives of these historically significant loci. In *Cartas*, I explored Bécquer's recourse to mysticism to convey his unease about the overwhelming vicissitudes of the modern age. While such changes met the needs of infrastructure and lifestyle, they also compelled writers like Bécquer to acknowledge and contemplate the gaps in Spain's spiritual architecture. I suggest that while Bécquer's *Historia* and *Cartas* communicate in a Romantic and melancholic fashion his acceptance of their current states, his *Leyendas* exhibit the depth of his longing to restore Spain's sacred and monastic past. My analyses of three tales from Bécquer's *Leyendas* dealt with aspects of holy horror and the sublime that are characteristic of Gothic and Romantic literature. In these fantastical stories, Bécquer sacralizes and solemnizes the sacred space by portraying sacrilege, trespassing, and damage as transgressions subject to divine retribution by unseen forces. In all these texts, Bécquer stresses the boundaries of the holy space, depicting it as indomitable in a world of increasingly secular tendencies and excessive human ambition. By examining his own personal experiences in relation to sacred spaces and ruins, Bécquer endeavored to make meaning out of a "ghost" world in a time of rapid secularization and sought to understand an uncertain future through the lingering echoes of the past.

I have traced how Böhl and Bécquer share similar concerns regarding religious life and its connections to cultural memory and future generations. Their anxiety led them to look to the religious traditions of the past. In contrast, Benito Pérez Galdós, whose works form the subject of the ensuing chapter, faces the future, addressing the modern maelstrom of political, economic, and scientific challenges and enterprises. I will examine how he comments on its perceived impact on the religious and spiritual foundations of Spanish society to fashion a vision of a harmonious, rational, yet still spiritual society.

CHAPTER 4

A New Vital Force

RECONSTRUCTING SPAIN'S SPIRITUAL BODY IN
BENITO PÉREZ GALDÓS'S *DOÑA PERFECTA* (1876),
GLORIA (1877), *MENDIZÁBAL* (1898),
AND *MONTES DE OCA* (1900)

No es, Señora, una fría especulación mercantil, ni una mera operación de crédito, por más que ésta sea la palanca que mueve y equilibra en nuestros días las naciones de Europa. Es un elemento de animación de vida y de ventura para España. Es, si puedo explicarme así, el complemento de su resurrección política.

[Madam, it is neither cold mercantile speculation nor a mere credit operation, even if it is the lever that moves and maintains steady the European nations of our day. It is an element that gives life and happiness to Spain. It is, if I may explain it thus, the complement of its political resurrection.]

—Juan Álvarez Mendizábal, *Gaceta de Madrid*, February 19, 1836

In his above address to the queen regent María Cristina in 1836, the progressive liberal Mendizábal justified ecclesiastical confiscation as a means of bringing life and fortune to Spain. Such was the rationale behind liberal proposals for economic and sociopolitical reform, although Mendizábal's laws were more extreme, as I mentioned in chapter 1. While the conservative Böhl and Bécquer conveyed their anxieties over the impact of the government's economic policies on Spain's cultural and religious traditions, the liberal Benito Pérez Galdós communicated the need to revive the national body through sociopolitical and spiritual reforms. Böhl and Bécquer's attention to the religious and spiritual fallout of ecclesiastical confiscation and declining faith prompted them to look to Spain's religious heritage and advocate its preservation. For his part, Galdós welcomed progressive reforms, counting himself among a high number of young intellectuals who favored the introduction of rationalist theories in universities and the shunning of old Aristotelian and Hippocratic approaches to science. This emphasis on advanced scientific inquiry influenced Krausism, a philosophical movement that attracted the intellectual elite, including the young Galdós.

Krausism was founded by the German philosopher Karl Christian Krause (1781–1832), who published his most famous treatise, *Das Urbild der Menschheit* [The ideal of humanity] in 1811. A form of religious modernism, Krausism aimed to reconcile God with science.[1] The Spanish philosopher and jurist Julián Sanz del Río (1814–1869) published *Ideal de la humanidad para la vida* [The ideal of humanity for life, 1860], a translation of Krause's seminal work, which not only placed Sanz del Río and his followers at the center of contemporary intellectual debates but also helped lead him to a position at the Universidad Central de Madrid in 1854.[2] The Enlightenment legacy of skepticism toward belief in the supernatural continued. Pitted against religious intransigence was the liberal project.[3]

I posit that the politicized religious metaphor of resurrection lends itself to the concept of a life force. Nicolás Fernández-Medina states that the discourse on *vis vitalis* [vital force] was a reaction to the mechanistic and physicalist philosophies undergirding the Scientific Revolution. Vitalism hypothesized that an immaterial element animated the body. In Spain especially, vitalism was much more than a rebellion; it sought to interpret the relations between the body and the world and to comprehend the very notion of life itself.[4] Spanish Krausist philosophy drew on vitalist ideas, melding notions such as soul, spirit, and mind to form a "theological modernism" that attempted to reconcile religion with evolutionary biology and panentheism (the belief in the interrelationship of God and the material world).[5] Juan López Morillas states that Krausism viewed Christianity as a phase in the religious evolution of humankind, the end of which was a religion without dogmas or miracles—the coexistence of humanity with God as supreme being.[6] In Spain, it became a platform to challenge and engage with the Church, given that, as Fernández-Medina declares, the rationalist religion-versus-science debate was central to the advent of modernity.[7]

Among the main principles of the Spanish Krausists regarding the religious institution of the Church were the simplification of Catholic rites, the distrust of papal infallibility, the trivialization of religious orders, the upholding of personal scriptural interpretation, tolerance, and an emphasis on Christianity's central doctrine of love.[8] Their hierarchical and liturgical reforms paralleled the liberals' political and economic justification of disentailment. These factors contributed to the liberals' desired excarnation of the material and doctrinal apparatus of institutional religion in favor of establishing an inward spirituality. I hold that Galdós's envisagement of such transformations draws on religious, corporeal, and scientific ideas associated with a vital force.

An advocate of modern progress, Galdós is considered one of the most incisive nineteenth-century commentators on Spanish society. In the repository of scholarship on Galdós, his realist novels have been regarded as portraits of

A NEW VITAL FORCE 99

social, cultural, and political change.[9] Galdós was born in the Canary Islands and raised in a religious household, where he regularly attended Mass.[10] He studied law in Madrid, only to switch to journalism before pursuing a writing career. His articles and essays influenced his *novelas de tesis* [ideological novels], which deal with sociopolitical issues, especially those pertaining to religion in Spain. Novels written in the last third of the 1800s, as Hazel Gold asserts, were essentially manifestos documenting national identity and life.[11] Blind faith, lingering doubt, and the search for religious tolerance form the key concepts in many of Galdós's novels. Regarding religious belief, Carlos M. Rodríguez López-Brea holds that as a heterodox, Galdós often struggled with his Catholic faith throughout his life.[12] Galdós's religion, although complicated, reflected the philosophical leanings of young intellectuals of his time. His discovery of Krausist philosophy took place at university and flourished in *tertulias* [literary salons] throughout Madrid. As a student, Galdós wrote critical reflections on Spanish society and its religious identity as a Catholic nation. In an 1865 essay, he lambasted "la dictadura del hisopo" [the dictatorship of the aspergill (receptacle for holy water)]—the theocratic ambitions that, as he saw it, were concomitant to religious observance and therefore detrimental to a liberal democratic future.[13]

I consider that Galdós's texts propose a new vital force for Spain's progress. This force would demand sociopolitical reforms to reject elements of organized religion and embrace an internalized spirituality. Building on the interconnecting Krausist and vitalist discourses that appealed to liberal Spaniards, Galdós, I argue, advocates a departure from institutionalized religion to bring about the spiritual renewal of Spain's national body. In his works, he deploys corporeal metaphors, religious imagery and symbolism, and marital and familial relations to reveal the extent to which this life force is impactful. By employing these literary strategies and themes in his ideological novels, Galdós challenges the Spanish nation's circumstances, which he perceives to be in a state of material, moral, and spiritual torpor. Whereas ecclesial buildings and monasticism are privileged in Böhl and Bécquer's nostalgic texts, Galdós scrutinizes the relevance of these hierarchical, traditional elements of the Church to Spain's future, thus challenging what he regards as the rigid doctrinal underpinnings of Catholicism.

My discussion will focus mainly on two thesis novels, *Doña Perfecta* (1876) and *Gloria* (1877), and I enhance my argument with brief incursions into *Mendizábal* (1898) and *Montes de Oca* (1900), the twenty-second and twenty-eighth installments of his series of historical novellas, *Episodios nacionales*. Finally, I will touch on how the key themes from these novels are represented in Galdós's noted play *Electra* (1901). Alluding to how Galdós's novels problematize the general inseparability of religion from Spanish society and culture, Federico Sopeña Ibáñez remarks that all the political, economic, and moral problems that arose from disentailment appear in Galdós's portrayals of his characters.[14] Disentailment features in several novels, especially *El audaz* [The bold one, 1871],

Halma (1895), and the *Torquemada* series, which explicitly mention ecclesiastical expropriation.[15] Likewise, I consider that spiritual problems not only accompanied ecclesiastical confiscation but also signaled wider changes in Spain's public sphere. Although ecclesiastical disentailment is mentioned in *Doña Perfecta* and *Gloria* and the historical novels *Mendizábal* and *Montes de Oca*, what remains to be addressed in these works is Galdós's literary treatment of its social and spiritual ramifications.

I will therefore examine Galdós's representation of the ideological apparatus of liberal progressivism, which sought the transformation of Spain's spiritual body. I have chosen to analyze *Doña Perfecta* and *Gloria* in particular to consider the religious and philosophical attitudes that constructed Spain's old order. Although *Doña Perfecta* and *Gloria* make no overt reference to the laws of ecclesiastical disentailment, they subtly portray the decline of the Church's influence in the hearts of the Spanish people. In Galdós's texts, churches are almost bereft of attendants, liturgical rites seem to have lost their meaning, and doctrines and norms are put to the test in an increasingly modernizing society. While Böhl and Bécquer consider the decreasing significance of religious expression to be a repercussion of cultural and political reforms, Galdós doubts the authenticity of such faith.

Religious indifference intrigued Galdós, who expressed this disquiet in his writings, shedding light on the politicized and variegated character of Spain's religious sentiment and the consequences of insincere and misapplied religious faith. He voiced his concerns regarding religion and politics in letters to his contemporary and friend, the Catholic and conservative Cantabrian author José María de Pereda, who also dealt with the same topics in his writings.[16] As I will point out later in this chapter, their correspondence and novels evince their constant debate on these matters. In an epistolary response to Pereda's critique of *Gloria* in February 1877, Galdós declares, "Con todo, hay en [el juicio que hace de *Gloria*] una aseveración que creo injusta, y es que yo hago novelas volterianas. Precisamente lo que quería combatir es la indiferencia religiosa (peste principal de España, donde nadie cree en nada, empezando por los neo-católicos)"[17] [Even so, there is in your argument concerning *Gloria* a claim that I consider unjust, and that is that I write Voltairean novels. What I precisely wished to challenge was religious indifference (the main plague of Spain, where nobody believes in anything, starting with the neo-Catholics)]. In his criticism of the neo-Catholics, Galdós decries politicized religion as the contributing factor to the Carlist Wars and the ruptures between the Church and the Spanish government. He also diagnoses Spain's spiritual body, labeling religious indifference as a pathological threat to the nation's health. This indifference arguably stems from changing and conflicting interpretations of the meaning of the Catholic religion in Spain, as Callahan has argued.

For Galdós, the Church's place in Spanish society had changed inevitably and definitively. New spiritual expressions and national goals were replacing the emphasis on Catholicism's traditional, conservative, and doctrinal institutions. Although article 11 of the 1876 Constitution had proclaimed that Catholicism was the religion of the State, it permitted and protected the private practice of other religious beliefs. In another letter to Pereda in June 1877, Galdós opined that Catholicism did not suit the nation's circumstances: "El catolicismo es la más perfecta de las religiones positivas, pero ninguna religión positiva, ni aun el catolicismo, satisface el pensamiento ni el *corazón* del hombre en nuestros días. No hay quien me arranque esta idea ni con tenazas. El catolicismo no puede seguir rigiendo en absoluto la vida"[18] [Catholicism is the most perfect of positive religions, but no positive religion, not even Catholicism, satisfies the thought or *heart* of man in our times. Nobody can strip me of this idea, not even with pincers. Catholicism cannot at all continue to govern life absolutely]. Galdós demonstrates here, as he does in his novels, that the demands of the modern age on Spanish hearts and minds cannot be satisfied by religious teachings and beliefs. Thus, a revitalization of the nation's spiritual body is in order, but whatever form this new expression of religion must take is the Galdosian question that seeks answers.

RELIGIOUS INTRANSIGENCE AND MODERNITY IN *DOÑA PERFECTA*

The first of Galdós's twenty-five novels describing nineteenth-century Spanish life and society, *Doña Perfecta* is also the first of three religion-centered novels, alongside *Gloria* and *La familia de León Roch*, which deal critically with the fundamentally bitter repercussions of the religious question.[19] The story begins with the thirty-four-year-old Pepe Rey, who, equipped with an engineering degree from Madrid, returns to the town of Orbajosa to seek Rosario's hand in marriage. His aunt, the eponymous Doña Perfecta Reyes, an outwardly devout woman, is controlling toward her young nephew. When she discovers that Pepe Rey is a freethinker, Doña Perfecta, along with the canon of Orbajosa's cathedral, Don Inocencio, does all she can to prevent Pepe Rey from marrying Rosario. In the end, Doña Perfecta commands the brutish horseman, Caballuco, to kill him. The novel closes with a comment on religious hypocrisy, principally embodied in the personage of Doña Perfecta: "Esto se acabó. Es cuanto por ahora podemos decir de las personas que parecen buenas y no lo son"[20] [Here's an end to it all. This is as much as we can say for the time being about people who seem good but are not].

The novel's principal themes of religious intransigence and intolerance, perpetuated through familial obligations, lead to profound divides between tradition and modern ambitions. This observation echoes Ignacio Javier López's thesis that the ideological novel in Restoration society was concerned with the theme of national division, encapsulated in the idea of the Two Spains put forth by both liberal and conservative thinkers.[21] In Orbajosa, the young professional Pepe Rey meets his ideological opponents, his aunt and the canon, who not only reside in Orbajosa, an underdeveloped town, but also represent it.

Scholarly interpretations of *Doña Perfecta* have mostly dealt with the novel's key characters. Wilfredo de Ràfols focuses on the use of irony in Galdós's characterization of figures like Doña Perfecta and Don Inocencio, arguing that Pepe Rey identifies their "toponymical misnomers not as lies but as rhetorical ironies."[22] In his study of *Doña Perfecta*, Mario Santana foregrounds the novel's preoccupation with appearances.[23] Contrasting it with Böhl's *La gaviota*, Santana points out that in reaction to the latter's conservative poetics, *Doña Perfecta* approximates a "secular metaphorization of national history."[24] For his part, Arnold M. Penuel asserts that this text, written by such a young author, constitutes "art of an uneven and often immature quality."[25] This scholar asserts that the rigid categorization of characters renders the novel less refined than Galdós's later ones. Concurring with Ràfols and Santana, I contend that Galdós's stark characterization suits *Doña Perfecta*'s quality as an ideological novel, representing the clash between old and young, past and future, and reactionary and progressive. These dichotomies serve to aid readers in envisioning Galdós's conceptualization of the Spanish nation as an inwardly spiritual body, the realization of which lies in a transformative departure from the old, conservative order.

The novel's regional setting of Orbajosa and its inhabitants are the principal metaphors of the reactionary attitude toward progress. It constitutes a locus of discord for the novel's principal neo-Catholic and liberal characters: Doña Perfecta and Don Inocencio on the one hand and Pepe Rey on the other. The novel opens with Pepe Rey's train ride from Madrid through rural areas and into Orbajosa, which denotes a departure from progress and a return to backwardness. Railway travel, one of the greatest industrial innovations of nineteenth-century Spain, represented modern progress and new directions for the future. As Wan Sonya Tang points out, the departure of Madrid's inaugural train on February 7, 1851, was doubtless a remarkable experience for people in the capital.[26]

. In comparison with the fast-paced and materially advancing Madrid, Orbajosa is barren in terms of infrastructure, industry, and intellectual progress.[27] Upon his arrival, Pepe Rey observes that the town is only alive through its inhabitants, who move around at a slow pace by horse or on foot. As far as the town's architecture is concerned, "era más bien de ruina y muerte que de progreso y vida"[28] [it reflected ruin and death rather than progress and life], with its residential areas composed of houses built with mud bricks, deformed walls, a few dark towers, and a decrepit castle. Mendicants roam the area. Only the ringing bells of the church indicate that "aquella momia tenía todavía un alma"[29] [that mummy still had a soul]. Although Anthony N. Zahareas considers that the settlement of Orbajosa purports to be a *locus amoenus*—an Arcadian landscape set aside from the busy, modern, and materialistic metropolis of Madrid[30]—ironically, its name, supposedly meaning "ciudad augusta" [august city; *urbs augusta*], denotes the most unpleasant city that Pepe Rey has ever seen. Even its natural surroundings

A NEW VITAL FORCE   103

evoke sparseness and barrenness, featuring a "pobrísimo río"[31] [miserly river] and few orchards.

Described with morbid imagery (*momia* [mummy], *ruina* [ruin], *muerte* [death]), Orbajosa is cast as an inactive settlement devoid of any viable chance of regeneration. Likewise, its cathedral, "cuya corpulenta fábrica dominaba todo el pueblo"[32] [whose corpulent edifice dominated the whole town], illustrates its negative influence.[33] I suggest that the phrase "corpulent edifice" ironizes the clerical hierarchy of Orbajosa by depicting it as antithetical to modern industry and commerce. Its corpulence also signifies an excessive authority and privilege symptomatic of the clergy themselves, rendering them inactive and unsound in body and soul. Such connotations mark Orbajosa as a place unfit for progress, a site of uncertainty or entropy. According to Sinclair, in liberal narratives, the lack of exchange or contact between the region and the outside world leads to the former's entropy and degeneration.[34]

The new order of modern pursuits is depicted as the remedy for Orbajosa's state of disuse and disorder. In contrast with its clergy and inhabitants, Pepe Rey, like Böhl's Stein, embodies modernity and its accomplishments, having studied in France and England prior to returning to Spain. Consequently, his physical description displays marked qualities of heroic strength and sophistication:

> Era de complexión fuerte y un tanto hercúlea, con rara perfección formado, y tan arrogante que, si llevara uniforme militar, ofrecería el más guerrero aspecto y talle que puede imaginarse. Rubios el cabello y la barba, no tenía en su rostro la flemática imperturbabilidad de los sajones, sino por el contrario, una viveza tal que sus ojos parecían negros sin serlo. Su persona bien podía pasar por un hermoso y acabado símbolo, y si fuera estatua, el escultor habría grabado en el pedestal estas palabras: *Inteligencia, fuerza*.[35]

> [He was of a strong and rather herculean build, formed with rare perfection, and so arrogant that if he wore a military uniform, he would present the most warrior-like aspect and figure imaginable. With blond hair and beard, his face reflected in his countenance not the unruffled serenity of the Saxons but rather a liveliness that made his eyes seem black. His person could well pass for a handsome, perfect symbol, and if he were a statue, a sculptor would have engraved on the pedestal the words *intelligence, strength*.]

Pepe Rey's liveliness, energy, mental capacities, and robustness are evident in his profession as an engineer. Displaying intelligence and strength, he embodies the height of usefulness and progress, mirroring what Ross terms the "new strong man," the emerging archetype of the two main masculine identities in the nineteenth century: the scientist and the capitalist-industrialist.[36] The scientist, Ross explains, searches for laws that are supposedly natural and universal and "originates powerful ways of applying these laws to transform the material conditions of society,"[37] whereas the capitalist-industrialist competes with the scientist in his own province of economic risk, power, and influence. It is in the "empire" of the competitive market that the capitalist expresses a confident dominance derived from self-creation. Both the scientist and capitalist-industrialist thus display a thirst for mastery and originality and a capacity for transformation.[38]

Such a process of self-creation affords stability to the new "strong man." The balance, creativity, and wholeness evident in Pepe Rey's educational background and physical aspect contrast starkly with Rosario, his beautiful yet sickly, vulnerable, and secluded cousin. Her timidity and meekness render her instantly loveable:

> Era Rosarito una muchacha de apariencia delicada y débil, que anunciaba inclinaciones a lo que los portugueses llaman *saudades*. En su rostro fino y puro se observaba algo de la pastosidad nacarada. . . . Pero lo principal en Rosario era que tenía tal expresión de dulzura y modestia, que al verla no se echaban de menos las perfecciones de que carecía. . . . La hermosura real de la niña de doña Perfecta consistía en una especie de transparencia. . . . Pero allí faltaba materia para que la persona fuese completa; faltaba cauce, faltaban orillas. El vasto caudal de su espíritu se desbordaba, amenazando devorar las estrechas riberas.[39]

> [Rosarito was, in appearance, a delicate, weak girl, who expressed tendencies toward what the Portuguese call melancholic nostalgia. In her fine, pure face could be seen something like a pearly pastiness. . . . But what most stood out about Rosario was an expression of such sweetness and modesty that, on seeing her, one did not miss the perfection that she lacked. . . . The real beauty of Doña Perfecta's girl was a kind of transparency. . . . But she lacked substance to make her whole; like a metaphorical river, she lacked a bed, banks. The vast torrent of her spirit overflowed, threatening to breach her narrow banks.]

The fluvial images in the passage (*cauce* [riverbed], *orillas* [shores], *caudal* [torrent], *riberas* [riverbank]) connote Rosario's lack of stability and her feared excess associated with an allegedly dangerous femininity. Given that she is devoid of any real substance and humanity, her body does not match her soul. As the personification of excess, she requires containment within the four walls of her home and restrictions to be placed on her because of familial and social expectations.[40]

Pepe Rey embodies the breath of life that promises to revitalize Rosario. When he and Rosario secretly declare their mutual love and their willingness to marry, Pepe Rey notices that Rosario is shivering, feverish, and suffering from "una pertubación moral"[41] [a moral agitation] that is harmful to her body and soul. After he confirms that he is not an atheist, Rosario fully accepts him, telling him, "Tus palabras resuenan en mi corazón como golpes violentos que, estremeciéndome, me dan nueva vida . . . una luz inefable sale de ti y me inunda el alma"[42] [Your words resound in my heart like violent blows that, shaking me, give me new life . . . you emit an indescribable light that floods my soul]. Pepe Rey, the symbol of balance and modernity, figures as her only chance of becoming a complete and holistic individual able to thrive in the world of the future: "Tú me darás aliento, tú me darás fuerzas"[43] [You will give me life, you will give me strength].

Galdós's anticlerical portrayal of Church officials arguably stems from the Krausist denunciation of perceived ecclesiastical excesses. This criticism is manifest in his characterization of the novel's two main clerical authorities: the canon Don Inocencio Tinieblas, whose surname conveys a sinister trait, and the unnamed dean of the cathedral, a victim of disentailment. Don Inocencio's name is an ironic comment on his lack of innocence. The following passage describes him as an educated and devout man:

> Era un santo varón piadoso y de no común saber, de intachables costumbres clericales, algo más de sexagenario, de afable trato, fino y comedido, gran repartidor de consejos y advertencias a hombres y mujeres. Desde luengos años era maestro de latinidad y retórica en el Instituto, cuya noble profesión dióle gran caudal de citas horacianas y de floridos tropos, que emplea con gracia y oportunidad.[44]

> [He was a holy, pious man, uncommonly knowledgeable, of priestly habits, a bit older than sixty, of kind, refined, and restrained behavior, a great giver of advice and warnings to men and women. For many long years, he had been master of Latin and rhetoric at the institute, a noble profession that had given him a great wealth of Horatian sayings and florid tropes that he used with flair and timeliness.]

Despite his veneer of kindness and piety, Don Inocencio is unwelcoming toward Pepe Rey, whom he sees as a liberal coming from the supposedly corrupt center of Madrid, and alienates him.

Sharing in Don Inocencio's distrust toward Pepe Rey, the dean of Orbajosa's cathedral represents clerical excess, unrestrained religious zeal, and vehement reactionism. Galdós's portrayal of the dean's physical appearance and demeanor echoes the progressive, liberal condemnation of the clergy's past privileges. His ungainliness is linked to the rationale behind excarnation, the desire to remove what progressives considered was useless and obstructive to secular modernity. The dean is the anthropomorphic manifestation of the overwhelming structure of the cathedral, which signifies the seemingly overbearing presence of the Church in Orbajosa:

> El señor deán era un viejo de edad avanzada, corpulento y encendido, pletórico, apoplético; un hombre que se salía fuera de sí mismo por no caber en su propio pellejo, según estaba de gordo y morcilludo. Procedía de la exclaustración; no

hablaba más que de asuntos religiosos, y desde el principio mostró hacia Pepe Rey el desdén más vivo.[45]

[The dean was a man of advanced age, corpulent and of ruddy complexion, ebullient, apoplectic. A man without corporeal limits because he did not fit in his own skin, he was plump and fleshy. He was a product of disentailment. He did not speak of anything other than religious matters, and from the start, he exhibited toward Pepe Rey the most intense disdain.]

For Gold, Galdós's fictional universe rests on the similitude between physiognomy and the moral self.[46] Likewise, the dean's character can be read as manifest in his physical appearance. His namelessness is also significant in that he becomes a stereotype of the Spanish clergy. Through his constant discourses on disentailment and religion, the dean is presented as an individual out of touch with the outside world.

In its portrayal of rigid priestly authority and the clergy's concomitant religious abuses, *Doña Perfecta* has been regarded as a classic work of liberal anticlericalism. Publishing the novel when he was thirty-three years old, Galdós adopts, as Timothy Mitchell explains, Böhl's realism but sits at the opposite end of the political spectrum by undermining Spanish ultra-Catholicism. Mitchell continues that for Spain's liberal governments, the provinces were linked with "religious dysfunction, clerical paranoia, Carlism, agrarian backwardness, and civil insurrection."[47] What triggered these antagonisms were liberal measures such as disentailment, which ultimately challenged Spain's Catholic identity.[48] Hence, the disdain shown by Don Inocencio and the cathedral dean toward the progressive-leaning Pepe Rey symbolizes the culmination of clerical grievances. Akin to Böhl's regional settings, Galdós's Spanish provincial town of Orbajosa is depicted as a bulwark against what its conservative inhabitants perceive as a hostile central government.[49]

Pepe Rey's lack of religiosity and his criticisms of excessive ecclesial ornamentation, music, and overly religious people in general demonstrate his progressive Krausist thought. Furthermore, his engineering profession, which primarily concerns technological advancement and convenience, puts him at odds with his aunt, whose obsession with the extravagant exteriors of religion transcends basic human concerns and passions. The clash between a youth symbolic of potential and progress and mature authority, which denotes an alleged tradition and wisdom acquired through experience, features prominently in the conflict between Pepe Rey and Doña Perfecta.

Unsurprisingly, when Pepe Rey asks for Rosario's hand in marriage, Doña Perfecta staunchly refuses. She considers Pepe Rey to be an active disbeliever due to his scientism and resultant rejection of outward shows of piety:

Nada de esto te diré, porque tampoco lo entenderás, Pepe. Eres matemático. Ves lo que tienes delante y nada más; rayas, ángulos, pesos y nada más. Ves el

A NEW VITAL FORCE

efecto y no la causa. El que no cree en Dios no ve causas. Dios es la suprema intención del mundo. El que le desconoce, necesariamente ha de juzgar de todo como juzgas tú, a lo tonto.[50]

[I will not tell you any of this, because you would not understand it either, Pepe. You're a mathematician. You see what is in front of you and nothing else: lines, angles, weights, and nothing more. You see the effect and not the cause. He who does not believe in God does not see causes. God is the supreme intention of the world. He who does not acknowledge him will certainly judge everything as you do—badly.]

Pepe Rey is hardly convinced by Doña Perfecta's "embrollada, sutil y mística dialéctica"[51] [complicated, subtle, and mystical reasoning]. Whereas Pepe Rey's vocabulary is modern and straightforward, Doña Perfecta's is vague and condescending. She finally finishes what seems to be a sermonette with an outright confession, which he actually appreciates, because she has openly admitted her antagonism toward him:

—Dado tu carácter arrebatado, dada tu incapacidad para comprenderme, debí abordar la cuestión de frente y decirte: "Sobrino mío: no quiero que seas esposo de mi hija."

—Ese es el lenguaje que debió emplear usted conmigo desde el primer día—repuso el ingeniero, respirando con desahogo, como quien se ve libre de enorme peso—. Agradezco mucho a usted esas palabras. Después de ser acuchillado en las tinieblas, ese bofetón a la luz del día me complace mucho.[52]

["Given your rash character, given your inability to understand me, I had to address the issue squarely and tell you: 'My nephew, I do not want you to be my daughter's spouse.'"

"That is the language that you should have used with me since the first day," replied the engineer, breathing with relief like someone freed from an enormous weight. "I appreciate those words very much. After being stabbed in the dark, that slap in open daylight pleases me greatly."]

Doña Perfecta's convoluted discourse reflects the absence of an enlightened and illuminating truth and honesty. The darkness and light imagery alludes to the obscurantism of superstition and the Enlightenment, respectively. Doña Perfecta is, therefore, a hypocrite and hardly the ardent believer in moral goodness that she claims to be. Separated by their distinct vocabularies, there is a long pause between the aunt and her nephew. He again asserts that he will marry Rosario, to which the panicking Doña Perfecta responds, "Y mi autoridad, y mi voluntad, yo . . . ¿yo no soy nada?"[53] [And my authority, and my will, I . . . am I nothing?]. It is her position of authority within the family that serves to validate her own sense of identity. Her influence on Rosario's marriage prospects mimics traditional paternal roles, reflecting Doña Perfecta's patriarchal influence on Rosario's life. The undaunted Pepe Rey calmly states that God knows him for who he truly is and that other opinions do not matter: "El mundo podrá tenerla a usted en olor de infabilidad. Yo no"[54] [The world may consider you to be infallible. I do not]. This direct reference to the doctrine of papal infallibility here confirms that Doña Perfecta also symbolizes the powerful head of the Church, whose authority the Spanish Krausists actively denounced.[55]

Embodying institutional resistance to the budding spirit of ideological and personal autonomy, Doña Perfecta is "anatema hecho mujer"[56] [anathema made woman]. Ronald Cueto thus describes the Catholic Church as "Doña Perfecta *par excellence*,"[57] while Pepe Rey represents the liberal State.[58] Pepe Rey's liberal convictions reflect the ideological conflict arising from the Restoration, particularly the controversy surrounding the eleventh article of the 1876 Constitution, which, in the same year that *Doña Perfecta* was published, once again acknowledged Catholicism as the official religion of the State. This contentious article sparked parliamentary and public debate, for although people were free to practice their own religion, no public manifestations of faith were acceptable except for those of the established Church.[59]

Notwithstanding its own national ecclesiastical history, the Spanish Church's ideological defensiveness coincided with the decisions of Rome, its spiritual center. Reactionism to the forces of modernity characterized the nineteenth-century Catholic Church, evidenced by the reign of Pius IX between 1846 and 1878, which saw the issue of the *Syllabus of Errors* and the doctrinal enshrinement of papal infallibility in the First Vatican Council (1869–1870).[60] Naturally, the ultramontane neo-Catholics in Spain, loyal to Rome, would regard Pius IX as an authority in all matters of faith and morals.

Denotative of the Church's augmented orthodoxy is Doña Perfecta's dominant, unyielding character, which contributes to Rosario's mental and emotional instability. Rosario's delicacy, caused by her upbringing within the filial and religious confines of her home, conforms to the norm of the "angel in the house," which limited women to the domestic sphere and its rarefied, spiritualized atmosphere.[61] In the domestic locus, Bridget Aldaraca argues, it is the woman who must establish order and peace by demonstrating self-denial and virtue.[62] In stark contrast with Galdós's Rosario are Böhl's young and transgressive female characters, Marisalada from *La gaviota* and Rita from *La familia de Alvareda*, who openly defy social norms pertinent to the roles of women, as previously mentioned.

In *Doña Perfecta*, a portrayal of that gendered delimitation of space occurs when Rosario, on showing Pepe Rey his new room and the scenery outdoors, exhorts him, "No abras las dos ventanas a un tiempo, porque las corrientes de aire son muy malas"[63] [Do not open both windows simultaneously because the draughts are very harmful]. An outsider and a purveyor of modern ideas, he

A NEW VITAL FORCE

embodies these "corrientes de aire" [air currents] that invade the enclave of Doña Perfecta's household. López thus holds that Galdós's proposed remedy for Spain's deterioration is "abrir España a todos los vientos y a todas las tendencias para sanear la opinión al mismo tiempo que los nativos se ejercitaban en la virtud de la tolerancia"[64] [to open Spain to all currents and trends to improve public opinion while the natives practiced the virtue of tolerance]. This metaphor of opening the home's windows to welcome in the fresh air of the outdoors was championed by the Spanish intellectual and writer Miguel de Unamuno, one of the principal figures of fin de siècle regenerationism. In "Sobre el marasmo actual de España" [On Spain's current stagnation], the fifth essay of his *En torno al casticismo* series published between 1894 and 1911, Unamuno argued that Spain's rebirth was dependent on an intellectual and cultural openness to modern Europe: "Quisiera sugerir con toda fuerza al lector la idea de que al despertar de la vida de la muchedumbre difusa y de las regiones tiene que ir de par y enlazado con el abrir de par en par las ventanas al campo europeo para que se oree la patria"[65] [I wished to suggest emphatically to the reader the idea that the awakening to life of the people in general and regions must go hand in hand with opening our windows to Europe so as to air the homeland].

Rigid conservatism hampers Pepe Rey's goal to marry Rosario and extends also to his relationship with the people of Orbajosa. In a letter to his father, Pepe Rey states that Doña Perfecta's dogged resistance causes the town's inhabitants to perceive him negatively. This dearth of openness symbolically constricts Orbajosa, rendering it more primitive. Pepe Rey especially criticizes Doña Perfecta's defensiveness and antiquated ideas, which are redolent of feudal society:

> La hostilidad contra nosotros y contra el Gobie[r]no la tienen los orbajosenses en su espíritu, formando parte de él como la fe religiosa. Concretándome a la cuestión particular con mi tía, diré a usted una cosa singular, y es que la pobre señora, que tiene el feudalismo en la médula de los huesos, ha imaginado que yo voy a atacar su casa para robarle su hija.... Excuso decir a usted que me tiene por un monstruo, por una especia de rey moro herejote.[66]

> [The inhabitants of Orbajosa feel in their very spirit hostility against us and the government, as it forms part of that spirit. Limiting myself to the particular issue with my aunt, I will tell you one thing, and it is that the poor woman, who has feudalism in the marrow of her bones, has imagined that I am going to attack her house to rob her of her daughter.... It's hardly necessary to tell you that she takes me for a monster, for some kind of heretic Moorish king.]

Galdós's melding of medieval, political, and theological terms ("rey moro herejote" [heretic Moorish king]) reflects Orbajosa's absolute rejection of the modern, rationalist ideas that Pepe Rey espouses in order to protect its identities, traditions, and ways of life. Galdós's negative portrayal of the townspeople's heightened, exclusive orthodoxy contrasts with Böhl's conceptualization of Catholic piety as a core facet of Spain's spiritual self. Yet Zahareas avows that Pepe Rey's perception of the conservatives' mindsets as outdated also exhibits the liberals' intolerant and patronizing attitude toward rural folk. Hence, Galdós underscores the lack of easy solutions to the problematic town-countryside relationship.[67] As Sierra argues, Pepe Rey's evocation of the historic confrontation of Moors and Christians denotes the ideological conflict that hampers a harmonious coexistence between liberals and conservatives.[68] By mentioning his surname in the aforementioned phrase ("rey moro herejote"), Pepe Rey includes himself in that heterodox group of progressive liberals.

Doña Perfecta's ascription of heresy to Pepe Rey's rationalism stresses both her unwavering defense of the Catholic faith and her fixation on piety. Through his female characters, Galdós elucidates a gendered concept of religious devotion. According to Raúl Mínguez Blasco, the nineteenth century saw the ascription of religious devotion to women, bolstered by the figure of the Virgin Mary. Moreover, the priesthood was considered a femininization of Catholicism in its involvement with private family life and promotion of values deemed highly feminine, such as chastity, patience, sensibility, generosity, and abnegation.[69] As paragons of domestic virtue, Doña Perfecta and Rosario's prominent trait is their piety. Catherine Jagoe holds that piety was the province of women in not only nineteenth-century Spain but also the rest of Western Europe.[70] Indeed, nineteenth-century European anticlerical fears arose from a perceived close alliance between women and the Church.[71] As I mentioned in my chapter on Böhl's writings, female piety, the prominent trait of Böhl's maternal characters, is portrayed as vital for familial stability and that of future generations. In contrast, Galdós depicts female religious devotion as the product of an inadequate formation, associating it with illness and underlining its dangerous potential. The learned Don Cayetano de Polentinos, Doña Perfecta's brother-in-law, warns Pepe Rey about a condition of madness that supposedly runs through the female members of his family.[72] The practical, forward-thinking personalities of Don Cayetano and Pepe Rey are therefore juxtaposed with Rosario's instability and Doña Perfecta's intransigence.

The religious zeal and mental frailty of Galdós's female characters are antithetical to the Spanish nation's revival and survival. The violent murder of Pepe Rey by Caballuco at the behest of Doña Perfecta represents the abrupt termination of progress and reason. The novel's tragic denouement, expressed in an epistolary manner, reveals that Rosario becomes insane after Pepe Rey's death. She not only exhibits deathly traits—"palabras incoherentes . . . atroz delirio . . . pálidez mortal"[73] [incoherent words . . . atrocious delirium . . . deathly pallidness]—but is subsequently transferred to the mental asylum of San Baudilio in Llobregat. Rosario's internment as a result of her psychological reaction to Pepe Rey's death echoes the common depiction of the nineteenth-century madwoman. As Elaine Showalter notes,

A NEW VITAL FORCE

at mid-century, the majority of patients in public lunatic asylums were women, resulting in the labeling of insanity as the "female malady."[74] Alba del Pozo adds that in the second half of the nineteenth century, degeneration discourse principally shaped associations of gender with infirmity.[75] While female madness was commonly regarded as a result of female sexuality and deviancy, Galdós's sheltered, innocent, and devout Rosario also suffers the same psychological fate.[76] Such a portrayal elucidates Showalter's thesis that the figure of the madwoman articulates the patriarchal binary opposition between female irrationality and male reason, which is evident in the intellectual juxtaposition of Rosario and Pepe Rey.[77]

Ideological and political differences between the liberal government and the traditionalist provinces, between the secular establishment and religious believers, form the basis of Don Inocencio's anxieties. In the following passage, the cleric condemns the government with emotionally charged language, referring to the politicians' activities as conquests, extermination, and infestation and thus revealing his reactionary traditionalism:

> Verdad es que si vamos a mirar atentamente las cosas, la fe peligra ahora más que antes. . . . Pues ¿qué representan esos ejércitos que ocupan nuestra ciudad y pueblos inmediatos? ¿Qué representan? ¿Son otra cosa más que el infame instrumento de que se valen para sus pérfidas conquistas y el exterminio de las creencias, los ateos y protestantes de que está infestado Madrid?[78]

> [It is true that if we will look at things closely, faith is in much greater danger now than before. . . . Well, what do those armies that occupy our city and neighboring towns represent? What do they symbolize? Are they anything other than the vile instrument that they use for their treacherous conquests and the extermination of beliefs—the atheists and Protestants that infest Madrid?]

Don Inocencio's defensiveness stems from his fears that the day will come when Spain will be drained of its spiritual blood. Referring to Madrid, he alludes to the extermination of not only Catholic beliefs but also the individuals who represent them. He predicts that the Spanish clergy will suffer yet again anticlerical persecution and violence in the future:

> Sé muy bien que nos aguardan días terribles; que cuantos vestimos el hábito sacerdotal tenemos la vida pendiente de un cabello, porque España, no lo duden ustedes, presenciará escenas como aquellas de la Revolución francesa, en que perecieron miles de sacerdotes piadosísimos en un mismo día. . . . Mas no me apuro. Cuando toquen a degollar presentaré mi cuello; ya he vivido bastante. ¿Para qué sirvo yo? Para nada, para nada.[79]

> [I know very well that terrible days await us, that those of us who dress in priestly garb have their life hanging by a thread, because Spain—do not doubt this—will witness scenes like those of the French Revolution, in which

thousands of very pious priests perished in a single day. . . . But I do not worry. When the time comes for my throat to be slit, I will present my neck. I have lived long enough. What purpose do I serve? Nothing. Nothing.]

In citing the French Revolution, Don Inocencio points out that anticlerical sentiment also prevailed elsewhere in Europe and was sometimes manifest in acts of violence. As Mitchell puts it, "Anarchist words became anarchist deeds."[80] Approximately one hundred clergy in 1822–1823 were killed in an anticlerical uprising.[81] More specifically in Spain, a massacre of seventy-eight Jesuits, Dominicans, Mercedarians, and Franciscans and the destruction of their residences took place in Madrid on July 17–18, 1834, after rumors circulated days before that the friars had poisoned the city's water supply and caused a cholera outbreak.[82] Decades later, in 1896, a bomb was detonated during a Corpus Christi procession in Barcelona, its alleged perpetrator a French anarchist named Jean Girault.[83] In Western Europe, the German political campaign under Otto von Bismarck to suppress Catholicism (*Kulturkampf*), the struggle between the Kingdom of Italy and the Papal States, and the anticlerical measures of the French Third Republic were among the many nineteenth-century religious-secular struggles.[84] Manuel Pérez Ledesma states that while anticlerical movements existed in other European nations, they were more intense in Spain.[85]

I consider that the symbolic names of *Perfecta* and *Inocencio* lend themselves to a double interpretation. While these names may be ironical, given that the two characters are partly responsible for Pepe Rey's death, I posit that they are also pertinent in Galdós's discourse against ecclesiasticism and clericalism. Doña Perfecta's namesake is Saint Perfectus of Córdoba, a devout Christian martyr under the Moorish occupation in the ninth century.[86] Don Inocencio recalls the fifth-century pontiff Pope Saint Innocent, who was one of the key opponents of the Pelagian heresy. Pelagianism downplayed the notion of divine grace for the salvation of humankind on earth, relying instead on the essential goodness of mortals.[87] Clerical authorities, such as Saints Augustine of Hippo and Pope Innocent I, condemned the layman Pelagius's theology; their self-interest, as John H. Beck suggests, was one of the driving factors behind their disapproval.[88] Don Inocencio conveys his self-interest by meddling in Doña Perfecta's and Pepe Rey's lives to carry out his own agenda. He personally disapproves of Pepe Rey and wants Rosario to marry his nephew Jacinto instead. The ironic and onomastic interpretations of Perfecta and Inocencio encapsulate aspects of the religious question, which was of a fundamentally sociopolitical nature in that it concerned the guiding principles and procedures that regulated Church-State dynamics.[89] These two ardent Catholics, Don Inocencio and Doña Perfecta, contrast with Pepe Rey in their observations on the state of affairs in a rapidly secularizing Spain.

Their interference in Pepe Rey's affairs leads to disastrous consequences, since Don Inocencio and Doña Perfecta both end up in a state of turmoil. Such

A NEW VITAL FORCE

a repercussion parallels the liberal condemnation of religion's perceived threat to modern progress. Germán Gullón asserts that

> la lucha entre la Ciencia y la Religión, tan ferozmente entablada, acaba en tragedia para Pepe, asesinado por un matón; los instigadores del crimen, Inocencio y Perfecta, terminan destruidos en un mar de remordimientos, víctimas de su propia conciencia, el castigo se lo imponen a sí mismos, les viene de dentro, de su conciencia, y no de fuera.[90]

> [the battle between Science and Religion, so fiercely initiated, ends in tragedy for Pepe, killed by a thug; the instigators of the crime, Inocencio and Perfecta, end up destroyed in a sea of regret, victims of their own conscience. The punishment they impose on themselves comes from within, from their own conscience, and not from the outside world.]

According to Gullón, the Church's rigid defense of the status quo was in reaction to secularization, which was seen as the progressive intellectuals' active attempt to "borrar la cara de Dios de la faz de la tierra" [erase the face of God from the face of the earth]. For her part, Valis avows that *Doña Perfecta*, one of Galdós's earliest thesis novels, conveys his rejection of politicized religion during the second major Carlist War in the years 1872–1876.[91]

INSTITUTIONAL RELIGION AND INTERFAITH DIALOGUE IN *GLORIA*

Religious intolerance and parental authoritarianism in *Doña Perfecta* are themes that continue to be paramount in *Gloria*. This novel focuses on not only Catholicism but also Judaism. Published just one year after *Doña Perfecta*, *Gloria*, as Walter T. Pattison notes, appeared not long after the Bourbon Restoration of Alfonso XII, the Second Carlist War, the article for freedom of religion from the constitution after the 1868 Revolution, and the removal of Krausist academics from university chairs. *Gloria*, Pattison continues, is akin to Octave Feuillet's 1874 *Histoire de Sybille* [The story of Sybil], which is also set in a small village and involves a priest rescuing the female protagonist's love interest. This novel was among a large collection of French and English novels in Galdós's possession, which included the works of Balzac and Dickens.[92]

In *Gloria*, the Catholic Lantigua family and the Jewish Morton family are opposed due to their religions. The control that the parents and extended families exert over the two young protagonists, Gloria Lantigua and Daniel Morton, restricts their individual liberty. Set in the fictional town of Ficóbriga, the story concerns a young Catholic woman, Gloria, whose father, Don Juan Lantigua, and uncle, Don Ángel, a bishop, are influential figures. When the steamboat *Plantagenet* capsizes in the estuary, Ficóbriga's parish priest, Don Silvestre Romero, rescues a young Jewish Englishman, Daniel Morton. Daniel and Gloria eventually fall in love and constantly discuss the meaning of religion and its place in the future. Opposing their marriage are their family members, particularly Gloria's relatives and Daniel's mother, Esther Spinoza. Although Gloria perishes after giving birth to Daniel's son and Daniel dies in England at the age of thirty-three, their child, Jesús el Nazarenito, a messianic figure, symbolizes a future of religious harmony and union.

Rodríguez López-Brea asserts that the novel's denouement is a "verdadero canto al ecumenismo"[93] [true hymn to ecumenism]. Ecumenism, in the sense of interfaith dialogue, as Madeea Axinciuc explains, can be considered a more potent form of religious tolerance in that it not only tolerates but also dismisses any differentiation between belief systems in order to avoid discrimination.[94] I hold that Galdós's Catholic and Jewish characters also problematize this notion of interreligious discourse, which calls for changes in character and identity and comes across as tentative and, at times, a mere ideal. Although Daniel Morton agrees to convert to Catholicism in order to marry Gloria, his purported conversion is so superficial that not even Gloria is convinced of his sincerity.

Daniel's shipwreck at the start of the novel is significant because shipwrecks in literature typically signify rebirth, a transformation in identity, and struggle. James V. Morrison observes that in biblical and classical narratives, shipwrecks involve the forces of nature acting upon travelers who, forced to escape the vessel, usually survive by divine intervention or rescue. Prime examples are Homer's *Odyssey* and Saint Paul's account of his shipwreck on the way to Malta in AD 60, whose protagonists reveal their initial helplessness and resultant survival through divine aid.[95]

Significantly, the wreckage of the *Plantagenet* occurs in the inlet of Ficóbriga, a narrow passage symbolically halting the arrival of modernity on the provincial shores. It thus suggests the impediment to progress that Ficóbriga represents, since steamboats were the epitome of progress and modern convenience.[96] Indeed, Daniel comes from the homeland of innovation, since steam power was invented in France but developed in Britain.[97] In contrast, just like Orbajosa in *Doña Perfecta*, Ficóbriga continues to be a place of agriculture. Taking its name from *ficus* ("fig tree" in Latin) and *briga* ("town" in Celtic), Ficóbriga resembles the countryside of Cantabria, where the seaside, fields, and mountains were utilized for fishing, hunting, mining, and farming.[98] Moreover, I suggest that the inlet of Ficóbriga is depicted as a kind of birth passage from which Don Silvestre Romero delivers Daniel, an action indicative of his vocation as a priest who seeks to save the spiritual lives of the parishioners under his care.

Several key similarities exist between *Doña Perfecta* and *Gloria*. These stories occur in provincial areas that oppose the values of the modern capital, and both narratives involve young protagonists pitted against strict familial authorities and clerical officials. In *Gloria*, Galdós depicts Don Silvestre Romero as an ardent Catholic priest whose discourses focus mainly on the irreligiosity caused by

A NEW VITAL FORCE

scandals and revolutionary philosophies. Like Don Inocencio in *Doña Perfecta*, he too recalls the French Revolution and its effects on Catholic Spain. Religiosity has always been lukewarm in Spain, he comments, but now it has completely disappeared from the lives of most Spaniards. As evident in the following passage, Don Silvestre holds the Spanish government accountable for promoting a public culture of atheism and antireligious mockery that impacts the nation's practice of faith:

> Los hombres que gobiernan al país predican públicamente el ateísmo, se burlan de los Santos Misterios, insultan a la Virgen María, denigran a Jesucristo, llaman bobos a los Santos, y mandan demoler las iglesias y profanar los altares. Los ministros del Señor hállanse hoy en la condición más precaria: se les trata peor que a los ladrones y asesinos: el culto, sin decoro ni magnificencia a causa de la general pobreza de la Iglesia, entristece el ánimo. Los hombres no piensan más que en reunir dinero, en reñir los unos con los otros y en disputarse el gobierno de las naciones, que al dejar de ser guiadas por la política cristiana y único gobierno posible, que es el de Cristo, marchan con paso ligero a su disolución y total ruina.[99]

> [The men governing the nation publicly preach atheism, mock the sacred mysteries, insult the Virgin Mary, denigrate Jesus Christ, call the saints stupid, and order the demolition of churches and profanation of altars. The ministers of the Lord find themselves today in a most precarious state. They are treated worse than thieves and murderers. Worship, without ornamentation or magnificence due to the Church's general poverty, saddens the soul. Men think of nothing else but acquiring money, fighting with each other, and competing to govern nations that, ceasing to be guided by Christian politics and the only government possible, which is that of Christ, walk swiftly toward their dissolution and total ruin.]

Here Don Silvestre, like Don Inocencio, laments the diminishing significance of the universal Church. The correlation between inadequate funding and the lack of magnificence in ecclesial decor evokes the disentailment laws that appropriated the Church's properties. The privation of the stuff of religion results in spiritual desolation. Moreover, López notes that attacks against the Church happened more frequently during the Revolutionary Sexenium because the revolutionaries considered that the time had come to put an end to Spain's historical dogmatism.[100]

The Restoration, however, saw a renewal of monarchical authority, a marked context in Galdós's novels. Akiko Tsuchiya observes the crystallization of social discipline in Restoration society in Galdós's depiction of asylums and convents as places of pronounced social control.[101] In *Doña Perfecta* and *Gloria*, I argue that the domestic space features also as the principal source and place of the interplay between authoritarian constriction and young female deviance. While it is at Doña Perfecta's home that Pepe Rey observes Rosario's bounded lifestyle and outlook, Gloria encounters Daniel Morton in the Lantigua family's residence, an event that marks the beginning of their relationship and their hopes of autonomy and religious harmony. According to Tsuchiya, the traversing of imposed boundaries by female subjects renders Galdós's novels not only transgressive but also foundational.[102]

Through her questioning of social traditions, Gloria commences her pursuit of selfhood, which primarily constitutes a departure from the precincts of her family's religious past. Her surname, Lantigua, evokes the conservatives' belief in the significance and longevity of tradition and connotes her descent from religious authorities from whom she has inherited certain religious and cultural beliefs and practices. She displays, however, a sense of independent inquiry in her satirical comment: "Cada cosa en su lugar. . . . Vivimos abajo y no arriba. Mi padre me ha dicho varias veces que si no corto las alas al pensamiento voy a ser muy desgraciada. Vengan, pues, las tijeras"[103] [Everything in its place. . . . We live below and not above. My father has often said that if I do not rein in my imagination, I will be very unhappy. Well then, bring on the scissors]. These words denote her rebellion against tradition and distinguish her from her father, Don Juan de Lantigua, who resembles the typical neo-Catholic: "Su inclinación contemplativa le llevó a considerar la fe religiosa, no sólo como gobernadora y maestra del individuo en su conciencia, sino como un instrumento oficial reglamentado que debía dirigir externamente todas las cosas humanas"[104] [His contemplative tendency led him to consider religious faith not only as the governor and master of the individual's conscience but as an official, regulated instrument that outwardly directed all human affairs]. Although the members of the powerful Lantigua family are very devout, the province of Ficóbriga itself seems to be losing its religious fervor: "Gloria penetró en la iglesia, gozosa de encontrarse sola y en sitio a propósito para soltar el freno a su imaginación. En el sagrado recinto no había ya sino cinco o seis personas"[105] [Gloria entered the church, happy to be alone and in a place fit for freeing her imagination. In the sacred place, there were only five or six persons]. The virtually empty church indicates Ficóbriga's gradual spiritual barrenness. This decreased attendance stems from changes in religion's social significance. During the Restoration, debates surrounding religion grew more intense. López maintains that even liberals believed that Spain was undergoing a profound spiritual crisis, although the proposed solutions to this great problem differed immensely. Galdós conveys that the idealized return to a spiritual source was impossible, as his headstrong and forward-thinking characters Pepe Rey, Daniel, and Mendizábal all demonstrate.[106]

In Krausism, religion was to be oriented toward virtue and harmony rather than ritual. In his religious novels, Galdós depicts nineteenth-century Spanish piety as heavily predicated upon external features of hierarchy and ritual. In

A NEW VITAL FORCE

Gloria, therefore, López maintains that religious sentiment stems not from sincere faith and belief but from social customs, while Sara E. Schyfter argues that Spanish Catholicism was merely "empty formalism."[107] Krausist ideals, which aligned themselves with a Protestant approach to Christianity rather than the doctrinal and ritualistic nature of Catholicism, offered a solution to the perceived superficiality of Spanish religiosity. As López points out, Julián Sanz del Río, Krausism's main disseminator in Spain, defended "una religión interior y personal, menos ritual"[108] [an interior and personal religion, less ritual]. In *Gloria*, the characters' perceptions of religion are important to represent its divisive nature in nineteenth-century Spain, as intellectuals, neo-Catholics, conservatives, liberals, and progressives differed in their perspectives on religious observance, ritual, doctrine, and societal significance. Conversations between Rafael del Horro and Don Silvestre Romero reveal the sociopolitical usage of religion, while Gloria and Daniel continue to discuss the importance of religious belief for all aspects of life.

Rafael del Horro, Gloria's potential suitor, is a successful journalist and orator with plans to enter politics. At the beginning of the novel, he joins a gathering in Gloria's home of important prelates and officials, including Gloria's uncle (the bishop Ángel Lantigua); her father (Don Juan), the parish priest (Don Silvestre Romero), the bishop's secretary (Don Juan Amarillo), and the mayor of Ficóbriga. Don Silvestre praises Rafael's religious devotion and modesty:

> Aquí está nuestro heroico joven, nuestro valiente soldado. Señores y amigos míos, saluden ustedes al benemérito campeón de los buenos principios, de las creencias religiosas, de la Iglesia católica, y al perseguidor del filosofismo, del ateísmo, de las irreverencias revolucionarias. ¡Gloria a la juventud creyente, fervorosa, llena de fe y de amor al catolicismo![109]

> [Here is our heroic youth, our brave soldier. Gentlemen, my friends, salute the worthy champion of good principles, of religious beliefs, of the Catholic Church, and the persecutor of spurious philosophy, of atheism, and revolutionary irreverence. Glory to the young believers—fervent, full of faith and love for Catholicism!]

Depicted as a soldier, a version of heroism pertaining most especially to the medieval era and rapidly becoming obsolete in the late nineteenth century, Rafael contrasts with the new entrepreneurial heroism personified by Daniel as well as Pepe Rey from *Doña Perfecta*. The ideal of the chivalric knight, as Marlon B. Ross states, emblematized masculine superiority and strength in the defense of the vulnerable and the search for the collective good. Yet this masculine power displayed through bodily might in combat was ceding to mental strength. In the modern era, the new emphasis on intellectual dominance was rapidly overriding the old chivalric system of physical prowess.[110] The difference between Rafael and Daniel lies, then, in how they have employed their skills, talents, and influence.

From the bishop's point of view, Daniel represents the youth who "se entrega a los vicios de la inteligencia y se corrompe con perniciosas lecturas"[111] [submits to the vices of intelligence and corrupts himself with dangerous readings]. In a later conversation with Don Silvestre, Rafael belies his role as a champion of the Church's beliefs and principles by revealing his own pretentiousness and insincerity in faith, to which the priest responds, "Usted también es de los que hablan mucho y creen poco"[112] [You are also one of those who speak much and believe little]. Viewing religion through an instrumentalist lens, Rafael replies that "sin religión no hay sociedad posible. ¿Adónde llegaría el frenesí de las masas estúpidas e ignorantes, si el lazo de la religión no enfrenara sus malas pasiones?"[113] [without religion, society is impossible. Where would the madness of the stupid and ignorant masses end up if the bond of religion did not restrain their evil passions?]. For Rafael, therefore, religious practice is a mere branch of the State's agenda, a tool to control the masses and class conflict. Its liturgies and discourses, Rafael asserts, "se han creado para coadyuvar a la gran obra del Estado, y rodear de garantías y seguridades a las clases pudientes e ilustradas"[114] [have been designed to contribute to the grand work of the State and surround the wealthy and enlightened classes with guarantees and security].

Conversely, Don Silvestre objects to this view of religion as a sociopolitical system of regulation, which means nothing more than "una especie de instrumento correccional contra los pillos"[115] [a kind of correctional instrument against scoundrels]. He points out that Rafael misunderstands the purpose of the Church's rites and teachings, remarking that not truly believing in basic religious teachings is a gross departure from true faith. Their disagreement mirrors the problematic religious situation in Spain, which is a product of opposing views on the external and internal aspects of Catholicism. As Don Silvestre remarks,

> Usted, Rafael . . . pertenece a la escuela de los que defienden la religión por egoísmo, es decir, porque les cuida sus intereses. Ven en ella una especie de guardería rural. Dicen: "La religión es muy buena, debe creerse: [la] verdad es que yo no creo; pero crean los demás para que tengan miedo a Dios y no me hagan daño." En tanto no se cuidan de los altos fines religiosos, ni de la vida eterna.[116]

> [You, Raphael . . . belong to the school of those who define religion out of selfishness—that is, because it protects your interests. You perceive in it a kind of rural guard. You say, "Religion is good, one must believe: the truth is that I do not believe, but let others believe so that they fear God and do me no harm." Meanwhile, you care nothing for religion's elevated goods or eternal life.]

Rafael's affectation and wavering convictions thus echo the superficiality and hypocrisy to which Schyfter and López refer in their above-cited appraisals of

A NEW VITAL FORCE

Spanish Catholicism in the nineteenth century. Rafael and Don Silvestre's differing stances reveal that religion can be perceived and observed variously.

Religion is also a serious matter for the Spinoza family, whose observance of the Jewish faith differs among its individual members. For Daniel, religion has advantages and disadvantages: "¿No ves que hablamos de religión? Y la religión es hermosa cuando une; horrible y cruel cuando separa"[117] [Do you not see we are talking about religion? And religion is beautiful when it unites; it is horrible and cruel when it divides]. He displays cynicism toward formulaic rites, believing that these are devoid of sincerity and authentic devotion. In Galdós's thesis novels, the institutionality of religion is pitted against the subjectivity of spirituality. As López notes, Daniel's criticisms foreground the hollowness of Spanish religion, advocating instead the inward expression of spirituality: "Lo que falta al español es espiritualidad, vida interior, necesidad que ha sustituido con los ritos religiosos públicos"[118] [What the Spaniard lacks is spirituality—interior life, a need that has been replaced with public religious rites].

While Daniel does not practice the Jewish faith, his mother adheres to Judaism out of respect for her ancestors, imitating the heroic queen Esther, who defended her Jewish compatriots in the Old Testament. Her emphasis on religion is buttressed by its social functions, of which the narrative voice is fully aware:

> No profesaba su religión con entusiasta fervor, pero sí con lealtad, es decir, con un sentimiento dulce y firme que era, más que devoción, respeto a los mayores, amor al nombre y a la historia de una casta desgraciada. Ésta era objeto de su pasión más viva, de un fanatismo capaz de reproducir en ella, si los tiempos lo consintieran, las grandes figuras de Débora la mujer juez, de Yáel la que con un clavo mataba al enemigo, de la trágica Judith y la dulce Esther. La moral la cautivaba; pero el rito no merecía de ella el mismo amor.[119]

> [She did not profess her religion with enthusiastic fervor but with loyalty—that is, a sweet and strong sentiment that was, more than devotion, respect toward elders and love for the name and history of a disgraced caste. This was the aim of her most fervent passion, of a fanatism capable of duplicating in her, if the times permitted it, the great figures of Deborah, the female judge, and Yael, who killed the enemy with a nail, of the tragic Judith, and the sweet Esther. Morality captivated her, but she did not have the same love for ritual.]

In distinguishing between religious rites and morals, Esther's religious observance leans toward an appreciation of Judaism's values, making it a starkly abstract system of religious beliefs and principles. Given that, as Schyfter argues, the Jewish religion is "a vague deism without emotional or ritual appeal,"[120] Esther is convinced that Daniel's disregard for Catholic rituals will impede the possibility of a harmonious relationship with the devout Gloria. The birth of their child, Jesusito, who emblematizes future unity, disproves this claim.

MENDIZÁBAL: ADDRESSING SPAIN'S INERTIA

Two novellas that reinforce Galdós's messages on reactionism put forward in *Doña Perfecta* and *Gloria* are *Mendizábal* and *Montes de Oca*. In these texts, Galdós examines the historical significance of political figures in order to critique their approaches to Spanish society and religious matters. According to Rodolfo Cardona, Mendizábal came to power during a difficult time in government, after the so-called Ominous Decade of Fernando VII's reign.[121] *Mendizábal* focuses on the eponymous figure's regime and legacy. Don Fernando Calpena is the young fictional protagonist who works as a civil servant in Mendizábal's government. In a conversation with his friend, the liberal priest Don Pedro Hillo, Calpena warns him about Mendizábal's decrees on disentailment:

> —[Mendizábal] dictó una larguísima carta a Martínez de la Rosa. . . . Expresaba su pensamiento con rapidez; rectificaba pocas veces; no se paraba en el estilo; iba derecho al asunto y a la idea sin cuidarse de la forma. Mandóme volver al día siguiente, y me dictó tres o cuatro decretos, uno de ellos suprimiendo las órdenes religiosas y haciendo tabla rasa de todos los frailes, monjas, clérigos y beatas que hay en estos reinos, estableciendo la reversión de todos los bienes al Estado para venderlos . . . y ¡qué sé yo!
>
> —¡María Santísima! Pero eso sería broma.
>
> —¿Broma? Ya verá usted las que gasta ese sujeto. No habíamos concluido aquella degollina de frailes y la repartición de sus riquezas, cuando entró un señor inglés.[122]

> ["Mendizábal dictated a lengthy letter to Martínez de la Rosa. . . . He expressed his thoughts quickly, corrected very little. He was not pedantic with style. He went straight to the matter and idea without caring about form. He ordered me to return the following day and dictated to me three or four decrees, one of them suppressing the religious orders and making a clean slate regarding friars, nuns, clerics, and holy women in these kingdoms, establishing the return of all goods to the State to be sold . . . and whatever else!"
>
> "Holy Mary! But that must be a joke."
>
> "A joke? You will soon see the kind of jokes that this individual makes. We had not finished slitting the throats of friars and distributing their wealth when an English gentleman walked in."]

Here the historical figure of Mendizábal, like Pepe Rey, is portrayed as an ambitious, forward-thinking, progressive politician, yet hardly a benign liberal. While Mendizábal's policies reflect the positivist and Krausist rationales behind disentailment, his contribution to the suppression and elimination of Spanish religious individuals renders him a ruthless leader. Mendizábal's brevity and conciseness of speech, like Pepe Rey's, exemplify a critique of the superfluous. This paring

A NEW VITAL FORCE

back of language—a removal of linguistic and sentimental excess—enacts the progressive liberal conceptualization of the Church as an externally extravagant institution that requires pruning.

The narrative voice intimates that the Church's wide influence in political, social, and cultural spheres restricts a liberal Spain's quest for freedom of thought. Willing to remain in Madrid to devote himself to his political career under Mendizábal instead of moving to Cádiz with the liberal Pedro Hillo, Calpena asserts his desire for independence:

> No sea usted inocente, Don Pedro. ¡El destinito! ¡Vivir amarrado al pesebre de la Administración! Pero ¿no comprende usted que el que una vez prueba las facilidades de ese pesebre ya está enviciado para toda la vida, ya no se pertenece, ya es una máquina, que los ministros paran o echan a andar, según les acomoda? No, no me digan que sea máquina.... En los empleos tiene usted la explicación de la inercia nacional, de esta parálisis, que se traduce luego en ignorancia, en envidia, en pobreza.[123]

> [Do not be naive, Don Pedro. The position! To live tethered to the trough of the administration! But do you not understand that he who once tastes the privileges of that trough will be hooked for life—he no longer belongs to himself, he is a machine that the ministers stop or put in motion as they see fit? No, don't tell me to be a machine.... In these positions, you have the reasons behind the nation's inertia, this paralysis that later converts to ignorance, envy, and poverty.]

In this passage, Calpena speaks not only of his own autonomy but also that of the Spanish nation. According to this character, Mendizábal represents Spain's only chance of emerging from a lifeless stagnation in the modern world. The respectively scientific and medical terms *inertia* and *paralysis*, which pertain to a positivistic vocabulary as well as to the metaphors of regenerationist writing, underline the young civil servant's awareness of the country's sluggishness. Akin to the self-sufficient and forward-thinking protagonists Daniel and Pepe Rey, Calpena adopts the role of the new strongman.

MONTES DE OCA: BETWEEN PROGRESSIVISM AND CONSERVATISM

Spain's internal struggle between progressivism and conservatism is also evident in *Montes de Oca*. The novella tells the story of the idealistic, rather obscure military general and politician Manuel Montes de Oca (1804–1841), who opposed Espartero, a statesman who was considered to be the "apóstol de todos los adelantos"[124] [apostle of all progress]. Espartero was appointed regent by the Cortes after María Cristina resigned in 1840. Montes de Oca joined María Cristina in exile and was executed upon his return to Spain in 1841. *Montes de Oca* recalls the regency of Espartero, who, on assuming power in 1840, was also a proponent of disentailment laws. Set in the period after the 1839 Convention of Vergara, which signaled the end of the First Carlist War, the novella explores Espartero's rise and the ensuing rebellion against him, in which Montes de Oca played a key role. The latter's loyalty toward and idealization of the increasingly unpopular María Cristina is portrayed as irrational.[125] As Shubert puts it, María Cristina symbolized the corruption of the former regime, and revolutionaries sought to put her on trial.[126]

As in *Gloria* and *Doña Perfecta*, regenerationist discourse is prevalent in *Montes de Oca*. In a *tertulia* in Madrid, a jeweler, Don Carlos Maturana, declares that the national body is in a degenerate, infirm state:

Ya no hay guerra, señores; ya no hay más que política, lo que a mí me parece un grave mal, pues España es un enfermo que no puede vivir sino a fuerza de sangrías. . . . No reírse. La política sola paréceme más mortífera que la política con guerra. La una corrompe, la otra purga.[127]

[There is now no war, gentlemen; there is nothing but politics, which seems to me a grave evil, because Spain is a sick nation that cannot live without bloodletting. . . . Do not laugh. For me, politics alone is deadlier than politics with war. The former corrupts; the latter purges.]

Along with the nation's political turmoil are its economic problems, dominated by a complicated view of the value of things. Colonel Don Santiago Ibero, a supporter of Espartero, has a conversation with the young Rafaela del Milagro about materialism. The resourceful Rafaela, who was abandoned by her husband, declares that modern society has made money the only remedy for the social ill of poverty. In the following passage, she brings up the situation of destitute friars and nuns, whose properties are now in the possession of newly wealthy buyers:

Es porque ahora hay ricos, y antes no los había . . . es porque nos hemos despabilado con la sacudida de las guerras. Pues otra: ¿y qué me cuenta de los ricos nuevos que van a salir, de todos esos que están comprando por un pedazo de pan las tierras y casas que fueron de frailes? ¿Y los que afanaron, como dice papá, el papel de deuda que tenían las monjas? Vamos, que habrá cada millonario que meta miedo, y eso, eso es lo que conviene.[128]

[It is because now there are wealthy people, and before there were none . . . it is because we have woken up with the shock of wars. And another thing: What can you tell me about the newly affluent who are emerging, about all those who are buying with a piece of bread the lands and houses that once belonged to the friars? And those who snaffled, as Father says, the debt papers of the nuns? Well now, there are all types of millionaires who can cause worry, and that, that is what is supposedly appropriate.]

A NEW VITAL FORCE

123

Peter Bush suggests that the character of Montes de Oca embodies an extreme idealism or quixotism, a trait often found in regenerationist reflections on moral principles.[129] Galdós's *Montes de Oca* rejected regenerationist quixotism, demonstrating that while the rest of Europe was inspired by notions of science and progress, Spain was still invested in nostalgic, heroic interpretations of its past. Thus, Bush asserts that Galdós's imaginative exploration of Montes de Oca, who aims to bring irrational idealism to the political sphere, is an admonition against the adoption of quixotism as a national creed.[130]

ELECTRA: RESUSCITATING THE NATIONAL BODY

Galdós's historical novellas and thesis novels highlight the conflicting ideals of the old world and the new. While a compromise is desired, it is impossible to reach. Galdós portrays this insurmountable difficulty in the hindered unions caused by intransigent authoritarian figures, a theme that is also manifest in his 1901 play *Electra*. This dramatic work draws on the same issues arising from the divide between religious tradition and modern faith in progress and science. The story revolves around Electra, a young orphaned girl who, after the death of her mother, Eleuteria, is raised in the convent of the Ursulines and adopted by Don Urbano García Yuste and his wife, Evarista. Electra's love interest, the play's male protagonist, is Máximo, a widowed scientist, father of two children, and nephew of Don Urbano. Described as "traviesa" [mischievous] and "juguetona"[131] [playful], Electra, like Rosario, is depicted as a woman who requires boundaries. The cleric, Don Salvador Pantoja, attempts to separate the couple by lying to Electra about her origins, stating that Electra and Máximo are siblings. It is implied, however, that Don Salvador is her father, who abandoned Eleuteria in her time of need.

At the conclusion of the play, Máximo and his family friend, the Marquis of Ronda, set out to rescue Electra from the convent, where Don Salvador Pantoja has placed her. Like the fragile Rosario's room in *Doña Perfecta*, the convent in *Electra* is depicted as an airless space. Consequently, Electra declares to Sor Dorotea, who accompanies her, "Aquí . . . Quiero respirar . . . Quiero vivir"[132] [Here . . . I want to breathe . . . I want to live]. Subsequently, as Sor Dorotea explains to Don Salvador Pantoja, "Salimos a respirar el aire puro. Electra se asfixiaba"[133] [We went outside to breathe the fresh air. Electra was suffocating]. Electra's need to breathe outside evokes the recurrent motif of air currents that Galdós associates with liberty and progress in *Doña Perfecta*. In her delirium, Electra sees the specter of her mother, Eleuteria, who not only confirms to her the truth of her paternity but also reminds her that "Dios está en todas partes. . . . Búscale en el mundo por senderos mejores que los míos"[134] [God is everywhere. . . . Search for him in the world on paths better than mine]. Through the mother's speech, the text communicates the Spanish nation's need for more viable pathways that connect God with the liberal interest in personal freedom. By conveying the monastic space as physically suffocating, the narrative voice represents the ecclesiastical space as a site of harmful restrictions. This final episode at the convent brings to the fore Galdós's envisagement of Spain's spiritual future, predicated on a departure from ecclesial formality and the privileging of a realm of love and liberty. In the end, Electra is reunited with Máximo, who informs Don Salvador that the newly liberated Electra "no huye. . . . Resucita"[135] [does not flee. . . . She has been resuscitated].

In a review for *El País* dated January 31, 1901, Pío Baroja commended Galdós's *Electra*, asserting that it proffered a genuine remedy for Spain's social ills in the form of "entusiasmo, rebeldía, amor, fe" [enthusiasm, rebellion, love, faith] as opposed to plans, dogmas, and formulas.[136] Baroja's concluding remarks, which draw on rationalist principles and religious imagery, expressed the progressive desire for an advanced secular future:

> La obra de Galdós en un país como el nuestro, que no es más que un feudo del papa, en donde el catolicismo absurdamente dogmático ha devorado todo, arte y ciencia, filosofía y moral . . . la obra de Galdós es una esperanza de purificación, es la visión vaga de la 'Jerusalén nueva' que aparece envuelta en nubes.[137]

> [Galdós's work in a country like ours, which is nothing more than a papal domain, where an absurdly dogmatic Catholicism has devoured everything—art and science, philosophy and morality. . . . Galdós's work is a hope for purification; it is the vague vision of the "New Jerusalem" that appears shrouded in cloud.]

The evocation of the New Jerusalem, a symbol of heaven in the New Testament's book of Revelation, conveys the progressive liberals' earnest commitment to Spain's social, cultural, and political evolution. Baroja's emphasis on newness responds to Galdós's reiteration of the ideal of national "resuscitation," an event that would transform Spain's identity, separating it from its past religious self and bringing about the nation's entry into a distinct mode of being.[138]

Evoking the motif of Spain's revival evident in Mendizábal's address in this chapter's opening excerpt, Galdós's play shares in the progressive intellectuals' mission to renew Spain's health to enable its participation in the modern world. Galdós's frequent motifs of life, youth, and energy are evident not only in Máximo's scientific experiments and Electra's "resuscitation" but also in the impact on the provinces of Pepe Rey and Daniel Morton, who cause controversy as young heralds of future progress. The constant allusions to life in Galdós's writings mirror the thoughts and principles of the liberal intellectuals in the latter part of the nineteenth century, whose visions of Spain, as Santos Juliá notes, harnessed ideologies such as Krausism, positivism, and regenerationism. Yet such images

A NEW VITAL FORCE   125

of ailment and renewal are inseparable from religion. As Juliá remarks, "Como en todo mito de salvación, el momento de la muerte no es más que el fundamento de la vida. España se dice muerta porque espera la resurrección"[139] [As in every myth of salvation, the moment of death is nothing more than the foundation of life. Spain is said to be dead because it awaits resurrection]. The religion of humanitarianism allied with rationalism, which the young protagonists in Galdós's works fervently uphold, is figured as a bridge between the Two Spains of conservative tradition and progressive liberalism.

Personal correspondence between Galdós and Pereda exhibits such an endeavor to establish a dialogue between visions of the old and new Spains. In a letter dated March 1, 1901, Galdós speaks of the successful reception of *Electra* and conveys his admiration for Pereda:

> Ya habrá recibido el tomo de *Electra*. Nunca sospeché que esta obra levantara tan gran polvareda, y el día anterior al ensayo general creía firmemente . . . que el drama produciría poco o ningún efecto. En fin, me equivoqué en aquella apreciación, y todavía no *he vuelto de mi apoteosis*. Quédese para cuando nos veamos (y ojalá fuera pronto) el disputar un poco amigablemente sobre el *quid* de esta endiablada cuestión que a todos nos trae medio locos, y entretanto me concreto a decirle, mi querido y admirable D. José, que su carta me supo a las puras mieles, porque en ella he visto su grandeza de alma, y pude apreciar cuánto vale el tenor de su amistad, bastante sólida para que no la quebranten las divergencias en el modo de apreciar creencias más o menos generales y . . . discordias recientes.[140]

> [You will have received the volume of *Electra*. I never anticipated that this work would cause such an outcry, and the previous day at the general rehearsal, I strongly believed . . . that the drama would produce little or no effect. In short, I was wrong in this judgment, and *I still have not returned from my grand finale*. Let's leave for when we meet again (hopefully soon) our friendly discussion about the *crux* of this diabolical matter that makes us all half mad. Meanwhile, I will limit myself to telling you, my dear, admirable friend Don Jose, that your letter tasted like the purest honey, because in it I saw the greatness of your soul, and I could appreciate how invaluable your kind of friendship is—solid enough so that it cannot be shattered by differences in beliefs that are quite general and . . . recent disagreements.]

Here Galdós alludes to the profound religious crisis manifest in Spanish society, denouncing it as an "endiablada cuestión" [diabolical matter] to reveal not only its polemical nature but also its questioning of the divine. This reference to the demonic contrasts with his ascribing a "grandeza de alma" [greatness of soul] to the devout Pereda, with whom he engages in honest, civil, and probing debates. Galdós claims to understand religious beliefs, principles, and customs just as well as Pereda.

126   MAKING MODERN SPAIN

Although Galdós promotes a dismissal of the external and material elements of Catholicism, he still understands its significance for Spanish culture and history. This awareness demonstrates that the shift from the tangible and visible to the internal would be a difficult process. In an earlier letter written on June 6, 1877, Galdós protests Pereda's claim that he does not comprehend Spain's religious heritage:

> Por cierto que al referirme V. las festividades religiosas de su país lo hace dándome a entender que yo no sé lo que son procesiones, ni monumentos, ni ceremonias religiosas de Semana Santa. De esto se desprende su opinión desfavorable respecto a mi irreligiosidad, que no debo dejar de protestar un poquillo. No tanto, don José, no tanto que ignore esas cosas tan cruciales.[141]

> [Certainly, when you mentioned to me the religious festivities of your country, you did so in such a way as to insinuate that I did not know what processions, monuments, and Holy Week ceremonies were. Consequently, I deduce that your opinion on my irreligiosity is unfavorable, an opinion that I must protest a little. Hardly, Don José; I am hardly ignorant of such crucial things.]

Galdós explains that he grew up witnessing the public expression of the Catholic faith and the celebration of Easter and Holy Week "con bastante esplendor" [with enough splendor]. But this religious observance in his youth has come to an end: "En mí está tan arraigada la duda de ciertas cosas que nada me la puede arrancar. Carezco de fe, carezco de ella en absoluto. He procurado poseerme de ella y no lo he podido conseguir"[142] [So ingrained in me is skepticism toward certain things that nothing can dispel it. I lack faith. I lack it completely. I have tried to possess it and have not succeeded in doing so]. Nevertheless, despite his disbelief in the doctrinal and supernatural aspects of religion, Galdós continues to maintain that religion plays a crucial role in human affairs, even though society's perceptions of its particular mission are varied and fluctuating. He privileges an abstract notion of religion as a social implement that trumps the "gori-gori"[143] [chanting] of rites, monuments, and tenets of faith. Political decisions and events, along with the ideological promotion of a new religion that foregrounds humanity and rationality, have contributed to the reform of the meaning of the Church and its spaces. Thus, in line with the aspirations of Galdós's youthful liberal protagonists, Spain's spiritual body must prepare for its rebirth.

In order to bring to fruition the nation's revival, Galdós urges sincere loyalty from his compatriots. In his 1909 manifesto "Al pueblo español" [To the Spanish people], published in the republican, Madrid-based periodical El País (1887–1921) in protest against the policies of Antonio Maura's government, Galdós seeks to persuade his countrymen to set aside their differences in political opinion and devote their energies to remedying the nation's ills. As he puts it, "Hablo sin que nadie me lo mande, y respondo sin que nadie me lo pregunte, por irresistible

A NEW VITAL FORCE

impulso de mi conciencia y exaltación de mi fe en el porvenir de la patria, sin invocar otro título ni otro fuero que el fuero y título de español, porque esto basta"[144] [I speak without anyone ordering me to, and I respond without anyone asking me to out of the irresistible impulse of my conscience and the exaltation of my faith in my country's future, without invoking any other titles or privileges expect those of being a Spaniard, because this is enough]. Love of country, Galdós declares, ought to be pure, disinterested, and without ambition, "sin distinción de partidos, sin distinción de doctrinas y afectos"[145] [without distinction in parties, doctrines, and affections]. As evidenced also in his *Doña Perfecta* and *Gloria*, Galdós promotes harmony in his manifesto for the purpose of national cohesion and stability.

Frustrated with the uncertainty and hidden dangers generated by the divisions within the Partido Liberal Conservador [Liberal Conservative Party], Galdós urges the Spanish people to mobilize and reform the country themselves: "Que la Nación hable, que la Nación actúe, que la Nación se levante . . . que no pida al Gobierno lo que éste, enredado en la maraña de sus desaciertos, no puede dar ya"[146] [Let the nation speak, let the nation act, let the nation rise . . . it mustn't ask from the government what the latter, entangled in the mess of its errors, cannot now give it]. In this statement, Galdós alludes to the hoped-for resurrection of the national body. Defining the conservative governments of Fernando VII and Maura as forms of political imperialism and barbarism, Galdós looks to republicanism to pave the way for Spain's democratic future: "Ya es tiempo de que se acabe tanta degradación y el infamante imperio de la mayor barbarie política que hemos sufrido desde el aborrecido Fernando VII. . . . Los republicanos serán los primeros que acudan a levantar un fuerte muro entre España y el abismo"[147] [Now is the time to end so much degradation and the dishonorable empire of the greatest political barbarity that we have suffered since the detested Fernando VII. . . . The republicans will be the first to build a strong wall between Spain and the abyss]. The image of erecting a wall to protect Spain from a metaphorical abyss confirms the necessity of establishing firm barriers and limits for the realization of progressive ideals. The partition and chasm, however, are also symbols that, connoting division, problematize the theme of harmony prevalent in Galdós's ideological novels.

CONCLUSION

Galdós's writings present a complicated portrait of the challenges of the religious question in a rapidly modernizing Spanish society. In his literary depictions of familial obligations to religion, impeded marriages, and the conflicting desires and priorities of older and younger generations, Galdós illuminates the societal restrictions of the conservative order that obstruct a more modern vision of individual and national selfhood. More significantly, issues of gender feature prominently in Galdós's criticism of traditionalist and patriarchal ideals. In his texts, women's piety is associated with narrow-mindedness, devitalization, and mental illness, whereas the foundations of new life and liberty are secured by the characters' deviation from established social codes and religious doctrines.

Galdós's texts scrutinize the changing face of Spanish society's relationship with Catholic beliefs, vocations, and liturgy. The spiritual and material relevance of the Church to the Spanish populace, as Galdós conveys in his works, is gradually decreasing. In criticizing intransigence in *Gloria* and *Doña Perfecta*, religious excess in *Mendizábal*, and idealism in *Montes de Oca*, Galdós demonstrates that the reactionary old order leads to stagnation. Crucial to Spain's move toward a modern world is a figurative resuscitation, a theme that Galdós conveys in *Electra* and "Al pueblo español." Galdós thus proposes Spain's approximation toward rationalism and internalized spirituality as solutions to the nation's ills.

Such changes hardly seem organic. They necessitate a range of sociocultural currents that dismantle the old and construct the new: a vital force that will animate the national body, to which this new spiritual identity is ancillary. I have claimed that this vital force responds to Spain's religious question because it opposes Catholicism's reactionary dogmatism in favor of broader intellectual and sociopolitical horizons. Yet this desired aperture also signals a passage toward uncertainty, a reorientation (or disorientation) in the dark, a concern manifest in Pereda's writings.

CHAPTER 5

The Abyss and the Mount

QUESTIONS OF FAITH, FAMILY, AND TRADITION
IN JOSÉ MARÍA DE PEREDA'S *EL TÍO CAYETANO*
(1858–1859 AND 1868–1869), *BLASONES
Y TALEGAS* (1869), *DE TAL PALO, TAL
ASTILLA* (1880), AND *SOTILEZA* (1885)

No hallo fundado motivo para que recibiera V. como jarro de agua mi "filípica" sobre *Gloria*, después de haberle asegurado que esta novela, en cuanto a la *forma*, era de intachable hermosura.... En cuanto a lo de *volteriano*, ya sabe V. que no se necesita negarlo *todo* para merecer ese título. "La gran infame" llamaba aquel asalariado adulador de todas las humanas grandezas, a la Iglesia Católica, y a ella fueron sus tiros constantemente. Como hombre de largos alcances, sabía demasiado que, demolido el *viejo edificio*, los demás caían ellos solos, por eso apuntaba siempre a la *vieja fe*, y por eso siguen llamándose volterianos en que, sin meter mucho ruido, socavan los mismos cimientos.

[I cannot see why you were discouraged by my "tirade" against *Gloria* after I assured you that this novel, with regard to its *form*, was of impeccable beauty.... Regarding the label of *Voltairean*, you already know that it is not necessary to deny *everything* to warrant this title. That salaried cajoler labeled the Catholic Church "the great infamy" and constantly directed shots at her. As a man who saw the long term, he knew all too well that once the *old edifice* was demolished, the others would follow suit. Thus, he always aimed at the *old faith*, and therefore Voltaireans continue calling themselves as such in that, without making too much noise, they undermine the same foundations.]

—José María de Pereda, letter to Benito Pérez Galdós,
March 14, 1877 (italics in original)

In the above letter to his contemporary, companion, and regular correspondent Galdós, José María de Pereda commends Galdós's writing style in *Gloria* yet

129

reproves his treatment of the Catholic religion. Critical of the negative portrayal of religious devotion and "clerigalla fanática" [fanatical clergy] in the novel, Pereda declares that *Gloria* evokes Voltaire's exhortation to "écrasez l'infâme" [crush the vile thing], a statement in which the Enlightenment philosopher referred to the Catholic Church, the spiritual base of the old order.[1] As a traditionalist and Carlist, Pereda was alarmed by what he considered to be the irreversible effects of the Revolution of 1868 and its liberal policies that continued under the Restoration in 1875. In describing the Catholic religion and Church as the "vieja fe" [old faith] and "viejo edificio" [old edifice], he reiterates his belief in the institution's authority and intended endurance. Nevertheless, the idea of an ancient building also implies fragility and impending collapse, just as old age links to gradual physical decline. The institution of Catholicism is vulnerable in that its opponents, as Pereda puts it, secretly pursue its destruction. This erosive act, I suggest, sheds light on the deeper, invisible aspects of religion. While Böhl and Bécquer explicitly describe the visible edificial apparatus of the Church in their nostalgic writings, Pereda aims to foreground the multifaceted ties that interlace religious belief, which, for him, depends largely on stable communal identities. For Pereda, the foundations of the Church constitute an intangible, stabilizing structure in the microcosm of the family and social order.

Most studies on Pereda foreground his life as well as the influences of regionalism, traditionalism, and folklore on his writings.[2] Evidently, Pereda expressed his reactionary political stance through a constant, frank defense of the Catholic Church and satirical interpretation of suggested reforms.[3] In their analyses, Labanyi, Sierra, and López mention Pereda's traditionalist ideas, which center on the "patria chica" [local homeland]. I add that Pereda regards the local homeland as conducive to fostering a sense of human belonging and spiritual belief. He depicts religious faith and familial and communal union as increasingly vulnerable when confronted with Spain's modernizing trends. Sinclair claims that the traditionalist authors Böhl and Pereda focus entirely on imagination and faith in their writings, whereas Galdós's novels are "socially concerned."[4] In my ensuing analysis, I will contend that Pereda's texts are also concerned with social realities, especially the decrease in faith, which he attributed to the lack of religious formation. In contrast with Galdós's association of spiritual growth with ideological movement and openness to modern changes, Pereda indicates that the idea of progress leads to the deterioration and collapse of the nation's spirit.

I will analyze how Pereda's articles and novels respond to the religious question by centering on the disinheritance of tradition and what he perceives as the spiritual disorientation of the modern world. I argue that in his writings, Pereda defines the rejection of one's ancestral faith as a form of disinheritance. The evolving situations of the Church and religious belief in modern Spain are the subjects of several of his articles in the periodical *El Tío Cayetano*, which he co-founded in 1858–1859 and renewed in 1868–1869 during La Gloriosa. In

THE ABYSS AND THE MOUNT   131

these articles, to which I turn shortly, Pereda voices his concerns about Catholicism's declining influence in Spain after its long history as the nation's official religion. References to ecclesiastical expropriation and exclaustration are more explicit in Pereda's works than in those of Böhl, Bécquer, and Galdós, and he overtly denounces these processes by portraying the resultant destitution of the religious orders. The idea of disowning religion is symbolically equated with the dismissal of social traditions such as marriage among the nobility.

Pereda communicates these conservative ideas in his novel *Blasones y talegas* (1869), where he depicts, as I will develop, the attitudes of the nobility toward bourgeois ideology and its effect on their families. In this novel, Pereda considers that interclass marriage changes the social order, which he represents as divinely ordained for the good of all. I will further examine the consequences of liberal ideology in *De tal palo, tal astilla* (1880), in which Pereda problematizes skepticism, foregrounding the role of religious belief in the critical, intimate contexts of family and marriage. Finally, his novel *Sotileza* (1885) focuses on the idea of the isolated province as a sanctuary from modern values. In my reading of this text, I maintain that Pereda renders the clerical presence indispensable to the harmony and well-being of a tight-knit community. Moreover, he reiterates the idea of stabilizing the old order through the marriage of individuals of the same social standing and the aligning of professional pursuits with the industrial priorities of traditional life. In *Sotileza*, expropriation and exclaustration are inextricably connected, much like the experiences of displacement and destitution suffered by religious characters such as Fray Gabriel in Böhl's *La gaviota* and the unnamed dean of Orbajosa's cathedral in Galdós's *Doña Perfecta*. Thus, Pereda responds to the question of the role of Catholicism in Spanish society by reinforcing the intermediary role of the provincial clergy in matters spiritual and earthly.

Pereda's Views on Religion and the Spanish Nation

Pereda's principles, beliefs, and familial background influenced his literary works. He was born into a conservative landowning family in Polanco, Cantabria, and came from a long line of *hidalguía*, or "lower nobility."[5] Having initially pursued a military career, he returned to Cantabria to write and publish costumbrist novels. A defender of traditional values and orthodox Catholicism, Pereda frequently interacted with like-minded thinkers interested in neo-Catholicism and Carlism.[6] His companions encouraged him to enter the Carlist Party, with which he and several family members were affiliated.[7] James Swain asserts that Pereda was an absolutist and a committed Catholic who in his writings signaled that the ideal of liberty had the potential to result in anarchy.[8] Given his noble familial background, it is apparent that his conception of fixed social relations was aligned with the hierarchical feudal system.

Central to Pereda's conservative ideals was his conceptualization of the Catholic religion in Spain. Like Böhl and Bécquer, Pereda responds to the religious question by looking back to what traditionalists construed as the heightened religious character of the old order. According to López, Pereda's realist texts blend his reactionary views with a focus on the gradual decline of the transcendental character—the religious beliefs and concerns—of the old order. Furthermore, Pereda regards tradition as a collective system.[9] Hence, disunity leads to the collapse of tradition due to the latter's reliance on social structures for its survival. I allude to Pereda's traditionalism in this chapter title's doubly significant images of the mountain and the abyss. On a sociocultural level, these motifs signify hierarchical structures reflecting the conservative, traditionalist, and Catholic standpoints of the Carlists, whose strongholds were in the mountainous Cantabrian region.[10] In a spiritual sense, ascending to the summit is symbolically associated with religion—the active and outward pursuit of the divine—while descending into the abyss recalls the fall and the loss or absence of faith.

While traditionalists like Pereda highly esteemed religion, Krausists and revolutionaries espoused the principle of intellectual freedom, which set them against the neo-Catholics, who upheld religious unity.[11] Catholic conservatives equated this religious unity with Spanish greatness, commending its isolation and immunity from progressive, "dissolvent" ideas ranging from Protestantism to Voltairean atheism and anticlericalism. The founding of the Unión Católica in 1881 by the neo-Catholic politician Alejandro Pidal y Mon (1846–1913) aimed to defend Catholic control over education to prevent the dissemination of new ideologies, or the propagation of "error."[12] Neo-Catholics vehemently opposed the reforms of the 1868 Revolution, especially article 11 of the 1869 Constitution, which "disinherited Catholicism" by allowing the expression of other religious beliefs.[13] Consequently, many clerics refused to swear to the constitution. Pereda disapproved of the mitigating policies of the leader of the Partido Liberal Conservador, Antonio Cánovas del Castillo (1828–1897), who, in endeavoring to consolidate the Spanish nation in 1875, sought to provide a compromise between the neo-Catholic ideal of religious unity and the liberals' principle of religious freedom.[14] The processes of modernization and their concomitant aperture to new ideas was a hazardous strategy for Pereda, who, as López asserts, firmly believed that "no hay comunicación sin contaminación"[15] [there is no communication without contamination]. This distrust of influential, "contagious" modern ideologies is evident in Pereda's characterization of nobles, ardent Catholics, and young, forward-thinking professionals.

The main setting in Pereda's novels is Cantabria, portrayed as a pristine, traditional region largely shielded from the influences of the modern. His novels, as Labanyi argues, foreground the family as a unit that fuses the private and public and stress the family's dependence on private property transmitted through inheritance, not commercially, as a way of keeping both land and power within

THE ABYSS AND THE MOUNT

the family.[16] Relatedly, Sierra argues that Pereda's novels are minute glimpses into shifts in identity boundaries, which are caused by the rift between regional ways of life and the broader national agenda.[17] Applied to the larger context of Spain's disentailment laws, these interpretations signal the struggle of Spanish provinces to maintain their tangible and intangible heritage—their possessions, customs, and identities—in the face of government legislation and increasing modernization. The Spanish novel of the 1880s, as Stephanie Sieburth argues, was preoccupied with confronting modernity and its transformations.[18]

Pereda saw the 1868 Revolution as a source of political and religious disharmony. Reflecting this political disorder was the conflict between parties. The revolution's provisional government under Serrano as regent and the progressive General Juan Prim as prime minister struggled to establish a constitutional monarchy that would command the loyalty of the coalition of unionists, progressives, and democrats.[19] While Prim considered the Italian Amadeo I of Savoy fit for the Spanish monarchy, the disparate movements of Carlists, Alfonsists (supporters of Alfonso XII), and republicans were willing to unite against his foreign dynasty. Carlists, similarly divided, now comprised activists in favor of uprisings and legalists who believed that the September regime would collapse into self-imposed anarchy and thus precipitate the Bourbon Restoration so as to renew social order.[20]

Clashing approaches to tackle the religious question was a political factor in the 1868 Revolution, which, as Swain states, was closely linked to attempts at secularization.[21] Following the end of the last Carlist War in 1876, Cánovas set about consolidating the Spanish nation along conservative monarchical lines.[22] Sierra observes that in Pereda's representation of the tensions between regional identities and broader national agendas, such a political project superimposed a system of "sacred nation" rather than "sacred religion." Cánovas introduced a novel set of cultural values that combined history with divine providence to pave the way for Spain's progress.[23] I consider that this liberal concept of the "sacred nation" recalls Mendizábal's religious metaphor of "resurrección política"[24] [political resurrection]. Such a political interpretation of providence, however, was incongruent with the religious notion of divine order. Thus, Pereda's works aim to preserve traditional regional identities and religious customs as an antidote to the State's modernizing impetus.

EL TÍO CAYETANO: DISENTAILMENT AND THE CHURCH

Pereda's acerbic perspective on the issues arising from the decline of the Church's influence is apparent in his articles in *El Tío Cayetano*.[25] He articulates his point of view through the character of Don Cayetano de Noriega, the fictional figurehead of the eponymous periodical.[26] The second epoch of *El Tío Cayetano* was established after the 1868 Revolution and dealt with matters that Pereda considered imperative to the religious identity of the Spanish nation. In the first issue of this second series, published in Santander on November 9, 1868, Pereda points out the main concerns of the newspaper in the leading article, "¡Loado sea Dios!" [Praise be to God!]. The fictional author begins this article by addressing his "amado pueblo" [beloved people]. This affective salutation is significant in Pereda's discourse in *El Tío Cayetano* in that it forges a link between the Spanish nation and its Catholic community, given that Pereda depicts the practicing Catholics as a *pueblo* [people] in their own right. Such an association of faith and the *pueblo* goes back to the medieval era, when, as Francisco José Aranda Pérez notes, the Church and its consecrated individuals were named the "pueblo de Dios"[27] [people of God]. Thus, Pereda conveys that expropriation and exclaustration disjoin the two *pueblos*: the Spanish nation and its Catholic community. Furthermore, in nineteenth-century Europe, the concept of *pueblo* assumed new layers of signification. Inspired by German Romantic thought, particularly Herder's *Kultur des Volkes* and the Grimm Brothers' *Volkskunde*, *pueblo* was to define the social entity that represented "la entraña de una nación"[28] [the nucleus of a nation]. In political terms, by 1820, the beginning of the three-year period of the liberal constitution, the term *pueblo* had become synonymous with "the popular," as opposed to the upper classes, in the sense of "el común de ciudadanos que, sin gozar de particulares distinciones, rentas ni empleos, vive de sus oficios"[29] [the majority of citizens who, without enjoying particular distinctions, rents, or professions, live off their trades].

Like Galdós, Pereda also perceives the need for the resurrection of the Spanish nation, but through conservative means. In the following passage of "¡Loado sea Dios!," he makes known, through the fictional voice of Tío Cayetano, the constancy of his journalistic objective to endorse traditional Spanish society:

> Diez años há que me lancé por primera vez a la vida periodística buscando una región más digna de mis aspiraciones; una sociedad más adecuada a mis levantados instintos; un terreno donde fructificar pudieran en todo vigor y lozanía las semillas de un ingenio derrochado sin gloria ni prestigio; en figones y plazuelas.[30]

> [It has been ten years since I first leaped into life as a journalist looking for a region that would be more worthy of my aspirations; a society more suited to my elevated instincts; a land where the seeds of an ingenuity wasted without glory or prestige might flourish in complete vigor and vitality, in modest inns and small squares.]

Given that the second epoch of *El Tío Cayetano* was established in 1868, the year of the revolution, Pereda reinforces his aims to defend the "higher" matters of the old order, in keeping with his "levantados instintos" [elevated instincts]. He holds that in the decade leading up to the revolution, the Spanish nation had already been undergoing great change.

THE ABYSS AND THE MOUNT   135

For Pereda, Spain's ideological and political conflicts undermine the nation and its history. He deploys combative imagery to allude to the civil disputes and violence (wars and revolutions) and ideological clashes (secularism, anticlericalism, fanaticism) that have influenced Spanish society and contributed to its collapse:

> Era un estruendo como el de cien batallas y otros tantos huracanes; un fragor inusitado, indescriptible: no parecía sino que sobre el techo de mi tumba se desmoronaban los siglos a docenas y que entre los escombros se retorcían jadeantes y aterrados, como si sobrevivir al cataclismo procurasen, las páginas de la historia patria, los gloriosos hechos, las grandes miserias; la religión, el fanatismo, la luz, la oscuridad; las artes, la literatura, el derecho, la conquista, el valor, la fuerza, la hidalguía, la fe de los mártires . . . todo en confuso montón y estridente vocerío.[31]

> [It was a turmoil akin to a hundred battles and just as many hurricanes. A rare, indescribable clamor: it only seemed that countless centuries were collapsing over my tomb's roof and that, writhing among the debris, panting and terrified, as if they attempting to survive the cataclysm, there were the nation's history pages, glorious deeds, great miseries, religion, fanaticism, light, darkness, the arts, literature, the law, conquest, courage, strength, nobility, the faith of the martyrs . . . all in a confused heap and with strident shouts.]

Metaphorically melding natural and manmade disasters (battles and hurricanes), Pereda conjures an image of a deeply calamitous Spain characterized by uproar, disorder, and collapse. Such violent connotations refer also to the loss of an intangible heritage, which has plunged the Spanish people into a state of confusion as to their origins. The act of collapsing alludes to the neglect and destruction of an allegedly enduring past, extending to the personified pages of Spain's social, political, and spiritual history. Pereda presents Spain—both knowing and ignorant, glorious and miserable—as a great paradox. Such a catastrophic envisagement is largely Romantic, recalling Bécquer's language of ruins.

By conceptualizing Spain's past and its faith, feats, and failures as inscribed in the nation's history, Pereda reveals a deeply nostalgic longing for a return to an impossible imperial splendor conveyed in the term *conquista* [conquest].[32] Moreover, he represents the nation's history in epic terms, given that elements of the epic are valorized, hierarchical, and focused on memory. Pereda's amalgamation of historical events, national myths, religion, and abstract notions of dark and light sacralizes the Spanish nation, casting it as a lofty entity that defies simple description. A sacred realm of its own, the nation's history commands respect, exaltation, and lamentation. As Mikhail Bakhtin categorically states, "The tradition of the past is sacred."[33] In his depiction of national history as a "confuso montón" [confused heap] from which emanate "estridente vocerío" [strident shouts], Pereda highlights the conflicting visions of the past and future. The perceived dismantling of the past—the nation's origins—adds to Spain's disorientation.

Writing five weeks after the 1868 September Revolution, Pereda states in a later passage of "¡Loado sea Dios!" that the Spanish nation, now a "miserable superficie" [wretched surface], is conceivably devoid of any trace of its sacralized past and has lost much of its historically imperialistic character that was much celebrated by Spanish traditionalists. What has engineered this loss is, as Pereda illustrates, an exponential modernization and the permutations of civil and religious authority. He conveys the transformation of Spanish religious observance as follows:

> Donde dejé el silencio y la apatía, encuentro la ebullición y el entusiasmo; donde estaba la fuerza, la debilidad . . . el trono vacante y el pueblo soberano; los curas en la calle y la filosofía en el púlpito; las letras dormitando, y las masas en las urnas pidiendo a gritos escuelas y ateneos.[34]

> [Where I left silence and apathy, I found ebullience and enthusiasm; weakness where there was formerly strength . . . a vacant throne and a sovereign people; priests on the street and philosophy at the pulpit; the humanities dozing and the voting masses crying out for schools and athenaeums.]

Pereda's cautioning undertones demonstrate his belief that the revolution was the cause of a major spiritual disorientation within the Spanish nation. Weakness, the result of lost vigor, evokes the fading piety and decreasing value that religion holds for many in Spanish society. Pereda's reference to the priests on the street signals the physical and economic repercussions of exclaustration on Spanish religious. His telling phrase "la filosofía en el púlpito" [philosophy at the pulpit] sheds light on the transition from the Church's emphasis on theological dogma to a more generic, humanity-based mode of thinking embodied by the Krausist movement. Headed by "professors as priests," Krausism continued to appeal to progressive liberal sectors.[35] Whereas Galdós finds regeneration in the Krausist proposal to transform religion, Pereda only sees the Spanish nation's fall into a state of fatigue and atrophy. For him, what gives life to the nation is not a scientific and rationalist education, as Galdós would argue, but religious belief. Pereda depicts traditional education as in a state of repose, while the "masas en las urnas" [voting masses] represent the call for universal male suffrage.[36] Illuminating the break between the old feudal order and the new rationalist order, Pereda regards the medieval humanities as the soul's source of life, while he considers sociopolitical reforms such as universal male suffrage as the death of tradition and spirituality. As I develop below, such a spiritual disorientation characterizes the experiences of Fernando Peñarrubia, the young scientist and protagonist of *De tal palo, tal astilla.*

THE ABYSS AND THE MOUNT   137

In his conclusion to "¡Loado sea Dios!," Pereda communicates the traditionalists' vision of a predetermined, hierarchical society, maintaining that the leveling forces of social stratification are unnatural: "Era innegable que el gran *rasero* había pasado sobre la haz de España transformando, al parecer, hasta la naturaleza de sus hijos, y no podía ser otra la causa del estrépito que me volvió a la vida en la mansión de los muertos"[37] [It was undeniable that the great *strickle* had passed over the face of Spain, apparently transforming the very nature of her children. There could be no other reason for the loud racket that revived me in the mansion of the dead]. The transformation of Spain's future populations through political and religious reforms involves not a silent, peaceful change but an aggressive "racket"—a flurry of multivalent national visions and imposing State policies. The final passage returns to the feudal metaphor of the medieval joust, with which Don Cayetano de Noriega rallies support for the defense of faith and tradition:

> Y sin más preámbulos ni bordaduras, sobre el terreno ya en que ha de darse la gran batalla, acampo en el que me pertenece; y, como los antiguos paladines, con la fe en la justicia de mi causa que es la tuya, y la esperanza en la ayuda de Dios, sin contar los enemigos avanzo, y, en ley de urbanidad, los saludo y entro en liza.[38]

> [Without further preamble or ornamentation, on the terrain where the great battle must take place, I camp on what belongs to me. And like the paladins of old, with faith in the justice of my cause, which is yours, and hope in God's help, without counting my enemies I advance, and in accordance with the laws of courtesy, I greet them and enter the fight.]

Pereda continues to defend religious tradition in two key articles on exclaustration in *El Tío Cayetano*, "La Iglesia libre" [The free Church, December 1868] and "Año nuevo" [New year, January 1869], which address the Church and Catholicism in the new Spain. In "La Iglesia libre," Pereda categorically declares that the State's enforced policies of disentailment and its constitutional belief in liberty are hypocritical. He maintains that while the State is free, the Church, as a result of anticlerical sentiment, is not. Revolutionary vertigo, another marker of the disorientation caused by social and political changes, characterizes the divide among liberals, whose only common stance is their antagonism toward the Church:

> El vértigo revolucionario ha llevado a muchos a pedir LA IGLESIA LIBRE EN EL ESTADO LIBRE. Cada vez que EL TÍO CAYETANO oye ese grito hipócrita, se le pone delante la desamortización de los bienes eclesiásticos. . . . Aunque revelan un antagonismo feroz, hay sin embargo un lazo para unirlas. Ese lazo es el odio a la iglesia. La iglesia es siempre el caballo de batalla de

algunos liberales. ¿Está la iglesia rica, tiene hermosas fincas, posee magnífi-
cos solares? Pues la iglesia no debe poseer nada, no debe tener libertad para
poseer nada. Vengan todos sus bienes. Ahí va la desamortización eclesiástica.
El estado se encarga de dar una dotación para el clero y para el culto. La iglesia
no debe ser libre. Necesita la tutela del Estado. . . . ¿Por qué el Estado ha de
sostenerla? El que quiera culto que le pague. El que quiera clero que le pague.
El Estado no necesita del uno ni del otro. La Nación, como ente colectivo, tampoco. Se declara la iglesia libre en el Estado libre. Es decir, se deja a la iglesia
abandonada a sí misma para que recoja una limosna de puerta en puerta.[39]

[Revolutionary vertigo has led many to ask for a FREE CHURCH IN A FREE
STATE. Every time UNCLE CAYETANO hears this hypocritical cry, he recalls
the disentailment of ecclesiastical goods. . . . Although these persons demonstrate a fierce antagonism, there is, however, one bond that unites them. This
bond is hatred toward the Church. The Church is always the battle horse for
some liberals. Is the Church wealthy? Does it own beautiful lands and magnificent plots? Well, the Church should possess nothing. It should not be free
to possess anything. Let it bring all its assets. This is ecclesiastical disentailment. The State will arrange to provide for clergy and liturgy. The Church must
not be free. It needs the State's guardianship. . . . Why should the State sustain her? He who desires worship must pay for it. He who desires clergy must
pay for them. The State needs neither. Neither does the nation, as a collective
entity. They declare a free Church in a free State. That is, they abandon the
Church so that it can collect alms from door to door.]

Here Pereda highlights the inherent clashes in interests between the modern
Spanish State and the Church. In his view, since the Church is the only entity
that values religious faith and practice, the State should keep out of its affairs and
assets:

Y ni el Estado tendrá nada que ver en ese caso con la iglesia, ni la iglesia con el
Estado. ¿Es esto lo que ustedes quieren, señores liberalísimos? Es decir que si
el Estado decretara: *fuera estos conventos, derríbense esas Iglesias, vengan esos
bienes*, la iglesia podría contestar: «señor Estado, métase usted en sus oficinas,
en sus edificios, en su dinero» y déjeme libre a campar por mis respetos; que
tan ama soy yo de lo mío como usted es amo de lo suyo.[40]

[And in this case, the State will have nothing to do with the Church and vice
versa. Is that what you want, most liberal gentlemen? That is, if the State decrees,
"Out with the convents, destroy those churches, bring those assets," the Church
can reply, "Mr. State, stick to your offices, buildings, and money" and let me
do as I please, because I am just as much the master of my own assets as you
are of yours.]

THE ABYSS AND THE MOUNT   139

By emphasizing the impact of disentailment on the Church, Pereda refutes the notion of the Church's liberty within a so-called free liberal State.[41] *El Tío Cayetano* disagrees with the illusory notion of the Church's freedom by pointing out that it is subject to the State:

> ¡La *libertad* de la iglesia . . . !! EL TÍO CAYETANO va a arrancar la máscara de ese grito. Se quiere que el Estado no sostenga ni el culto ni el clero; pero que pueda el ministro de Gracia y Justicia quitar cuantos conventos le dé la gana, y derribar cuantos templos quiera; y que la desamortización arrebate además a la iglesia sus bienes. *No debe, pues, gritarse: LA IGLESIA LIBRE EN EL ESTADO LIBRE, sino la iglesia esclava y pobre en el Estado omnipotente.*[42]
>
> [The Church's *freedom* . . . !! UNCLE CAYETANO will rip off the mask from this cry. They do not want the State to support worship or clergy, yet they want the minister of justice to confiscate as many convents as he wishes and destroy as many temples as he desires and for disentailment to snatch the Church's assets. *One should, therefore, shout not "A FREE CHURCH IN A FREE STATE" but rather "An enslaved and impoverished Church in an omnipotent State."*]

Pereda claims that the deified "Estado omnipotente" [omnipotent State] has trivialized the Church. The latter can no longer be considered an authority despite the historical nomination of Catholicism as the official state religion in the 1812 Constitution.

Fueling Pereda's distrust of the government are policies that continue to heavily impact the Church.[43] In "Año nuevo" [New year], Pereda criticizes anticlerical legislation effected by politicians such as Antonio Romero Ortiz (1822–1884), minister of justice in the provisional government from 1868 to 1869.[44] Pressured by the revolutionary juntas, the provisional government enforced decrees such as the suppression of the Jesuit order on October 12, 1868, and the forbidding of religious communities to possess and acquire property.[45] In Tío Cayetano's words, "Romero Ortiz despabila una lámpara sepulcral, después de no haber apagado las de los templos católicos, y la apaga también"[46] [Romero Ortiz fans a sepulchral lamp, after not extinguishing those of Catholic temples, and puts that one out too]. Here Pereda deploys the symbols of the sepulchre and temple, both icons reminiscent of Bécquer's imagery, to illustrate the threat of Romero Ortiz's laws for ecclesial buildings. Thus, Pereda reiterates that anticlerical legislation has repercussions for Spain's spiritual landscape. Extending the metaphors of light and darkness, Pereda asserts that Spain has been plunged into the darkness of what he considers to be religious persecution:

> España, pues, se ve a oscuras al comienzo de una senda llena de precipicios y de obstáculos, sin un solo punto claro que le sirva de norte, sin una mano que la guie, sin una voz que la aconseje. Y no puede retroceder, ni siquiera detenerse;

porque el tiempo y los sucesos la obligan a caminar. Por eso reniega de sus hombres, se enjuga una lágrima, tiendes [*sic*] las manos al vacío, y nada.[47]

[Thus, Spain finds itself in the dark before a path strewn with precipices and obstacles, without a single light to serve as true north, without a guiding hand or counseling voice. And it cannot retreat or even stop because time and events oblige it to move. Thus, it disowns its men, dries a tear, stretches out its hands to the abyss, and finds nothing.]

These images of obscurity and the abyss evoke a sense of loss, absence, and lack of direction. Representing the Church as a leader, a light to guide Spain out of its state of darkness and confusion, Pereda aligns the removal of religious spaces and communities with the displacement of the Spanish people from their spiritual journey.

Pereda's fixation on the *pueblo* is also evident in his regionalist novels, which explore the perceived negative challenges that materialism and the search for progress pose for the province and its smaller, tight-knit, traditionalist communities. Regionalism, Eric Storm maintains, was a response to the erosion of traditional structures of provincial society affected by the process of socioeconomic modernization.[48] I add that Pereda focuses on the immediate homeland precisely because it is more intimate and bounded compared with not just the modern city but also the larger, diverse, and evolving Spanish nation and its governments.

The Significance of Family and Tradition
in *Blasones y talegas*

Like Böhl and Galdós, Pereda draws on the symbolism of marriage to problematize the divide between tradition and modernity. His novel, *Blasones y talegas*, set in Santander, concerns the union between Verónica, the daughter of aristocrat Don Robustiano Tres-Solares y de la Calzada, and Antón, the son of a newly wealthy Toribio Mazorcas (also called Zancajos), who has made his fortune selling olive oil in Andalusia. Knowing that Toribio is only interested in the marriage for upward social mobility, Don Robustiano laments the imminent loss of his family's nobility and honor when the marriage between Verónica and Antón takes place. In the end, Don Robustiano voices his resentment of their interclass marriage in a rhetorical question to his daughter: "¿Qué has hecho del lustre de tu familia?"[49] [What have you done to your family's prestige?]. His disapproval of their marital union mirrors the traditionalist defense of nobility and the family, both building blocks of the old social order and important social units for conservative sectors.

From Pereda's perspective, materialism and secularization threaten the conservatives' perceived safeguards of religion, tradition, and familial heritage.

THE ABYSS AND THE MOUNT   141

He expresses these ideas through Don Robustiano's speech to his companions, which elucidates the philosophical, economic, and political changes that have assailed their tranquil coastal town:

> "Las revoluciones, el materialismo grosero de la época," aboliendo los derechos y las preeminencias que llenaron las escarcelas y los graneros de sus mayores . . . barrieron hasta el polvo de sus pergaminos . . . en una palabra, don Robustiano tenía pura la sangre de su linaje, pan para nutrirse y casa blasonada que le prestaba abrigo en el invierno y sombra en el verano. Es decir, tenía cuanto un pobre de su alcurnia, de sus ideas y de su carácter podía apetecer en los tiempos que corrían, y en ello fundaba su mayor vanidad.[50]

> ["The revolutions, the crude materialism of the age," abolishing all the rights and privileges that filled the bags and barns of his forebears . . . swept away even the dust from his titles of nobility . . . in a word, Robustiano had the pure blood of his lineage, bread to nourish himself, and an emblazoned house that sheltered him in winter and gave him shade in summer. That is, he had as much as a poor man of his ancestry, ideas, and character could fancy in current times, and on that he founded his greatest vanity.]

This passage demonstrates the waning influence of the nobility. As Labanyi notes, in the early stages of nineteenth-century liberalism, the imposition of central control was also perceived as a way of curtailing the influence of the traditional rural oligarchy. In 1833, local government reform divided Spain into forty-nine provinces to be ruled by centrally appointed provincial governors, thus abolishing traditional communities and historical kingdoms.[51] Through Don Robustiano's words, Pereda communicates the nobility's view that established social hierarchies are threatened by what they perceive as vulgar materialism. As an oligarchy, these nobles are determined to safeguard their past privileges. They equate the continuity of their elevated class with the maintenance of the old order and its values.

The experiences of Pereda's hidalgo characters reflect the changing relevance of the nobility in a social reality transformed by industrialization and the rise of the liberal bourgeoisie. As Carr explains, since the late eighteenth century, the "useful" bourgeois class of Spain had been set against the "useless" noble as a paradigm of social virtue.[52] Conversing with another hidalgo, Don Ramiro Seis-Regatos y Dos Portillas de la Vega, Don Robustiano denounces the characteristics of the new age, explaining that they do not feel at home in the modern world:

> Es a todas luces evidente que una estrecha y cordial inteligencia entre todos los nobles de cada país, nos hubiera dado una fuerza considerable. Lo vulgar, lo nuevo, lo ilustrado, como ahora se dice, nos desecha, nos acoquina: agrupémonos mutuamente; y de este modo, si no logramos vencer al torrente

desbordado, podremos, separándonos de él, vivir en un remanso aparte con nuestros recuerdos, nuestras ideas y nuestros mutuos auxilios.[53]

[It is clearly evident that a close and friendly understanding among all nobles of each country would have strengthened us considerably. The vulgar, the new, the enlightened, as it is called now, casts us aside, intimidates us. Let us come together mutually, and in this way, if we do not succeed in defeating the overflowing torrent, we will, by separating ourselves from it, live in a separate refuge with our memories, ideas, and mutual aid.]

Don Robustiano emphasizes that the forces of modernization, secularism, and commercialism are disastrous to the old order. As this metaphorical torrent is uncontrollable, it necessitates restraint, boundaries, and most importantly, unity, which Pereda portrays as dependent on a social cohesion founded on religious accord, a core principle for neo-Catholic traditionalists.

Through the nobles' discussion, Pereda foregrounds the dangers of disunity. Don Ramiro claims that the nobles' formerly fraternal union, which distinguishes them from the rest of Spanish society, has been debilitated by discord, which has been "entre las familias de calidad el pecado más común"[54] [the most common sin among distinguished families]. Don Robustiano perceives this sin differently, applying it instead to the "unholy" transformation of modern Spanish society, which now values the secular over past glories:

Pecado sublime, pecado magnífico, señor don Ramiro, en los tiempos de nuestra grandeza; porque teniéndonos en perpetua rivalidad, fructificaba en grandes empresas que redundaban en honra de la clase y lustre de la nación. Pero hoy es distinto: hoy somos pocos, estamos sin fuerzas y nos aqueja un infortunio común. Y pues no podemos vivir como señores, debemos tratar de no morir como esclavos.[55]

[A sublime sin, a magnificent sin, Don Ramiro, in our glory days, because by keeping alive our ongoing rivalry, it flourished in great undertakings that honored our class and brought prestige to our nation. But now it is different: we are few, we lack strength, and a common misfortune besets us. And as we cannot live like lords, we must try not to die like slaves.]

Through Don Robustiano's expressed fear of being declassed, Pereda conveys the experience of being displaced from a "home" dependent on social class, position, and family. In contrast, Don Ramiro disagrees with Don Robustiano's statement that the time of the nobles has come and gone. As a father of four daughters, Don Ramiro is concerned for their futures and is therefore not anxious about the social class into which his daughters will marry as long as these unions cover their necessities and ensure their survival. He perceives the rejection of class intermarriage as highly impractical in modern society, especially due to the abolition of the nobility's privileges.

THE ABYSS AND THE MOUNT

The upper class's rejection of the increasing strength of the new middle class is manifest in Don Robustiano's opposition to Toribio Mazurcas. Consequently, he calls Toribio several derogatory names to distinguish him from his own hidalgo class. Referring to the sectors of society behind the French Revolution, Don Robustiano defines Toribio as a rebellious, antireligious individual: "sanculote" [sansculotte], "francmasón" [Freemason], "Robespierre," and "Voltaire."[56] Alluding to biblical antagonists, Don Robustiano describes Toribio as evil, labeling him "Iscariote" [Iscariot] and "hijo de Lucifer"[57] [son of Lucifer]. Such derisive terms not only highlight interclass tensions but also demonstrate that Don Robustiano, like other members of the nobility, perceives his lineage as sacred and therefore worthy of protection. To transgress the limits of one's class defies the divinely ordained social order, an act that Don Robustiano ultimately considers blasphemous. His character therefore denotes the traditionalist and Carlist interlacing of earthly affairs with divine beliefs.

While Don Robustiano represents the old world, Toribio embodies the new. He defends his social class, stating that it was through hard work and emigration to Andalusia that he was able to achieve commercial success. Likening Don Toribio's noble status to a collapsing, ancient shield, he asserts that the end of the old order is inevitable. From Toribio's point of view, the nobility must now depend on the rising middle class:

> Que nosotros, no los impíos que usted cree (y yo se lo perdono), ni los bandoleros, ni los jacobinos, sino los hombres de bien, creyentes y laboriosos, que a fuerza de trabajo hemos hecho una fortuna; que nosotros, repito, somos los llamados a afirmar estos escudos que se caen de rancios, y estos techos minados por la polilla.[58]

> [We, not those impious that you think of (and I forgive you for it), nor the bandits, the Jacobins, but rather men of goodwill, believing and hardworking, who have made their fortune through hard graft. We, I repeat, are the ones called to secure these musty shields and those moth-eaten roofs that are crumbling away from age.]

Toribio's pursuit of upward social mobility is a sign of modern times, a break from the static old order and its perceived divinely appointed social standings. In this approach to work, he stands for modern enterprise, while Don Robustiano, "el fanático solariego"[59] [the fanatic of noble ancestry], adheres to the bygone era of titles and privileges despite his pending impoverishment. Hence, the distinction between both fathers lies in what they perceive as systems of worth. Don Robustiano values what is inherited, whereas Toribio exalts what is earned. Verónica and Antón's eventual marriage challenges the boundaries imposed by societal and familial expectations, thus creating an abyss between past and present. While Don Robustiano sees the change in the social hierarchy as a departure from the old order, Toribio is aware that the new order has come to stay.

DE TAL PALO, TAL ASTILLA: FAITH AS INHERITANCE AND THE BURDENS OF (DIS)BELIEF

Pereda presents similar traditionalist attitudes to religion and family in *De tal palo, tal astilla* (1880). The text concerns two young lovers whose parental expectations and spiritual upbringing ultimately influence their decision to marry. Thus, as suggested in the novel's title, *De tal palo, tal astilla* deals with the issues that arise from the passing down and inheriting of familial beliefs, values, and attitudes. Fernando Peñarrubia resides in the town of Perojales, an area physically and symbolically separated by a gorge from the hometown of his lover, Águeda Quincevillas, who lives in the mountain village of Valdecines. Despite their love, both clash due to their familial obligations and religious beliefs. Águeda's mother, Doña Marta Rubárcena, who is extremely devout and has raised her daughter in the Catholic faith, disapproves of their union, given that the young scientist Fernando is the son of the renowned nonreligious doctor Peñarrubia (informally named Pateta). After her mother's death from illness, Águeda rejects Fernando for his lack of religious belief, while Don Sotero, who had forged a friendship with Doña Marta during her illness, attempts to arrange a marriage between his illegitimate son, Bastián, and Águeda. Anguished, Fernando confides to his father his own doubts concerning religion and commits suicide in the end. Águeda is devastated, while a remorseful Pateta invokes God.

While scholars have generally considered Pereda's *De tal palo, tal astilla* to be a counterargument to Galdós's *Gloria*, Daniel Brown argues that Pereda was also indirectly engaging with French naturalism, spearheaded by the nineteenth-century author Émile Zola. Naturalism embraced the theory of determinism, which believed that human behavior and decisions were caused by preexisting conditions and actions. The novel's title itself, Brown argues, is a traditional Spanish adage purportedly validating the theory of hereditary determinism. This notion is evident in Pereda's sympathetic portrayal of Fernando's existential anguish and subsequent suicide, both of which are depicted as consequences of Pateta's refusal to instruct Fernando in the Catholic religion.[60] The narrative voice considers Pateta's refusal to commit to Fernando's spiritual formation to be a negligent act. Just as Sieburth asserts that Galdós deploys familial issues of defective and inadequate parenting and the forgetting of one's origins to reflect Spain's national crisis, I argue that the same can be said of Pereda's narratives.[61] Pateta's regret reflects Pereda's view of the disinheritance of religion as irremediable.

Like Böhl, Pereda focuses on the family as the crucial, original source of faith and personal development. Halbwachs asserts that the family fashions one's understanding of the world: "Our kin communicate to us our first notion about people and things."[62] For her part, Astrid Erll suggests that families and religious groups function as "mnemonic intersections" that can mediate, transmit, and develop cultural traditions.[63] As my chapter's title suggests, Pereda's novels situate

THE ABYSS AND THE MOUNT 145

characters within the physical, but always ideological, locales of the abyss and the mountain. For López, the former's relevance to Pereda relates to the ideological novel, which "surgió del vacío—de ideas, de proyectos, de esperanza—que siguió al fracaso de la revolución liberal"[64] [emerged from the abyss—of ideas, projects, hope—that followed the failure of the liberal revolution]. The image of the abyss denotes the unknown and the absence and loss of material and spiritual substance (faith and religious fervor). Conversely, as seen with regard to Bécquer's *Cartas*, the mountain signifies a place of authority, emblematic of the prophets.[65] Furthermore, in Pereda's works, it evokes the physically and ideologically remote villages of the Cantabrian landscape, signifying these communities' laborious cultivation of religious practices and traditions. *De tal palo, tal astilla* is a novel about faith and doubt and the influence of familial obligations on these spiritual conflicts. Central to discussions between Fernando and Pateta are notions concerning faith and religious heritage, while doubt is an essential aspect of Fernando's personal story. Joaquín Casalduero asserts that through the character of Fernando, Pereda endeavors to "plantear un problema entre el conocimiento racional y el revelado"[66] [consider a problem between rational and revealed knowledge]. By problematizing the gap between revelation and rationalism in Fernando, Pereda highlights the difficulty of separating religious belief from modern thought. The religious and clerical ambience, Casalduero argues, is impossible to ignore.[67]

For Fernando, the Catholic faith is a difficult set of beliefs to process due to the prevailing influences of positivism, anticlericalism, and materialism. The negative portrayals of dogmas related to purgatory and the confessional and the antagonistic depictions of decadent friars and ambitious Jesuits mold Fernando's interpretation of the religion that Águeda professes and loves:

> La fe católica, según él la había estudiado y combatido, le ofrecía el siguiente cuadro: Una nube de curas ignorantes y egoístas socavando la sociedad por el agujero del confesonario y con la fábula del purgatorio. Otra nube de frailes groseros, holgazanes, comilones y lascivos. . . . Otra nube de jesuitas ambiciosos, intrigantes y envenenadores, corruptores de las consciencias y opresores de los Estados; una gusanera de monjas rebelándose contra las leyes de la naturaleza, y cantando con voz gangosa salmos en latín contrahecho . . . el "catolicismo, conjunto de estas repugnantes indignidades, había sido negra mazmorra del entendimiento humano en los tres últimos siglos, y aún legítimo, desvirtuando así los generosos alientos del espíritu democrático del 'Filósofo' de Judea."[68]

> [The Catholic faith, according to what he had studied and challenged, painted him the following picture: a swarm of ignorant, selfish priests undermining society through the hole in the confessional and the fable of purgatory. Another

swarm of rude, idle, gluttonous, and lecherous men.... Another swarm of ambitious, scheming, and poisonous Jesuits, corruptors of consciences and oppressors of States; a maggot nest of nuns rebelling against natural laws and singing psalms in a deformed Latin ... "Catholicism, an amalgamation of these abhorrent disgraces, had been the dark dungeon of human understanding over the last three centuries and, although still legitimate, continued to distort the generous inspirations of the democratic spirit of the 'Philosopher' of Judea."]

Unable to understand Catholic religious vocations, Fernando regards the celibacy of nuns and their life of prayer as unnatural. He concludes that the Catholic religious have long exhibited traits of ignorance, egoism, and avarice. Consequently, Fernando's thinking centers on the figure of Jesus as the "Philosopher" of Judea, whom he cites, claiming that rather than being the divine head of the Catholic Church as an institution, Christ is a model of democracy and rationalism. I consider that this understanding of Christ renders him a quasi-religious benchmark of Krausist principles. Through Fernando's ideas, Pereda illuminates the Krausists' liberal position on religion.

However, Fernando's stereotype of the avaricious clergyman is ultimately belied by the house of the parish priest of Valdecines, whom he consults. The priest's open door reflects his openness to parishioners, indicating his faithful adherence to ongoing pastoral obligations:

La casita del cura de Valdecines, próxima a la iglesia, no se cerraba en todo el día; y como la escalera arrancaba de la misma puerta que daba a la calle, Fernando subió sus peldaños sin necesidad de preguntar a nadie por el camino que buscaba. En aquella pequeñez no había ni cabía más que uno, y no era posible el extravío.[69]

[The cottage of the priest of Valdecines, next to the church, was never closed during the day, and as the stairwell started from the same door facing the street, Fernando climbed its steps without needing to ask anyone where to go. Its smallness could only fit one person, and getting lost was impossible.]

The meager possessions of this "pobre cura de aldea"[70] [poor village priest] indicate that he does not grant importance to material comfort. Such a description also recalls the ascetic focus of medieval Christian monasticism, which entailed the voluntary renunciation of the secular world.[71] Also, since Pateta has played no role in his son's spiritual development, Fernando looks to the priest, a spiritual father, for help: "Pero es, señor cura, que en mi mente no cabe ... ¡ni la idea de Dios!"[72] [But the thing is, Reverend, my mind cannot comprehend ... even the idea of God!].

Fernando's genuine anxiety and despair are the result of Pateta's flaws, which in turn stem from his own upbringing. The relationship between Pateta's parents

THE ABYSS AND THE MOUNT   147

suggests that, for Pereda, a child's spiritual growth rests on the parents' joint effort. While Pateta's mother practiced the Catholic faith with devotion, she still held little influence over her son due to her lack of education and indolence, which was exacerbated by her husband's overbearing vanity. Although his mother took Pateta to church services and gave him sacramentals, she paid no heed to what he was learning from other servants living in the household.[73]

Consequently, Pateta received an expensive scientific education, "libre de ... *la tiranía del dogma*"[74] [free from ... *the tyranny of dogma*], and enjoyed a luxurious existence in Madrid. Although he raised Fernando to be "robusto y fuerte"[75] [robust and strong], Pateta did not teach him about God. The narrative voice depicts the neglect that Pateta displays toward Fernando's spiritual upbringing. Unlike his own devout mother, Pateta denies his son a knowledge of his faith and family:

> El ejemplo del padre forma el modo de ser de los hijos. . . . En el doctor germinaban de vez en cuando, entre los recuerdos de su infancia, las enseñanzas de su madre; en la memoria de Fernando no había semillas de esa especie: nada podía brotar allí en daño de otro cultivo: lo que en el padre fueron dudas, en el hijo, negaciones terminantes.[76]

> [The father's example forms the children's mode of being. . . . Among the doctor's childhood memories, his mother's teachings would surface from time to time. In Fernando's memory, there were no seeds of that kind. Nothing could sprout there to the detriment of another cultivation: what for the father were doubts were, for the son, categorical negations.]

Here Pereda's recourse to metaphors of cultivation denotes religious education, which he shows to be the principal source of spiritual faith. Tradition, which Pereda regards as a collective system, necessitates a continuity dependent on sustaining religious traditions, beliefs, and values.

When Fernando visits the parish priest of Valdecines, he confides in him that he never had a religious education. The priest tells him that an acknowledgment of God is the first step toward knowing the truth. In his response to Fernando, the priest again utilizes metaphors of cultivation:

> Hoy me presenta usted un terreno bravío y escabroso, y se trata de ponerle en buenas condiciones de cultivo. Hay que cortar las malezas; extirpar una a una sus raíces; remover el suelo hasta lo más profundo; pasarle . . . por un tamiz para que en él no quede ni un germen de sus impurezas; darle después condiciones vegetales, y por último, depositar en él buena semilla.[77]

> [Today you present a coarse and rugged terrain, which one tries to prepare well for cultivation. One must cut the weeds, remove their roots one by one,

turn over the soil to its very depths, pass it . . . through a sieve so no seed of impurity remains, give it good vegetable conditions, and finally, plant the good seed in it.]

Sowing seeds and ideas is an ancient trope; in classical literature, the female body denoted safety and cultivated earth.[78] The maternal symbolism that underlies the imagery of sowing, reaping, and raising relates to the perception of mothers as fertile ground for giving birth to and raising children. Not only does the mother reproduce biological offspring; she is also responsible for the continuation of traditions and religious observance, a concept dominant in late nineteenth-century liberal ideology. I assert that given the maternal role in sowing and reaping this cultural heritage, ideas and principles also become the mother's symbolic offspring. Brown specifies that the metaphoric and even linguistic feminization of *la tierra* [earth] and *la naturaleza* [nature] in Castilian reinforces this symbolic dissemination of beliefs and customs.[79] The images of land, cultivation, birth, and motherhood intersect in the characters of Pateta's mother and Doña Marta, who raises Águeda to love her faith and "suelo nativo"[80] [native soil]. Foreign thought is therefore meaningless to the "rooted" Spaniards, who have cultivated their own sense of identity and worldview.[81] The ideologically "foreign" Fernando, much like Galdós's Pepe Rey and Daniel, can hardly expect to be welcome either in Doña Marta's family or in the version of the Spanish nation that it represents.

Like Galdós's Daniel and Gloria, Fernando and Águeda discuss their incongruous religious beliefs and ideas, which make the prospect of their marriage problematic:

> Ya he dicho que Fernando fiaba mucho en la fuerza de sus convicciones filosóficas para desvanecer los reparos de Águeda. Que le dejaran hablar, discutirlos, y el triunfo era infalible. Porque, en su concepto, las ideas religiosas de aquella no tenían base ni arraigo; eran, más bien, reflejo de las ideas de su madre, que quizá tampoco las tuvo propias acerca de ese punto.[82]

> [I have already said that Fernando trusted the strength of his philosophical convictions to dispel Águeda's objections. Let him talk, argue them, and triumph was inevitable. Because in his view, Águeda's religious ideas had no base or support. Rather, they reflected her mother's ideas, who perhaps had none of her own on this point either.]

Implying that Águeda's mother has influenced her religious background, Fernando concludes that Águeda cannot think independently. Similarly, Fernando's personal background is also the result of his father's example and influence: "El padre construyó la senda; el hijo no tuvo más que caminar sobre ella. Hallábase en aquel terreno como el pez en el agua, convencido de que en otro elemento

THE ABYSS AND THE MOUNT   149

no se podía vivir"[83] [The father forged the path; the son only needed to walk it. He found himself in that terrain like a fish in water, convinced that there was no other way to live]. Pateta has established a specific terrain for Fernando, delimited by his rationalism, which impedes his son from engaging with Águeda on a metaphysical level.

It is Fernando's absence of belief that causes Águeda to refuse his hand, given that she prioritizes her religion in her plans for a future family. In the following passage, Fernando questions Águeda on the relation of love to her Catholic dogmatism:

> —Y aún conociéndote que la religión que profesas sea la mejor de todas las conocidas, la verdadera y única, como tú dices, ¿qué tiene que ver el amor con eso?
> —¿A qué llamas «eso»?
> —A tu religión, con su carácter divino y sus dogmas indiscutibles.
> —¡Qué tiene que ver el amor con esa religión! ¿Y qué es un hombre sin ella? ¿Qué es un hogar sin esa luz y sin ese calor? . . . Yo me imagino una familia que jamás invoca el nombre de Dios. ¡Qué cárcel! . . . , ¡qué lobreguez! Aquellos dolores sin consuelo; aquellas contrariedades sin la resignación cristiana; aquellos hijos creciendo sin mirar jamás hacia arriba.[84]

> ["And even were I to admit to you that the religion you profess is the best of all known religions, the true and only one, as you say, what does love have to do with all this?"
> "What do you mean by 'all this'?"
> "Your religion, with its divine character and indisputable dogmas."
> "What does love have to do with that religion! And what is man without it? What is a home without that light and warmth? . . . I can only imagine a family that never invokes God's name. What a prison! . . . What darkness! Those sorrows without consolation; those difficulties without Christian resignation; those children growing up without ever looking upward."]

Águeda values above all else her Catholic religion, regarding it as the adhesive that binds families together. Most significantly, she recognizes it as essential to the home, constructed as a place of refuge. Illustrating their home as a place of Christian resignation, Pereda demonstrates that it is in this domestic site that religious devotion is practiced and enhanced.

Águeda and her sister Pilar's home is therefore portrayed in terms of its "holgura, comodidad, abundancia, buen gusto y primores de limpieza" [space, comfort, abundance, good taste, and exquisite cleanliness], qualities that echo their familial unity and their parents' "feliz matrimonio"[85] [happy marriage]. Conversely, the home of the Peñarrubia family in Perojales is quite different. Pateta and Fernando do not fit in with their neighbors due to their disdain

150   MAKING MODERN SPAIN

for the Catholic faith. Fernando's house is described as old and surrounded by vegetation. It is implied that the Peñarrubias acquired church goods as private buyers of disentailed ecclesiastical property, given that their house features "un balcón de *púlpito*"[86] [a balcony like a *pulpit*]. This detail illuminates the "silent" fate of church property passing into private ownership through disentailment.

For Águeda, the home is also a place of religious upbringing akin to Rosario's dwelling in Galdós's *Perfecta*. From Doña Marta, Águeda learns about Catholicism, and its moral and religious teachings inform the foundations of her worldview: "La educación de Águeda . . . se fundó sobre los cimientos de la ley de Dios, sin salvedades acomodaticias ni comentarios sutiles. . . . Con la fuerza del convencimiento racional, arraigó sus creencias en el corazón. Así es la fe de los mártires; heroica, invencible, pero risueña y atractiva"[87] [Águeda's education . . . was built on the foundation of God's law, without flexible conditions or subtle comments. . . . With the force of rational conviction, her beliefs were ingrained in her heart. Such is the faith of the martyrs: heroic, invincible, but cheerful and inviting].

Doña Marta's instruction of Águeda in the faith is a form of cultivation. The narrator states that Águeda learned to apply ideas about the world to reality within "las extensas páginas del hermoso suelo patrio"[88] [the detailed pages of its beautiful native soil]; that is, the province and its traditionalist way of life, which produce sentiments of pride and belonging. Moreover, Valis notes that the mid-nineteenth century in Spain saw the Catholic Revival, with its increase in charitable practices and devotionalism. Such a movement grounded in religious fervor resurfaced in the 1870s and 1880s, coinciding with the last Carlist War and the renewed debate on the nature of Church and State.[89]

Foregrounding her religious devotion, Águeda adopts her late mother's disapproving attitude toward the disbelieving Fernando. When Fernando visits Águeda following her mother's death, she turns him away. Both individuals begin to acknowledge the vast ideological chasm between them:

> —Esto lo sabes tú muy bien, Águeda, o no me decías la verdad cuando el abismo no se había abierto aún entre nosotros. Pues bien, los abismos, o se llenan o se salvan, según sea su profundidad. Yo no conozco todavía la del nuestro; para conocerla hubiera vuelto aquí.
> —Te dije que este abismo no es de los que se salvan con puentes, y que es muy profundo para colmado.[90]

> ["You know this very well, Águeda, or you did not tell me the truth when the void had not yet opened up between us. Well, voids are either filled or survived depending on their depth. I still do not know how deep ours is; to find out, I should have come back."]

THE ABYSS AND THE MOUNT

"I told you this void is not like those that can be crossed with bridges and that it is too deep to be filled."]

Most significant in their exchange is the dual interpretation of religious vocabulary, which impedes their ability to understand each other. In contrast with Galdós's ideological bridging through the proposed interfaith unions in *Gloria* and *Doña Perfecta*, Pereda's Águeda refuses to marry Fernando precisely because of his lack of faith, considering Catholicism and atheism to be mutually exclusive.

Subsequently, Fernando tells Águeda that the barrier of their spiritual beliefs is what creates the deep chasm between them, making marriage impossible despite their love for each other: "No podemos entendernos así, Águeda; yo mido un hecho con el criterio humano, y tú le [*sic*] contemplas desde los ideales de tu fantasía religiosa. Desciende por un instante al mundo de la realidad, y júzgame entre los hombres y con la razón de los hombres"[91] [We cannot get on like this, Águeda. I assess a fact with human criteria, and you contemplate it from the ideals of your religious fantasy. Come down to the world of reality for a moment and judge me among men and with man's reason]. The binaries of high and low, of ascent and descent, which I have associated with the mountain and the abyss, elucidate the tensions that Pereda establishes between the "higher" matters of religion and the "lower" affairs and goals of humankind. Águeda's faith is envisaged as a mountain, a summit of beliefs and ideals hardly accessible to individuals like Fernando, for whom the world of religious faith is incomprehensible.

Águeda's inability to empathize with Fernando, and the latter's failure to comprehend the former's religious ideals, evoke the politico-religious tensions that characterized the 1868 Revolution and the 1875 Restoration. From Pereda's conservative perspective, an alliance between the traditionalist old order and the liberal new order can never come to fruition. At the end of their conversation, Águeda again brings up the topic of her faith, signaling the impossibility of compromise and further reinforcing her undivided loyalty to her inherited religious faith. Questions of faith and doubt are reiterated in terms of concepts of ascent and descent:

> —No la hay [la fe] tan grande en la vida humana, que no pueda ser vencida por la reflexión, cuando ésta se inspira en la fe que te falta.
> —¡Otra vez la fe! . . .
> —¡Otra vez, y siempre! . . .
> —Resueltamente, Águeda, no cabe inteligencia entre nosotros, si no desciendes de esas alturas ideales.
> —O si tú no subes a ellas.[92]

["There is no faith so great in human life that it cannot be conquered by reflection, when the latter is inspired by the faith that you lack."
"Here you go again with faith!"

"Again, and always!"

"Decidedly, Águeda, there can be no understanding between us unless you descend from those idealistic heights."

"Or unless you ascend to them."]

The spiritual distance between the devout Águeda and the skeptical Fernando, which renders their union impossible, stems from their personal backgrounds. Hence, as indicated in the novel's aphoristic title, Pereda stresses the role of parents as spiritual guides for future generations. After leaving Águeda, the distraught Fernando confronts his father, Pateta, about the latter's neglect of his religious instruction. Fernando declares that even though Pateta never implemented his own mother's religious beliefs in his life, he was still able to benefit from her spiritual assistance:

> Pero tú conociste a tu madre. Era piadosa. . . . Debió enseñarte a rezar; hablarte de Dios. . . . Dicen que «esas cosas» y otras semejantes son a manera de semilla que, aunque olvidada en esa edad, fructifica profusamente en cualquiera otra de la vida, si se la busca y se la cuida con esmero.[93]

> [But you knew your mother. She was pious. . . . She must have taught you to pray, told you about God. . . . They say that "those things" and similar such ones are like a seed that, although forgotten at the time, bears an abundance of fruit if you seek it and care for it conscientiously.]

Fernando is aware that his missed opportunity for spiritual development, which has resulted in his absence of faith, is not of his own doing but a consequence of his father's voluntary disregard for inherited religious beliefs.

The metaphor of cultivation in Fernando's reference to Pateta's mother also recalls the motif of the seed in Pereda's articles on the Catholic religion in *El Tío Cayetano*, deployed to refer to spiritual heritage and growth in the modern era. Inherent in the memory of Pateta's pious mother sowing the seeds of faith in her son is the allusion to the parable of the sower in the New Testament. There the seeds represent the teachings of the gospel, which are either planted in fertile soil or cast aside in rocky areas where they cannot thrive. Ironically, Pateta discarded these seeds of religion with marked indifference despite having received them during his childhood, whereas Fernando never received a religious upbringing and is tormented by this reality. Fernando's questioning of his path leads to a request for proper guidance from his father, whom Fernando considers a custodian of his past: "Quiero que te vayas penetrando poco a poco de la gravedad del trance en que me veo. Sabes cómo pasó mi niñez; cómo entré en la juventud; qué vientos me empujaron; en qué moldes se fundieron mis ideas"[94] [I want you to gradually understand the seriousness of the situation in which I find myself. You know how I spent my childhood, how I became a young man, what winds

THE ABYSS AND THE MOUNT

153

drove me forward, what molds shaped my ideas]. When Pateta asks him what he really desires, Fernando replies, "Que me guíes y me ayudes. . . . Si no puedes darme luz, dame aliento siquiera"[95] [I want you to guide and help me. . . . If you cannot give me light, at least give me breath]. Once again, the metaphor of light, representative of a profound, spiritual vision, features as the antithesis to doubt.

Consequently, the image of light in Pereda's novel not only carries great religious significance. It also subverts the modern association of light with Enlightenment ideals. In the description of Pateta's young adulthood as a student of medicine, the narrator alludes to God as the source of light, first introduced to Pateta by his mother. Pateta, however, chooses to suppress these memories:

> Por entonces le asaltaron las mientes los recuerdos de aquellos poéticos relatos de su madre sobre la vida futura y los milagros de la fe, cosas tan opuestas a las *verdades* que el dedo de la ciencia le iba señalando en las páginas que devoraba con creciente avidez; y sin detenerse a considerar si aquellas pequeñeces infantiles y candorosas eran el rayo tibio de la aurora, cuyo otro extremo llega hasta el Sol, foco de la luz y del calor del mundo, y pálido reflejo y hechura de otra Luz más grande; si con esta Luz por guía y aquel rayo por senda se podría llegar a ver las cosas del revés de como él las contemplaba o, por lo menos, en perfecta conformidad las unas con las otras.[96]

> [By then, his thoughts were struck by memories of his mother's poetic stories about the afterlife and miracles of the faith, matters so opposed to the *truths* that the finger of science signaled to him in the pages that he devoured with increasing greed. He went on without stopping to consider if those naive and childish trifles were a warm ray of dawn, whose other end reached the Sun, the source of the world's light and warmth, and a pale reflection and handiwork of another greater Light—if, with this Light as a guide and that ray as a path, he could succeed in seeing things contrary to how he contemplated them, or at least with everything in perfect conformity.]

Impressions of his mother's discourse on miracles and eternal salvation have remained in Pateta's conscience, who voices his desired balance between faith and science "en perfecta conformidad" [in perfect conformity]. Pateta's final words of regret and guilt signal his delayed recognition of his own createdness and the existence of a creator: "Si este martirio que me acongoja es un castigo del cielo . . . Señor, ¡tremenda es tu justicia!"[97] [If this martyrdom that grieves me is a punishment from heaven . . . Lord, how terrible is your justice!].

Fernando's autodefenestration at the end is an act of descent evocative of the fall. Pereda deploys this scriptural motif, I argue, to criticize modern egoism and hubris and to caution against the lack of religious belief, which he perceives as fatal. While the opening of doors and windows to breathe in the air outdoors is a symbolic and physical act of liberty for Galdós's Electra and

Rosario, Pereda's Fernando flings himself out of his window in a violent manner, literally descending into an abyss symbolic of his religious doubt and heartbreak. Arguably, Fernando's fall into the abyss, Pereda suggests, stems from his lack of a religious foundation. In turn, Pateta's remorse at his son's death constitutes his own symbolic fall due to failing to provide a spiritual foundation or roots for Fernando's life.

MODERNITY AND THE HOMELAND IN *SOTILEZA*

Rootedness, as well as the accompanying notions of anchoring and mooring, suggests a purportedly organic dependence on place.[98] This sense of dependence and belonging is both concrete and symbolic in Pereda's depiction of coastal village life in *Sotileza* (1885). This novel deals with the life and marriage prospects of the orphan Silda (short for Sotileza) and her wharf-side village in Santander, where Fray Apolinar is the parish priest. He takes the abused Silda to Tío Mechelín and Tía Sidora, who treat her better than her foster family, the mariner Tío Mocejón, his wife, and two children. Fray Apolinar continues his pastoral role by instructing the poor children of the village—including Silda—and providing them with clothing. Silda's lover, Andrés, is a young man who does not wish to follow his family's expectations regarding his future profession. He does not want to be a seaman like his father, Don Pedro Colindres, captain of *La Montañesa*. Andrés is not Silda's only suitor, as Muergo, Silda's impoverished childhood companion, and Cleto, the hardworking son of Tío Mocejón, also wish to marry her. In keeping with their societal standing, Silda ends up marrying Cleto, while Andrés marries Luisa, the daughter of the rich merchant Don Venancio.

The principal themes in *Sotileza* that I will discuss are exclaustration and familial tradition. As Pereda states in his dedication, he wrote this novel for his contemporaries in Santander and regards his texts as distinct from those of other writers of bygone times:

> Al fin y a la postre, lo que en él acontece no es más que un pretexto para resucitar gentes, cosas y lugares que apenas existen ya, y reconstruir un pueblo sepultado de la noche a la mañana, durante su patriarcal reposo, bajo la balumba de otras ideas y otras costumbres arrastradas hasta aquí por el torrente de una nueva y extraña civilización.[99]

> [After all, what happens in it is nothing more than a pretext to revive the persons, things, and places that barely exist now and reconstruct a people suddenly buried, during its patriarchal repose, under the mountain of other ideas and customs swept here by the torrent of a new, strange civilization.]

What most interests Pereda is an ostensibly buried past, which his text will endeavor to disinter and reconstruct. The idea that these people, places, and

THE ABYSS AND THE MOUNT

155

things—specific to a certain time and place—no longer exist indicates the author's profound nostalgia and championing of former times. He first places Santander within the broader context of the Spanish nation to then situate the latter within a new time and space. The "pueblo sepultado" [buried people] represents both Cantabria and Spain as a whole, now immersed in an extraneous mass. Pereda, therefore, seeks to resurrect the obscured site of the past by foregrounding its patriarchal religious identity.

In *Sotileza*, Pereda elucidates the concrete aspects of contemporary Spanish spiritual life by introducing an exclaustrated friar, Fray Apolinar, as one of the main characters. Evoking the mendicant orders, who had faced suppression ever since the start of the nineteenth century, the character of Fray Apolinar was inspired by the last friar to reside at the Dominican monastery of Ajo in Cantabria. This real Fray Apolinar, according to Luis de Escallada González, visited Ajo frequently after his exclaustration and resided in one of the cells of the former monastery with the assistance of neighbors from Camino.[100] Julio Caro Baroja asserts that such friars were the main victims of disentailment. While younger religious joined the Carlists or sought work, the old exclaustrated friars were abandoned to their fate. As Caro Baroja remarks, "La figura del viejo exclaustrado, soportando su miseria, escuálido, enlevitado, dando clases de latín en los colegios, o realizando otros trabajillos mal pagados, es el símbolo de la vida de la mayoría de los hombres que viven en épocas de violencia sin ser violentos"[101] [The figure of the old exclaustrated priest—enduring his misery, emaciated, dressed in religious garb, teaching Latin in schools or undertaking other poorly paid jobs—symbolizes the life of the majority of men who lived nonviolently in times of violence]. Both Pereda's and Böhl's respective friar characters, Fray Apolinar in *Sotileza* and Fray Gabriel in *La gaviota*, demonstrate that their displacement through disentailment and exclaustration places them in a state of uncertainty, neglect, and suffering. Attesting to the former's hardship are his physical appearance ("negra la dentadura" [blackened teeth]) and attire ("sotana remendada" [patched-up cassock]).[102] Despite these difficulties, both characters strive to observe the rules of their religious orders as if they still resided in their monasteries.

Evoking the negative social impact of exclaustration, Pereda dedicates substantial attention to the reduced circumstances and liberty of Fray Apolinar, which are manifest in his poor quarters and scanty possessions, much like the parish priest whom Fernando consults in *De tal palo, tal astilla*. Despite his financial situation, however, Fray Apolinar maintains his religious identity through the presence of a few essential sacramentals:

> El cuarto era angosto, bajo de techo y triste de luz; negreaban a partes las paredes, que habían sido blancas, y un espeso tapiz de roña, empedernida casi, cubría las carcomidas tablas del suelo. Contenía una mesa de pino, un

derrengado sillón de vaqueta y tres sillas desvencijadas, un crucifijo con un ramo de laurel seco, dos estampas de la Pasión y un rosario de Jerusalén, en las paredes; un tintero de cuerno con pluma de ave, un breviario muy recosido, una carpetilla de badana negra, un calendario y una palmatoria de hojalata, encima de la mesa.[103]

[The room was narrow, with a low roof and dim lighting. Parts of the wall, once white, were blackened, and a thick, almost hardened carpet of filth covered the floor's rotten planks. It had a pine table, a bent armchair made of calf leather, and three rickety chairs. On the walls, a crucifix with a dried laurel wreath, two religious images of the Passion, and a rosary from Jerusalem. On the table, a horn inkwell with a bird's feather, a well-mended breviary, a black leather folder, a calendar, and a tin candlestick.]

Consequently, in contrast with Galdós's religious characters, Pereda's treatment of the clergy is very positive. As Eugene Savaiano asserts, the Peredian clergyman remains faithful to the tenets of the Christian faith by continuing his pastoral duties and, as an extension of his ministerial obligations, goes out of his way to counsel and assist the rural folk with their individual and personal problems.[104] Hence, the village priest in *De tal palo, tal astilla* offers spiritual insights to the skeptical Fernando, while Fray Apolinar in *Sotileza* instructs the village children and helps Silda leave her abusive foster family.

The fictional Santander of the past is depicted as a neighborly and intimate town owing to a traditional infrastructure and way of life. Separated from transport and tourism, the town seems static and does not appear subject to the supposed threat of external innovations:

Aquel Santander sin escolleras ni ensanches, sin ferrocarril ni tranvías urbanos, sin la plaza de Velarde y sin vidrieras en las claustros de la catedral, sin hoteles en el Sardinero y sin ferias ni barracones en la Alameda segunda; en el Santander con dársena y con pataches hasta la Pescadería . . . el de la Huerta de los frailes en abertal . . . el de la casa de Botín, inaccesible, sola y deshabitada.[105]

[That Santander without breakwaters or city developments, without railway or urban trams, without the Velarde square or stained glass in the cathedral cloisters, without hotels on the Sardinero beach or markets and barracks along the Second Avenue. In the Santander with a dock and merchant boats up to the fish market . . . the Santander of the friars' unwalled orchard . . . of the house of the Botín family, inaccessible, isolated, and uninhabited.]

Such a description casts Santander as a distinctly traditional landscape, still untouched by modernity. As Sinclair puts it, conservative regional narratives extol the motif of isolation, as in the case of Böhl's Andalusian village and Pereda's Cantabrian hometown.[106] While Galdós's rural towns signify entropy due to their

THE ABYSS AND THE MOUNT   157

ideological and physical distance from modern progress, Pereda and Böhl depict the preservation of a "natural," untainted paradise before the fall in their isolated communities. Pereda imbues his description of Santander with nostalgia for a preexisting time, for an Edenic "original home" predicated upon the supposed virtues of religious belief and observance and a strong, sincere relationship among the townsfolk. In comparison with Böhl's costumbrist sketches of Andalusia, with its ruined edifices, Pereda's novels venerate a Cantabria that is pristine due to what Sinclair terms "the virtues of isolation."[107] The narrative voice privileges not only the town's landscape but also the inhabitants' peculiarities in their speech, especially the Cantabrian use of the diminutive (-*uco* / -*uca*) in names to display affection. As Labanyi notes, *Sotileza* garnered praise for Pereda's representation of speech, particularly the orality of the minimally educated and illiterate, which suggests a revival of an "original" plenitude of meaning prior to literacy.[108]

However, the theme of isolation is double edged in Pereda's novels. On the one hand, it denotes the allegedly untainted purity of the traditionalist province; on the other, it indicates the foreignness of the individualistic, modern liberal. According to López, Pereda held that liberalism was a value system based on egoism, discord, and avarice, which impacted negatively on a traditional way of life that for centuries had provided for the village's well-being and happiness. The original error lay in the dissemination of liberal values and ideas that Pereda regarded as false promises to the "gentes sencillas"[109] [common people]. López points out that although the 1868 Revolution was suffocated by the 1875 Restoration, Pereda still considered the former's effects to be long-lasting and irreversible, marking the separation between traditional society and the modern world.[110]

This aspect of isolation is also recurrent in *De tal palo, tal astilla*. Much like Galdós's young, progressive professionals Pepe Rey and Daniel, Fernando is alienated due to his lack of religious beliefs. His isolation mirrors that of the modernizing elites, for whom the liberal revolution, as Álvarez Junco explains, was weaker as a result of the dominating antimodern position of the rural Catholic masses.[111] Although the government's army defeated the three successive rebellions of the Carlists' self-proclaimed *ejército católico* [Catholic army], Spanish liberal elites had to accept that they were an isolated minority amid a rural and mostly Catholic nation.[112]

Rather than appreciating the renewal of conservatism during the 1875 Restoration, Pereda focuses instead on the damage that he considered to be inflicted irrevocably on the "paradisal" old order by the 1868 Revolution. As López argues, Pereda regarded this devastation as analogous to the fall.[113] Hence, Pereda's traditionalist discourse resembles that of Böhl and Bécquer, who also drew on the moral significance of the fall of humankind to represent what they perceived as the transgressions of excessive individualism and modern ambition.

Pereda's fixation on origins is pertinent to the metaphor of family in that it implies continuity and development. In *Sotileza*, the ideological gap between the young and old is manifest in conversations regarding professions and the future. Upon hearing that Andrés would like to be a mariner, the wealthy merchant Don Venancio Liencres admonishes Andrés's father, Captain Pedro Colindres (known as Bitadura), for not insisting otherwise, stating that it is wiser for the parent to select their child's profession:

> —Usted, por haber obtenido buenos frutos de su carrera y por no tener más que un hijo, puede darle a escoger entre lo que más le guste.
> —Nada le gusta tanto como la carrera de marino—se apresuró a replicar el capitán.
> —O escoger usted mismo—continuó el comerciante, fingiendo no haber oído la réplica—lo más conveniente para él; porque las inclinaciones de los niños obedecen, por lo común, a caprichos del momento . . . a fantasías pasajeras de la imaginación, al contagio de los entusiasmos de otro. . . . Ya usted me entiende.[114]

> ["As you have reaped good rewards from your career and have only one son, you can let him choose whatever he wants."
> "He wants nothing more than to become a mariner," the captain hastily responded.
> "Or you can choose yourself," continued the merchant, pretending not to have heard his reply, "what is most convenient for him, because children are generally inclined to obey momentary whims . . . fleeting fantasies . . . the contagion of others' passions. . . . You know what I mean."]

Don Venancio's paternalistic suggestion reflects the clash between traditionalism and modern individualism brought about by the pursuit of class mobility. Not only does Don Venancio's advice stress parental authority; it also prioritizes material wealth, considering it the marker of basic survival: "A cosa más sólida debe aspirar un padre para su hijo . . . y ríase de los que le digan que no sólo de pan viven las gentes; que esto suelen decirlo los que nunca han logrado hartar el estómago. ¡Pan, pan ante todo, mi señor don Pedro!"[115] [A father must aspire to something sounder for his child . . . and disregard those who tell him that people do not live on bread alone. Usually those who say this have never managed to fill their bellies. Bread, bread above all, my dear sir Pedro!]. Just as the marriages between the young protagonists in *Blasones y talegas* and *De tal palo, tal astilla* evince the older generation's influence on the younger, in *Sotileza*, Silda marries Cleto and Andrés marries Luisa. Parental authority therefore ensures the younger generations' futures and professions and the maintenance of class distinctions. This preservation of social stratification is premised upon a notion of tradition as a collective system. As López puts it, Pereda holds that solidarity strengthens the community. If every member does their part, they can beget harmony between the self and the world.[116]

THE ABYSS AND THE MOUNT

CONCLUSION

Pereda's articles in *El Tío Cayetano* denounce the ramifications of expropriation and exclaustration, while his novels explore the concept of belonging to a "home" that is composed of the pillars of family, social class, the hometown, and the religious community—all groups at risk from modernization and materialism. In *Sotileza*, *Blasones y talegas*, and *De tal palo, tal astilla*, marriage and family are represented as bounded worlds that are not receptive to "foreigners": those not of the same religion or social class. Thus, in *Sotileza*, Silda and Andrés are to marry Cleto and Luisa, respectively, in keeping with their social standing; in *Blasones y talegas*, the noble Don Robustiano laments his daughter Verónica's marriage to Antón; and Águeda's marriage to Fernando is impeded by his irreligion in *De tal palo, tal astilla*.

Through the motif of cultivation, Pereda portrays as indispensable the role of parents in passing down social traditions and tending to the religious formation of their children. In his writings, he deals with themes that underpin the causes and consequences of disentailment: lack of spiritual direction, loss of faith, and discontinuity of familial traditions and beliefs. In his criticism of the arrival of modernity in the province, Pereda condemns the shallowness of utilitarian thinking. By deploying realist depictions of provincial life, he instead ascribes a special meaning and worth to the repositories of religion and regional culture, which are threatened by modernization and secularization.

Arguably, Pereda favors stasis in that he vehemently supports tradition and the preservation of the old order, in contrast with Galdós's advocacy of progress. Like Böhl, Pereda deems upward mobility and the pursuit of profit at the expense of the sacred as acts that are dismissive of tradition. Recalling Bécquer, Pereda elucidates the functions of divinity in the world, representing religious faith as a unifier and disbelief as a factor of personal ruin. Pereda's Carlist beliefs, a blend of traditionalist and Catholic principles, set him against the forces and ideas of modernity. In his writings, he formulates his conceptualization of social classes and religion in a series of vertical relationships, with no middle ground between the divine firmament of religion and the earthly abyss of secularism. The modern pursuit of progress, which Galdós sees as the reorientation of Spain toward an optimal future, causes what Pereda interprets as a process of disorientation and descent. Particularly in his novels, the disinheritance of the institutions of religion, family, and society, which conservatives uphold as foundational for a strong nation, leads to confusion and collapse at individual and collective levels. Portraying modern ideology and ambition through pessimistic motifs of darkness, death, and the abyss, Pereda's texts reveal his belief that these sociopolitical and cultural changes are irreversible. Yet there is an ambivalence in his perception of these realities. Although he depicts the new order as a Pandora's box of sorts, as a point of no return, Pereda beckons his people to reclaim what might remain, restless in the rubble.

Final Reflections

It seems fitting that after opening this study with an image of a ruined portico in Oviedo, I end it with that of an intact one from the Museo de Bellas Artes in Seville. Formerly a Mercedarian convent founded in the late sixteenth century, the museum was established in 1835 under Mendizábal's disentailment laws.[1] As in all monuments, its stone exterior belies its intended fixity. It gives, as Mumford explains, a false sense of continuity. The material aspect of the monument only serves to indicate meaning, but even then, it first requires its beholder's acknowledgment. Thus, Mumford asserts that the "exterior form can only confirm an inner life: it is not a substitute. All living beliefs, all living desires and ideas, must be perpetually renewed, from generation to generation: re-thought, re-considered, re-willed, re-built, if they are to endure."[2] Although the Museo de Bellas Artes was never rebuilt but transformed, its perpetual renewal is still possible through its retention of previous features and accessibility.

No longer an abode for nuns, the museum today houses art, ceramics, and sculptures. Nevertheless, its intricate exterior and iconography signify its conventual past. For the crowds of tourists visiting and passing by, one glance might inspire a thought: Why does this museum look different from other museums? I consider that this nineteenth-century convent-turned-museum, with its extant religious features, is an embodiment of Spain's cultural history, a visible link between past and present. As Halbwachs puts it, memory relies on perception.[3] Ruminating on the Museo de Bellas Artes in Seville and the ruin in Oviedo's Campo de San Francisco, I recall Bécquer's Gothic imagery and conclude that throughout this study, I have observed that within the ideological and physical ruptures of the religious question linger the bones of ruins and the ghosts of meaning.

This study has explored the links between religion and culture in nineteenth-century Spain by examining literary responses to the religious question. In my

Figure 5. Portico, Museo de Bellas Artes, Seville.

analysis of a range of texts, I have endeavored to examine the indirect and direct consequences of disentailment and cultural attitudes toward the nature and role of religion in nineteenth-century Spanish society. Ideas of utility and authority have been pivotal for developing an understanding of the Spanish liberal governments' conceptualizations of the functions of the Church. Expropriation and its accompanying image of the ruin facilitate the perception of the religious question as a deep, multifaceted conflict between tradition and the modern world.

In chapter 1, I examined a selection of parliamentary speeches, pamphlets, and periodical articles that addressed the role of Catholicism, clergy, and religious orders. These various discourses from conservative and liberal members of parliament, the pulpit, and the press elucidated the new values ascribed to the Catholic identity of Spaniards and the meaning of religious orders. In the first Constitution of 1812, set out in liberal terms, nuns and monks were distinguished from the clergy in that the former were not valued as much as the latter. The State's emphasis on material utility influenced this conceptualization of Catholic religious groups.

Chapter 2 dealt with Cecilia Böhl de Faber's texts, which argue for a profound restoration of Spain's past religious character. Tied to the conservative emphasis on national and spiritual dominance, encapsulated in the historical "Reconquest," Böhl deems Spain's religious history a source of greatness and unity in need of renewal. I examined how Böhl regards the domestic sphere and the

FINAL REFLECTIONS

familial unit as intrinsic to safeguarding traditional values and sacraments. Her writings assert that transgressions of religious dogma only lead to the downfall of the individual and the family, symbolic in turn of a feared national decline.

Chapter 3 examined Gustavo Adolfo Bécquer's nostalgia for a fervent Catholic identity. I have argued that in his reflections on the sacred spaces of actual ruined or disentailed ecclesiastical buildings in his *Historia de los templos de España* and *Cartas desde mi celda*, Bécquer reinforces and reimagines the idea of the hallowed by drawing on Romantic and Gothic literary features. In his fantastical *Leyendas*, he casts new light on the idea of resurrection by presenting animated, spectral, and sublime bodies. Hence, I consider that Bécquer not only imbues his writings with sentiments of longing for a lost past. He also envisages a restoration of the holy in his unique and vividly artistic manner.

Chapter 4 focused on liberal views of the religious question, specifically in Benito Pérez Galdós's themes of reorientation and regeneration. In his writings and letters, Galdós urges Spain to address its need for new modalities of nationhood, identity, and spiritual character. From his perspective, the Church and its conservative adherents constitute an impediment to Spain's modern progress. In his development of the notion of a vital force throughout his texts, Galdós assesses the necessity for transformation in Spain's Church.

Contending Galdós's critical perceptions of religious and traditional social institutions is José María de Pereda, whose works form the subject of chapter 5. In his articles and novels, Pereda favors reclaiming the hallmarks of the old order. This call for a resolute spiritual identity and the repossession of conservative principles was fueled by Pereda's disapprobation of the changes he perceived in the Glorious Revolution and the Bourbon Restoration in the latter part of the nineteenth century. For him, the novel ideas that so appealed to Galdós and other like-minded liberals were foreign to the intimate realms of the regional homeland, the family, and the marital union. As a traditionalist and a Carlist, Pereda defends these domestic domains, to which he ascribes the desirable qualities of stability and duration.

Throughout these authors' texts, thematic parallels and symbols are prevalent. A thematic commonality in the novels by Böhl, Galdós, and Pereda is that of the pious dead mother who represents not only the origin of life but also religious formation and authority. In Böhl's *Lágrimas*, the protagonist's mother dies at the beginning of the novel, and her religious and fragile self is mirrored in her daughter. Galdós's maternal characters are multifaced. Doña Perfecta raises her daughter, Rosario, in a confined world, sheltering her from external ideas and influences, and continues to live beyond Pepe Rey's tragic demise. Nevertheless, the forward-thinking Gloria dies shortly after giving birth to her son, and as a ghost, Electra's mother visits her daughter, goading her to escape the constraints of institutional religion. Consequently, the maternal figure is absent from the lives of certain protagonists, as is the case with Böhl's Marisalada and

Lágrimas. In contrast, for Pereda, individuals depend on their mother's devotion after even after death. Águeda's mother has dutifully instructed her daughters in the faith to such an extent that not even her death can end the bonds that she has created between her family and their religion. Significantly, Pateta's mother was not able to accomplish the same feat in raising her son, and Pereda portrays the consequences of this fault through his allusion to the fall. Ultimately, the mother directly influences and indirectly represents one's past and future.

Two further major metaphors present in these authors' works are those of the body and the edifice. Since these symbols share qualities of boundedness, wholeness, and structuration, they are apt analogies for the Spanish nation, which the writers conceive of as a composite of body and soul. Whereas Böhl, Bécquer, and Pereda uphold the institutional Catholic position on sacred places and moral dogmas, Galdós stresses that the spirit of the nation is indeed a living, breathing, and evolving organism. Bécquer's ekphrastic contemplation and personification of religious buildings, Böhl's ode to historical and transformed convents, and Pereda's reference to the "viejo edificio" [old edifice] further sacralize ecclesial and monastic spaces and the old order that these sites represent. By focusing thus on the place of the Church and its apparatus in Spanish society, my writers' works demonstrate that disentailment and exclaustration were not only political and economic issues but also deeply felt cultural and spiritual ones.

On pondering the so-called religious question in today's terms, an issue beyond the boundaries of this study but, notwithstanding, pertinent to it, it becomes clear that sociocultural perceptions of religion are again undergoing transformation. The significance of religious belief is ambivalent, as Yves Lambert puts it, remarking that "God is neither as dead nor as alive as some now maintain." Modernity, he continues, has involved processes of secularization and countersecularization in constant evolution.[4] For his part, Lieven Boeve asserts that modernization in Europe has caused a transformation, not a disappearance, of religion. Spirituality nowadays is defined by "un-churching," with lower attendance rates at church services, especially among younger generations whose reliance on personal beliefs rather than collective associations constitutes an act of "believing without belonging."[5]

In spite of such changes to a broader religious landscape, Rodney Stark contends that these do not equate with decline.[6] Likewise, Joseba Louzao Villar holds that despite the complex, dynamic relationship between modernity and religion, the two are not mutually exclusive. In comparison with the scholarly view that religious change constitutes a "metamorphosis," Louzao Villar describes it as a "recomposition," with religion having to adapt to modern life, albeit not without resistance. The shift from religious culture to individualized belief characterized the nineteenth and twentieth centuries; today's situation is marked by religious pluralism.[7] Hence, Stark argues that religious "variation,"

FINAL REFLECTIONS

the rise and fall of aspects of religiousness, merits further exploration, given that secularization predicts a marked decline in individual religiousness.[8]

Speaking of Catholicism in his interview with Nicolas Diat, Cardinal Robert Sarah perceives a crisis of faith due to a lack of belief in the concrete manifestations of religion.[9] Lambert and Boeve's above observations also hold for Spain, and Sarah's statement uncannily echoes the conservative concerns of nineteenth-century Spanish clergymen. I perceive a link between Lambert's observation of God being neither living nor dead and my interpretation of Catholic religion today as struggling in a state of betweenness, situated in a liminal space between tradition and modernity, between spirit (the ghost) and body (the bones).

Catholic identities in contemporary Spain are more nominal in that they resemble the more "spiritual" brand of religious belief as opposed to institutional affiliation and a serious observance of the faith. According to Vincent, since the 1970s, the practice of religion in Spain has decreased rapidly, and in its place, a form of "cultural" Catholicism has remained, as seen in the annual celebrations of Holy Week, while fewer people attend Mass and receive the sacraments.[10] A question that remains amid the secular characteristics of modern Spain, and the West's privileging of the "spiritual" over religious doctrines and observation, is the fate of the ecclesial site.[11]

The concepts of patrimony, nation, and religion at stake in this study intersect in the emblem of the religious building, which continues to be of relevance nowadays. Resisting the current perception that the Church's buildings are relevant only in the past is the question of Church proprietorship over religious edifices in Spain, a topic hotly debated by national governments ever since the nineteenth century. This issue causes tension, for although the nation claims to be of nonconfessional status, its links to the Catholic Church remain solid. As Victor Urrutia Abaigar categorically states, the consolidation of Spain's nonconfessional status should still be viewed as an ongoing process.[12] In 2018, the secretary general and spokesperson of the Conferencia Episcopal Española (CEE), José María Gil Tamayo, announced that the government's investigation of the Church's buildings constituted "una desamortización encubierta" [an undercover disentailment].[13] Conservatives declare that according to José María Aznar's reformed Ley Hipotecaria [Mortgage Law] in 1998, the Church has the right to register certain buildings and properties for the first time. The first Mortgage Law was established in 1861 under Isabel II and permitted the Church to register churches, cathedrals, and hermitages.[14] Moreover, this law was created with the aim of protecting disentailed ecclesiastical buildings acquired by private buyers.[15] According to the 1861 decree's exposition written by the jurist Alejandro Díaz Zafra, the law was established for "la creación de bancos de crédito territorial, para dar certidumbre al dominio y a los demás derechos en la cosa, para poner límites a la mala fe, y para libertar al propietario del yugo de usureros despiadados"[16] [the creation of territorial credit banks, to render certainty regarding the ownership and other rights, to place limits on bad faith, and to liberate the owner from the yoke of ruthless usurers]. Under Franco, the 1946 Mortgage Law allowed for the registration of buildings without documentation, excluding places of worship. Aznar's 1998 reform of this law extended the registration process to cover places of worship.[17]

Yet in 2019, Elena G. Sevillano, writing for *El País*, noted that in almost two decades since the beginning of this century, the Spanish Church had registered around thirty thousand properties, a measure considered legally questionable. At that point, Church documents were still under the process of correction for possible errors and remained undisclosed to the public. With numerous properties to its name, particularly cultural attractions like the Mosque–Cathedral of Córdoba, the Church in Spain has benefited from tourism revenue over the years. Juan José Picó of the coordinating committee Recuperando [Recovering] declared that Spain's cathedrals, churches, and monasteries ought to be under public ownership due to their significance as "bienes de patrimonio" [assets of national patrimony].[18] In June 2020, *Europa Press* announced that the Spanish government had temporarily halted the elaboration of a legal report on the Church's registered goods due to the COVID-19 pandemic.[19]

This study has aimed to contribute to scholarly discussions on the intersections of religion, literature, memory, and nationhood in nineteenth-century Spain. As I pointed out in my introduction, many studies on disentailment examine its artistic, economic, and political outcomes. While some scholarship on my selected authors' works covers ideas pertaining to the religious question, I have traversed a different path by examining the perspectives of Catholicism from various constituents of the Spanish nation—government, press, and clergy—and by building on Taylor's idea of excarnation to probe the patterns of disjuncture between tradition and modernity in a wide range of fictional texts, epistolary exchanges, political speeches, and treatises.

What remains to be addressed in future studies are accounts of the effects of disentailment by nuns and monks themselves during the nineteenth century. An inquiry into how they viewed disentailment and suppression would necessitate extensive archival research and locating personal correspondence, where available. Moreover, it would be pertinent to analyze further the varied implementation of expropriation and exclaustration processes throughout the Spanish nation. Palomo Iglesias points out that Mendizábal's disentailment laws were carried out in Spain's provinces through different measures and not all at the same time.[20] I hope this study will inspire further critical interpretations of cultural responses to ecclesiastical confiscation in various areas and investigations into the individual and collective lives of excloistered populations.

By foregrounding the significant sociocultural changes that disentailment wrought, I have illuminated the role of the ruin, the monument, and the ecclesiastical edifice in the physical and literary landscapes of Spain. Overall, this

FINAL REFLECTIONS

study has demonstrated that in literary responses to the religious question, the peoples, properties, and principles of the Catholic religion became a palimpsest, their meanings subject to constant critiquing, reshaping, and renewing. Such perceptions (and problems) endure to this very day. It is imperative therefore to continue conversing about and commemorating facets of the past and their relation to ourselves, our presents, and our futures. Returning to the two archways in Oviedo and Seville, I cannot deny that time has carved many a life into their stone.

Acknowledgments

I owe a debt of gratitude to Christine Arkinstall for constantly guiding me in my work. I thank José Colmeiro for sharing his insights. I am grateful to Daniela Cavallaro for her gracious support and to Akiko Tsuchiya for her help and advice. Thanks to Alda Blanco and Kathryn Lehman for their valuable feedback. This young academic has learned so much from you all.

I thank Isabel Cuñado, Jason McCloskey, and the board of *Campos Ibéricos* for giving my first book a chance. I especially acknowledge the constructive critique of my anonymous reviewers, which has assisted me greatly in reviewing the manuscript. I am indebted to Suzanne Guiod, Pamelia Dailey, Catherine Denning, Hannah McGinnis, and the incredible teams at Bucknell University Press, Rutgers University Press, and Scribe.

Material from chapter 3 first appeared as "Recomposing Memory's Fragments: The Sacred Precinct in Gustavo Adolfo Bécquer's *Historia de los templos de España* (1857) and *Cartas desde mi celda* (1864)," *Decimonónica* 19, no. 1 (2022): 1–19, and is reprinted by kind permission of JP Spicer-Escalante and *Decimonónica*, for which I am grateful. This publication received the 2022 Association of Iberian and Latin American Studies of Australasia (AILASA) Early Career Researcher Prize. I thank Robert Mason and the judging panel for this award.

I am obliged to Ana Isabel Mendoza de Benito of the Casa-Museo Pérez Galdós, María Gallardo of Sevilla Venues, Miguel Romero of the Museo del Romanticismo in Madrid, and the staff of the Biblioteca Nacional in Madrid, the Palacio de Montemuzo in Zaragoza, and the Archivo Histórico Provincial in Salamanca.

I appreciate the support and generosity of Bronwen McShea, Francisco Javier Campos y Sevilla, James Mandrell, Derek Flitter, and Kieran Flanagan.

Many thanks to Noël Valis, Jennifer Smith, Linda Willem, and Wan Tang of the Asociación Internacional de Galdosistas for awarding me the 2021 Premio Peter Bly for Best Dissertation.

Finally, I am beholden to my parents, Betsabe and Eduardo; my siblings, Albraine, Mahaleel, Nain, Israel, Jairel, Tirzah, Carissime, Melchi, and Jerahmeel; and my extended family and friends. What started out as a question about family history led to myriad paths on which some kindled the fires and others showed me the stars.

Notes

INTRODUCTION

1. Pierre Nora, "Between Memory and History: *Les Lieux de Mémoire*," *Representations* 26 (Spring 1989): 7, https://www.jstor.org/stable/2928520.7.

2. Joseph Leo Koerner, "On Monuments," *Res: Anthropology and Aesthetics* 67, no. 1 (September 1, 2017): 9.

3. Nora, "Between Memory and History," 12.

4. Lewis Mumford, *The Culture of Cities* (New York: Open Road Media, 2016), 297.

5. Nora, "Between Memory and History," 24.

6. Claudia Granda, "¿Cómo ha llegado aquí este arco de más de ocho siglos?," *La Voz de Asturias*, August 10, 2018, https://www.lavozdeasturias.es/noticia/oviedo/2018/10/03/llegado-arco-ocho-siglos/00031538576132523829470.htm (accessed May 29, 2023).

7. "Convento de San Francisco," El Tesoro de Oviedo, http://el.tesorodeoviedo.es/index.php?title=Convento_de_San_Francisco (accessed December 30, 2022).

8. By *Church*, I refer to the Catholic Church. In mentioning the church building, I use its lowercase form.

9. E. Inman Fox, *La invención de España: Nacionalismo liberal e identidad nacional*, 2nd ed. (Madrid: Cátedra, 1998), 13.

10. Sara Medina Calzada, "The Felon King: Ferdinand VII in British Print Culture (1814–1833)," *Bulletin of Spanish Studies* 96, no. 6 (2019): 951–952, 972, https://doi.org/10.1080/14753820.2019.1633797.

11. Francisco Simón Segura, *La desamortización española en el siglo XIX* (Madrid: Ministerio de Hacienda, Instituto de Estudios Fiscales, 1973), 51.

12. Francisco Tomás y Valiente, "El proceso de desamortización de la tierra en España," *Agricultura y sociedad*, no. 7 (1978): 13.

13. Tomás y Valiente, 12–13. For an outline on this legislation from 1798 to 1875, see also Francisco Javier Campos y Fernández de Sevilla.

14. Francisco Tomás y Valiente, *El marco político de la desamortización de España* (Barcelona: Ediciones Ariel, 1971), 48.

15. Tomás y Valiente, "El proceso de desamortización," 15. Disentailment's breadth and legacy explain its aperture in research. In this respect, a symposium on ecclesiastical confiscation, titled "La desamortización: El expolio del patrimonio artístico y cultural de la Iglesia en España," was held on September 6–9, 2007, at the Real Centro Universitario Escorial–María Cristina in El Escorial, Madrid. Organized by Francisco Javier Campos y Fernández

de Sevilla, it focused on the effects of disentailment on cultural patrimony in nineteenth-century Spain. Recent additions to the literature include José Ramón López Rodríguez's work on disentailment and museums, José Luis Eugercios Arriero's analysis of the effects of expropriation and exclaustration on the Augustinian order in nineteenth-century Spain, and new studies on convents and exclaustration by Javier Gómez Cediel, Francisco Jesús Martínez Asensio, José María Velaz Pascual, and Manuel Villena Villar.

16. Francisco Javier Ramón Solans, "Introducción: Economía, sociedad y religión," in *El Trienio Liberal (1820–1823): Balance y perspectivas*, ed. Ivana Frasquet, Pedro Rújula, and Álvaro París (Zaragoza: Prensas de la Universidad de Zaragoza, 2022), 283.

17. "Representación que a la reina de las virtudes la Caridad dirige un quilibet exclaustrado, con solo el objeto de hallar el socorro y alivio de ella" (Madrid: Imprenta de D. J. Palacios, 1838).

18. Eustasio Esteban, *El siervo de Dios Fr. Diego José de Rejas: Religioso agustino exclaustrado de la provincia de Andalucía; Posiciones y artículos para la causa de su beatificación* (Madrid: Imprenta Helénica, 1919), 1, 3, 30.

19. Crescencio Palomo Iglesias, *Claudio Sancho de Contreras (1811–1886): Dominico exclaustrado* (Segovia: Imprenta Gabel, 1970), 5, 6, 13.

20. Antonio Iturbe Saíz, "Patrimonio artístico de tres conventos agustinos en Madrid antes y después de la desamortización de Mendizábal," in *La desamortización: El expolio del patrimonio artístico y cultural de la Iglesia en España; Actas del Simposium (6/9-IX-2007)*, ed. Francisco Javier Campos y Fernández de Sevilla (Alicante: Biblioteca Virtual Miguel de Cervantes, 2010), 368, http://www.cervantesvirtual.com/obra/la-desamortizacion-el-expolio-del-patrimonio-artistico-y-cultural-de-la-iglesia-en-espana-actas-del-simposium-69-ix-2007/ (accessed May 19, 2023).

21. José María Antequera, *La desamortización eclesiástica: Considerada en sus diferentes aspectos y relaciones* (Madrid: A. Pérez Dubrull, 1885), 456.

22. José Manuel Cuenca, *D. Pedro de Inguanzo y Rivero (1764–1836): Ultimo primado del antiguo régimen* (Pamplona: Universidad de Navarra, 1965), 183.

23. Antequera, *La desamortización eclesiástica*, 455–456.

24. Germán Rueda Hernanz, *España 1790–1900: Sociedad y condiciones económicas* (Madrid: Editorial ISTMO, 2006), 9.

25. See Josefina Bello.

26. Susan M. Griffin, *Anti-Catholicism and Nineteenth-Century Fiction* (Cambridge: Cambridge University Press, 2004), 4–5.

27. Mary Vincent, "Religion: The Idea of Catholic Spain," in *Metaphors of Spain: Representations of Spanish National Identity in the Twentieth Century*, ed. Javier Moreno-Luzón and Xosé Núñez Seixas (Oxford: Berghahn Books, 2017), 22.

28. Charles Taylor, *A Secular Age* (Cambridge, Mass.: Harvard University Press, 2007), 554.

29. Thomas Joseph White, *The Light of Christ: An Introduction to Catholicism* (Washington, D.C.: Catholic University of America Press, 2017), 148.

30. Kieran Flanagan, *Seen and Unseen: Visual Culture, Sociology and Theology* (London: Palgrave Macmillan, 2004), 155.

31. José Álvarez Junco, *Mater Dolorosa: La idea de España en el siglo XIX* (Madrid: Taurus, 2001), 316–317.

32. For case studies on transformed, expropriated buildings, see Alba Arboix and Jesús Abizanda Sanromán.

33. Astrid Erll and Ann Rigney, "Literature and the Production of Cultural Memory: Introduction," *European Journal of English Studies* 10, no. 2 (2006): 113, https://doi.org/10.1080/13825570600753394.

34. Jan Assmann, *Religion and Cultural Memory: Ten Studies*, trans. Rodney Livingstone (Stanford: Stanford University Press, 2006), 128.

35. Assmann, 123, 129.

NOTES TO PAGES 8–15

36. Assmann, 81.

37. Assmann, 107.

38. Michael Thompson, Richard Ellis, and Aaron Wildavsky, *Cultural Theory* (Boulder, Colo.: Westview Press, 1990), 1.

39. Fox, *La invención de España*, 22.

40. Mieke Bal, introduction to *Acts of Memory: Cultural Recall in the Present*, ed. Mieke Bal, Jonathan Crewe, and Leo Spitzer (Lebanon, N.H.: University Press of New England, 1999), vii.

41. Bal, xi.

42. Maurice Halbwachs, *On Collective Memory*, ed. and trans. Lewis A. Coser (Chicago: University of Chicago Press, 1992), 169.

43. Halbwachs, 168–169.

44. Halbwachs, 175.

45. Nora, "Between Memory and History," 19.

46. Nora, 22.

47. Laurajane Smith, "Intangible Heritage: A Challenge to the Authorised Heritage Discourse?," *Revista d'etnologia de Catalunya*, no. 40 (2015): 141, https://www.raco.cat/index .php/RevistaEtnologia/article/view/293392/381920.

48. Smith, 140.

49. Catholic Bishops' Conference of England and Wales, *Consecrated for Worship: A Directory on Church Building* (London: Catholic Truth Society, 2006), 14.

50. Kieran Flanagan, *Sociological Noir: Irruptions and the Darkness of Modernity* (London: Routledge, 2017), 120.

51. Anne Janowitz, *England's Ruins: Poetic Purpose and the National Landscape* (Oxford: Basil Blackwell, 1990), 10.

52. Raymond Carr, *Spain: A History* (Oxford: Oxford University Press, 2000), 209, 226, 228.

53. Throughout my study, I will refer to all primary texts by their shortened titles.

54. Xavier Andreu Miralles, *El descubrimiento de España: Mito Romántico e identidad nacional* (Madrid: Taurus, 2016), 321.

55. Raquel Gutiérrez Sebastián, prologue to *Blasones y talegas*, by José María de Pereda, ed. Raquel Gutiérrez Sebastián (Doral, Fla.: Stock Cero, 2006), xvi.

CHAPTER 1 — MODERN MATTER

1. Cathy Caruth, *Unclaimed Experience: Trauma, Narrative, and History* (Baltimore: Johns Hopkins University Press, 1996), 3.

2. Sigmund Freud, "Mourning and Melancholia," in *The Freud Reader*, ed. Peter Gay (New York: Vintage, 1995), 589.

3. Martin Hopkins, "St. Thomas and the Encyclical *Mystici Corporis*," *The Thomist: A Speculative Quarterly Review* 22, no. 1 (January 1959): 2, https://doi.org/10.1353/tho.1959.0000. Pius XII stressed the analogy of the Church as the body of Christ, recurrent in the Pauline Epistles, in his 1943 encyclical *Mystici Corporis Christi* [Mystical body of Christ]. Pius XII, *Mystici Corporis Christi*, June 29, 1943, Holy See, http://www.vatican.va/content/pius-xii/ en/encyclicals/documents/hf_p-xii_enc_29061943_mystici-corporis-christi.html (accessed May 19, 2023).

4. E. Inman Fox, *La invención de España: Nacionalismo liberal e identidad nacional*, 2nd ed. (Madrid: Cátedra, 1998), 38. Josefina Bello adds that the complex process of disentailment was an economic measure for liberals and an antiecclesiastical program for progressives. Josefina Bello, *Frailes, intendentes y políticos: Los bienes nacionales 1835–1850* (Madrid: Taurus, 1997), 18.

5. Jaime Vicens Vives, *An Economic History of Spain*, trans. Frances M. López-Morillas (Princeton, N.J.: Princeton University Press, 1969), 607.

6. Charles Esdaile, *Spain in the Liberal Age: From Constitution to Civil War, 1808–1939* (Hoboken, N.J.: Blackwell, 2000), 6.

7. Francisco Martí Gilabert, *La desamortización española* (Madrid: Ediciones Rialp, 2003), 23.

8. Martí Gilabert adds a religious meaning to the term *manos muertas*, stating that ecclesiastical communities, especially the regular orders, had "died" for the world through their services in health and education (19).

9. Vicens Vives, *Economic History of Spain*, 611.

10. The 1812 Constitution did not solely concern Spain. Bartolomé Clavero stresses that this constitution was not Spanish exclusively because it spanned both hemispheres and referred to Spain and its colonies. Bartolomé Clavero, "Cádiz and the Noise of a Constitutionalism Common to Both Hemispheres," *Giornale di Storia Costituzionale*, no. 21 (2011): 41.

Moreover, Marta Lorente Sariñena underlines that this bihemispheric constitution was affiliated with a plurisecular Catholic monarchy that was also linked to its peninsular, European, American, Philippine, and African territories. Marta Lorente Sariñena, "Crisis of the Catholic Monarchy and Regeneration of Its Constitution," *Giornale di Storia Costituzionale* 19 (2010): 67.

11. Stanley G. Payne, *Spain: A Unique History* (Madison: University of Wisconsin Press, 2011), 144.

12. Martí Gilabert, *La desamortización española*, 21.

13. Payne, *Spain*, 144–145. The development of Spanish liberalism was neither smooth nor completely successful. Payne states that the years between 1810 and 1814 were particularly chaotic for the Cortes to fully consolidate liberal ideals, and the 1820–1823 Liberal Triennium was similarly short-lived. From the death of Fernando VII in 1833 until 1923, much of Spain's liberalism was fairly conservative, punctuated by occasional progressive phases (143).

As E. Inman Fox sees it, Spanish governments in the latter part of the nineteenth century and the early twentieth century were characterized by a liberal hegemony oftentimes conflicting with traditionalist sectors. Fox, *La invención de España*, 12.

14. Isabel Burdiel, "Myths of Failure, Myths of Success: New Perspectives on Nineteenth-Century Liberalism," *Journal of Modern History* 70, no. 4 (December 1998): 901, https://www.jstor.org/stable/10.1086/235170901.

15. José Álvarez Junco, *Mater Dolorosa: La idea de España en el siglo XIX* (Madrid: Taurus, 2001), 305. Furthermore, the Church's reaction to the onset of the Enlightenment and its challenge to monarchical and ecclesial authority resulted in the clergy's adoption of a crusader mentality that sought to combat reforms and public ridicule of Catholicism. In Bonapartist Spain, pamphlets and polemics attacked the authority and practices of the Catholic Church, with lithographs in the periodical *Le Motín* portraying clerical excess with the figure of a plump and decadent friar. Noël Valis, *Sacred Realism: Religion and the Imagination in Modern Spanish Narrative* (New Haven, Conn.: Yale University Press, 2010), 83, 101–102.

16. Gregorio Alonso, *La nación en capilla: Ciudadanía católica y cuestión religiosa en España, 1793–1874* (Granada: Comares, 2014), 58; Sara Medina Calzada, "The Felon King: Ferdinand VII in British Print Culture (1814–1833)," *Bulletin of Spanish Studies* 96, no. 6 (2019): 951, https://doi.org/10.1080/14753820.2019.1633797. Moreover, the 1820–1823 Liberal Triennium saw Ferdinand VII giving way to constitutionalism, although this would end after the French invasion in 1823, which restored him to absolutist power. By the time of his death in 1833, Spain had lost most of its colonies in the Americas and was subsequently entangled in a web of economic, political, dynastic, and social crises that relegated the former imperial power to a "second-rate" nation in Europe. Medina Calzada, "Felon King," 951, 952, 972.

17. Álvarez Junco, "La nación en duda," in *Más se perdió en Cuba: España, 1898 y la crisis de fin de siglo*, ed. Juan Pan-Montojo (Madrid: Alianza: 1998), 426–427.

NOTES TO PAGES 17–21

18. Fox, *La invención de España*, 14.

19. Fox, 17–18.

20. Fox, 25.

21. Fox, 20–21.

22. Jaime Balmes, "Dos escollos," *El Pensamiento de la Nación*, no. 70 (1845): 353.

23. Balmes, 354.

24. The so-called Two Spains was discussed by prominent liberal thinkers in the late nineteenth century such as Vicente Blasco Ibáñez and Ramiro de Maeztu. The metaphor was also important for Marcelino Menéndez y Pelayo and regenerationist writers such as José Ortega y Gasset and Miguel de Unamuno. Santos Juliá, *Historias de las dos Españas* (Madrid: Taurus, 2004), 147.

25. Balmes, "Dos escollos," 355.

26. Balmes, 359.

27. Juliá, *Historias de las dos Españas*, 149.

28. José Álvarez Junco, *A las barricadas: Cultura, identidad, y movilización política* (Madrid: Ediciones Complutense, 2009), 276.

29. William J. Callahan, "Two Spains and Two Churches 1760–1835," *Historical Reflections* 2, no. 2 (Winter 1976): 157, http://www.jstor.org/stable/41298665.

30. Xavier Andreu Miralles, *El descubrimiento de España: Mito Romántico e identidad nacional* (Madrid: Taurus, 2016), 200–201.

31. Hartmut Pogge von Strandmann, "1848–1849: A European Revolution?," in *The Revolutions in Europe, 1848–1849: From Reform to Reaction*, ed. Robert Evans and Hartmut Pogge von Strandmann (Oxford: Oxford University Press, 2011), 1.

32. Frank J. Coppa, *Politics and the Papacy in the Modern World* (Santa Barbara, Calif.: ABC-CLIO, 2008), 45.

33. Solange Hibbs-Lissorgues, *Iglesia, prensa y sociedad en España (1868–1904)* (Alicante: Instituto de Cultura "Juan Gil-Albert" y Diputación de Alicante, 1995), 21.

34. Eamonn Rodgers, "Religious Freedom and the Rule of Law in Nineteenth-Century Spain," *Irish Jurist* 22, no. 1 (1987): 115, https://www.jstor.org/stable/44027198.

35. Begoña Urigüen, *Orígenes y evolución de la derecha española: El neo-catolicismo* (Madrid: Consejo Superior de Investigaciones Científicas, 1986), 56.

36. Urigüen, 57.

37. Marcelino Menéndez y Pelayo, *Historia de los heterodoxos españoles: Heterodoxia en el siglo XIX*, vol. 6, ed. Enrique Sánchez Reyes (Alicante: Biblioteca Virtual Miguel de Cervantes, 2008), 508.

38. Doris Moreno and Ricardo García Cárcel, introduction to *The Complexity of Hispanic Religious Life in the 16th–18th Centuries*, ed. Doris Moreno, trans. Phil Grayston (Leiden: Brill, 2020), 1.

39. Vicens Vives, *Economic History of Spain*, 633–635.

40. Rocío Román Collado, "Andaluces en el pensamiento económico del siglo XIX," in *Economía y economistas andaluces: Siglos XVI al XX*, ed. Rocío Sánchez Lissen (Madrid: Eco-Book Economista, 2013), 329.

41. Vicens Vives, *Economic History of Spain*, 633–635. Furthermore, Noël Valis explains that the political and economic problems arising from Napoleonic anticlericalism and expropriation and the Cortes' abolition of the Inquisition and ecclesiastical privileges all contributed to the steady decline of the Church from the very start of the nineteenth century. Valis, *Sacred Realism*, 94.

42. María G. Moreno Antón, *La enajenación de bienes eclesiásticos en el ordenamiento jurídico español* (Salamanca: Universidad Pontificia de Salamanca, 1987), 67; Joaquín Varela Suanzes-Carpegna, "La construcción del Estado en la España del siglo XIX: Una perspectiva constitucional," Biblioteca Virtual Miguel de Cervantes, http://www.cervantesvirtual .com/obra-visor/la-construccion-del-estado-en-la-espaa-del-siglo-xix-una-perspectiva

-constitucional/html/dcd3569e-2dc6-11e2-b417-000475f5bda5_2.html#I_0_ (accessed December 31, 2022).

43. After the Carlists' defeat in the Third Carlist War (1872–1876), the "Integralists," a faction of the Carlist movement, ceased to support Carlos María Isidro de Borbón's heirs. According to Christopher J. Ross, the Carlists focused instead on more reactionary demands, particularly those regarding the Church's status. The movement would later reunite to form the Traditionalist Party in 1932. Christopher J. Ross, *Spain, 1812–1996* (New York: Oxford University Press, 2000), 12, 82.

44. Vicens Vives, *Economic History of Spain*, 637.

45. Moreno Antón, *La enajenación de bienes eclesiásticos*, 66.

46. For a comprehensive outline of disentailment legislation, see Javier Francisco Campos de Sevilla, María G. Moreno Antón, Jaime Vicens Vives, and Martí Gilabert. According to the Code of Canon Law, the expropriation of ecclesial properties undermined papal authority and the purpose of the Church's temporal goods: "To order divine worship, to care for the decent support of the clergy and other ministers, and to exercise works of the sacred apostolate and of charity, especially toward the needy." The pontiff's opposition to the confiscation laws increased tensions between Rome and Spain, an issue that would be partially resolved by the 1851 Concordat. "Code of Canon Law: Book V; The Temporal Goods of the Church," Holy See, http://www.vatican.va/archive/cod-iuris -canonici/eng/documents/cic_lib5-cann1254-1310_en.html#TITLE_II (accessed December 31, 2022).

47. Francisco Javier Campos y Fernández de Sevilla, "Textos legales de las desamortizaciones eclesiásticas españolas y con ellas relacionados," in *La desamortización: El expolio del patrimonio artístico y cultural de la Iglesia en España; Actas del Simposium (6/9-IX-2007)*, ed. Francisco Javier Campos y Fernández de Sevilla (Alicante: Biblioteca Virtual Miguel de Cervantes, 2010), 17–19, http://www.cervantesvirtual.com/obra/la-desamortizacion-el-expolio -del-patrimonio-artistico-y-cultural-de-la-iglesia-en-espana-actas-del-simposium-69-ix -2007/ (accessed May 19, 2023); Moreno Antón, *La enajenación de bienes eclesiásticos*, 66–67.

Furthermore, because of the War of Independence and growing secularization, Spanish clergy dwindled from around 200,000 priests in 1797 to 56,000 in 1860. Vicens Vives, *Economic History of Spain*, 624.

48. Esdaile, *Spain in the Liberal Age*, 77, 79, 82.

49. Adrian Shubert, *A Social History of Modern Spain* (London: Routledge, 1990), 146.

50. Vicens Vives, *Economic History of Spain*, 632.

51. Martí Gilabert, *La desamortización española*, 75.

52. Congreso de los Diputados, "Número 117: Sesión del sábado 4 de julio de 1840," Diario de sesiones: Serie histórica, 2994, https://app.congreso.es/est_sesiones/web/viewer.html ?file=https%3A%2F%2Fapp.congreso.es%2Fest_sesiones%2Fresource%3Fid%3D1840%2F07 %2FC-0117-02991.pdf#page=8&zoom=auto,-53,593 (accessed January 3, 2023).

53. Martí Gilabert, *La desamortización española*, 75.

54. Moreno Antón, *La enajenación de bienes eclesiásticos*, 68–70.

55. Carolyn P. Boyd, *Historia Patria: Politics, History, and National Identity in Spain, 1875–1975* (Princeton, N.J.: Princeton University Press, 1997), 99.

56. Moreno Antón, *La enajenación de bienes eclesiásticos*, 76.

57. Menéndez y Pelayo, *Historia de los heterodoxos españoles*, 256. This view has dominated historiography, as Ángel Ramón del Valle Calzado explains. Among the clerics who debated ecclesiastical disentailment were the chief archbishop of Toledo, Pedro de Inguanzo, author of the two-volume treatise *El dominio sagrado de la Iglesia en sus bienes temporales: Cartas contra los impugnadores de esta propiedad, especialmente en ciertos libelos de estos tiempos* [The Church's sacred dominion over its temporal goods: Letters against those who challenge this property, especially in certain libels of these times]; the canon José Vicente Mier y Terán; and, as noted above, Jaime Balmes. Ángel Ramón del Valle Calzado,

NOTES TO PAGES 23–29

"Desamortización eclesiástica en la provincia de Ciudad Real, 1836–1854" (PhD diss., Universidad de Castilla–La Mancha, 1995), 5.

58. Juan Martín Carramolino, *La Iglesia de España económicamente considerada* (Madrid: Imprenta del Colegio de Sordo-Mudos, 1850), v.

59. Martín Carramolino, 18.

60. Martín Carramolino's treatise on the Church's patrimony and its relation to the poor echoes that of the seventeenth-century French prelate and historian Jacques Bénigne Bossuet, who addresses monarchs in the seventh volume of his *Politics Drawn from Holy Scripture*, stating that protecting the assets of the Church protects those of the poor. José María Antequera, *La desamortización eclesiástica: Considerada en sus diferentes aspectos y relaciones* (Madrid: A. Pérez Dubrull, 1885), 41.

61. Yang Yongjiao, Iain Brennan, and Mick Wilkinson, "Public Trust and Performance Measurement in Charitable Organizations," *International Journal of Productivity and Performance Management* 63, no. 6 (2014): 782, 789, https://doi.org/10.1108/IJPPM-09-2013-0159.

62. El Solitario [pseud.], *Juicio histórico-canónico-político de la autoridad de las naciones en los bienes eclesiásticos, o Disertación sobre la pertenencia de su dominio según el espíritu invariable de la iglesia y los principios inconclusos del derecho público* (Alicante: Manuel Muñoz, 1813), 26.

63. Hermano Bartolo, *El Anacoreta* (Alicante: Oficina de Nicolás Carratalá e Hijos, 1813), 10.

64. Hermano Bartolo, 21.

65. Hermano Bartolo, 27.

66. Gabino Tejado, *El catolicismo liberal* (Madrid: Librería Católica Internacional, 1875), 9 (emphasis in original).

67. Tejado, 10 (emphasis in original).

68. Tejado, 13.

69. Joaquín Casalduero, introduction to *De tal palo, tal astilla*, by José María de Pereda, 4th ed., ed. Joaquín Casalduero (Madrid: Cátedra, 1981), 25.

70. Congreso de los Diputados, *Constitución de la monarquía española*, 1837, http://www.congreso.es/docu/constituciones/1837/ce37_cd.pdf (accessed December 29, 2022).

71. Congreso de los Diputados, "Número 90: Sesión del viernes 5 de junio de 1840," Diario de Sesiones: Serie histórica, 2246, https://app.congreso.es/est_sesiones/web/viewer.html?file=https%3A%2F%2Fapp.congreso.es%2Fest_sesiones%2Fresource%3Fid%3D1840%2F06%2FC-0090-02245.pdf#page=2&zoom=auto,-53,421 (accessed January 3, 2023).

72. Congreso de los Diputados, 2247.

73. Shubert, *Social History of Modern Spain*, 144.

74. Álvarez Junco, *A las barricadas*, 277.

75. Raymond Carr, *Spain, 1808–1939* (Oxford: Oxford University Press, 1966), 45–46.

76. Callahan, "Two Spains," 175–176. Moreover, the Cortes demonstrated their determination to subdue clerical backlash by exiling the Benedictine friar and archbishop of Valencia Veremundo Arias Teixeiro y Rodríguez, who criticized the law on regular clergy, and expelling from their dioceses the bishops of Oviedo, Tarazona, León, Salamanca, Cádiz, Ceuta, and Málaga to subsequently replace their episcopates with liberal clerics (177).

77. Congreso de los Diputados, "Número 100: Sesión del lunes 15 de junio de 1840," Diario de sesiones: Serie histórica, 2520, https://app.congreso.es/est_sesiones/web/viewer.html?file=https%3A%2F%2Fapp.congreso.es%2Fest_sesiones%2Fresource%3Fid%3D1840%2F06%2FC-0100-02517.pdf#page=1&zoom=auto,-53,742 (accessed January 3, 2023).

78. Richard Stites, *The Four Horsemen: Riding to Liberty in Post-Napoleonic Europe* (Oxford: Oxford University Press, 2014), 76.

79. Congreso de los Diputados, "Número 100," 2520 (emphasis in original).

80. Congreso de los Diputados, 2520–2521.

81. Congreso de los Diputados, 2521.

82. Congreso de los Diputados, "Número 112: Sesión extraordinaria de la noche del martes 20 de julio de 1841," *Diario de sesiones: Serie histórica*, 2485, https://app.congreso.es/est_sesiones/web/viewer.html?file=https%3A%2F%2Fapp.congreso.es%2Fest_sesiones%2Fresource%3Fid%3D1841%2F07%2FC-0112-02481.pdf#page=1&zoom=auto,-52,602 (accessed January 3, 2023).

83. Congreso de los Diputados, 2488.

84. Congreso de los Diputados, 2487.

85. Congreso de los Diputados, 2487.

86. Congreso de los Diputados, 2487.

87. Congreso de los Diputados, 2495.

88. Congreso de los Diputados, 2496.

89. Congreso de los Diputados, 2496.

90. Congreso de los Diputados, 2497.

91. Congreso de los Diputados, 2499.

92. Shubert, *Social History of Modern Spain*, 144.

93. Callahan, "Two Spains," 168.

94. Jean Antoine Llorente, *History of the Inquisition of Spain, from the Time of Its Establishment to the Reign of Ferdinand VII: Composed from the Original Documents of the Archives of the Supreme Council and from Those of Subordinate Tribunals of the Holy Office* (London: Geo. B. Whittaker, 1827), 567. https://www.gutenberg.org/files/38354/38354-h/38354-h.htm (accessed May 29, 2023).

95. Julián Juderías, *La leyenda negra* (Barcelona: Araluce, 1917), 21, 22, 316.

96. Juderías, 272, 275.

97. Daniel Muñoz Sempere, *La Inquisición española como tema literario: Política, historia y ficción en la crisis del antiguo régimen* (Suffolk: Tamesis, 2008), 39, 100.

98. Llorente, *History of the Inquisition*, 568–569.

99. Quoted in Íñigo Sánchez Llama, *Galería de escritoras isabelinas: La prensa periódica entre 1833 y 1895* (Madrid: Cátedra, 2000), 191.

100. Shubert, *Social History of Modern Spain*, 146.

101. Álvarez Junco, "La nación en duda," 447.

102. Callahan, "Two Spains," 158, 160.

103. Shubert, *Social History of Modern Spain*, 148, 150–152.

104. Callahan, "Two Spains," 160–162.

105. Shubert, *Social History of Modern Spain*, 164.

106. Shubert, 163.

107. Julio de la Cueva Merino and Ángel Luis López Villaverde, "A modo de introducción: Reflexiones en torno al clericalismo y al asociacionismo católico," in *Clericalismo y asociacionismo católica en España: De la Restauración a la Transición; Un siglo entre el palio y el consiliario*, ed. Julio de la Cueva Merino and Ángel Luis López Villaverde (Ciudad Real: Ediciones de la Universidad de Castilla–La Mancha, 2005), 24.

108. Cueva Merino and López Villaverde, *Clericalismo y asociacionismo católica*, 39.

109. Francisco Javier Ramón Solans, "Mary into Combat: Marian Devotions and Political Mobilizations during the European Culture Wars," *European History Quarterly* 51, no. 3 (2021): 331, https://doi.org/10.1177/02656914211024943.

110. Ramón Solans, 338.

111. Ramón Solans, 339.

112. José Manuel Cuenca, *D. Pedro de Inguanzo y Rivero (1764–1836): Ultimo primado del antiguo régimen* (Pamplona: Universidad de Navarra, 1965), 214–215.

113. David Martínez Vilches, "'Católicos conciudadanos': Los sermones del clero liberal en el trienio constitucional (1820–1823)," in *El Trienio Liberal (1820–1823): Balance y perspectivas*, ed. Ivana Frasquet, Pedro Rújula, and Álvaro París (Zaragoza: Prensas de la Universidad de Zaragoza, 2022), 546, 552.

NOTES TO PAGES 35–40

114. Cuenca, *D. Pedro*, 141.

115. Rafael de Vélez, *Apología del altar y del trono, o Historia de las reformas hechas en España en tiempo de las llamadas cortes, e impugnación de algunas doctrinas publicadas en·la Constitución, diarios, y otros escritos contra la religión y el estado* (Madrid: Cano, 1818), 334.

116. Anthony D. Smith, *Nationalism and Modernism: A Critical Survey of Recent Theories of Nations and Nationalism* (London: Routledge, 1998), 23.

117. Smith, 19–20.

118. Carr, *Spain*, 39, 43.

119. Maryellen Bieder, "Historical Background: From Wars and Revolution to Constitutional Monarchies; Spain's Sporadic Path to Modernity, 1808–1919," in *A New History of Iberian Feminisms*, ed. Silvia Bermúdez and Roberta Johnson (Toronto: University of Toronto Press, 2008), 95.

120. Bieder, 97.

121. Moreno Antón, *La enajenación de bienes eclesiásticos*, 76.

122. Francisco Simón Segura, *La desamortización española en el siglo XIX* (Madrid: Ministerio de Hacienda, Instituto de Estudios Fiscales, 1973), 276.

123. Francisco Tomás y Valiente, *El marco político de la desamortización de España* (Barcelona: Ediciones Ariel, 1971), 73.

124. Menéndez y Pelayo, *Historia de los heterodoxos españoles*, 835, 837.

125. Menéndez y Pelayo, 299.

CHAPTER 2 — AT THE HEART OF THE NATION

1. Marieta Cantos Casenave, *Fernán Caballero: Entre el folklore y la literatura de creación; De la relación al teatro* (Cádiz: Ayuntamiento de El Puerto de Santa María, 1999), 379.

2. The notion of "patrimony" in Western Europe was largely influenced by the French legal term *patrimoine*. The concept of heritage after the French Revolution extended from familial inheritance to a wider cultural patrimony determined by the nation. Marilena Vecco, "A Definition of Cultural Heritage: From the Tangible to the Intangible," *Journal of Cultural Heritage* 11, no. 3 (2010): 321, https://doi.org/10.1016/j.culher.2010.01.006.

3. Susan Kirkpatrick, *Las Románticas: Escritoras y subjetividad en España, 1835–1850* (Madrid: Cátedra, 1991), 229.

4. Cantos Casenave, *Fernán Caballero*, 380.

5. Carmen Bravo-Villasante, introduction to *La gaviota*, by Cecilia Böhl de Faber, ed. Carmen Bravo-Villasante (Madrid: Castalia, 1979), 25.

6. Gabriel Tortella, *El desarrollo de la España contemporánea: Historia económica de los siglos XIX y XX* (Madrid: Alianza, 1994), 51.

7. Derek Flitter, *Spanish Romantic Literary Theory and Criticism* (Cambridge: Cambridge University Press, 1992), 162–163.

8. *La familia de Alvareda* was Böhl's first long novel, set in 1810. Flitter, *Spanish Romantic Literary Theory*, 153.

Julio Rodríguez-Luis contends that *Magdalena* is Böhl's oldest work, probably written between 1816 and 1820 during her first marriage. The exact dates of writing of Böhl's novels are largely unknown, owing to the fact that Böhl wrote in secret long before she published. Julio Rodríguez-Luis, introduction to *La familia de Alvareda*, ed. Julio Rodríguez-Luis (Madrid: Castalia, 1979), 21–22.

9. Cecilia Böhl de Faber (Fernán Caballero), *Callar en vida y perdonar en muerte*, in *Obras de Fernán Caballero: 2*, ed. José María Castro Calvo (Madrid: Atlas, 1961), 244.

10. Íñigo Sánchez Llama, *Galería de escritoras isabelinas: La prensa periódica entre 1833 y 1895* (Madrid: Cátedra, 2000), 100.

11. Xavier Andreu Miralles, "La mujer católica y la regeneración de España: Género, nación y modernidad en Fernán Caballero," *Género, sexo y nación: Representaciones y prácticas políticas en España (siglos XIX–XX)*, Mélanges de la Casa de Velázquez, n.s., vol. 42, no. 2 (2012): 32.

12. Quoted in Sánchez Llama, *Galería de escritoras isabelinas*, 101. Furthermore, Böhl's support from the neo-Catholic establishment was met with fierce criticism from author and politician Juan Valera (1824–1905), who claimed that Böhl was politicizing her novels "para ensalzar el Antiguo Régimen y condenar la civilización de nuestro siglo" [to extol the ancien régime and condemn the civilization of our century]. Quoted in Sánchez Llama, *Galería de escritoras isabelinas*, 101.

13. Derek Flitter, *Spanish Romanticism and the Uses of History: Ideology and the Historical Imagination* (Oxford: Legenda, 2006), 29; Kirkpatrick, *Las Románticas*, 232.

14. Carol Tully, "How German Romanticism Travelled to Spain: The Intellectual Journey of Johann Nikolas Böhl von Faber," *Publications of the English Goethe Society* 71, no. 1 (2016): 80, https://doi.org/10.1080/09593683.2001.11716326.

15. Salvador García Castañeda argues that Romanticism arrived in Spain from abroad to be imitated in its external features, with little regard for ideological and doctrinal implications. Typified by a tardy development, it scarcely made an impact throughout its brief run before culminating in the rise of realism. After all, the idea of Romantic liberty was limited on ideological, moral, and religious grounds. Salvador García Castañeda, *Las ideas literarias en España entre 1843 y 1850* (Berkeley: University of California Press, 1971), 3–4. Although Romanticism returned "a dar vida a la historia" [to give life to history], García Castañeda asserts that the nation and the past also constitute literary resources (5).

16. Flitter, *Spanish Romanticism*, 52; Tully, "How German Romanticism," 82.

17. Philip W. Silver, *Ruin and Restitution: Reinterpreting Romanticism in Spain* (Nashville: Vanderbilt University Press, 1997), 38.

18. Silver, 7–8.

19. Silver, 8–10.

20. Jo Labanyi, "Liberal Individualism and the Fear of the Feminine in Spanish Romantic Drama," in *Culture and Gender in Nineteenth-Century Spain*, ed. Lou Charnon-Deutsch and Jo Labanyi (Oxford: Clarendon Press, 1995), 8.

21. Flitter, *Spanish Romanticism*, 20.

22. Labanyi, "Liberal Individualism," 10.

23. Kirkpatrick, *Las Románticas*, 118.

24. Labanyi, "Liberal Individualism," 10–11.

25. Quoted in Karl Menges, "Particular Universals: Herder on National Literature, Popular Literature, and World Literature," in *A Companion to the Works of Johann Gottfried Herder*, ed. Hans Adler and Wulf Koepke (Columbia, S.C.: Camden House, 2009), 198–199, https://www.jstor.org/stable/10.7722/j.ctt14brrn7.13.

26. Menges, 199.

27. Flitter, *Spanish Romanticism*, 153.

28. Flitter, 158. Other Spanish Romantic writers who also shared Böhl's ideas were Ramón López Soler and Agustín Durán (153).

29. Joaquín Álvarez Barrientos, "En torno a las nociones de andalucismo y costumbrismo," in *Costumbrismo andaluz*, ed. Joaquín Álvarez Barrientos and Alberto Romero Ferrer (Seville: Universidad de Sevilla, 1998), 11.

30. Costumbrismo celebrated *Volksgeist*, claiming that each *pueblo* [people] was equipped with what Herder called *Nazionalkarakter* [national character]. This search for a permanent "character," applied to Herder's native Germany from the late eighteenth to the early nineteenth centuries, responded to the imperialistic and universalistic strains of the Napoleonic project. Carlos Serrano, "Conciencia de la crisis, conciencias en crisis," in *Más se perdió en Cuba: España, 1898 y la crisis de fin de siglo*, ed. Juan Pan-Montojo (Madrid: Alianza, 1988), 355–56.

NOTES TO PAGES 42–45

31. Flitter, *Spanish Romantic Literary Theory*, 152.

32. Susan Kirkpatrick suggests that although Böhl's subject matter associates her with the Spanish peasantry, her own familial background and educational and cultural formation were more European than Spanish. Indeed, Böhl wrote almost all her novels in French, and some in German and Spanish. Even though she had spent years collecting material and was composing from 1822 onward, she only started writing officially in 1842. Kirkpatrick, *Las Románticas*, 230–231.

33. Böhl respected her father's literary achievements. Flitter notes that Böhl once negotiated, although unsuccessfully, with a German bookseller to secure the publication of the second volume of her father's 1832 work, *Teatro español anterior a Lope de Vega*. I posit that the first name of Böhl's pseudonym recalls the medieval Spanish king Ferdinand III. Venerated as a saint and hero, this figure embodied heroic, monarchical, and Christian qualities, which summarized the traditionalist Spanish Romantic response to the Middle Ages. Flitter, *Spanish Romantic Literary Theory*, 153–154.

34. Teresa González Pérez, "Identidad cultural y discurso de género: Las mujeres patriotas en el imaginario nacional," *Cadernos de História da Educação* 10, no. 1 (2011): 228–229.

35. Alison Sinclair, "The Regional Novel: Evolution and Consolation," in *The Cambridge Companion to the Spanish Novel: From 1600 to the Present*, ed. Harriet Turner and Adelaida López de Martínez (Cambridge: Cambridge University Press, 2006), 55.

36. Álvarez Barrientos, "En torno a las nociones," 12.

37. Álvarez Barrientos, 12.

38. Alejandro Pizarroso Quintero, "Prensa y propaganda bélica 1808–1814," *Cuadernos dieciochistas* 8 (2007): 221.

39. Álvarez Barrientos, "En torno a las nociones," 12–13; Pizarroso Quintero, "Prensa y propaganda bélica," 220.

40. Álvarez Barrientos, "En torno a las nociones," 13.

41. At the end of 1800s, the main urbanized cities were Madrid and Barcelona. However, only 9 percent of the Spanish population were big-city dwellers, with the majority remaining in rural and small provincial areas. Tortella, *El desarrollo de la España*, 36–37.

42. Marisalada's affair with a bullfighter echoes that of the eponymous Andalusian gypsy in the French writer Prosper Mérimée's *Carmen* (1845), which, as José Colmeiro argues, reflected the nineteenth-century European orientalization of Spain. José F. Colmeiro, "Exorcising Exoticism: *Carmen* and the Construction of Oriental Spain," *Comparative Literature* 54, no. 2 (Spring 2002): 127, https://www.jstor.org/stable/4122479. Given that *La gaviota* was published four years after *Carmen*, it seems that Böhl, in her aim to establish a national literature for Spain, "rewrites" the story by having the flighty Marisalada live and Pepe Vera perish instead.

43. Böhl, *La gaviota*, 39–40.

Although both terms are often used interchangeably, Álvarez Junco states that *nación* [nation] entailed the creation of a mythology for an existing collective entity, while *patria* [homeland] exalted monarchy, religion, and the traditions and fundamental institutions typical of the old order. José Álvarez Junco, *Mater Dolorosa: La idea de España en el siglo XIX* (Madrid: Taurus, 2001), 363.

44. Xavier Andreu Miralles, *El descubrimiento de España: Mito Romántico e identidad nacional* (Madrid: Taurus, 2016), 321.

45. Andreu Miralles, 197.

46. Andreu Miralles, 197.

47. Andreu Miralles, 321.

48. Ian Duncan, "The Provincial or Regional Novel," in *A Companion to the Victorian Novel*, ed. Patrick Brantlinger and William B. Thesing (Hoboken, N.J.: Blackwell, 2005), 320.

49. Tortella, *El desarrollo de la España*, 51.

50. Quoted in Bravo-Villasante, introduction, 25.

51. Bravo-Villasante, 25.

52. Duncan, "Provincial or Regional Novel," 322.

53. Ferran Archilés, "La nación narrada, la nación vivida: Nación y región como horizonte textual en *Arroz y Tartana* (1894) de Vicente Blasco Ibáñez," in *Ondear la nación: Nacionalismo banal en España*, ed. Alejandro Quiroga and Ferran Archilés (Granada: Editorial Comares, 2018), 79.

54. Böhl, *La gaviota*, 41.

55. Böhl, 41.

56. Duncan, "Provincial or Regional Novel," 322.

57. Regarding transformed convents in Seville, see Antonio Cubero Hernández and María Teresa Pérez Cano.

58. Böhl, *La gaviota*, 202.

59. Böhl, 202.

60. Böhl, 204.

61. Böhl, 206.

62. Böhl, 70.

63. Böhl, 121.

64. Böhl, 170.

65. Böhl, 90. Also, in Spanish, the term *convento* can mean both a nunnery for women and also a monastery for men.

66. Böhl, 75.

67. Matthew 4:19.

68. Böhl, *La gaviota*, 165.

69. Böhl, 65.

70. Álvarez Barrientos, "En torno a las nociones," 13.

71. Ben Dodds, "Representations of Bandits in Mid-Nineteenth-Century Spain," *Cultural and Social History* 9, no. 2 (2012): 208, https://doi.org/10.2752/147800412X13270753068803.

72. Lou Charnon-Deutsch, *The Spanish Gypsy: The History of a European Obsession* (University Park: Pennsylvania State University Press, 2004), 179, 59. Racialized orientalist discourses, such as those of the French diplomat and theorist Joseph Arthur de Gobineau (1816–1882), conceptualized the gypsies as a "passionate race of pariahs" (45).

73. Zoe Beenstock, *The Politics of Romanticism: The Social Contract and Literature* (Edinburgh: Edinburgh University Press, 2016), 45.

74. Böhl, *La gaviota*, 180.

75. Böhl, 176–177.

76. Böhl, 176–177.

77. Böhl, 177.

78. Böhl, 177.

79. Böhl, 177.

80. Böhl, 177.

81. Cecilia Böhl de Faber, *La familia de Alvareda*, ed. Julio Rodríguez-Luis (Madrid: Castalia, 1979), 80–81.

82. Böhl, 75.

83. Javier Herrero, "El naranjo romántico: Esencia del costumbrismo," *Hispanic Review* 46, no. 3 (Summer 1978): 346, https://www.jstor.org/stable/472418.

84. Timothy W. Luke, "Identity, Meaning, and Globalization: Detraditionalization in Postmodern Space-Time Compression," in *Detraditionalization: Critical Reflections on Authority and Identity*, ed. Paul Heelas, Scott Lash, and Paul Morris (Hoboken, N.J.: Blackwell, 1996), 122.

85. Böhl, *La familia de Alvareda*, 80.

86. Böhl, 80.

87. Böhl, 75.

NOTES TO PAGES 54–66

88. Antonio A. Gómez Yebra, "Actualidad de los elementos folclóricos recopilados por Fernán Caballero," in *Actas del encuentro Fernán Caballero, hoy: Homenaje en el bicentenario del nacimiento de Cecilia Böhl de Faber 1996*, ed. Milagros Fernández Poza and Mercedes García Pazos (Cádiz: Ayuntamiento de El Puerto de Santa María, 1998), 77.

89. Böhl, *La familia de Alvareda*, 87.

90. Böhl, 87.

91. Kirkpatrick, *Las Románticas*, 233–234.

92. Böhl, *La familia de Alvareda*, 134.

93. Böhl, 135.

94. Böhl, 136.

95. Böhl, 87.

96. Böhl, 134.

97. Böhl, 144.

98. Böhl, 111.

99. Böhl, 152.

100. Böhl, 152.

101. Teresa Brennan and Carole Pateman, "Mere Auxiliaries to the Commonwealth: Women and the Origins of Liberalism," *Political Studies* 27, no. 2 (1979): 94, https://doi.org/10.1111/j.1467-9248.1979.tb01198.x.

102. Böhl, *Callar en vida*, 244.

103. Böhl, 247 (italics in original).

104. Cecilia Böhl de Faber, *Lágrimas: Novela de costumbres contemporáneas* (Madrid: Mellado, 1862), 311.

105. Javier Moreno-Luzón and Xosé Núñez Seixas, "The Flag and the Anthem: The Disputed Official Symbols of Spain," in *Metaphors of Spain: Representations of Spanish National Identity in the Twentieth Century*, ed. Javier Moreno-Luzón and Xosé Núñez Seixas (Oxford: Berghahn Books, 2017), 34, 57.

106. Böhl, *Lágrimas*, 49 (italics in original).

107. Böhl, 295.

108. Böhl, 48–49. Gabriel Tortella notes that in 1850, 75 percent of the Spanish population was illiterate. Tortella, *El desarrollo de la España*, 12.

109. Kirkpatrick, *Las Románticas*, 234.

110. Böhl, *Lágrimas*, 10.

111. Böhl, 10.

112. Böhl, 309.

113. Böhl, 309 (emphasis in original).

114. Böhl, 309.

115. See also Juan Rico y Amat.

116. Böhl, *Lágrimas*, 311 (emphasis in original).

117. Böhl, 325.

118. Böhl, 325.

119. Böhl, 342 (emphasis in original).

120. Böhl, 342.

121. Flitter, *Spanish Romantic Literary Theory*, 163.

122. Böhl, *Lágrimas*, 178–179.

CHAPTER 3 — THE HALLOWED, THE HAUNTING

1. Quoted in Susan J. Brison, "Trauma Narratives and the Remaking of the Self," in *Acts of Memory*, ed. Mieke Bal, Jonathan Crewe, and Leo Spitzer (Lebanon, N.H.: University Press of New England, 1999), 39.

184 NOTES TO PAGES 66–72

2. Franz Schneider, "Gustavo Adolfo Bécquer as 'Poeta' and His Knowledge of Heine's 'Leider," *Modern Philology* 19, no. 3 (1922): 251, https://www.jstor.org/stable/433441251.

3. Rubén Benítez, *Bécquer tradicionalista* (Madrid: Editorial Gredos, 1971), 51.

4. Jesús Rubio Jiménez, *Los Bécquer en Veruela: Un viaje artístico-literario* (Zaragoza: Iber-Caja, 1990), 34–35.

5. Leo Spitzer, "Back through the Future: Nostalgic Memory and Critical Memory in a Refuge from Nazism," in Bal, Crewe, and Spitzer, *Acts of Memory*, 90.

6. Barbara Cassin, *Nostalgia: When Are We Ever at Home?*, trans. Pascale-Anne Brault (New York: Fordham University Press, 2016), 5.

7. Kieran Flanagan, *Sociological Noir: Irruptions and the Darkness of Modernity* (London: Routledge, 2017), 75.

8. Svetlana Boym, *The Future of Nostalgia* (New York: Basic Books, 2001), 41, 49.

9. These texts have received considerably less attention compared to Bécquer's *Rimas* and *Leyendas*. See Sarah Sierra, Enrique Rull Fernández, and Francisco Javier Díez de Revenga Torres.

10. Flanagan, *Sociological Noir*, 120.

11. Benítez, *Bécquer tradicionalista*, 51.

12. Tom Lewis, "Gender, Discourse, and Modernity in Bécquer's *Rimas*," *Revista de Estudios Hispánicos* 31, no. 3 (October 1, 1997): 423.

13. Sarah Sierra, "Modernity and the Cultural Memory Crisis in Gustavo Adolfo Bécquer's *La cruz del diablo* and *El monte de las ánimas*," *Modern Language Review* 10, no. 2 (April 2015): 473, https://www.jstor.org/stable/10.5699/modelangrevi.110.2.0473.

14. Philip W. Silver, *Ruin and Restitution: Reinterpreting Romanticism in Spain* (Nashville: Vanderbilt University Press, 1997), xiii.

15. Silver, 66.

16. Silver, 74.

17. Benítez, *Bécquer tradicionalista*, 56.

18. Patricio de la Escosura, *España artística y monumental: Vistas y descripción de los sitios y monumentos más notables de España* (Paris: Imprenta de Fain y Thunot, 1842), 13.

19. Paul Patrick Rogers, "New Facts on Bécquer's *Historia de los templos de España*," *Hispanic Review* 8, no. 4 (October 1940): 311–312, http://www.jstor.org/stable/469761.

20. Gustavo Adolfo Bécquer, *Historia de los templos de España*, in *Gustavo Adolfo Bécquer: Obras completas*, 13th ed., ed. Dionisio Gamallo Fierros (Madrid: Aguilar, 1969), 771–773.

21. Miguel González-Gerth, "The Poetics of Gustavo Adolfo Bécquer," *MLN* 80, no. 2 (March 1965): 185, 186, 191, https://www.jstor.org/stable/3042609.

22. Bécquer, *Historia de los templos*, 770.

23. Rubio Jiménez, *Los Bécquer en Veruela*, 35.

24. Peter Linehan, *History and the Historians of Medieval Spain* (Oxford: Oxford University Press, 1993), 22–23.

25. Rafael Domínguez Casas, "San Juan de los Reyes: Espacio funerario y aposento regio," *Academia: Boletín de la Real Academia de Bellas Artes de San Fernando*, no. 78 (1994): 364.

26. Antolín Abad Pérez, "San Juan de los Reyes en la historia, la literatura y el arte," *Anales toledanos* 11 (1976): 120, 123.

27. Abad Pérez, 123.

28. Domínguez Casas, "San Juan de los Reyes," 373.

29. Daniel Ortiz Pradas, *San Juan de los Reyes de Toledo: Historia, construcción y restauración de un monumento medieval* (Madrid: La Ergástula, 2015), 57–58.

30. Pierre Nora, introduction to *Rethinking France: Les Lieux de Mémoire*, vol. 4, *Histories and Memories*, ed. Pierre Nora (Chicago: University of Chicago Press, 2010), vii.

31. Nora, viii.

32. Pedro Navascués Palacio, "Bécquer y San Juan de los Reyes," *Descubrir el arte*, no. 17 (2000): 96.

NOTES TO PAGES 72–78

33. Navascués Palacio, 98.

34. Navascués Palacio, 96. See also Manuel Peláez del Rosal regarding outcomes of disentailment and exclaustration on Franciscans.

35. Bécquer, *Historia de los templos*, 830.

36. Bécquer, 773.

37. Mary Douglas, *Purity and Danger: An Analysis of Concepts of Pollution and Taboo* (New York: Frederick A. Praeger, 1966), 115.

38. Bécquer, *Historia de los templos*, 812.

39. Duncan Stroik, *The Church Building as a Sacred Place: Beauty, Transcendence, and the Eternal* (Mundelein, Ill.: Hillenbrand Books, 2012), 64.

40. Bécquer, *Historia de los templos*, 769.

41. Bécquer, 770 (italics in original).

42. Bécquer, 775.

43. Bécquer, 770.

44. Brison, "Trauma Narratives," 45.

45. Brison, 48 (emphasis in original).

46. Brison, 48.

47. Brison, 46.

48. Bécquer, *Historia de los templos*, 771.

49. Bécquer, 837.

50. Bécquer, 835.

51. Bécquer, 836.

52. Bécquer, 836.

53. David Kennedy, *Elegy* (London: Routledge, 2007), 4.

54. Kennedy, 6.

55. Isabel Burdiel notes that the Bécquer brothers belonged to the artist collective SEM, which produced satirical, pornographic caricatures of figures like Isabel II and her confessor, Antonio María Claret. However, scholars argue that the Bécquers, sponsored by moderates such as Ramón María Narváez and Luis González Bravo, did not share the radical, progressive, republican, anticlerical, and antimonarchical principles displayed in these illustrations, some of which were also accredited to the republican artist Francisco Ortego, among others. Arguably, SEM could have been a pseudonymous collective or used by diverse creators since 1865. Isabel Burdiel, *Los Borbones en Pelota* (Zaragoza: Institución Fernando el Católico, 2012), 9–10.

56. Rubio Jiménez, *Los Bécquer en Veruela*, 22.

57. Rubio Jiménez, 46, 49, 51.

58. Rubio Jiménez, 17.

59. Marlon B. Ross, "Troping Masculine Power in the Crisis of Poetic Identity," in *Romanticism and Feminism*, ed. Anne Mellor (Bloomington: Indiana University Press, 1988), 44.

60. Gustavo Adolfo Bécquer, "El Monasterio de Veruela en Aragón," in Gamallo Fierros, *Gustavo Adolfo Bécquer*, 989.

While Bécquer regards the attention of artists, antiquarians, and tourists as necessary for the upkeep of the monastery, Böhl criticizes such materialistic aesthetes, who form the new group of occupants (see chapter 2). Bécquer's description of the state of the monastery makes no mention of its former inhabitants, indicating their absence. Thus, both writers, in their own ways, articulate a silent "loss."

61. Gustavo Adolfo Bécquer, "Carta IV," in Gamallo Fierros, *Gustavo Adolfo Bécquer*, 541 (emphasis mine).

62. Anthony D. Smith, *The Antiquity of Nations* (Cambridge: Polity, 2004), 75.

63. Smith, 14.

64. Gustavo Adolfo Bécquer, "Carta II," in Gamallo Fierros, *Gustavo Adolfo Bécquer*, 522–523.

186   NOTES TO PAGES 79–82

65. Bonnie Young, "A Medieval Bell," *Metropolitan Museum of Art Bulletin*, n.s., vol. 11, no. 10 (June 1953): 293, https://doi.org/10.2307/3258293. Matthew D. Herrera, however, traces the practice of ringing church bells back to the fifth century, when Saint Paulinus, the bishop of Nola, introduced the practice to summon monks to prayer. Two centuries later, Pope Sabinianus approved of bell ringing to call the faithful to Mass. By the ninth century, the custom had spread to all parishes of the Western Roman Empire. Matthew D. Herrera, "Sanctus Bells: Their History and Use in the Catholic Church," *Adoremus Bulletin* 11, no. 1 (March 2005), https://adoremus.org/2005/03/sanctus-bells/ (accessed May 29, 2023).

66. Jacques Le Goff, "Church Time and Merchant Time in the Middle Ages," trans. Christophe Campos, *Annales* 15, no. 3 (May–June 1960): 159.

67. Mircea Eliade, *Images and Symbols: Studies in Religious Symbolism*, trans. Philip Mairet (London: Harvill Press, 1961), 158.

68. Eliade, 155.

69. Eliade, 152.

70. Eliade, 151 (emphasis in original).

71. Sierra, "Modernity and the Cultural Memory," 473.

72. Benítez, *Bécquer tradicionalista*, 31.

73. Benítez, 36.

74. Benítez, 38.

75. Benítez, 60–61. Much like other European nations, Spain began to treat the past as "heritage" by establishing national provincial museums during the mid-nineteenth century to house expropriated religious and civil artifacts. Josefina Bello, *Frailes, intendentes y políticos: Los bienes nacionales 1835–1850* (Madrid: Taurus, 1997), 13–14. Several of these provincial museums were former convents and monasteries, such as the Museo do Pobo Galego in Galicia, the Museo de Bellas Artes in Seville, and the Museo de la Trinidad in Madrid, which became part of the Museo del Prado in 1872. Benítez observes that the denunciation of confiscation and demolition was also common, for instance, in the writings of José de Espronceda and the editorials of the periodical *El Semanario Pintoresco Español* [The picturesque Spanish weekly]. Benítez, *Bécquer tradicionalista*, 61.

76. Bécquer, "Carta IV," 541. In his phrase "poéticas tradiciones" [poetic traditions], Bécquer alludes to Spain's rich cultural heritage, combining it with religion, to which he pays homage in his ninth letter, where he refers to the "verdadera poesía de la religión" [true poetry of religion]. Gustavo Adolfo Bécquer, "Carta IX: La Virgen de Veruela," in Gamallo Fierros, *Gustavo Adolfo Bécquer*, 612.

77. Joe Bailey, *Pessimism* (London: Routledge, 1988), 43.

78. Rubio Jiménez, *Los Bécquer en Veruela*, 51.

79. Pierre Nora, "Between Memory and History: Les Lieux de Mémoire," *Representations* 26 (Spring 1989): 19, https://www.jstor.org/stable/2928520.7.

80. Bécquer, "Carta IV," 544.

81. Bécquer, 543.

82. Bécquer, 546.

83. Fray Luis de León, *Poesía*, 8th ed., ed. Jesús Manuel Alda Tesán (Zaragoza: Editorial Ebro, 1967), 24.

84. Armando López Castro, "Bécquer y los poetas del Siglo de Oro," in *Lógos hellenikós: Homenaje al profesor Gaspar Morocho Gayo*, vol. 2, ed. Jesús María Nieto Ibáñez (León: Universidad de León, Secretariado de Publicaciones y Medios Audiovisuales, 2003), 976.

85. Bécquer, "Carta IV," 543. The wars to which Bécquer refers here (sixty years prior to his *Cartas*) were the devastating Spanish War of Independence (1808–1814), which was fought against the French invaders; the Wars of Independence in Spanish America (1808–1826); and two of the three Carlist Wars that divided Spain (1833–1840 and 1846–1849).

86. During the Liberal Triennium, the politicians behind the 1812 Constitution of Cádiz (*doceañistas* [men of 1812]) implemented their economic reforms and sought stability to

NOTES TO PAGES 82–87

enjoy their gains. Christopher J. Ross, *Spain, 1812–1996* (New York: Oxford University Press, 2000), 9.

87. Sarah L. White, "Liberty, Honor, Order: Gender and Political Discourse in Nineteenth-Century Spain," in *Constructing Spanish Womanhood: Female Identity in Modern Spain*, ed. Victoria Lorée Enders and Pamela Beth Radcliff (Albany: State University of New York Press, 1999), 246.

88. San Juan de la Cruz, "Llama de amor viva," in *The Collected Works of Saint John of the Cross*, trans. Kieran Kavanaugh and Otilio Rodriguez (Washington, DC: Institute of Carmelite Studies, 1991), 52, ll. 1–6.

89. San Juan de la Cruz, "Cántico espiritual," in Kavanaugh and Rodriguez, *Collected Works*, 44.

90. Michel de Certeau, *Heterologies: Discourse on the Other*, trans. Brian Massumi (Minneapolis: University of Minnesota Press, 1986), 90 (emphasis in original).

91. De Certeau, 94.

92. De Certeau, 88. Moreover, the shattering of language—the mode of expressibility—is also pertinent to Romanticism, especially Romantic fragmentary poetics. As John Beer notes, Bécquer's *Rimas*, in particular, exhibit features of the Romantic "fragment" poem, which explained little yet suggested much. John Beer, "Fragmentations and Ironies," in *Questioning Romanticism*, ed. John Beer (Baltimore: Johns Hopkins University Press, 1995), 238–239. The fragment, he continues, is a reaction to "the current fascination for the resonant incident or experience where observation breaks off, leaving a space for the operation of imaginative suggestion" (241).

93. De Certeau, *Heterologies*, 86.

94. Gustavo Adolfo Bécquer, "Carta X," in Gamallo Fierros, *Gustavo Adolfo Bécquer*, 614.

95. Bécquer, *Historia de los templos*, 773.

96. Jane Donohoe, *Remembering Places: A Phenomenological Study of the Relationship between Memory and Place* (London: Lexington Books, 2014), 74.

97. Pedro Cerezo Galán, *El mal del siglo: El conflicto entre Ilustración y Romanticismo en la crisis finisecular del siglo XIX* (Granada: Biblioteca Nueva, Editorial Universidad de Granada, 2003), 365. Nevertheless, to believe earnestly in positivism's technological advances was a demonstration of faith. In this sense, positivism became a variant of religion, as the French philosopher John Ernest Renan observed (366).

98. Ross, "Troping Masculine Power," 27.

99. Fernando Darío González Grueso, "Lo tradicional y el elemento del miedo en las leyendas de Gustavo Adolfo Bécquer: Vínculos y poética," *Revista de Letras* 57, no. 1 (2017): 58.

100. Flanagan, *Sociological Noir*, 120.

101. Flanagan, 67.

102. Flanagan, 119.

103. Euan Cameron, *Enchanted Europe: Superstition, Reason, and Religion, 1250–1750* (Oxford: Oxford University Press, 2010), 241.

104. Cameron, 196.

105. It is relevant that, as indicated in chapter 1, the archbishop of Toledo, Pedro de Inguanzo y Rivero, died in 1836, Bécquer's birth year, and a year after the enactment of Mendizábal's extreme disentailment policies. Following his death was an eleven-year vacancy in the archepiscopate of Toledo, which ended with the nomination of Cardinal Juan José Bonel y Orbe in 1847. "Edad contemporánea (siglos XIX–XX)," Archidiócesis de Toledo, https://www.architoledo.org/archidiocesis/historia/#tab6 (accessed January 1, 2023).

106. Jane Garry, "Transformation, Motifs D0–D699," in *Archetypes and Motifs in Folklore and Literature: A Handbook*, ed. Jane Garry and Hasan M. El-Shamy (London: Routledge, 2004), 131.

107. James Mandrell, *Don Juan and the Point of Honor: Seduction, Patriarchal Society, and Literary Tradition* (University Park: Penn State University Press, 1992), 75.

108. Antonio Risco, *Literatura y fantasía* (Madrid: Taurus, 1982), 23.

NOTES TO PAGES 88–98

109. Risco, 110.

110. Edmund Burke, *A Philosophical Enquiry into the Sublime and Beautiful* (London: Routledge Classics, 2008), 59.

111. Burke, 61–62.

112. Thomas Weiskel, *The Romantic Sublime: Studies in the Structure and Psychology of Transcendence* (Baltimore: Johns Hopkins University Press, 1976), 16–17.

113. The arboreal image of the forest is a religious symbol. Mircea Eliade affirms that Christianity employed and reworked the symbol of the world tree in universal cosmologies. The cross, made of the wood of the tree of the knowledge of good and evil in the Garden of Eden, replaces the cosmic tree. The Lenten hymn "Crux fidelis" [Faithful cross], chanted on Good Friday, acknowledges Christ's sacrifice on this tree: "Faithful Cross! above all other / One and only noble Tree! None / in foliage, none in blossom, None / in fruit thy peer may be." *The Roman Catholic Daily Missal* (St. Marys, Kans.: Angelus Press, 1962), 556.

114. Gustavo Adolfo Bécquer, "La ajorca de oro," in Gamallo Fierros, *Gustavo Adolfo Bécquer*, 118–119.

115. Bécquer, 121.

116. Bécquer, 119.

117. Gustavo Adolfo Bécquer, "El beso," in Gamallo Fierros, *Gustavo Adolfo Bécquer*, 285.

118. Bécquer, 277.

119. Bécquer, "La ajorca de oro," 119.

120. Bécquer, 119.

121. Bécquer, 119.

122. Flanagan, *Sociological Noir*, 77–79.

123. Tzvetan Todorov, "Definition of the Fantastic," in *The Horror Reader*, ed. Ken Gelder (London: Routledge, 2000), 18.

124. Todorov, 18.

125. Bécquer, "La ajorca de oro," 120.

126. Bécquer, 122.

127. Philip Shaw, *The Sublime* (London: Routledge, 2006), 4.

128. Bécquer, "La ajorca de oro," 122.

129. Bécquer, "El beso," 290.

130. Gustavo Adolfo Bécquer, "El miserere," in Gamallo Fierros, *Gustavo Adolfo Bécquer*, 198.

131. Bécquer, 195–196.

132. Bécquer, 196.

133. Terry Castle, "Phantasmagoria: Spectral Technology and the Metaphorics of Modern Reverie," *Critical Inquiry* 15, no. 1 (Autumn 1988): 43, https://www.jstor.org/stable/1343603. Phantasmagoria was originally a "ghost-show" in late eighteenth-century and early nineteenth-century Europe. It made use of illusions and light to create "spectres" for public entertainment (27).

134. Castle, 43.

135. Shoshana Felman, *The Juridical Unconscious: Trials and Traumas in the Twentieth Century* (Cambridge, Mass.: Harvard University Press, 2002), 15 (emphasis in original).

136. Felman, 33.

137. Felman, 33.

138. Cathy Caruth, *Unclaimed Experience: Trauma, Narrative, and History* (Baltimore: Johns Hopkins University Press, 1996), 22.

CHAPTER 4 — A NEW VITAL FORCE

1. Carlos M. Rodríguez López-Brea, "Galdós, un cristiano heterodoxo," in *Galdós en su tiempo*, ed. Yolanda Arencibia and Ángel Bahamonde (Santa Cruz de Tenerife: Parlamentos de Cantabria y Canarias, 2006), 138.

NOTES TO PAGES 98-102

2. Antonio Jiménez García, *El Krausismo y la Institución Libre de Enseñanza* (Madrid: Cincel, 1985), 20; Daniel Rueda Garrido, "Aproximación a la teoría del conocimiento del krausismo español," *Revista de Filosofía* 43, no. 1 (2018): 69, https://doi.org/10.5209/RESF.60200.

3. By 1876, a "formidable laicist intelligentsia" had begun to form in Spanish universities, where young progressives adopted new ideologies, including Krausism, scientism, Hegelianism, regenerationism, socialism, and anarchism, partially as a response to political upheavals. While the 1873 failure of the First Republic led to the Restoration's relatively stable Spanish State, it also resulted in a corrupt parliamentary monarchy. For the politicized intellectual, the Restoration was too conservative; for the clerical faction, it was too liberal. Timothy Mitchell, *Betrayal of the Innocents: Desire, Power, and the Catholic Church in Spain* (Philadelphia: University of Pennsylvania Press, 1998), 38.

4. Nicolás Fernández-Medina, *Life Embodied: The Promise of Vital Force in Spanish Modernity* (Montreal: McGill–Queen's University Press, 2018), 4.

5. Denise DuPont, "Krausism and Modernism," *Hispanic Journal* 34, no. 2 (Fall 2013): 20, http://www.jstor.com/stable/44287191.

6. Juan López Morillas, *El krausismo español: Perfil de una aventura intelectual* (Mexico City: Fondo de Cultura Económica, 1956), 161.

7. Fernández-Medina, *Life Embodied*, 221. Fernández-Medina indicates that contrary to European historiography on Spain's backwardness due to its reputation as a defender of Catholicism in the Baroque era, several of its scholars did challenge the Church and its apologists, although their responses were hardly uniform and straightforward. Among the luminaries of the Spanish Enlightenment were clerics such as the Cistercian astronomer and mathematician Juan Caramuel y Lobkowitz, the Jesuit philosopher Baltasar Gracián y Morales, and the Benedictine scholar Benito Jerónimo Feijóo y Montenegro. (7–8).

8. Rodríguez López-Brea, "Galdós," 138.

9. Regarding sociopolitical and cultural changes in Galdós's novels, see also Hazel Gold and William H. Shoemaker.

10. Rodríguez López-Brea, "Galdós," 137.

11. Hazel Gold, *The Reframing of Realism: Galdós and Discourses of the Nineteenth-Century Spanish Novel* (Durham, N.C.: Duke University Press, 1993), 174.

12. Rodríguez López-Brea, "Galdós," 136, 164.

13. Benito Pérez Galdós, "Calor en la atmósfera y efervescencia en los ánimos. Furor neocatólico. Firmas y exposiciones. Partes telegráficos de la granja. Sudores, soponcios y vahídos" [July 16, 1865], in *Crónica de Madrid: (1865–1866) Obra inédita* (Madrid: Castro, 1933), 76.

14. Federico Sopeña Ibáñez, "Galdós y la desamortización," *Cuenta y razón* 2 (Spring 1981): 69.

15. Sopeña Ibáñez, 69.

16. Alfonso Armas Ayala, "Pérez Galdós y Pereda a través de sus cartas," in *Actas del Primer Congreso Internacional de Estudios Galdosianos*, ed. Government of Gran Canaria (Las Palmas: Cabildo Insular de Gran Canaria, 1977), 24.

17. Carmen Bravo-Villasante, "Veintiocho cartas de Galdós a Pereda," *Cuadernos Hispano-americanos*, nos. 250-251-252 (October 1970–January 1971): 15, http://www.cervantesvirtual.com/nd/ark:/59851/bmcgx4x9.

18. Quoted in Bravo-Villasante, 25.

19. William H. Shoemaker, *The Novelistic Art of Galdós*, vol. 2 (Valencia: Albatros-Hispanófila, 1980), 49.

20. Benito Pérez Galdós, *Doña Perfecta* (Madrid: Hernando, 1942), 279.

21. Ignacio Javier López, *La novela ideológica (1875–1880): La literatura de ideas en la España de la Restauración* (Madrid: Ediciones de la Torre, 2014), 21.

22. Wilfredo de Ràfols, "Lies, Irony, Satire, and the Parody of Ideology in *Doña Perfecta*," *Hispanic Review* 64, no. 4 (Autumn 1996): 475, https://www.jstor.org/stable/474883.

23. Mario Santana, "The Conflict of Narratives in Pérez Galdós *Doña Perfecta*," *MLN* 113, no. 2 (March 1998): 294, https://www.jstor.org/stable/3251476.

24. Santana, 302.

25. Arnold M. Penuel, "The Problem of Ambiguity in Galdós' *Doña Perfecta*," *Anales Galdosianos* 11 (1976): 74, http://www.cervantesvirtual.com/obra-visor/anales-galdosianos--7/html/0255070e-82b2-11df-acc7-002185ce6064_34.html#I_17_.

26. Wan Sonya Tang, "Sacred, Sublime, and Supernatural: Religion and the Spanish Capital in Nineteenth-Century Fantastic Narratives," in *The Sacred and Modernity in Urban Spain: Beyond the Secular City*, ed. Antonio Cordoba and Daniel García-Donoso (London: Palgrave Macmillan, 2016), 25.

27. Writing in 1896 to the painter Aureliano de Beruete, who produced an artistic rendition of Orbajosa (*Vista de Orbajosa*), Galdós revealed that Orbajosa was not just a fictitious town but a symbol of a dreary future. In his letter, Galdós employs Orbajosa as an adjective to demonstrate the danger of its reactionism, thus conveying pessimism for Spain's fate:

> Ya no hay en España provincia ni capital que no sea más ó menos Orbajosoido. Orbajosa encontrará Vd. en las aldeas . . . en las ciudades ricas y populosas. Orbajosa revive en las cabañas y en los dorados palacios. Todo es y todo será mañana Orbajosa, si Dios no se apiada de nosotros . . . Madrijosa.

> [There is no longer a province or capital in Spain that is not more or less like Orbajosa. Orbajosa can be found in the hamlets . . . in rich and populated cities. Orbajosa is reborn in huts and golden palaces. Everything is and will be Orbajosa tomorrow unless God pities us . . . Madrijosa.]

Quoted in Leo J. Hoar, "Galdós y Aureliano de Beruete, visión renovada de 'Orbajosa,'" *Anuario de Estudios Atlánticos* 1, no. 20 (1974): 707. As Leo J. Hoar indicates, Galdós's letter reaffirms that nothing has changed in the twenty years since the publication of *Doña Perfecta* and that the source of Spain's problems continues to be its "dolencia nacional" [national malady]—the array of social ills, conditions, and mindsets symbolized in Orbajosa (702).

28. Galdós, *Doña Perfecta*, 21.

29. Galdós, 22.

30. Anthony N. Zahareas, "Galdós' *Doña Perfecta*: Fiction, History and Ideology," *Anales Galdosianos* 11 (1976): 43, http://www.cervantesvirtual.com/obra-visor/anales-galdosianos--7/html/0255070e-82b2-11df-acc7-002185ce6064_32.html#I_11_.

31. Galdós, *Doña Perfecta*, 21.

32. Galdós, 32.

33. Zahareas, "Galdós' *Doña Perfecta*," 32.

34. Alison Sinclair, "The Regional Novel: Evolution and Consolation," in *The Cambridge Companion to the Spanish Novel: From 1600 to the Present*, ed. Harriet Turner and Adelaida López de Martínez (Cambridge: Cambridge University Press, 2006), 61.

35. Galdós, *Doña Perfecta*, 30 (italics in original).

36. Marlon B. Ross, "Troping Masculine Power in the Crisis of Poetic Identity," in *Romanticism and Feminism*, ed. Anne Mellor (Bloomington: Indiana University Press, 1988), 32.

37. Ross, 32.

38. Ross, 32–33.

39. Galdós, *Doña Perfecta*, 33–34 (italics in original).

40. Helen M. Malson observes that women have always signified excess in speech, emotion, and insecurity. According to the Cartesian mind-body dualism, femininity relates to the body and sentiment, while masculinity is associated with the mind and rationality. Helen M. Malson, "Anorexic Bodies and the Discursive Production of Feminine Excess," in *Body Talk: The Material and Discursive Regulation of Sexuality, Madness and Reproduction*, ed. Jane Ussher (London: Routledge, 1997), 237.

NOTES TO PAGES 104–110

41. Galdós, *Doña Perfecta*, 146–147.
42. Galdós, 147.
43. Galdós, 148.
44. Galdós, 33.
45. Galdós, 88.
46. Gold, *Reframing of Realism*, 25.
47. Mitchell, *Betrayal of the Innocents*, 44.
48. Mitchell, 47.
49. The common consequence of regional frustrations with the controlling "landholding plutocracy" was violence. Consequently, the Civil Guard was founded in 1844 to protect the rights of new landholders and to suppress dissidents. Mitchell, 47.
50. Galdós, *Doña Perfecta*, 170.
51. Galdós, 170.
52. Galdós, 171.
53. Galdós, 173.
54. Galdós, 173.
55. Ronald Cueto, "Our Lady, the French Revolution and Don Benito Pérez Galdós," in *A Face Not Turned to the Wall: Essays on Hispanic Themes for Gareth Alban Davies*, ed. Carlos A. Longhurst (Leeds: University of Leeds, 1987), 167.
56. Galdós, *Doña Perfecta*, 172.
57. Cueto, "Our Lady," 164.
58. Cueto, 166.
59. Cueto, 164.
60. López, *La novela ideológica*, 83; "Pope Pius IX," Holy See, http://www.vatican.va/news _services/liturgy/saints/ns_lit_doc_20000903_pius-ix_en.html (accessed May 29, 2023); "The Syllabus of Errors," Papal Encyclicals Online, https://www.papalencyclicals.net/pius09/p9syll .htm (accessed May 29, 2023).
61. Regarding the Anglo-Saxon context, Sandra M. Gilbert and Susan Gubar state that this paradigm of femininity was prevalent during the nineteenth century, when women were prepared for lives of privacy and reticence by being conditioned to fear public, open, and unconfined spaces. Sandra M. Gilbert and Susan Gubar, *The Madwoman in the Attic: The Woman Writer and the Nineteenth-Century Literary Imagination* (New Haven, Conn.: Yale University Press, 1980), 54.
62. Bridget Aldaraca, "El ángel del hogar: The Cult of Domesticity in Nineteenth-Century Spain in Theory and Practice of Feminist Literary Criticism," in *Theory and Practice of Feminist Literary Criticism*, ed. Gabriela Mora and Karen S. Van Hooft (Ypsilanti, Mich.: Bilingual P/Editorial Bilingüe, 1982), 63–66.
63. Galdós, *Doña Perfecta*, 36.
64. López, *La novela ideológica*, 199.
65. Miguel de Unamuno, "Sobre el marasmo actual de España," in *Obras completas*, vol. 8, *Ensayos*, ed. Ricardo Senabre (Madrid: Fundación José Antonio Fernández de Castro, 2007), 196.
66. Galdós, *Doña Perfecta*, 254.
67. Zahareas, "Galdós' *Doña Perfecta*," 38.
68. Sarah Sierra, "*Moros y cristianos*: Performing Ideological Dissent in Benito Pérez Galdós's *Doña Perfecta*," *Hispanófila*, no. 165 (May 2012): 31.
69. Raúl Mínguez Blasco, "Between Virgins and Priests: The Feminisation of Catholicism and Priestly Masculinity in Nineteenth-Century Spain," *Gender & History* 33, no. 1 (March 1, 2021): 94, 100.
70. Catherine Jagoe, *Ambiguous Angels* (Berkeley: University of California Press, 1994), 75.
71. Mínguez Blasco, "Between Virgins and Priests," 94.
72. It is likely that Galdós's Cayetano is named after Pereda's *El Tío Cayetano*, another factor indicative of the dialogue between the two writers.

73. Galdós, *Doña Perfecta*, 275.

74. Elaine Showalter, *The Female Malady: Women, Madness and English Culture, 1830–1980* (London: Virago, 1987), 3.

75. Alba del Pozo, "Degeneración, tienes nombre de mujer: Género y enfermedad en la cultura del fin de siglo XIX–XX," *Lectora* 19 (2013): 138, https://doi.org/10.1344/105.000002032.

76. Jane M. Ussher, *Women's Madness: Misogyny or Mental Illness?* (London: Harvester Wheatsheaf, 1991), 71.

77. Showalter, *Female Malady*, 4.

78. Galdós, *Doña Perfecta*, 201.

79. Galdós, 201.

80. Mitchell, *Betrayal of the Innocents*, 41.

81. Manuel Pérez Ledesma, "Studies on Anticlericalism in Contemporary Spain," *International Review of Social History* 46, no. 2 (August 2001): 244, https://www.jstor.org/stable/44583482.

82. Antonio Moliner Prado, "El anticlericalismo popular durante el bienio 1834–1835," *Hispania Sacra* 49, no. 100 (1997): 508.

83. Mitchell, *Betrayal of the Innocents*, 41.

84. Noël Valis, *Sacred Realism: Religion and the Imagination in Modern Spanish Narrative* (New Haven, Conn.: Yale University Press, 2010), 8.

85. Pérez Ledesma, "Studies on Anticlericalism," 244. From 1822 to 1936, at least 235 members of the clergy were killed and around five hundred churches and religious centers were burned, and during the three years of the Spanish Civil War, almost seven thousand priests, monks, and nuns were killed (227).

86. Cueto, "Our Lady," 159.

87. John H. Beck, "The Pelagian Controversy: An Economic Analysis," *American Journal of Economics and Sociology* 66, no. 4 (October 2007): 685, https://www.jstor.org/stable/27739661.

88. Beck, 692.

89. Gregorio Alonso, *La nación en capilla: Ciudadanía católica y cuestión religiosa en España, 1793–1874* (Granada: Comares, 2014), 6.

90. Germán Gullón, "'Sustituyendo el azogue del espejo': La novelización de la ideología decimonónica en *Doña Perfecta*," in *Galdós y la historia*, Ottawa Hispanic Studies 1, ed. Peter Bly (Ottawa: Dovehouse Editions Canada, 1988), 142.

91. Valis, *Sacred Realism*, 125.

92. Walter T. Pattison, *Benito Pérez Galdós and the Creative Process* (Minneapolis: University of Minnesota Press, 1954), 53, 59.

93. Rodríguez López-Brea, "Galdós," 146.

94. Madeea Axinciuc, "On Ecumenism and the Peace of Religions," *Journal for the Study of Religions and Ideologies* 10, no. 30 (Winter 2011): 173.

95. James V. Morrison, *Shipwrecked: Disaster and Transformation in Homer, Shakespeare, Defoe, and the Modern World* (Ann Arbor: University of Michigan Press, 2014), 12.

96. Paul Johnson, *The Birth of the Modern: World Society 1815–1830* (New York: Harper-Collins, 1991), 201.

97. Johnson, 188.

98. Benito Pérez Galdós, *Gloria*, ed. Ignacio Javier López (Madrid: Cátedra, 2011), 167.

99. Galdós, 207–208.

100. López, *La novela ideológica*, 208.

101. Akiko Tsuchiya, *Marginal Subjects: Gender and Deviance in Nineteenth Century Spain* (Toronto: University of Toronto Press, 2011), 29.

102. Tsuchiya, 56.

103. Galdós, *Gloria*, 224.

104. Galdós, 181.

NOTES TO PAGES 116–127

105. Galdós, 229.

106. López, *La novela ideológica*, 114–115.

107. Ignacio Javier López, introduction to Galdós, *Gloria*, 79; Sara E. Schyfter, *The Jew in the Novels of Benito Pérez Galdós* (Suffolk: Tamesis, 1978), 27.

108. López, introduction, 81.

109. Galdós, *Gloria*, 209.

110. Ross, "Troping Masculine Power," 31–32.

111. Galdós, *Gloria*, 209.

112. Galdós, 271.

113. Galdós, 271–272.

114. Galdós, 272.

115. Galdós, 272.

116. Galdós, 274.

117. Galdós, 317.

118. López, *La novela ideológica*, 199.

119. Galdós, *Gloria*, 561.

120. Sara E. Schyfter, "The Judaism of Galdós' Daniel Morton," *Hispania* 59, no. 1 (March 1976): 25, https://www.jstor.org/stable/339368.

121. Rodolfo Cardona, "*Mendizábal*: Grandes esperanzas," in Bly, *Galdós y la historia*, 99.

122. Benito Pérez Galdós, *Mendizábal: Episodios nacionales 22* (Madrid: Alianza, 2003), 29.

123. Galdós, 207.

124. Benito Pérez Galdós, *Montes de Oca: Episodios nacionales 28* (Madrid: Hernando, 1978), 13.

125. Peter Bush, "*Montes de Oca*: Galdós' Critique of 1898 *quijotismo*," *Bulletin of Hispanic Studies* 61, no. 4 (1984): 475, 479–801.

126. Adrian Shubert, *The Sword of Luchana: Baldomero Espartero and the Making of Modern Spain, 1793–1879* (Toronto: University of Toronto Press, 2021), 234.

127. Galdós, *Montes de Oca*, 16.

128. Galdós, 74.

129. Bush, "*Montes de Oca*," 472.

130. Bush, 472, 474.

131. Benito Pérez Galdós, *Electra*, in *La de San Quintín: Electra*, ed. Luis F. Díaz Larios (Madrid: Cátedra, 2002), 208.

132. Galdós, 338.

133. Galdós, 341.

134. Galdós, 337.

135. Galdós, 341.

136. Pío Baroja, "Galdós Vidente," in *Hojas sueltas*, ed. Luis Urrutia Salaverri (Madrid: Editorial Caro Raggio, 1973), 104.

137. Baroja, 106.

138. See María Victoria Nuñez.

139. Santos Juliá, *Historias de las dos Españas* (Madrid: Taurus, 2004), 92.

140. Benito Pérez Galdós, "Madrid, 1.º de marzo de 1901," in *Veintiocho cartas de Galdós a Pereda*, ed. Carmen Bravo-Villasante (Alicante: Biblioteca Virtual Miguel de Cervantes, 2012), 51 (italics in original).

141. Benito Pérez Galdós, letter to José María de Pereda, June 6, 1877, in Carmen Bravo-Villasante, *Veintiocho cartas*, 23.

142. Galdós, 23.

143. Galdós, 23.

144. Benito Pérez Galdós, "Al pueblo español," *El País: Diario Republicano* 23, no. 8087 (October 6, 1909), 1.

145. Galdós, 1.

146. Galdós, 1.

147. Galdós, 1.

CHAPTER 5 — THE ABYSS AND THE MOUNT

1. Sabina Kruszyńska, "*Écrasez l'infâme*: Voltaire's Philosophy of Religion," *Miscellanea Anthropologica et Sociologica* 16, no. 1 (2015): 125.

2. See Luz Colina de Rodríguez, Willis Knapp Jones, Judith E. Gale, Benito Madariaga de la Campa, and Henry Addy Bradley.

3. James O. Swain, "Reactionism in Pereda's *Tío Cayetano*," *Hispania* 17, no. 1 (February 1934): 84, https://www.jstor.org/stable/332410.

4. Alison Sinclair, "The Regional Novel: Evolution and Consolation," in *The Cambridge Companion to the Spanish Novel: From 1600 to the Present*, ed. Harriet Turner and Adelaida López de Martínez (Cambridge: Cambridge University Press, 2006), 54.

5. Benito Madariaga de la Campa, *José María de Pereda y su tiempo* (Polanco: Ayuntamiento de Polanco, 2003), 65.

6. Raquel Gutiérrez Sebastián, prologue to *Blasones y talegas*, by José María de Pereda, ed. Raquel Gutiérrez Sebastián (Doral, Fla.: Stock Cero, 2006), iv.

7. Benito Madariaga de la Campa, *Pereda: Biografía de un novelista* (Santander: Ediciones de Librería de Estudio, 1991), 71–72.

8. Swain, "Reactionism," 94.

9. Ignacio Javier López, "Pereda y la revolución liberal: *Don Gonzalo González de la Gonzalera* (1878)," *Bulletin of Hispanic Studies* 97, no. 4 (2020): 387–401, https://doi.org/10.3828/bhs.2020.22.

10. In the 1870s, Carlist militancy grew weaker, as it was confined to the north and thus lacked the necessary artillery and cavalry to expand. Raymond Carr, *Spain, 1808–1939* (Oxford: Oxford University Press, 1966), 339.

11. Carr, 303.

12. Carr, 351, 354.

13. Carr, 345.

14. López, "Pereda y la revolución," 388; Carr, *Spain*, 345, 351.

15. López, "Pereda y la revolución," 388.

16. Jo Labanyi, *Gender and Modernization in the Spanish Realist Novel* (Oxford: Oxford University Press, 2000), 300.

17. Sarah Sierra, "From Sacred Religion to Sacred Nation: Ritual Crisis in *Don Gonzalo González de la Gonzalera*," *Bulletin of Hispanic Studies* 91, no. 2 (2014): 128.

18. Stephanie Sieburth, *Inventing High and Low: Literature, Mass Culture, and Uneven Modernity in Spain* (Durham, N.C.: Duke University Press, 1994), 27.

19. Carr, *Spain*, 305.

20. Carr, 318–319, 337. Social and economic factors also contributed to the ideological and political crisis of the 1868 Revolution. Regarding the social question, peasant revolts in Andalusia and revolutionary workers' uprisings in Catalonia were becoming common in the 1860s. Also, economic struggles between 1865 and 1868 involved commercial setbacks and budgetary problems, which resulted from the cotton crisis of the American Civil War, European recession, and railway expenses. Decreased exports and railway construction, along with the decline of the cotton trade, contributed to Spain's ebbing economic power (209, 299–300).

21. Swain, "Reactionism," 84.

22. López, "Pereda y la revolución," 388.

23. Sierra, "From Sacred Religion," 128–129.

NOTES TO PAGES 133–142

24. Juan Álvarez Mendizábal, "Exposición a S. M. la Reina gobernadora," *Gaceta de Madrid*, February 21, 1836, 1, https://www.boe.es/gazeta/dias/1836/02/21/pdfs/GMD-1836-426.pdf (accessed May 24, 2023).

25. Pereda's *El Tío Cayetano* was published in two series: the first of thirteen issues between 1858 and 1859, and the second of thirty-two issues from 1868 to 1869. Swain, "Reactionism," 83.

26. Swain, 84.

27. Francisco José Aranda Pérez, "Pueblo o sociedad en el pensamiento político español de la modernidad: De la república y la comunidad, los súbditos y los vasallos, hacia la soberanía y la ciudadanía," *Cahiers d'études romanes*, no. 35 (2017): 173, https://doi.org/10.4000/etudesromanes.5844.

28. Honorio Manuel Velasco Maíllo, "Los significados de cultura y los significados de pueblo una historia inacabada." *Revista Española de Investigaciones Sociológicas*, no. 60 (1992): 14.

29. José Álvarez Junco, *Mater Dolorosa: La idea de España en el siglo XIX* (Madrid: Taurus, 2001), 139.

30. José María de Pereda, "¡Loado sea Dios!," *El Tío Cayetano*, no. 1 (November 9, 1868): 1.

31. Pereda, 1.

32. Carolyn P. Boyd, *Historia Patria: Politics, History, and National Identity in Spain, 1875–1975* (Princeton, N.J.: Princeton University Press, 1997), 71.

33. Mikhail Bakhtin, *The Dialogic Imagination: Four Essays* (Austin: University of Texas Press, 1981), 15.

34. Pereda, "¡Loado sea Dios!," 1.

35. Carr, *Spain*, 303.

36. Universal male suffrage was not made law until 1890. José María Jover and Guadalupe Gómez-Ferrer, "Sociedad, civilización y cultura," in *España: Sociedad, política y civilización (siglos XIX–XX)*, ed. José María Jover Zamora, Guadalupe Gómez-Ferrer, and Juan Pablo Fusi Aizpúrua (Madrid: Areté, 2001), 363.

37. Pereda, "¡Loado sea Dios!," 1 (emphasis in original).

38. Pereda, 1.

39. José María de Pereda, "La Iglesia libre," *El Tío Cayetano*, no. 6 (December 13, 1868): 1 (emphasis in original).

40. Pereda, 1 (emphasis in original).

41. Regarding the Church in liberal states, see also Manlio Graziano and Sergio Romano.

42. Pereda, "La Iglesia libre," 1 (emphasis in original).

43. Carr notes that aside from government legislation, there were also physical attacks on Church property throughout the revolution, which outraged Catholics, thereby weakening their loyalty to Amadeo of Savoy and attracting more Spaniards to the Carlist longing for a Bourbon Restoration. Carr, *Spain*, 345.

44. See Gregorio L. de la Fuente Monge.

45. Vicente Cárcel Ortí, *Historia de la Iglesia en la España contemporánea (siglos XIX y XX)* (Madrid: Ediciones Palabra, 2002), 84–85.

46. José María de Pereda, "Año nuevo," *El Tío Cayetano*, no. 9 (January 3, 1869): 1.

47. Pereda, 1.

48. Eric Storm, "La cultura regionalista en España, Francia y Alemania: Una perspectiva comparada (1890–1937)," *Ayer*, no. 82 (2011): 164, https://www.jstor.org/stable/41326125.

49. Pereda, *Blasones y talegas*, 59.

50. Pereda, 17.

51. Labanyi, *Gender and Modernization*, 301.

52. Carr, *Spain*, 43.

53. Pereda, *Blasones y talegas*, 48.

54. Pereda, 49.

55. Pereda, 49.

56. Pereda, *Blasones y talegas*, 36–37. *Sanculote*, a Gallicism transcribed by Pereda, comes from the term *sans-culotte* [without breeches], used to define the eighteenth-century working class and revolutionaries of France, who wore plain trousers as opposed to the aristocrats' culottes. Michael Sonenscher, "The Sans-culottes of the Year II: Rethinking the Language of Labour in Revolutionary France," *Social History* 9, no. 3 (October 1984): 303–304, https://www.jstor.org/stable/4285370.

57. Pereda, *Blasones y talegas*, 38–39.

58. Pereda, 39.

59. Pereda, 39.

60. Daniel Brown, "Commonsensical Determinism: A Reconsideration of Pereda's *De tal palo, tal astilla*," *Confluencia* 30, no. 1 (2014): 113, 120, https://www.jstor.org/stable/43490077.

61. Sieburth, *Inventing High and Low*, 184.

62. Maurice Halbwachs, *On Collective Memory*, ed. and trans. Lewis A. Coser (Chicago: University of Chicago Press, 1992), 61.

63. Astrid Erll, "Locating Family in Cultural Memory Studies," *Journal of Comparative Family Studies* 42, no. 3 (May–June 2011): 308, https://www.jstor.org/stable/41604447.

64. Ignacio Javier López, *La novela ideológica (1875–1880): La literatura de ideas en la España de la Restauración* (Madrid: Ediciones de la Torre, 2014), 281.

65. Marlon B. Ross, "Troping Masculine Power in the Crisis of Poetic Identity," in *Romanticism and Feminism*, ed. Anne Mellor (Bloomington: Indiana University Press, 1988), 44.

66. Joaquín Casalduero, introduction to *De tal palo, tal astilla*, by José María de Pereda, 4th ed., ed. Joaquín Casalduero (Madrid: Cátedra, 1981), 27.

67. Ignacio Javier López, introduction to *Gloria*, by Benito Pérez Galdós, ed. Ignacio Javier López (Madrid: Cátedra, 2011), 28–29.

68. Pereda, *De tal palo*, 196–197.

69. Pereda, 209.

70. Pereda, 212.

71. Christopher Dawson, *Religion and the Rise of Western Culture: The Classic Study of Medieval Civilisation* (New York: Doubleday, 1957), 45.

72. Pereda, *De tal palo*, 216.

73. Pereda, 81.

74. Pereda, 84 (italics in original).

75. Pereda, 86.

76. Pereda, 86.

77. Pereda, 217.

78. Page DuBois, *Sowing the Body: Psychoanalysis and Ancient Representations of Women* (Chicago: University of Chicago Press, 1988), 77.

79. Brown, "Commonsensical Determinism," 119.

80. Brown, 115.

81. Brown, 119.

82. Pereda, *De tal palo*, 173–174.

83. Pereda, 86–87.

84. Pereda, 176.

85. Pereda, 111.

86. Pereda, 90 (italics in original).

87. Pereda, 114.

88. Pereda, 115.

89. Noël Valis, *Sacred Realism: Religion and the Imagination in Modern Spanish Narrative* (New Haven, Conn.: Yale University Press, 2010), 11.

90. Pereda, *De tal palo*, 126.

91. Pereda, 128.

NOTES TO PAGES 151–164

92. Pereda, 182.

93. Pereda, 189.

94. Pereda, 189.

95. Pereda, 189.

96. Pereda, 82 (emphasis in original).

97. Pereda, 323.

98. Bernard Debarbieux, "Rootedness—Anchoring—Mooring: Reviving Metaphors," *L'Espace géographique* 43, no. 1 (2014): 68, https://archive-ouverte.unige.ch/unige:74912.

99. José María de Pereda, *Sotileza* (Madrid: Editorial Tesoro, 1962), 189.

100. Luis de Escallada González, "Inventarios sobre la fundación y desamortización del convento de San Ildefonso de Ajo," *Altamira: Revista del Centro de Estudiosos Montañeses*, no. 72 (2007): 181.

101. Julio Caro Baroja, *Introducción a una historia contemporánea del anticlericalismo español* (Madrid: Ediciones ISTMO, 1980), 170.

102. Pereda, *Sotileza*, 5.

103. Pereda, 5.

104. Eugene Savaiano, "Pereda's Portrayal of Nineteenth Century Clergymen," *Modern Language Journal* 36, no. 5 (May 1952): 225, https://www.jstor.org/stable/318381.

105. Pereda, *Sotileza*, 15–16.

106. Sinclair, "Regional Novel," 61.

107. Sinclair, 61.

108. Labanyi, *Gender and Modernization*, 331.

109. López, "Pereda y la revolución," 385, 396.

110. López, 393–394.

111. José Álvarez Junco, "The Formation of Spanish Identity and Its Adaptation to the Age of Nations," *History & Memory* 14, no. 1/2 (Fall 2002): 34, https://doi.org/10.1353/ham.2002 .0006.

112. Álvarez Junco, 27.

113. López, "Pereda y la revolución," 386.

114. Pereda, *Sotileza*, 81–82.

115. Pereda, 82.

116. López, "Pereda y la revolución," 401.

FINAL REFLECTIONS

1. Ana María Mendióroz Lacambra, "Miguel de Quintana, autor de la portada del convento de la Merced, actual Museo de Bellas Artes de Sevilla," *Laboratorio de Arte: Revista del Departamento de Historia del Arte*, no. 2 (1989): 261; Juan Aguilar Gutiérrez and Luis Francisco Martínez Montiel, "Las pinturas murales del Museo de Bellas Artes de Sevilla y su restauración," *Laboratorio de Arte: Revista del Departamento de Historia del Arte* 2, no. 5 (1992): 11.

2. Lewis Mumford, *The Culture of Cities* (New York: Open Road Media, 2016), 296.

3. Maurice Halbwachs, *On Collective Memory*, ed. and trans. Lewis A. Coser (Chicago: University of Chicago Press, 1992), 169.

4. Yves Lambert, "A Turning Point in Religious Evolution in Europe," *Journal of Contemporary Religion* 19, no. 1 (2004): 44, https://doi.org/10.1080/1353790032000165104.

5. Lieven Boeve, "Religion after Detraditionalization: Christian Faith in a Postsecular Europe," in *The New Visibility of Religion: Studies in Religion and Cultural Hermeneutics*, ed. Graham Ward and Michael Hoelzl (London: Continuum, 2008), 189.

6. Rodney Stark, "Secularization, R.I.P.," *Sociology of Religion* 60, no. 3 (1999): 269, https:// www.jstor.org/stable/3711936.

7. Joseba Louzao Villar, "La recomposición religiosa en la modernidad: Un marco conceptual para comprender el enfrentamiento entre laicidad y confesionalidad en la España contemporánea," *Hispania Sacra* 60, no. 121 (2008): 341.

8. Stark, "Secularization," 253, 269.

9. Robert Sarah and Nicolas Diat, *The Day Is Now Far Spent*, trans. Michael J. Miller (San Francisco: Ignatius Press, 2019), 39.

10. Mary Vincent, "Religion: The Idea of Catholic Spain," in *Metaphors of Spain: Representations of Spanish National Identity in the Twentieth Century*, ed. Javier Moreno-Luzón and Xosé Núñez Seixas (Oxford: Berghahn Books, 2017), 122, 139.

11. See, for instance, Carmen Bachiller and José Carlos Vizuete Mendoza.

12. Victor Urrutia Abaigar, "Church and State after Transition to Democracy: The Case of Spain," in *The Secular and the Sacred: Nation, Religion and Politics*, ed. William Safran (London: Routledge, 2002), 120.

13. "Alarma entre los obispos tras la reclamación de bienes a la Iglesia: 'Es una desamortización encubierta,'" *Público*, September 11, 2018, https://www.publico.es/espana/iglesia-alarma-obispos-reclamacion-bienes-iglesia-desamortizacion-encubierta.html (accessed December 23, 2022).

14. Óscar Morejón Hermosa, "Cinco grandes mentiras sobre las inmatriculaciones de la Iglesia," Libre Mercado, August 19, 2019, https://www.libremercado.com/2019-08-18/autores-invitados-cinco-grandes-mentiras-sobre-las-inmatriculaciones-de-la-iglesia-88564/ (accessed December 29, 2022).

15. Alicia Fiestas Loza, "La protección registral de los compradores de bienes eclesiásticos desamortizados (1863–1869)," *Anuario de historia del derecho español*, no. 53 (1983): 334, https://www.boe.es/biblioteca_juridica/anuarios_derecho/abrir_pdf.php?id=ANU-H-1983-10033400365 (accessed May 29, 2023).

16. Alejandro Díaz Zafra, "Exposición de los motivos y fundamentos del proyecto de Ley Hipotecaria," in *Ley Hipotecaria: Reglamento general para su ejecución e instrucción sobre la manera de redactar los instrumentos públicos sujetos a registro*, ed. Ministerio de Gracia y Justicia (Madrid: Ministerio de Gracia y Justicia, 1861), 3.

17. Javier Martín-Arroyo, "La Mezquita de Córdoba no es de los obispos, según un comité oficial," *El País*, September 17, 2018, https://elpais.com/sociedad/2018/09/14/actualidad/1536956121_483715.html (accessed December 31, 2022).

18. Elena G. Sevillano, "La Iglesia inscribió como propios 30.000 bienes en casi dos décadas," *El País*, August 13, 2019, https://elpais.com/sociedad/2019/08/11/actualidad/1565552360_678366.html (accessed December 31, 2022).

19. "El gobierno 'paraliza' por la pandemia el informe de los bienes inmatriculados por la Iglesia," *Europa Press*, June 10, 2020, https://www.europapress.es/sociedad/noticia-gobierno-paraliza-pandemia-informe-bienes-inmatriculados-iglesia-20200610141003.html (accessed December 26, 2022).

20. Crescencio Palomo Iglesias, *Claudio Sancho de Contreras (1811–1886): Dominico exclaustrado* (Segovia: Imprenta Gabel, 1970), 5.

Bibliography

Abad Pérez, Antolín. "San Juan de los Reyes en la historia, la literatura y el arte." *Anales toledanos* 11 (1976): 111–206.

Abellán, José Luís. Prologue to *El Krausismo y la Institución Libre de Enseñanza*, edited by Antonio Jiménez García, 11–17. Madrid: Cincel, 1985.

Abizanda Sanromán, Jesús. *El convento de los Trinitarios de Barbastro*. Barbastro: J. Abizanda, 2018.

Aguilar Gutiérrez, Juan, and Luis Francisco Martínez Montiel. "Las pinturas murales del Museo de Bellas Artes de Sevilla y su restauración." *Laboratorio de Arte: Revista del Departamento de Historia del Arte* 2, no. 5 (1992): 11–34.

Aldaraca, Bridget. "El ángel del hogar: The Cult of Domesticity in Nineteenth-Century Spain." In *Theory and Practice of Feminist Literary Criticism*, edited by Gabriela Mora and Karen S. Van Hooft, 62–87. Ypsilanti, Mich.: Bilingual P/Editorial Bilingüe, 1982.

Alonso, Gregorio. *La nación en capilla: Ciudadanía católica y cuestión religiosa en España, 1793–1874*. Granada: Comares, 2014.

Álvarez Barrientos, Joaquín. "En torno a las nociones de andalucismo y costumbrismo." In *Costumbrismo andaluz*, edited by Joaquín Álvarez Barrientos and Alberto Romero Ferrer, 11–18. Seville: Universidad de Sevilla, 1998.

Álvarez Junco, José. *A las barricadas: Cultura, identidad, y movilización política*. Madrid: Ediciones Complutense, 2009.

———. "The Formation of Spanish Identity and Its Adaptation to the Age of Nations." *History & Memory* 14, no. 1/2 (Fall 2002): 13–36. https://doi.org/10.1353/ham.2002.0006.

———. "La nación en duda." In Pan-Montojo, *Más se perdió en Cuba*, 405–476.

———. *Mater Dolorosa: La idea de España en el siglo XIX*. Madrid: Taurus, 2001.

Andreu Miralles, Xavier. *El descubrimiento de España: Mito Romántico e identidad nacional*. Madrid: Taurus, 2016.

———. "La mujer católica y la regeneración de España: Género, nación y modernidad en Fernán Caballero." *Género, sexo y nación: Representaciones y prácticas políticas en España (siglos XIX–XX)*, Mélanges de la Casa de Velázquez, n.s., vol. 42, no. 2 (2012): 17–35.

Antequera, José María. *La desamortización eclesiástica: Considerada en sus diferentes aspectos y relaciones*. Madrid: A. Pérez Dubrull, 1885.

Aranda Pérez, Francisco José. "Pueblo o sociedad en el pensamiento político español de la modernidad: De la república y la comunidad, los súbditos y los vasallos, hacia la soberanía y la ciudadanía." *Cahiers d'études romanes*, no. 35 (2017): 167–192. https://doi.org/10.4000/etudesromanes.5844.

Arboix, Alba. *Barcelona: Esglésies i construcció de la ciutat*. Barcelona: Ajuntament de Barcelona, 2018.

Archidiócesis de Toledo. "Edad contemporánea (siglos XIX–XX)." https://www.architoledo.org/archidiocesis/historia/#tab6 (accessed January 1, 2023).

Archilés, Ferran. "La nación narrada, la nación vivida: Nación y región como horizonte textual en *Arroz y Tartana* (1894) de Vicente Blasco Ibáñez." In *Ondear la nación: Nacionalismo banal en España*, edited by Alejandro Quiroga and Ferran Archilés, 73–96. Granada: Editorial Comares, 2018.

Armas Ayala, Alfonso. "Pérez Galdós y Pereda a través de sus cartas." In *Actas del Primer Congreso Internacional de Estudios Galdosianos*, edited by Government of Gran Canaria, 23–33. Las Palmas: Cabildo Insular de Gran Canaria, 1977.

Asín, Francisco, and Alfonso Bullón de Mendoza. *Carlismo y sociedad, 1833–1840*. Zaragoza: Aportes XIX, 1987.

Assmann, Jan. *Religion and Cultural Memory: Ten Studies*. Translated by Rodney Livingstone. Stanford: Stanford University Press, 2006.

Axinciuc, Madeea. "On Ecumenism and the Peace of Religions." *Journal for the Study of Religions and Ideologies* 10, no. 30 (Winter 2011): 159–182.

Bachiller, Carmen. "Conventos de Toledo, sin solución para un patrimonio en peligro de extinción." *El Diario*, June 14, 2017. https://www.eldiario.es/clm/Conventos-Toledo-solucion-patrimonio-extincion_0_657934259.html (accessed May 19, 2023).

Bailey, Joe. *Pessimism*. London: Routledge, 1988.

Bakhtin, Mikhail. *The Dialogic Imagination: Four Essays*. Austin: University of Texas Press, 1981.

Bal, Mieke. Introduction to Bal, Crewe, and Spitzer, *Acts of Memory*, vii–xvii.

Bal, Mieke, Jonathan Crewe, and Leo Spitzer, eds. *Acts of Memory: Cultural Recall in the Present*. Lebanon, N.H.: University Press of New England, 1999.

Balmes, Jaime. "Dos escollos." *El Pensamiento de la Nación*, no. 70 (1845): 353–360.

Baroja, Pío. "Galdós Vidente." In *Hojas sueltas*, edited by Luis Urrutia Salaverri, 104–106. Madrid: Editorial Caro Raggio, 1973.

Beck, John H. "The Pelagian Controversy: An Economic Analysis." *American Journal of Economics and Sociology* 66, no. 4 (October 2007): 681–696. https://www.jstor.org/stable/27739661.

Bécquer, Gustavo Adolfo. "Carta II." In Gamallo Fierros, *Gustavo Adolfo Bécquer*, 516–526.

——. "Carta IV." In Gamallo Fierros, *Gustavo Adolfo Bécquer*, 540–549.

——. "Carta IX: La Virgen de Veruela." In Gamallo Fierros, *Gustavo Adolfo Bécquer*, 602–612.

——. "Carta X." In Gamallo Fierros, *Gustavo Adolfo Bécquer*, 613–614.

——. *Cartas desde mi celda*. In Gamallo Fierros, *Gustavo Adolfo Bécquer*, 499–614.

——. "El beso." In Gamallo Fierros, *Gustavo Adolfo Bécquer*, 275–290.

——. "El miserere." In Gamallo Fierros, *Gustavo Adolfo Bécquer*, 189–200.

——. "El Monasterio de Veruela en Aragón." In Gamallo Fierros, *Gustavo Adolfo Bécquer*, 984–989.

——. *Historia de los templos de España*. In Gamallo Fierros, *Gustavo Adolfo Bécquer*, 767–947.

——. "La ajorca de oro." In Gamallo Fierros, *Gustavo Adolfo Bécquer*, 115–122.

Beenstock, Zoe. *The Politics of Romanticism: The Social Contract and Literature*. Edinburgh: Edinburgh University Press, 2016.

Beer, John. "Fragmentations and Ironies." In *Questioning Romanticism*, edited by John Beer, 234–264. Baltimore: Johns Hopkins University Press, 1995.

——. *Questioning Romanticism*. Baltimore: Johns Hopkins University Press, 1995.

Bello, Josefina. *Frailes, intendentes y políticos: Los bienes nacionales 1835–1850*. Madrid: Taurus, 1997.

BIBLIOGRAPHY

Benítez, Rubén. *Bécquer tradicionalista*. Madrid: Editorial Gredos, 1971.

Berger, Joachim. "The Great Divide: Transatlantic Brothering and Masonic Internationalism, c. 1870–c. 1930." *Atlantic Studies* 16, no. 3 (2019): 405–422.

Bieder, Maryellen. "Historical Background: From Wars and Revolution to Constitutional Monarchies; Spain's Sporadic Path to Modernity, 1808–1919." In *A New History of Iberian Feminisms*, edited by Silvia Bermúdez and Roberta Johnson, 93–100. Toronto: University of Toronto Press, 2008.

Bly, Peter, ed. *Galdós y la historia*. Ottawa Hispanic Studies 1. Ottawa: Dovehouse Editions Canada, 1988.

Boeve, Lieven. "Religion after Detraditionalization: Christian Faith in a Postsecular Europe." In *The New Visibility of Religion: Studies in Religion and Cultural Hermeneutics*, edited by Graham Ward and Michael Hoelzl, 187–209. London: Continuum, 2008.

Böhl de Faber, Cecilia [Fernán Caballero, pseud.]. *Callar en vida y perdonar en muerte*. In *Obras de Fernán Caballero: 2*, edited by José María Castro Calvo, 235–249. Madrid: Atlas, 1961.

———. *La familia de Alvareda*. Edited by Julio Rodríguez-Luis. Madrid: Castalia, 1979.

———. *La gaviota*. Edited by Carmen Bravo-Villasante. Madrid: Editorial Castalia, 1979.

———. *Lágrimas: Novela de costumbres contemporáneas*. Madrid: Mellado, 1862.

Bossuet, Jacques Bénigne. *Politics Drawn from Holy Scripture*. Edited by Patrick Riley. Cambridge: Cambridge University Press, 1990.

Boyd, Carolyn P. *Historia Patria: Politics, History, and National Identity in Spain, 1875–1975*. Princeton, N.J.: Princeton University Press, 1997.

Boym, Svetlana. *The Future of Nostalgia*. New York: Basic Books, 2001.

Bradley, Henry Addy. "Pereda and Galdós: A Comparison of Their Political, Religious and Social Ideas." PhD diss., University of Southern California, 1966.

Bravo-Villasante, Carmen. *Galdós visto por sí mismo*. Madrid: Editorial Magisterio, 1979.

———. Introduction to *La gaviota*, by Cecilia Böhl de Faber, edited by Carmen Bravo-Villasante, 7–30. Madrid: Castalia, 1979.

———, ed. *Veintiocho cartas de Galdós a Pereda*. Alicante: Biblioteca Virtual Miguel de Cervantes, 2012.

———. "Veintiocho cartas de Galdós a Pereda." *Cuadernos Hispanoamericanos*, nos. 250-251-252 (October 1970–January 1971): 9–51. http://www.cervantesvirtual.com/nd/ark:/59851/bmcgx4x9.

Brennan, Teresa, and Carole Pateman. "Mere Auxiliaries to the Commonwealth: Women and the Origins of Liberalism." *Political Studies* 27, no. 2 (1979): 183–200. https://doi.org/10.1111/j.1467-9248.1979.tb01198.x.

Brennan, Timothy. "The National Longing for Form." In *Nation and Narration*, edited by Homi Bhabha, 44–70. London: Routledge, 1990.

Brison, Susan J. "Trauma Narratives and the Remaking of the Self." In Bal, Crewe, and Spitzer, *Acts of Memory*, 39–54.

Brown, Daniel. "Commonsensical Determinism: A Reconsideration of Pereda's *De tal palo, tal astilla*." *Confluencia* 30, no. 1 (2014): 113–125. https://www.jstor.org/stable/43490077.

Burdiel, Isabel. *Los Borbones en Pelota*. Zaragoza: Institución Fernando el Católico, 2012.

———. "Myths of Failure, Myths of Success: New Perspectives on Nineteenth-Century Liberalism." *Journal of Modern History* 70, no. 4 (December 1998): 892–912. https://www.jstor.org/stable/10.1086/235170.

Burke, Edmund. *A Philosophical Enquiry into the Sublime and Beautiful*. London: Routledge Classics, 2008.

Bush, Peter. "*Montes de Oca*: Galdós' Critique of 1898 *quijotismo*." *Bulletin of Hispanic Studies* 61, no. 4 (1984): 472–482.

Callahan, William J. "Two Spains and Two Churches 1760–1835." *Historical Reflections* 2, no. 2 (Winter 1976): 157–181. http://www.jstor.org/stable/41298665.

Cameron, Euan. *Enchanted Europe: Superstition, Reason, and Religion, 1250–1750.* Oxford: Oxford University Press, 2010.

Campos y Fernández de Sevilla, Francisco Javier, ed. *La desamortización: El expolio del patrimonio artístico y cultural de la Iglesia en España; Actas del Simposium (6/9-IX-2007).* Alicante: Biblioteca Virtual Miguel de Cervantes, 2010. http://www.cervantesvirtual.com/obra/la-desamortizacion-el-expolio-del-patrimonio-artistico-y-cultural-de-la-iglesia-en-espana-actas-del-simposium-69-ix-2007/ (accessed May 19, 2023).

———. "Textos legales de las desamortizaciones eclesiásticas españolas y con ellas relacionados." In Campos y Fernández de Sevilla, *La desamortización,* 5–30.

Cantos Casenave, Marieta. *Fernán Caballero: Entre el folklore y la literatura de creación; De la relación al teatro.* Cádiz: Ayuntamiento de El Puerto de Santa María, 1999.

Cárcel Ortí, Vicente. *Historia de la Iglesia en la España contemporánea (siglos XIX y XX).* Madrid: Ediciones Palabra, 2002.

Cardona, Rodolfo. "*Mendizábal:* Grandes esperanzas." In Bly, *Galdós y la historia,* 99–112.

Caro Baroja, Julio. *Introducción a una historia contemporánea del anticlericalismo español.* Madrid: Ediciones ISTMO, 1980.

Carr, Raymond. *Spain: A History.* Oxford: Oxford University Press, 2000.

———. *Spain, 1808–1939.* Oxford: Oxford University Press, 1966.

Caruth, Cathy. *Unclaimed Experience: Trauma, Narrative, and History.* Baltimore: Johns Hopkins University Press, 1996.

Casalduero, Joaquín. Introduction to *De tal palo, tal astilla,* by José María de Pereda, 4th ed., edited by Joaquín Casalduero, 9–39. Madrid: Cátedra, 1981.

Cassin, Barbara. *Nostalgia: When Are We Ever at Home?* Translated by Pascale-Anne Brault. New York: Fordham University Press, 2016.

Castle, Terry. "Phantasmagoria: Spectral Technology and the Metaphorics of Modern Reverie." *Critical Inquiry* 15, no. 1 (Autumn 1988): 26–61. https://www.jstor.org/stable/1343603.

Castro Alfín, Demetrio. "Jacobinos y populistas: El republicanismo español a mediados del siglo XIX." In *Populismo, caudillaje y discurso demagógico,* edited by José Álvarez Junco, 181–217. Madrid: Centro de Investigaciones Sociológicas / Siglo XXI, 1987.

Catholic Bishops' Conference of England and Wales. *Consecrated for Worship: A Directory on Church Building.* London: Catholic Truth Society, 2006.

Cerezo Galán, Pedro. *El mal del siglo: El conflicto entre Ilustración y Romanticismo en la crisis finisecular del siglo XIX.* Granada: Biblioteca Nueva, Editorial Universidad de Granada, 2003.

Charnon-Deutsch, Lou. *The Spanish Gypsy: The History of a European Obsession.* University Park: Pennsylvania State University Press, 2004.

Clavero, Bartolomé. "Cádiz and the Noise of a Constitutionalism Common to Both Hemispheres." *Giornale di Storia Costituzionale,* no. 21 (2011): 41–58.

Colina de Rodríguez, Luz. *El folklore en la obra de José María de Pereda.* Santander: Institución Cultural de Cantabria, 1987.

Colmeiro, José F. "Exorcising Exoticism: *Carmen* and the Construction of Oriental Spain." *Comparative Literature* 54, no. 2 (Spring 2002): 127–144. https://www.jstor.org/stable/4122479.

Congreso de los Diputados. *Constitución de 1845: Senado de España.* https://www.senado.es/web/wcm/idc/groups/public/@cta_senhis/documents/document/mdaw/mde5/~edisp/senpre_018544.pdf (accessed May 19, 2023).

———. *Constitución de la monarquía española.* 1837. http://www.congreso.es/docu/constituciones/1837/ce37_cd.pdf (accessed December 29, 2022).

———. *Constitución de la nación española.* June 6, 1869. http://www.congreso.es/docu/constituciones/1869/1869_cd.pdf (accessed May 19, 2023).

———. *Constitución política de la monarquía española.* March 19, 1812. http://www.congreso.es/docu/constituciones/1812/P-0004-00002.pdf (accessed May 19, 2023).

BIBLIOGRAPHY

———. "Número 90: Sesión del viernes 5 de junio de 1840." Diario de sesiones: Serie histórica, 2245–2261. https://app.congreso.es/est_sesiones/web/viewer.html?file=https%3A%2F%2Fapp .congreso.es%2Fest_sesiones%2Fresource%3Fid%3D1840%2F06%2FC-0090-02245.pdf#page =2&zoom=auto,-53,421 (accessed January 3, 2023).

———. "Número 100: Sesión del lunes 15 de junio de 1840." Diario de sesiones: Serie histórica, 2517–2538. https://app.congreso.es/est_sesiones/web/viewer.html?file=https%3A %2F%2Fapp.congreso.es%2Fest_sesiones%2Fresource%3Fid%3D1840%2F06%2FC-0100 -02517.pdf#page=1&zoom=auto,-53,742 (accessed January 3, 2023).

———. "Número 112: Sesión extraordinaria de la noche del martes 20 de julio de 1841." Diario de sesiones: Serie histórica, 2481–2500. https://app.congreso.es/est_sesiones/web/viewer .html?file=https%3A%2F%2Fapp.congreso.es%2Fest_sesiones%2Fresource%3Fid%3D1841 %2F07%2FC-0112-02481.pdf#page=1&zoom=auto,-52,602 (accessed January 3, 2023).

———. "Número 117: Sesión del sábado 4 de julio de 1840." Diario de sesiones: Serie histórica, 2991–3013. https://app.congreso.es/est_sesiones/web/viewer.html?file=https%3A%2F%2Fapp .congreso.es%2Fest_sesiones%2Fresource%3Fid%3D1840%2F07%2FC-0117-02991.pdf#page= 8&zoom=auto,-53,593 (accessed January 3, 2023).

———. *Proyecto de constitución de la monarquía española.* June 30, 1876. http://www.congreso .es/docu/constituciones/1876/1876_cd.pdf (accessed May 19, 2023).

Coppa, Frank J. *Politics and the Papacy in the Modern World.* Santa Barbara, Calif.: ABC-CLIO, 2008.

Cruz, San Juan de la. "Cántico espiritual." In Kavanaugh and Rodriguez, *Collected Works*, 44–50.

———. "Llama de amor viva." In Kavanaugh and Rodriguez, *Collected Works*, 52–53.

Cubero Hernández, Antonio, and María Teresa Pérez Cano. "Permanence, Adaptation or Reuse: Transformations in the Convents of the City of Seville." *Open Engineering* 1 (2016): 281–290. https://doi.org/10.1515/eng-2016-0023.

Cuenca, José Manuel. *D. Pedro de Inguanzo y Rivero (1764–1836): Ultimo primado del antiguo régimen.* Pamplona: Universidad de Navarra, 1965.

Cueto, Ronald. "Our Lady, the French Revolution and Don Benito Pérez Galdós." In *A Face Not Turned to the Wall: Essays on Hispanic Themes for Gareth Alban Davies*, edited by Carlos A. Longhurst, 159–170. Leeds: University of Leeds, 1987.

Cueva Merino, Julio de la. "Clericalismo y movilización católica durante la Restauración." In Cueva Merino and López Villaverde, *Clericalismo y asociacionismo católica*, 27–50.

Cueva Merino, Julio de la, and Ángel Luis López Villaverde. "A modo de introducción: Reflexiones en torno al clericalismo y al asociacionismo católico." In Cueva Merino and López Villaverde, *Clericalismo y asociacionismo católica*, 17–25.

———, eds. *Clericalismo y asociacionismo católica en España: De la Restauración a la Transición; Un siglo entre el palio y el consiliario.* Ciudad Real: Ediciones de la Universidad de Castilla–La Mancha, 2005.

Dawson, Christopher. *Religion and the Rise of Western Culture: The Classic Study of Medieval Civilisation.* New York: Doubleday, 1957.

Debarbieux, Bernard. "Rootedness—Anchoring—Mooring: Reviving Metaphors." *L'Espace géographique* 43, no. 1 (2014): 68–80. https://archive-ouverte.unige.ch/unige:74912.

de Certeau, Michel. *Heterologies: Discourse on the Other.* Translated by Brian Massumi. Minneapolis: University of Minnesota Press, 1986.

Díaz Zafra, Alejandro. "Exposición de los motivos y fundamentos del proyecto de Ley Hipotecaria." In *Ley Hipotecaria: Reglamento general para su ejecución e instrucción sobre la manera de redactar los instrumentos públicos sujetos a registro*, edited by Ministerio de Gracia y Justicia, 3–130. Madrid: Ministerio de Gracia y Justicia, 1861.

Díez de Revenga Torres, Francisco Javier. "Brujas en Gustavo Adolfo Bécquer, 'Cartas desde mi celda.'" *Estudios románicos* 16–17, no. 1 (2007–2008): 369–388.

Dittrich, Lisa. "European Connections, Obstacles, and the Search for a New Concept of Religion: The Freethought Movement as an Example of Transnational Anti-Catholicism in the Second Half of the Nineteenth Century." *Journal of Religious History* 39, no. 2 (2015): 261–279.

Dodds, Ben. "Representations of Bandits in Mid-Nineteenth-Century Spain." *Cultural and Social History* 9, no. 2 (2012): 207–225. https://doi.org/10.2752/147800412X13270753068803.

Domínguez Casas, Rafael. "San Juan de los Reyes: Espacio funerario y aposento regio." *Academia: Boletín de la Real Academia de Bellas Artes de San Fernando*, no. 78 (1994): 315–350.

Donohoe, Janet. *Remembering Places: A Phenomenological Study of the Relationship between Memory and Place*. London: Lexington Books, 2014.

Donoso Cortés, Juan. *Ensayo sobre el catolicismo, el liberalismo y el socialismo considerados en sus principios fundamentales*. Madrid: Imprenta de La Publicidad, 1851.

Douglas, Mary. *Purity and Danger: An Analysis of Concepts of Pollution and Taboo*. New York: Frederick A. Praeger, 1966.

DuBois, Page. *Sowing the Body: Psychoanalysis and Ancient Representations of Women*. Chicago: University of Chicago Press, 1988.

Duncan, Ian. "The Provincial or Regional Novel." In *A Companion to the Victorian Novel*, edited by Patrick Brantlinger and William B. Thesing, 318–335. Hoboken, N.J.: Blackwell, 2005.

DuPont, Denise. "Krausism and Modernism." *Hispanic Journal* 34, no. 2 (Fall 2013): 13–28. http://www.jstor.com/stable/44287191.

Edensor, Tim. *National Identity, Popular Culture, and Everyday Life*. Oxford: Berg, 2002.

Eliade, Mircea. *Images and Symbols: Studies in Religious Symbolism*. Translated by Philip Mairet. London: Harvill Press, 1961.

El Solitario [pseud.]. *Juicio histórico-canónico-político de la autoridad de las naciones en los bienes eclesiásticos, o Disertación sobre la pertenencia de su dominio según el espíritu invariable de la iglesia y los principios inconclusos del derecho público*. Alicante: Manuel Muñoz, 1813.

El Tesoro de Oviedo. "Convento de San Francisco." http://el.tesorodeoviedo.es/index.php?title=Convento_de_San_Francisco (accessed December 30, 2022).

Erll, Astrid. "Locating Family in Cultural Memory Studies." *Journal of Comparative Family Studies* 42, no. 3 (May–June 2011): 303–318. https://www.jstor.org/stable/41604447.

Erll, Astrid, and Ann Rigney. "Literature and the Production of Cultural Memory: Introduction." *European Journal of English Studies* 10, no. 2 (2006): 111–115. https://doi.org/10.1080/13825570600753394.

Escallada González, Luis de. "Inventarios sobre la fundación y desamortización del convento de San Ildefonso de Ajo." *Altamira: Revista del Centro de Estudiosos Montañeses*, no. 72 (2007): 167–245.

Escosura, Patricio de la. *España artística y monumental: Vistas y descripción de los sitios y monumentos más notables de España*. Paris: Imprenta de Fain y Thunot, 1842.

Esdaile, Charles. *Spain in the Liberal Age: From Constitution to Civil War, 1808–1939*. Hoboken, N.J.: Blackwell, 2000.

Esteban, Eustasio. *El siervo de Dios Fr. Diego José de Rejas: Religioso agustino exclaustrado de la provincia de Andalucía; Posiciones y artículos para la causa de su beatificación*. Madrid: Imprenta Helénica, 1919.

Eugercios Arriero, José Luis. "Expropiados y exclaustrados efectos de los procesos desamortizadores del XIX en la Orden de San Agustín en España." *Revista Historia Autónoma*, no. 18 (2021): 209–211.

Europa Press. "El gobierno 'paraliza' por la pandemia el informe de los bienes inmatriculados por la Iglesia." June 10, 2020. https://www.europapress.es/sociedad/noticia-gobierno-paraliza-pandemia-informe-bienes-inmatriculados-iglesia-20200610141003.html (accessed December 26, 2022).

Felman, Shoshana. *The Juridical Unconscious: Trials and Traumas in the Twentieth Century*. Cambridge, Mass.: Harvard University Press, 2002.

BIBLIOGRAPHY

Fernández-Medina, Nicolás. *Life Embodied: The Promise of Vital Force in Spanish Modernity.* Montreal: McGill–Queen's University Press, 2018.

Fiestas Loza, Alicia. "La protección registral de los compradores de bienes eclesiásticos desamortizados (1863–1869)." *Anuario de historia del derecho español*, no. 53 (1983): 334–365. https://www.boe.es/biblioteca_juridica/anuarios_derecho/abrir_pdf.php?id=ANU-H-1983-10033400365 (accessed May 29, 2023).

Flanagan, Kieran. *Seen and Unseen: Visual Culture, Sociology and Theology.* London: Palgrave Macmillan, 2004.

———. *Sociological Noir: Irruptions and the Darkness of Modernity.* London: Routledge, 2017.

Flitter, Derek. *Spanish Romanticism and the Uses of History: Ideology and the Historical Imagination.* Oxford: Legenda, 2006.

———. *Spanish Romantic Literary Theory and Criticism.* Cambridge: Cambridge University Press, 1992.

Fox, E. Inman. *La invención de España: Nacionalismo liberal e identidad nacional.* 2nd ed. Madrid: Cátedra, 1998.

Freud, Sigmund. "Mourning and Melancholia." In *The Freud Reader*, edited by Peter Gay, 584–589. New York: Vintage, 1995.

Fuente Monge, Gregorio L. de la. *Los revolucionarios de 1868: Elites y poder en la España liberal.* Madrid: Marcial Pons, 2000.

Gale, Judith E. *El regionalismo en la obra de José María de Pereda.* Madrid: Pliegos de Bibliofilia, 1990.

Gamallo Fierros, Dionisio, ed. *Gustavo Adolfo Bécquer: Obras completas.* 13th ed. Madrid: Aguilar, 1969.

García Castañeda, Salvador. *Las ideas literarias en España entre 1843 y 1850.* Berkeley: University of California Press, 1971.

Garry, Jane. "Transformation, Motifs D0–D699." In *Archetypes and Motifs in Folklore and Literature: A Handbook*, edited by Jane Garry and Hasan M. El-Shamy, 125–132. London: Routledge, 2004.

Gilbert, Sandra M., and Susan Gubar. *The Madwoman in the Attic: The Woman Writer and the Nineteenth-Century Literary Imagination.* New Haven, Conn.: Yale University Press, 1980.

Gold, Hazel. *The Reframing of Realism: Galdós and Discourses of the Nineteenth-Century Spanish Novel.* Durham, N.C.: Duke University Press, 1993.

Gómez Cediel, Javier. "El convento de Santa Ana de Jumilla ante la exclaustración de 1836." *Archivo Ibero-Americano* 82, no. 294 (2022): 273–287. https://doi.org/10.48030/v82i294.253.

Gómez Yebra, Antonio A. "Actualidad de los elementos folclóricos recopilados por Fernán Caballero." In *Actas del encuentro Fernán Caballero, hoy: Homenaje en el bicentenario del nacimiento de Cecilia Böhl de Faber 1996*, edited by Milagros Fernández Poza and Mercedes García Pazos, 67–88. Cádiz: Ayuntamiento de El Puerto de Santa María, 1998.

González-Gerth, Miguel. "The Poetics of Gustavo Adolfo Bécquer." *MLN* 80, no. 2 (March 1965): 185–201. https://www.jstor.org/stable/3042609.

González Grueso, Fernando Darío. "Lo tradicional y el elemento del miedo en las leyendas de Gustavo Adolfo Bécquer: Vínculos y poética." *Revista de Letras* 57, no. 1 (2017): 57–70.

González Pérez, Teresa. "Identidad cultural y discurso de género: Las mujeres patriotas en el imaginario nacional." *Cadernos de História da Educação* 10, no. 1 (2011): 219–236.

Goodson, A. C. "Romantic Theory and the Critique of Language." In *Questioning Romanticism*, edited by John Beer, 3–28. Baltimore: Johns Hopkins University Press, 1995.

Granda, Claudia. "¿Cómo ha llegado aquí este arco de más de ocho siglos?" *La Voz de Asturias*, August 10, 2018. https://www.lavozdeasturias.es/noticia/oviedo/2018/10/03/llegado-arco-ocho-siglos/00031538576132523829470.htm (accessed May 29, 2023).

Griffin, Susan M. *Anti-Catholicism and Nineteenth-Century Fiction.* Cambridge: Cambridge University Press, 2004.

Guest, Matthew. "In Search of Spiritual Capital: The Spiritual as Cultural Resource." In *A Sociology of Spirituality,* edited by Kieran Flanagan and Peter C. Jupp, 181–200. Surrey: Ashgate, 2007.

Gullón, Germán. "'Sustituyendo el azogue del espejo': La novelización de la ideología decimonónica en *Doña Perfecta.*" In Bly, *Galdós y la historia,* 131–144.

Gutiérrez Sebastián, Raquel. Prologue to *Blasones y talegas,* by José María de Pereda, edited by Raquel Gutiérrez Sebastián, ix–xxiii. Doral, Fla.: Stock Cero, 2006.

Halbwachs, Maurice. *On Collective Memory.* Edited and translated by Lewis A. Coser. Chicago: University of Chicago Press, 1992.

Hermano Bartolo. *El Anacoreta.* Alicante: Oficina de Nicolás Carratalá e Hijos, 1813.

Herrera, Matthew D. "Sanctus Bells: Their History and Use in the Catholic Church." *Adoremus Bulletin* 11, no. 1 (March 2005). https://adoremus.org/2005/03/sanctus-bells/ (accessed May 29, 2023).

Herrero, Javier. "El naranjo romántico: Esencia del costumbrismo." *Hispanic Review* 46, no. 3 (Summer 1978): 343–354. https://www.jstor.org/stable/472418.

Hibbs-Lissorgues, Solange. *Iglesia, prensa y sociedad en España (1868–1904).* Alicante: Instituto de Cultura "Juan Gil-Albert" y Diputación de Alicante, 1995.

Hoar, Leo J. "Galdós y Aureliano de Beruete, visión renovada de 'Orbajosa.'" *Anuario de Estudios Atlánticos* 1, no. 20 (1974): 693–707.

Holy See. "Code of Canon Law: Book V; The Temporal Goods of the Church." http://www.vatican.va/archive/cod-iuris-canonici/eng/documents/cic_lib5-cann1254-1310_en.html#TITLE_II (accessed December 31, 2022).

———. "Pope Pius IX." http://www.vatican.va/news_services/liturgy/saints/ns_lit_doc_2000 0903_pius-ix_en.html (accessed May 29, 2023).

Hopkins, Martin. "St. Thomas and the Encyclical *Mystici Corporis.*" *The Thomist: A Speculative Quarterly Review* 22, no. 1 (January 1959): 1–24. https://doi.org/10.1353/tho.1959.0000.

Hutton, Patrick H. *History as an Art of Memory.* Lebanon, N.H.: University Press of New England, 1993.

Ibán, Iván C., and Marcos González. *Textos de derecho eclesiástico (siglos XIX y XX).* Madrid: Centro de Estudios Políticos y Constitucionales, Boletín Oficial del Estado, 2001.

Iturbe Saíz, Antonio. "Patrimonio artístico de tres conventos agustinos en Madrid antes y después de la desamortización de Mendizábal." In Campos y Fernández de Sevilla, *La desamortización,* 335–368.

Jagoe, Catherine. *Ambiguous Angels.* Berkeley: University of California Press, 1994.

Janowitz, Anne. *England's Ruins: Poetic Purpose and the National Landscape.* Oxford: Basil Blackwell, 1990.

Jiménez García, Antonio, ed. *El Krausismo y la Institución Libre de Enseñanza.* Madrid: Cincel, 1985.

Johnson, Paul. *The Birth of the Modern: World Society 1815–1830.* New York: HarperCollins, 1991.

Jones, Willis Knapp. "Regionalism: Advantage or Handicap?" *Hispania* 36, no. 4 (1953): 427–431. https://www.jstor.org/stable/334780.

Jover, José María, and Guadalupe Gómez-Ferrer. "Sociedad, civilización y cultura." In *España: Sociedad, política y civilización (siglos XIX–XX),* ed. José María Jover Zamora, Guadalupe Gómez-Ferrer, and Juan Pablo Fusi Aizpúrua, 203–258. Madrid: Areté, 2001.

Juderías, Julián. *La leyenda negra.* Barcelona: Araluce, 1917.

Juliá, Santos. *Historias de las dos Españas.* Madrid: Taurus, 2004.

Kavanaugh, Kieran, and Otilio Rodriguez, trans. *The Collected Works of Saint John of the Cross.* Washington, D.C.: Institute of Carmelite Studies, 1991.

BIBLIOGRAPHY

Kennedy, David. *Elegy*. London: Routledge, 2007.

Kirkpatrick, Susan. *Las Románticas: Escritoras y subjetividad en España, 1835–1850*. Madrid: Cátedra, 1991.

Koerner, Joseph Leo. "On Monuments." *Res: Anthropology and Aesthetics* 67, no. 1 (September 1, 2017): 5–20.

Kruszyńska, Sabina. "*Écrasez l'infâme*: Voltaire's Philosophy of Religion." *Miscellanea Anthropologica et Sociologica* 16, no. 1 (2015): 125–137.

Labanyi, Jo. *Gender and Modernization in the Spanish Realist Novel*. Oxford: Oxford University Press, 2000.

———. "Liberal Individualism and the Fear of the Feminine in Spanish Romantic Drama." In *Culture and Gender in Nineteenth-Century Spain*, edited by Lou Charnon-Deutsch and Jo Labanyi, 8–26. Oxford: Clarendon Press, 1995.

Lambert, Yves. "A Turning Point in Religious Evolution in Europe." *Journal of Contemporary Religion* 19, no. 1 (2004): 29–45. https://doi.org/10.1080/1353790032000165104.

Lázaro Lorente, Luis Miguel. "Con Barrabás o con Cristo: El acoso a la escuela laica en España, 1880–1910." *Historia de la Educación* 31 (2012): 209–230.

Le Goff, Jacques. "Church Time and Merchant Time in the Middle Ages." Translated by Christophe Campos. *Annales* 15, no. 3 (May–June 1960): 151–167.

León, Fray Luis de. *Poesía*. 8th ed. Edited by Jesús Manuel Alda Tesán. Zaragoza: Editorial Ebro, 1967.

Lewis, Tom. "Gender, Discourse, and Modernity in Bécquer's *Rimas*." *Revista de Estudios Hispánicos* 31, no. 3 (October 1, 1997): 419–447.

Linehan, Peter. *History and the Historians of Medieval Spain*. Oxford: Oxford University Press, 1993.

Llorente, Jean Antoine. *History of the Inquisition of Spain, from the Time of Its Establishment to the Reign of Ferdinand VII: Composed from the Original Documents of the Archives of the Supreme Council and from Those of Subordinate Tribunals of the Holy Office*. London: Geo. B. Whittaker, 1827. https://www.gutenberg.org/files/38354/38354-h/38354-h.htm (accessed May 29, 2023).

López, Ignacio Javier. Introduction to *Gloria*, by Benito Pérez Galdós, edited by Ignacio Javier López, 11–149. Madrid: Cátedra, 2011.

———. *La novela ideológica (1875–1880): La literatura de ideas en la España de la Restauración*. Madrid: Ediciones de la Torre, 2014.

———. "Pereda y la revolución liberal: *Don Gonzalo González de la Gonzalera* (1878)." *Bulletin of Hispanic Studies* 97, no. 4 (2020): 383–402. https://doi.org/10.3828/bhs.2020.22.

López Castro, Armando. "Bécquer y los poetas del Siglo de Oro." In *Lógos hellenikós: Homenaje al profesor Gaspar Morocho Gayo*, vol. 2, edited by Jesús María Nieto Ibáñez, 959–976. León: Universidad de León, Secretariado de Publicaciones y Medios Audiovisuales, 2003.

López Morillas, Juan. *El krausismo español: Perfil de una aventura intelectual*. Mexico City: Fondo de Cultura Económica, 1956.

López Rodríguez, José Ramón. "Museos y desamortización en la España del siglo XIX." In *El patrimonio arqueológico en España en el siglo XIX: El impacto de las desamortizaciones*, edited by Concha Papí Rodes et al., 163–179. Madrid: Ministerio de Educación, Cultura y Deporte, 2011.

Lorente Sariñena, Marta. "Crisis of the Catholic Monarchy and Regeneration of Its Constitution." *Giornale di Storia Costituzionale* 19 (2010): 67–92.

Louzao Villar, Joseba. "La recomposición religiosa en la modernidad: Un marco conceptual para comprender el enfrentamiento entre laicidad y confesionalidad en la España contemporánea." *Hispania Sacra* 60, no. 121 (2008): 33–354.

Luke, Timothy W. "Identity, Meaning, and Globalization: Detraditionalization in Postmodern Space-Time Compression." In *Detraditionalization: Critical Reflections on Authority and Identity*, edited by Paul Heelas, Scott Lash, and Paul Morris, 109–133. Hoboken, N.J.: Blackwell, 1996.

Madariaga de la Campa, Benito. *José María de Pereda y su tiempo*. Polanco: Ayuntamiento de Polanco, 2003.

———. *Pereda: Biografía de un novelista*. Santander: Ediciones de Librería de Estudio, 1991.

Malson, Helen M. "Anorexic Bodies and the Discursive Production of Feminine Excess." In *Body Talk: The Material and Discursive Regulation of Sexuality, Madness and Reproduction*, edited by Jane Ussher, 223–245. London: Routledge, 1997.

Mandrell, James. *Don Juan and the Point of Honor: Seduction, Patriarchal Society, and Literary Tradition*. University Park: Penn State University Press, 1992.

Manlio, Graziano. *Il secolo cattolico: La strategia geopolitica della Chiesa*. Rome: Laterza, 2010.

Martí Gilabert, Francisco. *La desamortización española*. Madrid: Ediciones Rialp, 2003.

Martín-Arroyo, Javier. "La Mezquita de Córdoba no es de los obispos, según un comité oficial." *El País*, September 17, 2018. https://elpais.com/sociedad/2018/09/14/actualidad/1536956121_483715.html (accessed December 31, 2022).

Martín Carramolino, Juan. *La Iglesia de España económicamente considerada*. Madrid: Imprenta del Colegio de Sordo-Mudos, 1850.

Martínez Alcubilla, Marcelo. *Diccionario de la Administración Española, Peninsular y Ultramarina: Compilación ilustrada de la novísima legislación de España en todos los ramos de la administración pública*. 2nd ed. Vol. 5. Madrid: Imprenta de la Viuda e Hijas de A. Peñuelas, 1869.

Martínez Vilches, David. "'Católicos conciudadanos': Los sermones del clero liberal en el trienio constitucional (1820–1823)." In *El Trienio Liberal (1820–1823): Balance y perspectivas*, edited by Ivana Frasquet, Pedro Rújula, and Álvaro París, 545–555. Zaragoza: Prensas de la Universidad de Zaragoza, 2022.

Medina Calzada, Sara. "The Felon King: Ferdinand VII in British Print Culture (1814–1833)." *Bulletin of Spanish Studies* 96, no. 6 (2019): 951–973. https://doi.org/10.1080/14753820.2019.1633797.

Mendióroz Lacambra, Ana María. "Miguel de Quintana, autor de la portada del convento de la Merced, actual Museo de Bellas Artes de Sevilla." *Laboratorio de Arte: Revista del Departamento de Historia del Arte*, no. 2 (1989): 261–266.

Mendizábal, Juan Álvarez. "Exposición a S. M. la Reina gobernadora." *Gaceta de Madrid*, February 21, 1836. https://www.boe.es/gazeta/dias/1836/02/21/pdfs/GMD-1836-426.pdf (accessed May 24, 2023).

Menéndez y Pelayo, Marcelino. *Historia de los heterodoxos españoles: Heterodoxia en el siglo XIX*. Vol. 6. Edited by Enrique Sánchez Reyes. Alicante: Biblioteca Virtual Miguel de Cervantes, 2008.

Menges, Karl. "Particular Universals: Herder on National Literature, Popular Literature, and World Literature." In *A Companion to the Works of Johann Gottfried Herder*, edited by Hans Adler and Wulf Koepke, 189–214. Columbia, S.C.: Camden House, 2009.

Mínguez Blasco, Raúl. "Between Virgins and Priests: The Feminisation of Catholicism and Priestly Masculinity in Nineteenth-Century Spain." *Gender & History* 33, no. 1 (March 1, 2021): 94–110.

Mitchell, Timothy. *Betrayal of the Innocents: Desire, Power, and the Catholic Church in Spain*. Philadelphia: University of Pennsylvania Press, 1998.

Moliner Prado, Antonio. "El anticlericalismo popular durante el bienio 1834–1835." *Hispania Sacra* 49, no. 100 (1997): 497–541.

Morejón Hermosa, Óscar. "Cinco grandes mentiras sobre las inmatriculaciones de la Iglesia." Libre Mercado, August 19, 2019. https://www.libremercado.com/2019-08-18/autores-invitados-cinco-grandes-mentiras-sobre-las-inmatriculaciones-de-la-iglesia-88564/ (accessed December 29, 2022).

BIBLIOGRAPHY

Moreno, Doris, and Ricardo García Cárcel. Introduction to *The Complexity of Hispanic Religious Life in the 16th–18th Centuries*, edited by Doris Moreno, translated by Phil Grayston, 1–12. Leiden: Brill, 2020.

Moreno Antón, María G. *La enajenación de bienes eclesiásticos en el ordenamiento jurídico español*. Salamanca: Universidad Pontificia de Salamanca, 1987.

Moreno-Luzón, Javier, and Xosé Núñez Seixas. "The Flag and the Anthem: The Disputed Official Symbols of Spain." In *Metaphors of Spain: Representations of Spanish National Identity in the Twentieth Century*, edited by Javier Moreno-Luzón and Xosé Núñez Seixas, 33–62. Oxford: Berghahn Books, 2017.

Moreno Seco, Mónica, and Alicia Abad Mira. "Mujeres y sociabilidad laica (1875–1931)." *Asparkía*, no. 17 (2006): 61–80.

Morrison, James V. *Shipwrecked: Disaster and Transformation in Homer, Shakespeare, Defoe, and the Modern World*. Ann Arbor: University of Michigan Press, 2014.

Mumford, Lewis. *The Culture of Cities*. New York: Open Road Media, 2016.

Muñoz Sempere, Daniel. *La Inquisición española como tema literario: Política, historia y ficción en la crisis del antiguo régimen*. Suffolk: Tamesis, 2008.

Navascués Palacio, Pedro. "Bécquer y San Juan de los Reyes." *Descubrir el arte*, no. 17 (2000): 96–98.

Nelson, Thomas J. "'Most Musicall, Most Melancholy': Avian Aesthetics of Lament in Greek and Roman Elegy." *Dictynna*, no. 16 (2019): 1–47. https://doi.org/10.4000/dictynna.1914.

Nora, Pierre. "Between Memory and History: Les Lieux de Mémoire." *Representations* 26 (Spring 1989): 7–24. https://www.jstor.org/stable/2928520.

———. Introduction to *Rethinking France: Les Lieux de Mémoire*, vol. 4, *Histories and Memories*, edited by Pierre Nora, vii–xiv. Chicago: University of Chicago Press, 2010.

Nuñez, María Victoria. "Electra se convirtió en el grito de guerra: Una aproximación a las reacciones del estreno cordobés de la obra teatral de Pérez Galdós." *Itinerantes: Revista de Historia y Religión*, no. 13 (2020): 141–165.

Ortiz Armengol, Pedro. *Vida de Galdós*. Barcelona: Crítica, 2000.

Ortiz Pradas, Daniel. *San Juan de los Reyes de Toledo: Historia, construcción y restauración de un monumento medieval*. Madrid: La Ergástula, 2015.

Palomo Iglesias, Crescencio. *Claudio Sancho de Contreras (1811–1886): Dominico exclaustrado*. Segovia: Imprenta Gabel, 1970.

Pan-Montojo, Juan, ed. *Más se perdió en Cuba: España, 1898 y la crisis de fin de siglo*. Madrid: Alianza, 1998.

Papal Encyclicals Online. "The Syllabus of Errors." https://www.papalencyclicals.net/pius09/p9syll.htm (accessed May 29, 2023).

Pattison, Walter T. *Benito Pérez Galdós and the Creative Process*. Minneapolis: University of Minnesota Press, 1954.

Payne, Stanley G. *Spain: A Unique History*. Madison: University of Wisconsin Press, 2011.

Peláez del Rosal, Manuel, ed. *El Franciscanismo en Andalucía: Actas del XIII Curso de Verano: Exclaustración y desamortización de los conventos franciscanos andaluces*. Córdoba: El Almendro, 2009.

Penuel, Arnold M. "The Problem of Ambiguity in Galdós' *Doña Perfecta*." *Anales Galdosianos* 11 (1976): 71–86. http://www.cervantesvirtual.com/obra-visor/anales-galdosianos--7/html/0255070e-82b2-11df-acc7-002185ce6064_34.html#I_17_.

Pereda, José María de. "Año nuevo." *El Tío Cayetano*, no. 9 (January 3, 1869): 1.

———. *Blasones y talegas*. Edited by Raquel Gutiérrez Sebastián. Doral, Fla.: Stock Cero, 2006.

———. *De tal palo, tal astilla*. 4th ed. Edited by Joaquín Casalduero. Madrid: Cátedra, 1981.

———. "La Iglesia libre." *El Tío Cayetano*, no. 6 (December 13, 1868): 1.

———. Letter from José María de Pereda to Benito Pérez Galdós. March 14, 1877. Colecciones Documentales de Benito Pérez Galdós. EPG3637. Las Palmas: Casa-Museo Pérez Galdós, Cabildo de Gran Canaria, 1–19.

———. "¡Loado sea Dios!" *El Tío Cayetano*, no. 1 (November 9, 1868): 1.

———. *Obras completas*. Vol. 2. 8th ed. Madrid: Aguilar, 1975.

———. *Sotileza*. Madrid: Editorial Tesoro, 1962.

Pérez Galdós, Benito. "Al pueblo español." *El País: Diario Republicano* 23, no. 8087 (October 6, 1909): 1.

———. "Calor en la atmósfera y efervescencia en los ánimos. Furor neocatólico. Firmas y exposiciones. Partes telegráficos de la granja. Sudores, soponcios y vahídos" [July 16, 1865]. In *Crónica de Madrid: (1865–1866) Obra inédita*, 75–77. Madrid: Castro, 1933.

———. *Doña Perfecta*. Madrid: Hernando, 1942.

———. *Electra*. In *La de San Quintín: Electra*, edited by Luis F. Díaz Larios, 203–341. Madrid: Cátedra, 2002.

———. *Gloria*. Edited by Ignacio Javier López. Madrid: Cátedra, 2011.

———. Letter to José María de Pereda, June 6, 1877. In Bravo-Villasante, *Veintiocho cartas*, 23–24.

———. "Madrid, 1.° de marzo de 1901." In Bravo-Villasante, *Veintiocho cartas*, 51.

———. *Mendizábal: Episodios nacionales 22*. Madrid: Alianza, 2003.

———. *Montes de Oca: Episodios nacionales 28*. Madrid: Hernando, 1978.

Pérez Ledesma, Manuel. "Studies on Anticlericalism in Contemporary Spain." *International Review of Social History* 46, no. 2 (August 2001): 227–255. https://www.jstor.org/stable/44583482.

Pius IX. "Quanta Cura: Condemning Current Errors." December 8, 1864. Papal Encyclicals Online. https://www.papalencyclicals.net/pius09/p9quanta.htm (accessed December 27, 2022).

Pius XII. *Mystici Corporis Christi*. June 29, 1943. Holy See. http://www.vatican.va/content/pius-xii/en/encyclicals/documents/hf_p-xii_enc_29061943_mystici-corporis-christi.html (accessed May 19, 2023).

Pizarroso Quintero, Alejandro. "Prensa y propaganda bélica 1808–1814." *Cuadernos dieciochistas* 8 (2007): 203–222.

Pogge von Strandmann, Hartmut. "1848–1849: A European Revolution?" In *The Revolutions in Europe, 1848–1849: From Reform to Reaction*, edited by Robert Evans and Hartmut Pogge von Strandmann, 1–8. Oxford: Oxford University Press, 2011.

Pozo, Alba del. "Degeneración, tienes nombre de mujer: Género y enfermedad en la cultura del fin de siglo XIX–XX." *Lectora* 19 (2013): 137–151. https://doi.org/10.1344/105.000002032.

Público. "Alarma entre los obispos tras la reclamación de bienes a la Iglesia: 'Es una desamortización encubierta.'" September 11, 2018. https://www.publico.es/espana/iglesia-alarma-obispos-reclamacion-bienes-iglesia-desamortizacion-encubierta.html (accessed December 23, 2022).

Ràfols, Wilfredo de. "Lies, Irony, Satire, and the Parody of Ideology in *Doña Perfecta*." *Hispanic Review* 64, no. 4 (Autumn 1996): 467–489. https://www.jstor.org/stable/474883.

Ramón Solans, Francisco Javier. "Introducción: Economía, sociedad y religión." In *El Trienio Liberal (1820–1823): Balance y perspectivas*, edited by Ivana Frasquet, Pedro Rújula, and Álvaro París, 277–283. Zaragoza: Prensas de la Universidad de Zaragoza, 2022.

———. "Mary into Combat: Marian Devotions and Political Mobilizations during the European Culture Wars." *European History Quarterly* 51, no. 3 (2021): 324–344. https://doi.org/10.1177/02656914211024943.

"Representación que a la reina de las virtudes la Caridad dirige un quilibet exclaustrado, con solo el objeto de hallar el socorro y alivio de ella." Madrid: Imprenta de D. J. Palacios, 1838.

BIBLIOGRAPHY

Rico y Amat, Juan. *Historia política y parlamentaria de España (desde los tiempos primitivos hasta nuestros días) escrita y dedicada a S. M. La Reina Doña Isabel II*. Vol. 1. Madrid: Escuelas Pías, 1860.

Risco, Antonio. *Literatura y fantasía*. Madrid: Taurus, 1982.

Rodgers, Eamonn. "Religious Freedom and the Rule of Law in Nineteenth-Century Spain." *Irish Jurist* 22, no. 1 (1987): 112–124. https://www.jstor.org/stable/44027198.

Rodríguez López-Brea, Carlos M. "Galdós, un cristiano heterodoxo." In *Galdós en su tiempo*, edited by Yolanda Arencibia and Ángel Bahamonde, 135–164. Santa Cruz de Tenerife: Parlamentos de Cantabria y Canarias, 2006.

Rodríguez-Luis, Julio. Introduction to *La familia de Alvareda*, by Cecilia Böhl de Faber, edited by Julio Rodríguez-Luis, 7–52. Madrid: Castalia, 1979.

Rogers, Paul Patrick. "New Facts on Bécquer's *Historia de los templos de España*." *Hispanic Review* 8, no. 4 (October 1940): 311–320. http://www.jstor.org/stable/469761.

The Roman Catholic Daily Missal. St. Marys, Kans.: Angelus Press, 1962.

Román Collado, Rocío. "Andaluces en el pensamiento económico del siglo XIX." In *Economía y economistas andaluces: Siglos XVI al XX*, edited by Rocío Sánchez Lissen, 329–337. Madrid: Eco-Book Economista, 2013.

Romano, Sergio. *Libera Chiesa: Libero Stato? Il Vaticano e l'Italia da Pio IX a Benedetto XVI*. Milan: Longanesi, 2005.

Ross, Christopher J. *Spain, 1812–1996*. New York: Oxford University Press, 2000.

Ross, Marlon B. "Troping Masculine Power in the Crisis of Poetic Identity." In *Romanticism and Feminism*, edited by Anne Mellor, 26–51. Bloomington: Indiana University Press, 1988.

Rubio Jiménez, Jesús. *Los Bécquer en Veruela: Un viaje artístico-literario*. Zaragoza: IberCaja, 1990.

Rueda, Ana. "La Electra de Galdós y sus redes de conducción eléctrica." *Anales Galdosianos* 54 (2019): 59–72. https://doi.org/10.1353/ang.2019.0003.

Rueda Garrido, Daniel. "Aproximación a la teoría del conocimiento del krausismo español." *Revista de Filosofía* 43, no. 1 (2018): 67–84. https://doi.org/10.5209/RESF.60200.

Rueda Hernanz, Germán. *España 1790–1900: Sociedad y condiciones económicas*. Madrid: Editorial ISTMO, 2006.

Rull Fernández, Enrique. "Estructura poética de las cartas desde mi celda." In *Bécquer, origen y estética de la modernidad: Actas del VII Congreso de Literatura Española Contemporánea, Universidad de Málaga, 9, 10, 11 y 12 de Noviembre de 1993*, edited by Cristóbal Cuevas García and Enrique Baena Peña, 251–264. Alicante: Biblioteca Virtual Miguel de Cervantes, 2015.

Sánchez Llama, Íñigo. *Galería de escritoras isabelinas: La prensa periódica entre 1833 y 1895*. Madrid: Cátedra, 2000.

Santana, Mario. "The Conflict of Narratives in Pérez Galdós *Doña Perfecta*." *MLN* 113, no. 2 (March 1998): 283–304. https://www.jstor.org/stable/3251476.

Sarah, Robert, and Nicolas Diat. *The Day Is Now Far Spent*. Translated by Michael J. Miller. San Francisco: Ignatius Press, 2019.

Savaiano, Eugene. "Pereda's Portrayal of Nineteenth Century Clergymen." *Modern Language Journal* 36, no. 5 (May 1952): 223–229. https://www.jstor.org/stable/318381.

Schneider, Franz. "Gustavo Adolfo Bécquer as 'Poeta' and His Knowledge of Heine's 'Leider.'" *Modern Philology* 19, no. 3 (1922): 245–256. https://www.jstor.org/stable/433441.

Schyfter, Sara E. *The Jew in the Novels of Benito Pérez Galdós*. Suffolk: Tamesis, 1978.

———. "The Judaism of Galdós' Daniel Morton." *Hispania* 59, no. 1 (March 1976): 24–33. https://www.jstor.org/stable/339368.

Serrano, Carlos. "Conciencia de la crisis, conciencias en crisis." In Pan-Montojo, *Más se perdió en Cuba*, 335–403.

Sevillano, Elena G. "La Iglesia inscribió como propios 30.000 bienes en casi dos décadas." *El País*, August 13, 2019. https://elpais.com/sociedad/2019/08/11/actualidad/1565552360 _678366.html (accessed December 31, 2022).

Shaw, Philip. *The Sublime*. London: Routledge, 2006.

Shoemaker, William H. *The Novelistic Art of Galdós*. Vol. 2. Valencia: Albatros-Hispanófila, 1980.

Showalter, Elaine. *The Female Malady: Women, Madness and English Culture, 1830–1980*. London: Virago, 1987.

Shubert, Adrian. *A Social History of Modern Spain*. London: Routledge, 1990.

———. *The Sword of Luchana: Baldomero Espartero and the Making of Modern Spain, 1793–1879*. Toronto: University of Toronto Press, 2021.

Sieburth, Stephanie. *Inventing High and Low: Literature, Mass Culture, and Uneven Modernity in Spain*. Durham, N.C.: Duke University Press, 1994.

Sierra, Sarah. "From Sacred Religion to Sacred Nation: Ritual Crisis in *Don Gonzalo González de la Gonzalera*." *Bulletin of Hispanic Studies* 91, no. 2 (2014): 127–145.

———. "Modernity and the Cultural Memory Crisis in Gustavo Adolfo Bécquer's *La cruz del diablo* and *El monte de las ánimas*." *Modern Language Review* 10, no. 2 (April 2015): 473–490. https://www.jstor.org/stable/10.5699/modelangrevi.110.2.0473.

———. "*Moros y cristianos*: Performing Ideological Dissent in Benito Pérez Galdós's *Doña Perfecta*." *Hispanofila*, no. 165 (May 2012): 31–50.

Silver, Philip W. *Ruin and Restitution: Reinterpreting Romanticism in Spain*. Nashville: Vanderbilt University Press, 1997.

Simón Segura, Francisco. *La desamortización española en el siglo XIX*. Madrid: Ministerio de Hacienda, Instituto de Estudios Fiscales, 1973.

Sinclair, Alison. "The Regional Novel: Evolution and Consolation." In *The Cambridge Companion to the Spanish Novel: From 1600 to the Present*, edited by Harriet Turner and Adelaida López de Martínez, 49–64. Cambridge: Cambridge University Press, 2006.

Smith, Anthony D. *The Antiquity of Nations*. Cambridge: Polity, 2004.

———. *Nationalism and Modernism: A Critical Survey of Recent Theories of Nations and Nationalism*. London: Routledge, 1998.

Smith, Laurajane. "Intangible Heritage: A Challenge to the Authorised Heritage Discourse?" *Revista d'etnologia de Catalunya*, no. 40 (2015): 133–142. https://www.raco.cat/index.php/RevistaEtnologia/article/view/293392/381920.

Sonenscher, Michael. "The Sans-culottes of the Year II: Rethinking the Language of Labour in Revolutionary France." *Social History* 9, no. 3 (October 1984): 301–328. https://www.jstor .org/stable/4285370.

Sopeña Ibáñez, Federico. "Galdós y la desamortización." *Cuenta y razón* 2 (Spring 1981): 69–76.

Spitzer, Leo. "Back through the Future: Nostalgic Memory and Critical Memory in a Refuge from Nazism." In Bal, Crewe, and Spitzer, *Acts of Memory*, 87–104.

Stark, Rodney. "Secularization, R.I.P." *Sociology of Religion* 60, no. 3 (1999): 249–273. https://www.jstor.org/stable/3711936.

Stites, Richard. *The Four Horsemen: Riding to Liberty in Post-Napoleonic Europe*. Oxford: Oxford University Press, 2014.

Storm, Eric. "La cultura regionalista en España, Francia y Alemania: Una perspectiva comparada (1890–1937)." *Ayer*, no. 82 (2011): 161–185. https://www.jstor.org/stable/41326125.

Stroik, Duncan. *The Church Building as a Sacred Place: Beauty, Transcendence, and the Eternal*. Mundelein, Ill.: Hillenbrand Books, 2012.

Swain, James O. "Reactionism in Pereda's *Tío Cayetano*." *Hispania* 17, no. 1 (February 1934): 83–96. https://www.jstor.org/stable/332410.

Tang, Wan Sonya. "Sacred, Sublime, and Supernatural: Religion and the Spanish Capital in Nineteenth-Century Fantastic Narratives." In *The Sacred and Modernity in Urban Spain*:

BIBLIOGRAPHY

Beyond the Secular City, edited by Antonio Cordoba and Daniel García-Donoso, 21–40. London: Palgrave Macmillan, 2016.

Tanner, Tony. *Adultery in the Novel*. Baltimore: Johns Hopkins University Press, 1979.

Taylor, Charles. *A Secular Age*. Cambridge, Mass.: Harvard University Press, 2007.

Tejado, Gabino. *El catolicismo liberal*. Madrid: Librería Católica Internacional, 1875.

Thompson, Michael, Richard Ellis, and Aaron Wildavsky. *Cultural Theory*. Boulder, Colo.: Westview Press, 1990.

Todorov, Tzvetan. "Definition of the Fantastic." In *The Horror Reader*, edited by Ken Gelder 14–19. London: Routledge, 2000.

Tomás y Valiente, Francisco. *El marco político de la desamortización de España*. Barcelona: Ediciones Ariel, 1971.

———. "El proceso de desamortización de la tierra en España." *Agricultura y sociedad*, no. 7 (1978): 11–33.

Tortella, Gabriel. *El desarrollo de la España contemporánea: Historia económica de los siglos XIX y XX*. Madrid: Alianza, 1994.

Tsuchiya, Akiko. *Images of the Sign: Semiotic Consciousness in the Novels of Benito Pérez Galdós*. Columbia: University of Missouri Press, 1990.

———. *Marginal Subjects: Gender and Deviance in Nineteenth Century Spain*. Toronto: University of Toronto Press, 2011.

Tully, Carol. "How German Romanticism Travelled to Spain: The Intellectual Journey of Johann Nikolas Böhl von Faber." *Publications of the English Goethe Society* 71, no. 1 (2016): 78–90. https://doi.org/10.1080/09593683.2001.11716326.

Unamuno, Miguel de. "Sobre el marasmo actual de España." In *Obras completas*, vol. 8, *Ensayos*, edited by Ricardo Senabre, 177–199. Madrid: Fundación José Antonio Fernández de Castro, 2007.

Urigüen, Begoña. *Orígenes y evolución de la derecha española: El neo-catolicismo*. Madrid: Consejo Superior de Investigaciones Cientificas, 1986.

Urrutia Abaigar, Victor. "Church and State after Transition to Democracy: The Case of Spain." In *The Secular and the Sacred: Nation, Religion and Politics*, edited by William Safran, 116–129. London: Routledge, 2002.

Ussher, Jane M. *Women's Madness: Misogyny or Mental Illness?* London: Harvester Wheatsheaf, 1991.

Valis, Noël. *Sacred Realism: Religion and the Imagination in Modern Spanish Narrative*. New Haven, Conn.: Yale University Press, 2010.

Valle Calzado, Ángel Ramón. "Desamortización eclesiástica en la provincia de Ciudad Real, 1836–1854." PhD diss., Universidad de Castilla–La Mancha, 1995.

Varela Suanzes-Carpegna, Joaquín. "La construcción del Estado en la España del siglo XIX: Una perspectiva constitucional." Biblioteca Virtual Miguel de Cervantes. http://www.cervantesvirtual.com/obra-visor/la-construccion-del-estado-en-la-espaa-del-siglo-xix-una-perspectiva-constitucional/html/dcd3569e-2dc6-11e2-b417-000475f5bda5_2.html#I_0_ (accessed December 31, 2022).

Vecco, Marilena. "A Definition of Cultural Heritage: From the Tangible to the Intangible." *Journal of Cultural Heritage* 11, no. 3 (2010): 321–324. https://doi.org/10.1016/j.culher.2010.01.006.

Velasco Maíllo, Honorio Manuel. "Los significados de cultura y los significados de pueblo una historia inacabada." *Revista Española de Investigaciones Sociológicas*, no. 60 (1992): 7–26.

Velaz Pascual, José María. "El convento de San Antonio de Padua, de Garrovillas de Alconétar (Cáceres): Un ejemplo de patrimonio olvidado." *Revista de estudios extremeños* 77, no. 1 (2021): 485–543.

Vélez, Rafael de. *Apología del altar y del trono, o Historia de las reformas hechas en España en tiempo de las llamadas cortes, e impugnación de algunas doctrinas publicadas en la Constitución, diarios, y otros escritos contra la religión y el estado.* Madrid: Cano, 1818.

Vicens Vives, Jaime. *An Economic History of Spain.* Translated by Frances M. López-Morillas. Princeton, N.J.: Princeton University Press, 1969.

Villena Villar, Manuel. "La observancia franciscana en Sevilla: Laicos y frailes entre la exclaustración y la restauración (1835–1881)." *Archivo hispalense: Revista histórica, literaria y artística* 104, nos. 315–317 (2021): 197–222.

Vincent, Mary. "Religion: The Idea of Catholic Spain." In *Metaphors of Spain: Representations of Spanish National Identity in the Twentieth Century,* edited by Javier Moreno-Luzón and Xosé Núñez Seixas, 22–41. Oxford: Berghahn Books, 2017.

Vizuete Mendoza, José Carlos. "Agonía de los conventos femeninos en España." *Anuario jurídico y económico escurialense,* no. 52 (2019): 603–612.

Weiskel, Thomas. *The Romantic Sublime: Studies in the Structure and Psychology of Transcendence.* Baltimore: Johns Hopkins University Press, 1976.

White, Sarah L. "Liberty, Honor, Order: Gender and Political Discourse in Nineteenth-Century Spain." In *Constructing Spanish Womanhood: Female Identity in Modern Spain,* edited by Victoria Lorée Enders and Pamela Beth Radcliff, 233–257. Albany: State University of New York Press, 1999.

White, Thomas Joseph. *The Light of Christ: An Introduction to Catholicism.* Washington, D.C.: Catholic University of America Press, 2017.

Yongjiao, Yang, Iain Brennan, and Mick Wilkinson. "Public Trust and Performance Measurement in Charitable Organizations." *International Journal of Productivity and Performance Management* 63, no. 6 (2014): 779–796. https://doi.org/10.1108/IJPPM-09-2013-0159.

Young, Bonnie. "A Medieval Bell." *Metropolitan Museum of Art Bulletin,* n.s., vol. 11, no. 10 (June 1953): 293–296. https://doi.org/10.2307/3258293.

Zafirovski, Milan. *The Enlightenment and Its Effects on Modern Society.* New York: Springer, 2011.

Zahareas, Anthony N. "Galdós' *Doña Perfecta*: Fiction, History and Ideology." *Anales Galdosianos* 11 (1976): 29–51. http://www.cervantesvirtual.com/obra-visor/anales-galdosianos--7/html/0255070e-82b2-11df-acc7-002185ce6064_32.html#I_11_.

Index

abbey, 68, 73, 82, 84; Fitero, 87; Fleury, 72
agriculture, 41
Alfonso XII, 5, 113, 133
Alfonso XIII, 5
Amadeo I, 5, 133, 195n43
Americas, the, 4, 174n16; as symbol, 61
anarchism, 39, 112, 189n3
ancien régime, antiguo régimen (old regime), 5, 21, 180n12
Andalusia, 11, 16, 40, 43, 55, 56, 143, 157, 194n20; stereotypes, 44, 51, 52
anticlericalism, 110, 132, 175n41, 185n55, 192n85; and Galdós, 105–106; and Pereda, 132, 135, 137, 139, 145; violence, 111–112
Argüelles, Agustín, 31–32, 37
Assmann, Jan, 8
asylums. See madness

Babel, 74, 83
Balmes, Jaime, 17–19, 176n57
bandits, 51, 52, 87, 143. See also Andalusia
baptism, 70, 79
Baroque, 8, 17, 91, 189n7
Bécquer, Gustavo Adolfo, 3, 66, 163; and Catholicism, 80, 86, 91; and monasteries, 185n60; and poetry, 186n76
bells, 57, 78–79, 91, 93, 102, 186n65
Black Legend, the (La leyenda negra), 33
Böhl de Faber, Cecilia, 3, 10, 38, 47, 162; and Catholicism, 38, 40, 45, 52; and costumbrismo, 42–43; and marriage, 38, 39
Böhl de Faber, Johann Nikolaus, 40
Borbón-Dos Sicilias, María Cristina de, 11, 21
Bourbon monarchy, 5, 34; Bourbon Restoration, 11, 101, 113, 133, 163, 195n43

bourgeoisie, 36, 41, 131, 141; liberal bourgeois revolution, 5, 15, 21
Boym, Svetlana, 66, 95
Burke, Edmund, 88

Caballero, Fernán. See Böhl de Faber, Cecilia
Cádiz, 35; and Böhl de Faber, 42, 44, 60. See also Constitutions of Spain; Cortes of Cádiz
Callahan, William J., 19, 27, 34, 100
Campo de San Francisco, Oviedo, 1, 61
Cánovas del Castillo, Antonio, 132–133
Cantabria, 114, 132; and Pereda, 100, 131–132, 145, 155, 156–157
Carlists, 21, 34, 106, 132–133, 155, 176n43, 194n10, 195n43; Carlist Wars, 6, 22, 31, 113, 122, 150, 157, 186n85; and Galdós, 100; and Pereda, 130–131, 143, 159, 163
Carlos III, 5
Carlos IV, 5, 15
cathedral, 28, 69, 165–166; and Bécquer, 86, 89–93; and Galdós, 101, 103, 105–106, 131; and Pereda, 156; of Toledo, 87, 88
Catholic Church (Iglesia Católica). See Catholicism
Catholicism, 34, 51, 108, 112, 118, 130, 146, 174n15; dogma, 7, 11; faith, 165; intransigence, 113; and liberalism, 17, 25; observance, 12; priesthood, 110; and progress, 27; religious vocations, 146; and Spain, 7–8, 16, 20, 79, 80, 106, 117, 119, 189n7. See also neo-Catholics; sacrament; theology; worship
Chateaubriand, François-Auguste-René, 66, 69

church building, 3, 13, 62
Church-State relations, 34, 80, 112, 150
Cistercians, 77, 87, 189n7
clergy, 7, 16, 18, 36, 162, 165–166, 174n15;
    Carlism, 21, 31; criticism, 103, 105–106,
    130; and disentailment, 26, 176nn46–47;
    exclaustrated clergy, 5, 13, 67, 94; and
    liberalism, 34–35, 37; and Pereda,
    138–139, 146, 156; perspectives, 24–26,
    37; property, 28–30; regular clergy,
    27, 177n76; rural clergy, 34, 131;
    secular clergy, 7, 10, 21. *See also*
    anticlericalism
Comte, Auguste, 85. *See also* positivism
Constitutions of Spain, 4, 16, 26, 28–29,
    72, 79, 84, 101; clerical resistance, 132;
    Constitution of Cádiz, 4, 16, 33–35,
    174n10, 177n76, 186n86; and Galdós,
    108
Contreras, Claudio, 6
convents and monasteries, 3, 6, 8, 13, 21, 22,
    70–71, 161; and Bécquer, 67–68, 74–75,
    94; and Böhl de Faber, 40, 47–51, 58–63;
    and Galdós, 115, 123–124; and Pereda,
    138–139. *See also* church building; San
    Juan de los Reyes
Cortes of Cádiz, 5, 15, 21–22, 33
costumbrismo, 10, 65. *See also* Böhl de
    Faber, Cecilia
Counter-Reformation, 82, 91. *See also*
    Baroque
Cuba, 44, 60
cultivation, 148, 152; as educational
    metaphor, 147; as religious symbol, 145,
    150, 152, 159
culture, 8–9, 36; and Böhl de Faber, 38–39,
    42–43; Catholic visual culture, 8; Spanish
    national culture, 3, 17, 42. *See also* nation:
    national spirit

de Certeau, Michel, 83
determinism, 144
devotionalism. *See* religious devotion
disentailment (*desamortización*), 3;
    and Böhl de Faber, 38–39, 45; civil
    disentailment, 20; ecclesiastical
    disentailment, 98, 165–166; and Galdós,
    115, 120; legislation, 4, 29, 36–37, 64, 77;
    and Pereda, 12, 133–134; studies, 5–7,
    13. *See also* Mendizábal, Juan Álvarez;
    Espartero, Baldomero; exclaustration;
    Madoz, Pascual
disjuncture, 3, 13, 166

dogma, 7–8, 11, 20, 32; and Bécquer, 79; and
    Böhl de Faber, 45, 65; and Galdós, 98, 115,
    124, 128; and Pereda, 136, 145, 147, 149. *See
    also* Catholicism
Dominicans, 6, 112
Donoso Cortés, Juan, 19, 20

ecclesiastical tithe (*diezmo*), 22
ecumenism. *See* interfaith relations
education, 36; inadequacy of, 34; religious
    formation, 147, 150; religious orders, 174;
    religious versus secular education, 132,
    136, 147
ekphrasis, 11, 164
elegy, 76
Enlightenment, the, 7, 16, 19–20; and
    Bécquer, 86, 88, 94; and Böhl de Faber,
    39, 41, 57–60; and Galdós, 107; and
    Pereda, 107; and Spanish clergy, 189n7
Espartero, Baldomero, 4, 5, 7, 21, 121–122
Europe, 5, 33, 43–44, 52, 79, 87, 134;
    modernity, 19, 109–110, 112, 164; as
    symbol, 60–61
excarnation, 7, 15, 39, 98, 106, 166. *See also*
    secularization; Taylor, Charles
exclaustration (*exclaustración*), 3–8, 13, 22,
    72, 79, 164, 166; and Bécquer, 94; and
    Böhl de Faber, 51; and Pereda, 131, 134,
    136–137, 155, 159
expropriation (*expropriación*). *See*
    disentailment

Fernando VII, 4, 16–17, 21, 33, 37, 120, 127,
    174n13
feudal society, 15, 43, 109, 131, 136–137
Flanagan, Kieran, 10, 66–67, 86, 92, 95
forest symbolism, 88–89, 188n113
France, 5, 17, 19, 33, 66, 72, 114; Catholic
    mobilization, 34; clergy, 27; French
    invasion, 174; French Revolution, 41, 66,
    111–112, 115, 143; French Third Republic,
    34; influences, 43, 113, 144, 177n60,
    179n2, 181n32; Romanticism, 41–42. *See
    also* Chateaubriand, François-Auguste-
    René; Napoleonic occupation; War of
    Independence
Freud, Sigmund, 13, 95
friars, 5, 6, 10, 27, 34; and Böhl de Faber,
    47–48; and Galdós, 120, 122; massacre of,
    112; and Pereda, 134, 145, 155–156

Genesis, Book of, 74
Gloriosa, La. *See* Glorious Revolution, the

INDEX

Glorious Revolution, the (La Gloriosa), 5, 130, 163
Godoy, Manuel, 5, 7
Gothic, 11, 85–86, 94, 161, 163; terror, 68
gypsies, 181n42. *See also* Andalusia

Halbwachs, Maurice, 9, 144, 161
Herder, Johann Gottfried, 41–42, 66; *Kultur des Volkes*, 134; *Nationalkarakter* (national character), 180n30
heritage, 7, 9, 140, 179n2, 186nn75–76; cultural heritage, 148; religious and spiritual heritage, 11, 32, 39, 50, 64, 67–68, 97, 126; Spanish national heritage, 11, 43, 82, 133, 135
Hermano Bartolo, 24–25
hidalguía. See nobility

industrialization, 32, 41, 68, 81, 141
inertia, 94, 121
Inguanzo y Rivero, Pedro de, 177n57, 187n105
interfaith relations, 113–114, 151
Isabel II, 4, 15, 21, 33, 36, 69, 165, 185n55

Jesuits, 21–22, 27–28, 34, 112, 139, 145–146, 189n7
Jesus Christ, 16, 23, 32, 77, 115, 146; Sacred Heart, 34
José I (Joseph Bonaparte), 4, 15, 21, 56
Judaism, 113, 119

Krause, Karl Christian, 98
Krausism, 98, 99, 113, 116–117, 132, 189n2; and Galdós, 105–106, 108, 120, 124; and Pereda, 136, 146. *See also* neo-Catholics

laicism, 38
Larrea, Frasquita, 42
liberalism, 17; and Bécquer, 76, 80; and nation, 43; and Pereda, 141, 157; and Spain, 10, 17, 19–20, 174n13; versus traditionalism, 41, 125
Liberal Revolution, 4, 44, 145, 147
Liberal Triennium, 4, 16, 21, 35, 174n13, 174n16, 186n86
lieux de mémoire, 1–2, 9, 72
light and dark imagery, 88, 140, 153. *See also* Burke, Edmund
liturgy. *See* worship

madness, 110, 111, 115; nineteenth-century madwoman, 111–112
Madoz, Pascual, 5, 22, 36, 64

Madrid, 78, 80, 102; as center of progressive liberalism, 10, 102, 105, 111
manos muertas, 15–16, 45, 174n8
Martín Carramolino, Juan, 23, 177n60
Martínez de la Rosa, Francisco, 27–29, 120
memory, 1, 8–10, 66, 81, 135, 161. *See also* Boym, Svetlana; Halbwachs, Maurice; nostalgia
Mendizábal, Juan Álvarez, 3, 11, 22, 30, 36, 63, 77, 97, 116, 120, 124, 133, 187n105; disentailment laws, 3–7, 13, 21–22, 77, 97; *Mendizábal*, 100, 116, 120–121, 161, 166. *See also* disentailment
moderates (*moderados*), 10, 11, 15–16, 22, 28, 36, 79, 185n55
Monasterio de Veruela, 11, 69, 77, 85
monasticism, 99, 146, 162, 166, 186n65, 192n85
Montes de Oca, Manuel, 11, 121–123; *Montes de Oca*, 121–123, 128
monument, 1–2, 63, 66, 68–69, 71–72, 80, 82, 161. *See also* church building; *lieux de mémoire*
Mortgage Law (Ley Hipotecaria), 165–166
Moses, 72, 77
Museo de Bellas Artes, Seville, 47, 161, 186n75, 197n1
mystical body of Christ, 173n3
mysticism, 67, 77, 83, 90, 96; and ruins, 83; Spanish mystics, 67, 83. *See also* San Juan de la Cruz

Napoleonic occupation, 33, 42, 56; and Bécquer, 72, 77, 87
nation, 36, 163; national history, 71–72, 84, 102, 135; national spirit, 3, 43, 46. *See also* heritage
naturalism, 144
neo-Catholics, 19–20, 26, 40, 80, 108, 132, 142, 180n12; and Galdós, 100; and Pereda, 131
nobility, 36, 41, 131, 140–143
Nocedal, Cándido, 40
Nora, Pierre, 1–2, 9, 72, 81
nostalgia, 9–10; and Bécquer, 65–69; and Böhl de Faber, 60, 65; and Pereda, 155, 157. *See also* Boym, Svetlana; memory
nuns, 22

Old Testament, 119
Ominous Decade, the, 4, 120
Orbajosa, 101–103, 105–106, 109, 131; and Ficóbriga, 114
Oviedo, 1, 161, 167, 177n76

Pacheco, Joaquín Francisco, 29–32, 37
parliament, 24, 26, 28, 31, 108, 189n3
Partido Liberal Conservador, 127, 132
patria, 42, 44, 109, 127, 130, 181n43
Pelagianism, 112
Pereda, José María de, 3, 12, 163; and
Catholicism, 130, 131, 139, 151; Galdós,
129. *See also* disentailment;
exclaustration
Pérez Galdós, Benito, 3, 11, 97; and
Catholicism, 99, 101, 126, 128, 163; and
Pereda, 129; vital force, 11, 98–99,
128, 163
phantasmagoria, 94, 188n133
Pidal y Mon, Alejandro, 1
Pius VII, 15, 33
Pius IX, 19–20, 108
positivism, 7, 38, 187n97; and Bécquer,
84–85; and Böhl de Faber, 47, 62; and
Galdós, 124; and Pereda, 145
Prim, Juan, 133
progressives (*progresistas*), 10, 15, 18,
105, 117, 133, 173n4, 189n3; progressive
reforms, 97; progressivism, 56, 100,
121. *See also* Mendizábal, Juan Álvarez;
Espartero, Baldomero; Montes de Oca,
Manuel; Pérez Galdós, Benito

Quanta Cura, 19

rationalism, 7, 12, 18; and Böhl de Faber, 57,
59; and Galdós, 110, 125, 128; and Pereda,
145–146, 149
Reformation, 83, 86. *See also*
Counter-Reformation
regionalism, 130, 140
Rejas, Diego José de, 6
religious devotion, 40, 56, 65, 75, 117, 130,
149–150; female piety, 110
religious indifference, 100
religious pluralism, 164
religious question, the, 3–5, 14–16, 26, 33,
101, 112, 128, 133
republicanism, 4, 127
Revolutionary Sexenium, 12, 34, 113, 115,
132–133, 151, 157, 194n20. *See also* Glorious
Revolution, the
Romanticism, 40–42; and conservatism,
52; and liberalism, 41–42, 55
Romero Ortiz, Antonio, 139
ruins, 9–10; and Bécquer, 66–67, 70, 72,
83–84, 86–87, 95–96, 135; and Böhl de
Faber, 51, 61–63. *See also* Flanagan,
Kieran

sacrament, 38, 79, 86, 91, 163, 165;
sacramentals, 147, 155–156
sacred horror, 85, 87, 90
sacrilege, 22, 36, 52, 86, 96
saeta, 57
Salamanca, 13, 177n76
San Juan de la Cruz, 81–82, 85
San Juan de los Reyes, 67, 69–73, 76
sans-culotte, 196n56
Santander, 12, 22, 154–157
Sanz del Río, Julián, 98, 117
Saragossa (Zaragoza), 11, 13, 77
Schlegel, August Wilhelm, and Friedrich,
40, 42, 66
secularization, 15, 37, 39, 41, 70, 74, 113,
176n47; church buildings, 3, 13, 34, 61–62;
legislation, 34; and materialism, 140; and
modernity, 164; and modernization, 159;
processes, 164; and revolution, 133. *See
also* excarnation
sepulchre, 69, 73, 87, 93, 95, 139
Seville, 22, 46–47, 51, 56, 161, 167,
186n75
shipwreck, 114
Silver, Philip W., 41
Solitario, El, 24
Spanish backwardness, 43, 189n7
Spanish Golden Age, 42, 81
Spanish Inquisition, the, 32. *See also* Black
Legend, the
sublime, the, 67, 77, 85, 88, 96. *See also*
Burke, Edmund; Romanticism
superstition, 59, 85, 88, 107
Syllabus of Errors, 19–20, 108

Taylor, Charles, 7–8, 166
technology, 41, 81, 106, 187n97
Tejado, Gabino, 25–26
theology, 8, 19, 32, 73, 79, 85, 98, 136; and
politics, 35; theological reform, 24;
virtues, 52
Toledo, 11, 36, 67, 69–71, 77, 86–89, 91,
95. *See also* Bécquer, Gustavo Adolfo;
Inguanzo y Rivero, Pedro de
tolerance, 16, 98–99, 109, 114; lack of, 101,
113
traditionalism, 20–21; and Bécquer, 66,
80; and Böhl de Faber, 10, 38, 42; and
Galdós, 111; and Pereda, 130, 132, 158–159,
163; in Spain, 3, 14–15, 20, 41, 174n13,
176n43, 181n33
transgression, 39, 51, 56, 85, 87, 92, 96, 163
trauma, 13, 69, 74, 83–84, 89, 95. *See also*
Freud, Sigmund

INDEX

Two Spains, the, 19, 41, 101, 125, 175n24. *See also* Callahan, William J.; Silver, Philip W.

Unión Católica, 132
utilitarianism, 22, 27–29, 36, 45, 64, 78, 159, 162

Visigoths, 70
vital force (*vis vitalis*), 98–99, 128; devitalization, 128; revitalization, 101, 104

Volksgeist, 40, 42, 180n30
Voltaire, 100, 129–130, 132, 143

War of Independence, 15–16, 71, 186n85
worship, 9, 16, 22–29, 35–36, 48, 59, 166, 176n46; and Bécquer, 68, 78, 80, 84, 89, 92; and Böhl, 59; and Galdós, 115; and Pereda, 138–139. *See also* Catholicism; worship

About the Author

AZARIAH ALFANTE obtained her PhD at the University of Auckland, New Zealand, where currently she is a professional teaching fellow and teaches Spanish language, culture, and history. Her doctoral thesis was awarded the Premio Peter Bly in 2021. She has published on Spanish Romanticism and Philippine nationalist writing in the late modern period. Her current research interests lie in the intersections between religion, memory, and culture.